The twelve essay[...] York St John [...]dy of musical performance. Three areas are investigated: the psychology of performance, the semantics of performance, and the relation between performance and analysis. The first section broaches fundamental issues such as text, expression, musical motion and the role of practice in the acquisition of expertise. The next four chapters address the shaping of structure and the projection of meaning in performance, while the last four consider performance as analytical paradigm, as dramatic narrative, as act of criticism, as temporal process. By combining speculative enquiry with detailed case-studies and by approaching from disparate perspectives an activity of central importance to all musicians, the volume has a wide appeal, and it achieves this without sacrificing scholarly rigour or artistic viability. Among the distinguished international authorship are many accomplished performers whose practical experience ensures that the book contains unusually vital and stimulating insights into musical interpretation.

# The Practice
# of Performance

Studies in Musical Interpretation

■

# The Practice
# of Performance

## Studies in Musical Interpretation

EDITED BY

## JOHN RINK

SENIOR LECTURER IN MUSIC, ROYAL HOLLOWAY, UNIVERSITY OF LONDON

CAMBRIDGE
UNIVERSITY PRESS

PUBLISHED BY THE PRESS SYNDICATE OF THE UNIVERSITY OF CAMBRIDGE
The Pitt Building, Trumpington Street, Cambridge, United Kingdom

CAMBRIDGE UNIVERSITY PRESS
The Edinburgh Building, Cambridge CB2 2RU, UK
40 West 20th Street, New York NY 10011–4211, USA
477 Williamstown Road, Port Melbourne, VIC 3207, Australia
Ruiz de Alarcón 13, 28014 Madrid, Spain
Dock House, The Waterfront, Cape Town 8001, South Africa

http://www.cambridge.org

First published 1995
First paperback edition 2005

*A catalogue record for this book is available from the British Library*

*Library of Congress cataloguing in publication data*

The Practice of Performance: Studies in Musical Interpretation / edited by John Rink
p.  cm.
Includes bibliographical references and index.
ISBN 0 521 45374 7 (hardback)
1. Music – Performance. I. Rink, John.
ML457.P473 1995
781.4'3 – dc20   94–42747 CIP

ISBN 0 521 45374 7 hardback
ISBN 0 521 61939 4 paperback

# Contents

# Preface

The past few decades have witnessed a virtual explosion in scholarly writing about musical performance. A vast literature on historical performance practice,[1] the psychology of performance,[2] the relation between analysis and performance,[3] and 'interpretation'[4] broadly defined has emerged during that time, but until now, no attempt has been made to distil the principal trends of performance scholarship into a single volume more accessible in style and content than the highly specialised – and often obscure – publications of its various subdisciplines. This book provides such a forum, and it does so by means of the 'studies' format widely used in music publishing. Whereas most collections of 'studies' focus on a single composer, however, this volume targets a musical *activity* of importance to all musicians – professional and amateur, academic and nonacademic. As a result, the book has a wide appeal lacking in much specialist writing, at the same time achieving a remarkable depth of insight into musical interpretation. Furthermore, it reflects the growing recognition of performance studies as a discipline in its own right.[5] Among the international authorship are distinguished scholars in a range of subject areas; many are also accomplished performers whose

---

[1] For bibliographic information see H. M. Brown and S. Sadie, eds., *Performance Practice: Music before 1600* and *Performance Practice: Music after 1600* (London: Macmillan, 1989), and R. Jackson, *Performance Practice, Medieval to Contemporary: A Bibliographic Guide* (New York: Garland, 1987). See also N. Kenyon, ed., *Authenticity and Early Music* (Oxford: Oxford University Press, 1988).

[2] Details of past research can be found in J. A. Sloboda, *The Musical Mind: The Cognitive Psychology of Music* (Oxford: Clarendon, 1985) and 'Psychological structures in music: core research 1980–1990', in J. Paynter et al., eds., *Companion to Contemporary Musical Thought*, 2 vols. (London: Routledge, 1992), vol. II, pp. 803–39. See also J. A. Sloboda, ed., *Generative Processes in Music* (Oxford: Clarendon, 1989), and J. Sundberg, ed., *Studies of Music Performance* (Stockholm: Royal Swedish Academy of Music, 1983).

[3] Bibliographic information is given in J. Rink, Review of W. Berry, *Musical Structure and Performance*, in *Music Analysis* 9/3 (1990): 319–39, and T. Howell, 'Analysis and performance: the search for a middleground', in J. Paynter et al., eds., *Companion to Contemporary Musical Thought*, 2 vols. (London: Routledge, 1992), vol. II, pp. 692–714.

[4] Examples include A. Brendel, *Musical Thoughts and Afterthoughts* (London: Robson, 1976) and J. Dunsby, *Performing Music: Shared Concerns* (Oxford: Clarendon, 1995).

[5] The increasing number of 'performance studies' courses at British universities and conservatories offers proof of this. See also 'Musical performance studies as a "discipline"', in Dunsby, *Performing Music*, pp. 17–28.

considerable practical experience shapes their writing and lends the book particular
vitality and cogency.

Despite the broad spectrum of topics, resonances between chapters are abundant.
Indeed, the division into three sections – fundamentals, structure and meaning in
performance, and performance as process – is neither rigid nor intended to sever the
threads running through the volume, which include such diverse themes as performance 'architecture'; the relation between musical moment and narrative process;
shape as diachronic counterpart to structure; the role of intuition in performance; the
relation between composer, performer and listener; the 'text(s)' of performance; and
the inevitable partiality of interpretation and the need for choice among more or less
plausible alternatives. That these recurrent themes have 'naturally' arisen attests to their
general significance and topicality. It is hoped that the book will serve as a research
tool for the further scholarly study of musical performance; to that end several authors
offer useful overviews of past work in their respective subdisciplines and set agendas
for future investigations.

In the first essay, Roy Howat claims that it is not music but 'notation' (the score,
analytical diagrams, theoretical treatises, composers' own performances, etc.) that we
interpret. Works by Mozart, Schubert, Debussy, Ravel, Bartók and Gershwin are discussed along with such topics as ornamentation, rubato, tempo and pedalling. Howat
concludes that performers must often 're-edit' notation in order to express the music
as felt by the composer, rather than merely follow the dictates of received tradition.

Eric Clarke explores the paradox that musical performance can have immense
rhetorical force even though the expressive principles underlying it are quite simple.
He surveys three existing models of expression before proposing a more inclusive
semiotic framework which recognises and indeed celebrates the multiplicity of function of expressive features. Adducing data from a range of performances of Chopin
and Beethoven, Clarke proposes that certain expressive details act as clues for varying
conceptions of the music, rather than as empirical determinants.

One area identified by Clarke as warranting further investigation concerns the
relationship between musical motion and performance, which is the very topic
addressed in Patrick Shove and Bruno Repp's chapter. Noting that composers,
performers and listeners alike experience movement in music, they locate its source
not within the music itself but in human motion, specifically, that of the performer,
whose articulatory movements are shown to be sound-structuring movements. Shove
and Repp draw upon the theories of James Gibson and the empirical research of three
German 'pioneers' as well as more recent investigators to demonstrate that performed
music has the potential to represent forms of natural motion and to elicit corresponding movements in a human listener, and they go on to suggest that this potential must
be maximised to achieve 'aesthetically satisfying performance'. According to them,
expert performers have a profound understanding of principles of natural movement
which they exploit in interpreting music.

Expertise in performance is also considered by Ralf Krampe and Anders Ericsson,
who define a model of 'elite' (encompassing both 'expert', or professional, and

'eminent', or innovative) performance based not on the prevailing notion of talent but on the amount of 'deliberate practice' engaged in by musicians. Their developmental framework, empirical evaluations and provocative conclusions pose a fundamental challenge to the generally accepted view of the grounding of musical excellence.

Nicholas Cook's reappraisal of a particular 'historical performance practice' – that of Wilhelm Furtwängler – offers a similar challenge. After closely examining two of Furtwängler's recordings of Beethoven's Ninth Symphony, Cook claims that these interpretations represent a correlate in sound of a Schenkerian structural hierarchy, realised by means of carefully calculated 'tempo gradients' analogous to spans in a voice-leading graph. In short, Furtwängler's 'long-range conducting' creates nothing less than 'analyses in sound'.

Focusing on a structurally critical passage in Schumann's Fourth Symphony, David Epstein justifies his 'emotional' response when conducting the music, a response which at first seemed to contradict the composer's dynamic marking in the score. He adduces recent research on affect, analyses the music's form and thematic construction, and scrutinises manuscript evidence to make sense of his interpretation. Epstein's conclusion – that the passage in question belongs to a *Steigerung*, an intensity gradient not unlike those defined by Cook – reveals a sensitivity to the 'total language of the music', the ambiguity of which requires interpretative choices to be made sometimes at odds with the apparent wishes of the composer.

Janet Levy homes in on ambiguity and the implications of choice in interpretation, investigating the central question faced by performing musicians: what to project in performance and with what consequences – not only for the performance itself, but for those listening to it. She defines several types of musical ambiguity (often involving tiny details invested with 'immense communicative power' – a point also made by Eric Clarke), whether between immediately successive events, events separated in time or simultaneous ones. By treating ambiguity as an 'empowering' tool, Levy broadens the range of meaning that the performer can effectively convey.

Musical meaning is also explored in Ronald Woodley's chapter – specifically, ironic layers of meaning intrinsic to Prokofiev's Violin Sonata Op. 80. Woodley traces the 'ironising process' manifested throughout the work, which employs such agents as tonality, rhythm, metre and timbre in a fundamental struggle towards an ultimately unattainable, 'pure' spiritual realm free from irony. His conclusions of how performers 'can/should locate themselves' in transmitting that struggle point to the 'multivocality of artistic utterance' alluded to by several authors in this book.

The four chapters in the final section concentrate in different ways on the relation between analysis and performance, attending in particular to the temporal basis of performance. Joel Lester advocates the use of performance as an analytical paradigm, arguing that analysts would do well not only to refer directly to specific renditions of a work but also to introduce the terms of performance into the analytical premise. Like Roy Howat, he regards the score as merely a 'recipe'; each interpretation thereof reflects one and only one option. This, he says, is as true of analysis as of performance, and he encourages analysts to weigh up multiple strategies (as the performer must) and to avoid musically limiting black-and-white judgements.

Further discussion of how and when to project analytical findings in performance follows in the essay by William Rothstein, who argues (as I do in my chapter) that merely 'bringing out' the results of an analysis can all too easily distort the music. Instead, he favours 'synthesis' as a goal – i.e. an all-encompassing musical statement, a coherent 'dramatic' act. Rothstein supports his argument by studying thematic and motivic elements, metre, phrase structure and voice-leading in pieces by Bach, Beethoven and Chopin. In Chopin's Waltz Op. 42, for instance, he encourages the pianist to celebrate ambiguity by keeping more than one hypermetrical option alive.

Whereas Joel Lester casts performance in the role of analytical paradigm, Edward Cone's chapter defines it as a critical statement. Cone claims that the choice of a work and the building of a programme are both acts of criticism, as are basic decisions concerning relative and absolute tempo. Convincing performance, he says, results from the adoption of particular interpretative strategies to which the musician feels a deep personal commitment. Tempo decisions are especially crucial, and he discusses works by Schubert and Chopin to show the relation between tempo, expressive content and formal structure.

Many of the foregoing points are echoed in my own chapter, which uses Brahms's *Fantasien* Op. 116 to investigate the projection of large-scale temporal unity in performance, the shaping of smaller-scale gestures within that temporal background, and the style-historical basis of the 'intuitive' interpretation evaluated throughout the essay. My central aim is to show how analytical and historical awareness can together shape an interpretation without dominating it to the point of distortion; in short, 'synthesis' as defined by Rothstein is the goal of this reading of the work, which also demonstrates a novel kind of 'historical performance practice'.

As this overview suggests, the twelve chapters unite speculative enquiry with empirical case-studies, many of which refer to master recordings or to authors' own performances. The focus on music from the mid eighteenth to early twentieth centuries inspires discussion of a wide range of relevant topics, and this breadth is balanced by a concentration on piano music, orchestral repertoire and violin/piano works. By raising issues of concern to soloists, conductors and chamber players alike, the volume has the potential to speak to anyone actively engaged in making music, as well as to musicologists and music-lovers. Indeed, it is hoped that for all readers new light will be shed on the act of interpretation, the practice of performance, the very life of music.

A few prefatory guidelines will facilitate use of the book. An author–date citation system has been employed throughout: that is, an author's surname, date of publication and, where relevant, page number(s) of a given quotation are provided in the text rather than the footnotes, in the form 'Smith 1990: 24–5', etc. Subsequent references in immediate succession to a full citation are abbreviated ': 26', etc. rather than with 'ibid.' Dates in square brackets within a citation (e.g. 'Wagner [1869] 1966: 290') refer to the year of original publication, with the following date that of the later source from which the quotation was taken. In all cases, complete bibliographic (or, in some cases, discographic) details are given in the reference lists at the end of each chapter.

In both the text and the examples, upper- and lower-case Roman numerals depict major and minor harmonies respectively. Careted numerals designate either scale degrees or structural pitches in Schenkerian contexts. Pitch classes are represented by capital letters; the Helmholtz system is used to denote specific pitches where necessary.

As a last preliminary, a few words of acknowledgement are in order. I should like to thank in particular Lucy Passmore of the University of Surrey for her generous assistance, especially in preparing the index; John Sloboda, Eric Clarke and Alf Gabrielsson for helpful advice; the Department of Music, University of Surrey for financial support; and Penny Souster at Cambridge University Press for her warm encouragement and practical guidance.

John Rink

# PART ONE

# Fundamentals

# CHAPTER ONE

# What do we perform?

## ROY HOWAT

∎

What is the 'music' that we play or study? Other languages are more explicit than English, with words like *partition* and *Musiknoten*, in defining that musical scores are not music per se.[1] The relationship between notation and music is well illustrated by Stravinsky's claim that he could play the 'Danse sacrale' from the *Rite of Spring* for some time before he was able to write it down (Stravinsky and Craft 1962: 141). Although this distinction may seem hairsplitting to performers, we can hear all around us the results of regarding music as the symbols on the page, which one must then 'make interesting'. 'Put some expression into it!' is still a ubiquitous cry even at conservatories, notwithstanding the contradiction in terms.

Ravel's request that pianists should 'just play' rather than 'interpret my music' (Long [1960] 1972: 21) focuses the question for performers: can we actually 'interpret music'? Surely not, except by distorting it. What we can interpret – indeed, can only interpret – is its notation. Since notation, to quote the ever-literal French, 'partitions' music (that is, represents or encodes it in a welter of mostly binary symbols, involving variable conventions and shorthands), it cannot avoid distorting it, and our task is to 'read back through' the distortions on paper, employing aural and visual awareness, skill and sensitivity.

Although scores are the most fixed point of reference for our classical repertoire, far from being absolutes they rest on sand,[2] and what we scientifically trust least, our musical feeling, remains the strongest and final link to what the composer sensed and heard before subjecting it to notation. Debussy, one of the most technically meticulous of all notators, still considered it necessary to write in bar 1 of his Prelude 'Des pas sur la neige', 'Ce rythme doit avoir la valeur sonore d'un fond de paysage triste et glacé'. This direct appeal to feeling, characteristic of his scores, reminds us that notation too can only follow in music's footsteps, mapping where and how inspiration has passed.

---

[1] English is full of transferred epithets unthinkable in other languages, such as 'the kettle is boiling'.
[2] The Russian-trained French pianist Brigitte Engerer commented: 'you might ask a Russian pianist and a French pianist to play the same work *with an exact observation of the nuances*, and you would get two very different interpretations' (Timbrell 1982: 184; my emphasis).

We should observe straight away the distinction between alert feeling, which is a state of awareness, and wilfulness, which is a state of deliberate ignorance. The performer who ignores or overrides a composer's indications simply because 'I feel it this way' is often no better than the obedient dullard who merely shelters behind the notation: neither is truly exploring the feeling of what the composer committed to notation. Musical feeling also demands that we explore what we read, question it and be prepared to amend what does not make sense after thorough investigation and acquaintance with that composer's idiom. Manuscript study quickly reveals how riddled printed scores are with inaccuracies (of which more below), although subjectivity is inevitable, even when original sources are available. To try to efface subjectivity, as we sometimes do, is only more subjective, and our one link with objectivity is to acknowledge and accept our subjectivity, and within that the variety of expression inherent in what the composer heard and notated.[3]

Since notation provides the main access to classical repertoire (unless we want to throw ourselves into the lion's den of received tradition), notation is the principal focus here – specifically, its definitions and limitations (in different eras and traditions), how composers use it and how we read and interpret it. One form of notation is composers' manuscripts, often the source of essential information hard to convey in print (among the *Urtext* editor's subtler tasks) which can also help one read between the lines in other printed scores where manuscripts are lost. Composers' own recorded performances are a second kind of notation, providing insights as well as questions (they can mislead, as we shall see). Analytical diagrams are yet another notational category, useful if we can distinguish between where they reveal the music and where they merely prop up their own theories. Like performance, analysis only follows music's footprints, and its focus on a particular set of features at a time – usually pitch relationships (or more rarely rhythmic ones), mostly to the exclusion of nuance and indications of feeling – can distract from one's perception of the whole. As with the painter, close work on the canvas necessitates a balancing view from afar, eyes half closed to avoid distraction by detail. Nevertheless, whatever the dangers of analysis, ignorance is worse: we need to analyse, consciously or otherwise, if we want to follow a composer's train of aural thought and feeling through basic motivic, rhythmic and tonal relationships.[4] Analysis is equally vital for reliable memorising, the 'analytical memory' described by performers like Claudio Arrau (Elder 1982: 45–6). Above all, analysis needs to clarify our relationship to the music, not congest it with information which we cannot relate to our listening or playing.

---

[3]  This is well illustrated by the story of Brahms who, when asked why he had played a passage differently in separate performances, allegedly opened the score in front of his critic and challenged him to identify where it was written that the music always had to be the same.

[4]  This was presumably the sort of analysis that Chopin demanded of his piano pupils, addressing the music's 'formal structure, as well as . . . the feelings and psychological processes which it evokes'. (This phrase, originally from Mikuli's foreword to his 1879 collected edition of Chopin, is quoted in Eigeldinger 1986: 59.) It also doubtless involved Chopin's habit of relating musical performance to verbal declamation (: 42–4). See Eigeldinger 1986: 77 for Chopin's simple analysis of his Nocturne Op. 9 No. 2, as reported by Wilhelm von Lenz.

Example 1.1a   Mozart, Clarinet Trio K. 498, I, bars 1–4

Example 1.1b   Mozart, Piano Concerto K. 488, III, bars 270–3 (piano part)

Analytical alertness also aids stylistic awareness. Style, like expression, is inherent in music (Mozart's music audibly has more style and expression than Salieri's), and though composers from one era and national background naturally share elements of style, to derive and impose retrospective rules risks wagging the dog by the tail. Even the treatises (of all eras) that deal with 'style' are both retrospective and themselves forms of notation: their usual *raison d'être* is to document past usage against contemporary change. While our era has benefited enormously from learning about upper-note trills and on-the-beat ornaments in eighteenth-century music, we must use our ears to judge whether a stylistically approved practice is or is not working. In bar 4 of Mozart's Clarinet Trio K. 498 (see Example 1.1a), elementary analysis tells us that to start the grace notes on the beat (as is now done more often than not) causes parallel octaves and a doubled leading note, all the uglier for being strongly accented on the main beat. Similarly, a crotchet grace note in the finale of the Piano Concerto in A major K. 488 (Example 1.1b), if treated as a full appoggiatura, only undermines the larger appoggiatura under it, weakening the dissonant G to a consonant A. The passage makes sense if we understand the A as an acciaccatura emphasising the appoggiatura G, and the fact that it is notated as a crotchet (in all sources of the work) is simply a quirk of Mozart's notation.

Trills in eighteenth-century music also have a happier life if, instead of imposing rules about trill starts, we hear them more basically as a reiterated appoggiatura and

Example 1.2    Mozart, Piano Concerto K. 503, II, bars 100–2 (piano part)

Example 1.3    Chopin, Ballade Op. 47, bars 134–6

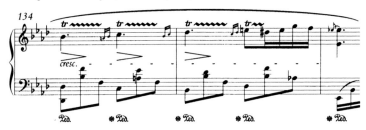

resolution – hence the upper-note beginning and variable tempo. Example 1.2, from Mozart's Piano Concerto K. 503, puts this in a more complex context. To start a trill from A here before resolving the chromatic descent to G sounds like a false step, robbing the A♭ of its passing-note function and frustrating the downward melodic impetus to the G of the dominant chord. If we allow the melody to resolve first to G and *then* begin a trill from the upper note, a more sensitive ornament results, as well as a more convincing melodic shape.

Nowadays, when performing traditions of different eras live side by side, we need to be especially circumspect. One of the more ridiculous side-effects of over-generalised stylistic rules is that performances of César Franck's Violin Sonata can now be heard, as often as not, with the third-movement trills (bars 4 and 25) starting from the upper note. Doubtless this is a semiconscious reaction to the passage's antique recitative setting, but it ignores the piece's wider context, a late-nineteenth-century tradition which played older music with main-note trill starts (as well as thickened accompaniments). An upper-note start here falls grotesquely between two stools, sounding absurdly precious against the piano's solid texture and Wagnerian chromaticism, and losing the strong fanfare-like repetition of the main note.

On the other hand, we have only begun to awaken to Chopin's baroque usage of ornamentation (as documented in Eigeldinger 1986), according to which the trills of Example 1.3 (from the Ballade Op. 47) should begin on the auxiliary note – a practice almost never observed by modern performers. I say 'auxiliary' rather than 'upper' because the fourth trill has a catch in its notation, requiring a little analytical thinking (or simple aural awareness): in harmonic terms it is really a lower-note trill from F, necessitating a start on the more dissonant E to maintain the appoggiatura effect of the three preceding upper-note starts. This also makes stronger sequential sense, with a rising third after each *Nachschlag*.

Chopin's notation here reminds us that, like a cookbook, a musical score has two basic ways of indicating the recipe for a performance: either by the method 'add fifty grams of flour' or by the method 'add enough flour to achieve a smooth consistency'. The former is prescriptive, like instrumental tablature, the latter descriptive, like pure staff notation. With most composers a natural preponderance of one or the other can usually be observed, although the two are often freely mixed (and this very mixture attests to the subjectivity inherent in our musical notation). Elsewhere (Howat, in press) I have described in detail Debussy's combinations of prescriptive rhythmic writing (where indicated contrasts of rhythm and tempo are often written into the note values) and descriptive performing indications (which capture the musical feeling and, in the case of tempo, sometimes simply confirm what is already written into the notation). In his music for piano we also find some purely descriptive open-score part-writing. Examples include the three-stave opening of the *Image* 'Cloches à travers les feuilles', which in effect must be arranged for two hands, and the last system of 'Feux d'artifice', where the bass continuity has to be 'faked' (one assumes) with pedal. The latter case supports an 'orchestral' or descriptive reading of other passages barely manageable as written, such as the opening of 'Poissons d'or' at or even near the composer's indicated tempo. Debussy's mania over the visual presentation of his editions as they appeared during his lifetime (later reprints rapidly degenerated) is part of this 'descriptive' setting of the scene, as is his extravagant use of three-stave notation in passages which technically do not require it, for example in the second series of *Images* or second book of Preludes.[5]

Understanding this balance in Debussy is important when performing a piece like the Sonata for Flute, Viola and Harp, whose contrasted sections in the first movement are linked by a virtually constant quaver pulse, with the contrasts written into the note values themselves. Widespread unawareness of this (which reflects a lapse of analytical awareness) results in performances that shred the movement's architecture, ironically by trying to obey Debussy's instructions. I have seen ensembles sigh with relief at this discovery in rehearsal, as the opening harp arpeggio becomes redolent of a graceful baroque flourish, not a dirge. We also learn literally to 'observe' Debussy's indicated nuances without adding uninvited ones. Memoirs such as Marguerite Long's (1960) confirm Debussy's detestation of parasitic tempo fluctuations, and his audio recordings[6] with Mary Garden reveal an identical 'unimpressionistic' strictness – one quite at variance with the surrounding romantic pianism. Passages of indicated rubato then stand in subtle relief, often intensifying the rhythmic surge rather than vice versa.

---

[5] The autograph of the second book of Preludes (Bibliothèque Nationale, Paris, Music MS 1006) brackets four staves to a system throughout the first four Preludes, though the music never occupies more than three at a time.

Ravel is more thoroughly prescriptive than Debussy: the hushed climax of 'Le gibet' is laconically marked 'un peu en dehors, mais sans expression', to prevent performers from botching the effect by emoting; and the score of 'Scarbo' – whose virtuosity demands every practical help – carefully indicates the most practical layout for the pianist's hands, often letting polyphonic lines emerge of their own accord.

[6] Reissued on EMI Références CHS 7 61038 2. Jean-Jacques Eigeldinger (1986: 49) documents the same strictness relative to Chopin, and Claire Croiza recalled that Fauré, when accompanying singers, 'was a metronome incarnate' (Nectoux [1990] 1991: 294).

Example 1.4a   Debussy, 'Hommage à Rameau', bar 14

Example 1.4b   Debussy, 'Mouvement', bars 30–1

This French habit of an underlying strict tempo preserves, via Chopin, a dance-inspired Mozartian tradition which was lost in much subsequent Germanic music. It is ironic that Beethoven is typically taught in strict tempo, and Chopin and French music in a haze of rubato, when first-hand memoirs tend to indicate the very opposite. What caused the reversal? A probable answer is laziness. The relative rhythmic uniformity and motoric drive of much older music facilitates and encourages uniform tempos (even when variation is desirable to avoid monotony). By contrast, the highly varied rhythmic surface of both Chopin and later French music (regarded by some as 'frivolous') makes a steady underlying tempo much harder to maintain, even if more necessary for architectural coherence. Ravel was reportedly strictest about this in pieces like 'Une barque sur l'océan', whose beat is all but submerged in the rolling piano figurations, and the similarly fluid 'Ondine', both of which he later indicated ♩ = 58.[7]

The classical nature of Debussy's notation is evident from the minim tempo shared between two consecutive *Images* for piano, the slow sarabande 'Hommage à Rameau' (headed 'Lent et grave') and the fast saltarello 'Mouvement' (headed 'Animé'), as shown in Example 1.4. The huge tempo contrast sensed between them is effected almost uniquely through the latter's running triplet semiquavers. Debussy is not alone in following the ear rather than the eye in this way: a similar identity of notated pulse links the finales of Brahms's Cello Sonata Op. 99 and Violin Sonata Op. 100, both in 2/2 but contrastingly headed 'Allegro molto' and 'Allegretto grazioso (quasi Andante)'.

---

[7]   Verbal information from Vlado Perlemuter in the late 1970s. The metronomic tempo for 'Une barque' appears in Ravel's orchestral transcription, and for 'Ondine' was indicated by Ravel to Vlado Perlemuter (printed in Ravel 1991: 7). The relation of firm tempos to the dance forms endemic to Debussy's music is discussed in Howat (in press).

Unawareness of how the difference is already written into the textures and harmonic rhythm causes many rushed performances of the Cello Sonata's finale, unbalancing the whole work to a tadpole shape – though the fault is rarer from German cellists who know the finale's main melody as a folksong. This descriptive usage of tempo markings contrasts with Mozart's 'Allegro' heading to his Piano Concerto K. 503 – a purely prescriptive 4/4 crotchet instruction for the performer, since the effect to the listener is of a Largo introduction, until the true Allegro modulates into the notation with the upbeat quavers to bar 19. (Mozart's appended 'maestoso' is the descriptive part of the indication.)

Pedalling is another highly subjective aspect of Western notation. Surprisingly, no major composer of the last 150 years has indicated this as thoroughly, or as prescriptively, as Chopin did (for the damper pedal), and even his indications leave questions. For example, Saint-Saëns stated categorically that the pedal was not to be used where Chopin had left no pedal marking (Saint-Saëns 1910: 387). This seems highly implausible, and it was probably that statement with which Debussy took issue in a letter recounting what he had learnt of Chopin pedalling from his childhood teacher Mme Mauté, an ostensible pupil of Chopin's (Durand 1927: 150). Nor do pianists generally pay much attention, anyway: Chopin's very interesting off-beat pedal releases in the F major episode of the Ballade Op. 47, yielding a beautiful 'Forlane'-like lilt if treated gently, are still largely ignored.

Debussy's pedalling is much more implicitly – or descriptively – incorporated into his notation of bass note values, ties and suchlike, including many rarely observed pedal lifts implied by phrase ends and staccatos (see Howat, in press). Debussy's explanation to Maurice Dumesnil was that 'Pedalling cannot be written down: it varies from one instrument to another, from one room, or one hall, to another' (Nichols 1992: 163). Source study also teaches us to read between the lines: for example, the printed indication 'Ped.' at bar 1 of 'Pagodes' (from the *Estampes*) changes sense upon discovering that Debussy wrote this indication in brackets (see Debussy 1991: 2 and 155), which the engraver presumably considered inessential.

A similar qualification suggests itself with Schubert, whose frequent staccato bass notes in piano music often call for a pizzicato-like treatment under higher legato lines. When this notation appears in conjunction with the indication 'col pedale', as at the beginning of the Andante sostenuto of the Sonata in B♭ major D. 960, the implication seems to be not to pedal through (as Paul Badura-Skoda reluctantly assumes – see Elder 1982: 121), but rather to use the pedal discriminatingly to avoid dryness (the texture is pure string quintet). Probably Schubert's most problematic printed pedal marking is in the fourth *Moment musical* D. 780 (Example 1.5): the indication seems banal if applied only to the half bar, or causes an unpleasant clash if carried over the barline. Various explanations for this have been proposed by editors (the different resonance of old pianos, etc.), but none refers to the autograph fair copy of the Sonata in A major D. 959, in which Schubert's 'pedale' indication nine bars from the end of the first movement is written towards the middle of the bar (his semibreves are often similarly positioned), though it is obviously intended (and always printed) from the

Example 1.5    Schubert, *Moment musical* No. 4, bars 21–5

first beat.[8] This is surely also the case in the *Moment musical* (whose autograph is long lost): the pedal is implied for that whole bar and similar bars. The confusion doubtless arose because (ironically) the only surviving source of the *Moment musical*, the notoriously sloppy first edition, for once probably followed the autograph exactly, unlike the more intelligently prepared posthumous first edition of the Sonata. The problem here is further masked by the fact that virtually all modern editions tacitly adjust the reprise (bar 135) to read as in Example 1.5, although the first edition there revealingly prints 'Ped.' from the fourth, not the fifth, semiquaver.

Modern technology has provided another form of notation: recordings by composers or their close associates. These show that our age of 'period performance' must still catch up with Elgar and Gershwin, among others, who adopted some much livelier tempos than are now prevalent. A major problem is the change over just a few decades in tone projection, vibrato and phrasing, often in response to larger halls. Few classical brass players can now float a line like the semi-jazz musicians on the 1924 Gershwin–Whiteman recording of *Rhapsody in Blue* (Ross Gorman's amazing clarinet antics are also noteworthy), or string sections judge portamentos as in the recordings conducted by Elgar.[9] As a result, modern imitations – like Georg Solti's recordings of Elgar's symphonies with tempos based on the latter's own, or Michael Tilson Thomas's orchestral accompaniments to Gershwin's Duo-Art piano roll of *Rhapsody in Blue* – tend to sound breathless in comparison with the flexibility of the originals.[10] Gershwin's piano-roll tempo through the tuttis is only marginally faster than the 1924 audio recording; however, that marginal difference – probably attributable to the fact that the piano's tone speaks faster than an orchestra's and then decays – is enough to cramp the phrasing of Tilson Thomas's band in trying to keep up with it. The faster attack and decay of piano tone may also account for Fauré consistently playing his *Pavane* on the piano 'at crotchet 100 or even faster' (Boult 1976: 490), as against his indication ♩ = 84 in the orchestral score.

[8]   For complete source details see Schubert 1979: 122. Access to the fair copy is not straightforward; a microfilm copy exists in the Library of Congress, Washington, and print copies are held by the Pendlebury Library, Cambridge.

[9]   The 1924 Gershwin–Whiteman recording of the *Rhapsody* was reissued on RCA Victrola LP AVM1-1740; Elgar's recordings are reissued on CD by EMI (CDS 7 54560 2 and 54568 2). In the booklet accompanying the Elgar CDs, Robert Philip discusses the treatment of notation like overdotting, and Jerrold Northrop Moore argues that Elgar's fast tempos were not a result of limitations in recording time.

[10]  The Solti recordings, with the London Philharmonic Orchestra, are reissued on CD (Decca 421 387-2 and 421 386-2); the Tilson Thomas recording is an LP issue by CBS (76509). On the latter's sleeve note Andrew Kazdin explains that for the recording the piano-roll perforations corresponding to the tuttis were covered over, so the orchestra had to maintain the same tempo.

In many such examples, tradition has slowed the music over even a few decades as a result of losing touch with an original dance idiom.[11] In one respect the process recalls Japanese *gagaku*, originally a repertoire of medieval Chinese popular tunes which over centuries grew progressively slower and overlaid with counterpoint until it became a new art form and an object of tradition worship when its original context was forgotten. Gershwin's *Rhapsody in Blue* suffered especially through Ferdie Grofe's rescoring for a much larger orchestra after the composer's death (he also changed Gershwin's *alla breve* through most of the work to 4/4) in response to the piece's enormous popularity – a fate parallel to that of Handel's *Messiah*, again reflecting a *gagaku*-like iconisation. Other relatively recent works which have experienced a similar history include Debussy's *Prélude à l'après-midi d'un faune* (perhaps because of Nijinsky's laborious choreography): Debussy's own printed copy of the score contains metronomic tempos which he added around 1908–13, much nimbler than habitually heard, including ♩. = 44 at the opening and ♩ = 84 for the recapitulation at figure 8 (as printed in Debussy 1970). (The difference between these indications confirms that the indicated 'Mouv$^t$ du début' at figure 8 is in effect written into the note values rather than externally imposed.) César Franck's *Symphonic Variations* are another case of an imposed, excessively slow tradition, probably through overassociation with Wagner rather than Saint-Saëns, from whose lively concertante tradition this work really springs.

On the other hand, a faulty metronome has probably caused Chabrier's magnificent piano music, virtually unplayable at many of his indicated tempos, to suffer neglect. In the *Bourrée fantasque* not only does the central section (indicated both 'Istesso tempo' and 'molto espressivo') become quite 'inexpressible' at the composer's ♩ = 152, but also Chabrier's unfinished orchestration of the piece has articulation quite implausible – especially from such a master orchestrator – at that speed.[12] (The 'bourrée d'Auvergne', from Chabrier's native region, is a clog dance, which suggests how to pace the opening repeated semiquavers in both the *Bourrée fantasque* and the similar central section of 'Paysage', from the *Pièces pittoresques*.) Wider study of Chabrier's piano music shows that much of it makes technical and musical sense two to five metronome notches slower than marked, and this is confirmed by comparison with those few pieces that do work at his metronomic indications, notably *España* and 'Mélancolie', 'Sous bois' and 'Idylle' from the *Pièces pittoresques*.[13]

A ludicrously fast printed metronome marking (♩. = 104), probably the result of a misunderstanding, has also caused the undeserved neglect of Debussy's *Masques*, a piece which rhythmically is best understood in relation to the tempo defined at bar 7 of its companion piece *L'isle joyeuse* ('Modéré et très souple' – see Debussy 1991: xvii–xviii). Debussy's recorded piano roll of *Children's Corner*, sometimes cited for its very fast tempos, is another suspect source: closer study reveals a possible error in the

[11] See Nectoux [1990] 1991: 108 concerning the dance setting of Fauré's *Pavane*, arranged by Fauré and Robert de Montesquiou.
[12] Chabrier's unfinished orchestration is in the Bibliothèque Nationale, Paris, Music MS 19201.
[13] Possibly he used a different metronome on occasion, for example while away from home.

encoding of the roll and suggests that the original recorded tempos were significantly slower.[14]

The case of Ravel's Concerto in G major is more complex because of the
influential 1932 recording made by its dedicatee Marguerite Long and allegedly
(though in fact not) conducted by Ravel,[15] while the two artists were touring the
work through Europe. Significant departures from Ravel's indications audible on this
recording include large tempo fluctuations in the first movement's second subject
group; a 'poco a poco accelerando' through the movement's long build-ups to the
recapitulation and end (reaching $\downarrow$ = 152, far above Ravel's specified $\downarrow$ = 116), with a
prestissimo blur in the quaver run-up to the recapitulation; wide rubato in the Adagio
(a movement whose main inspiration came from the Adagio of Mozart's Clarinet
Quintet); and again a 'prestissimo possibile' finale (versus Ravel's presto) which virtually
ensures its encoring by making it too short for the rest of the Concerto. Through
Long's enormous influence as a teacher, those quirks have become a received tradition
unthinkingly emulated by nearly all performers since (the Concerto is hardly ever
heard as Ravel conceived and notated it).[16] The point here is not to condemn the
colourful Marguerite Long, but simply to start reversing the damage inflicted by this
particular received tradition. The main problem is that the excessive, unsteady speeds
defeat much of Ravel's meticulous orchestration and breadth of architecture (for
example, at the solo run into the first movement's recapitulation, which, in Ravel's
notation, carries a long build-up of quaver momentum through to the recapitulation).

Though we must regard them with caution, memoirs of composers' associates
sometimes indicate important details not made explicit in the score. Vlado Perlemuter's
and Gaby Casadesus's separate reminiscences specify two moments pointed out by
Ravel where his usually exact notation does not quite suffice: in 'Oiseaux tristes' of
*Miroirs*, the triplet figure in bar 2 has to be slightly compressed (Perlemuter and
Jourdan-Morhange 1988: 21), and in 'Alborada del gracioso' the demisemiquaver turns
at bars 126–9 and 157–60 conversely must be slightly stretched out (Elder 1982: 75).[17]
Debussy's stepdaughter Mme de Tinan (the former Dolly Bardac) likewise recalled
that Debussy made a characteristic sarabande lift in a gestural context shared by the
'Sarabande' of *Pour le piano* and 'Hommage à Rameau' (*Images*, I), a nuance only partly
implied by the notated staccato dots and tenuto dashes (Example 1.6).[18]

---

[14]  Welte roll 2733, recorded, together with Debussy's other piano-roll recordings for Edwin Welte, between
      1910 and 1912. A less widely known reissue of roll 2733 in the early 1920s slows the tempos by
      approximately 30 per cent. For more technical discussion see Howat 1994 and Debussy (in press).
[15]  This commercial recording (reissued on LP on EMI World Records (SH209)) was conducted not by Ravel
      (who was not only a poor conductor but also, at the time of the tour, already in the first grips of his final
      illness) but by Pedro de Freitas-Branco, although Ravel was present and gave advice (Orenstein 1990:
      535–6). Thanks are expressed to Arbie Orenstein and Howard Ferguson for kindly supplying information
      useful to the present chapter.
[16]  Long's memoirs (1971) say nothing of Ravel's reaction to those liberties, but some severe dissent between
      them was witnessed by Felix Aprahamian, who overheard their furious arguments in 1932 while they
      rehearsed the Concerto in G major in the Queen's Hall, London (verbal information from Aprahamian).
[17]  In his orchestral version Ravel renotates this turn in semiquavers.
[18]  Mme de Tinan (1893–1985) provided this information when I played the pieces to her in the late 1970s.

Example 1.6   Debussy's reported 'sarabande' lifts

a. 'Sarabande' from *Pour le piano*, bars 1–2

b. 'Hommage à Rameau', bars 8–9

Debussy's sarabande lifts are of course suggested by his headings to the two pieces concerned. If this reference seems indirect, it is as prescriptive to anyone familiar with the dance idiom as is Bach's heading 'Gigue' to the binary notation in the finale of his Partita in E minor BWV 830.[19] For Debussy, the association of heading and gesture was obvious: his friend Emile Vuillermoz describes how he played a sarabande 'with the easy simplicity of a good dancer from the sixteenth century' (Nichols 1992: 156). The fault mostly lies in our era's loss of contact (so soon after Debussy's time!) with dance, which would allow immediate recognition of the gestures. This applies equally to the dance shorthand in Debussy's 'La soirée dans Grenade' and 'La Puerta del Vino', both headed 'Mouvᵗ de Habanera': according to Marcel Ciampi, Debussy wanted the ostinato rhythm 'overdotted' in habanera style, a stretching as natural as the overdotting in Mozart's sicilianos.[20] Debussy's piano-roll recording of 'La soirée dans Grenade' reveals an analogous stretching of the rhythms ♪., ♪♪ and ♪♪ at bars 33–6 towards ♪♪, ♪♪♪ and ♪♪♪ respectively.[21]

Notational stretching of this sort remains more endemic to the twentieth century than we are normally taught. A recording by Béla and Ditta Bartók of the Sonata for Two Pianos and Percussion demonstrates both pianists' natural compression of the first movement's iambs (♪ ♩), as characteristic of Hungarian speech or song as the light *parlando rubato* they apply to singing lines as in bars 317ff.[22] Again the context alone

---

19   See Ferguson 1975: 92 regarding other gigues notated in binary metre, some of which exist in additional ternary sources.

20   Information kindly supplied by Ciampi's former pupil Julie Hennig.

21   Welte roll 2735; for more information see Howat 1994 and Debussy 1991: 152.

22   Bartók's complete recordings were first reissued on LP by Hungaroton LPX 12326-33 (commercial recordings) and 12334-38 (private recordings). They are now on the CD set HCD 1 2326/31.

makes the reference plain to those familiar with the idiom; to those unfamiliar, the exact nuance is unnotatable. For the latter, probably the best initiation is to listen not only to recordings of Bartók playing (as well as east European folksong in general), but also to the remarkable recording of Bartók reciting, in Hungarian, the libretto of his beloved *Cantata profana*.[23] As with any form of rubato, unfeeling obedience to the abstract notation will miss the mark as widely as an inexpert guess or – as more often happens – a hopeful 'meno mosso' resulting in rhythmic collapse.

The other twentieth-century idiom where baroque notation and practice are still endemic is notated jazz or 'syncopated' swing. The piano music of Gershwin or Billy Mayerl mixes dotted and undotted notation as well as semiquaver and quaver upbeats, which in practice share the same 'swung' value, as in some of Handel's notation. Likewise, the second of Gershwin's Preludes for piano, in blues form, falls flat unless played slightly *inégal* – subtly though not blatantly 'swung', and not too slow, for the blues of the 1920s had not yet slowed to the blues of the 1940s.[24] Received tradition sometimes puts the boot on the wrong foot here, for instance by habitually applying a heavy swing to the D major Allegro episode (figure 57) in *An American in Paris*: the 1929 recording of this work directed by Nat Shilkret, with Gershwin playing celesta, makes much more vivid sense by playing the passage in quick, straight quavers marked by the side drum.[25]

Schubert on the other hand straddles the border of a particular nineteenth-century tradition in which a consistent metre entails some unmarked fluctuation. In a single decade he moved from a Haydnesque idiom to the massive architectural sophistication of his last works, and to understand his tempo and metric indications often means going beyond the context of a single work. His 'Great' Symphony in C major is an excellent example, its first movement specifying only the opening Andante, the ensuing Allegro ma non troppo and the coda's Più moto. In practice this movement demands, and nearly always receives, some degree of fluctuation to link those large-scale energy levels, and many performances extend this to layering the main Allegro. The problem is summed up by the movement's last twenty-three bars, which must clearly relate not only to the Più moto immediately before, but also to the opening Andante. Wilhelm Furtwängler's famous 1951 recording of the Symphony is probably the most daring, its range of tempo even contrasting the same thematic material across different contexts – for example, the Allegro first subject just before and then just after the double bar, or its initial *forte* appearance against the *piano* recapitulation.[26] While few would take the huge risks that Furtwängler, with his extraordinary architectonic sense, was able to carry off on one particular occasion, it is interesting that a recent live performance on period instruments, conducted by Simon Rattle, also conveyed some

[23]  See note 22. Incidentally, Robert Casadesus recalled that Bartók's piano playing reminded him of Debussy's (Elder 1982: 33).

[24]  Gershwin's audio recording of the three Preludes (reissued on RCA Victrola LP AVM1-1740) conveys something of this, though a little uncharacteristic unsteadiness suggests that he was being raced against the clock to fit all three on a single 78 rpm side.

[25]  See note 24 for discographic details.

[26]  Reissue on CD: Deutsche Grammophon 427 405-2GDO.

Example 1.7a   Schubert, Sonata D. 845, I, bars 40–4

Example 1.7b   Schubert, Sonata D. 894, IV, bars 181–5

such flexibility, so that the natural pace and dance-like character of all the varied material had a sense of continuity without being forced into uniformity.[27]

Other Schubert works confirm this implicit terracing of tempo as an essential part of the music's architecture. Radu Lupu's recording of the Sonata in A minor D. 845 illustrates this (perhaps inadvertently) by adhering to a single tempo throughout the first movement, set by the recitative-like opening Moderato and the development section's semiquavers.[28] Even Lupu's persuasive artistry cannot get the dancelike second subject (Example 1.7a) on its toes at this pace, and comparison with the E♭ episode from the finale of the later Sonata in G major D. 894, also *alla breve* (Example 1.7b), virtually pleads with us to let Example 1.7a move faster. (The faster tempo layer really needs to, and easily can, take effect from bar 10 or bar 26.)

The first movement of Schubert's late Sonata in A major D. 959 has a similar 'intertextual' link, through its running triplets, to the opening *alla breve* of the Sonata in D major D. 850, and it is doubtless because of this that Schubert's preparatory draft for D. 959 indicates ¢.[29] His change to C for the fair copy reflects the broader character of the two main subjects, but the variant also draws attention to dual rhythmic levels in this exposition, with the running triplets suggesting a slightly faster tempo if they are not to sag. Such a layering of tempo, far from distorting, is of the architectural and dramatic essence, as it sets off the main thematic statements (bars 1–6, 16–21, 55–81 and 117–22), with their melodic breadth and diatonic rising bass, against the more

27  Concert by the Orchestra of the Age of Enlightenment, Queen Elizabeth Hall, London, 11 February 1994. In a conversation afterwards, Simon Rattle described this pulse as a 'single heartbeat that sometimes moves faster or slower'.

28  Decca CD: 417 640-2DH.

29  See the facsimile in Schubert 1987: II, 1. The edition of D. 850 published in Schubert's lifetime conversely reads C, though that could be a misprint. In his 1979 edition of Schubert's sonatas, Howard Ferguson also draws attention to the variable tempo necessary especially for the first movements of D. 845 and D. 959.

mobile bridge passages (from bars 8, 28, 82 and 123), with their triplets and chromatic rising bass (from E each time).

A crucial point here is that judicious tempo adjustment is less intrusive or discernible to listeners than the sagging or cramping that results from imposing a uniform tempo on local material which does not suit it. For this reason it is understandable that Schubert does not specifically mark small intrinsic fluctuations, as these might risk exaggeration and musical fragmentation. On the other hand, he usually indicates tempo layering with care when it has to be audible as such, for example between scherzos and trios, or in rondo episodes or dance movements.

Though it need not imply uniformity, larger-scale temporal balance also has its say. Alfred Brendel remarks that a recent tendency to perform the first movement of the Sonata in B♭ major D. 960 at an ultra-slow tempo, besides misinterpreting the 'moderato' marking, 'makes for a movement longer than the other three' (Brendel 1990: 79).[30] In any case, the 'Molto' (of Molto moderato) in the heading to D. 960 was an afterthought, for Schubert's preparatory draft is merely headed 'Moderato' (see Schubert 1987: III, 1). The opposite is true of his draft of the Sonata in C minor D. 958, which reveals a cautionary 'moderato' appended to the first movement's 'Allegro' heading (: I, 1). (Schubert probably had in mind not only the second subject in its various guises, but also the passage before and just into the recapitulation, where the ostinato must be carried through without an ungainly lurch.) In all, the tempo indications in Schubert's drafts – the 'moderate' Allegro in D. 958, the ¢ in D. 959 and the unqualified 'Moderato' in D. 960 – put one another in context and help to avoid any exaggerated readings of the final markings.

That is one of many reasons why *Urtext* editions – especially if they take the word at all literally – could assist performers by showing variants from early versions: even if a later reading has supplanted them, they often play an important qualifying role. Nor can we be sure that a grammatically correct final version always overrides earlier readings. Schubert's working draft of the finale of the Sonata in A major D. 959 (Schubert 1987: II, 11) shows two interesting accidentals unmentioned in any existing edition – natural signs before the left hand's C and F in bar 231 (Example 1.8). Was their omission in the fair copy an oversight or a deliberate decision? Grammatically both versions are plausible, and for editors to make a passive decision by leaving the early reading unmentioned is highly subjective. Knowing about the natural signs also influences the performer's understanding of the surrounding context, specifically the anticipatory G♮ in bar 229.

Preparation of the Debussy complete edition has also taught the importance of early sources. Debussy's preliminary draft of the Etudes shows some accidentals not found in later sources,[31] possibly omitted by error, whereas his autograph of the first book of

---

[30] Compare Clifford Curzon's recording of the Sonata in D major D. 850, which, characterised by very reasonable tempos but no exposition repeat, has a first movement exactly half the duration of the second movement's thirteen minutes (Decca Jubilee LP: JB145).

[31] They appear on auxiliary staves in the *Oeuvres complètes*, series 1, vol. VI; see in addition Debussy 1989: 9.

Example 1.8   Schubert, Sonata D. 959, IV, bars 229–32 and preparatory draft, bar 231

Preludes conversely contains many indications added only after proofs had been engraved from it (see Debussy 1985: 159–60), the additions then being copied onto the proofs with a few inevitable slips of the pen. In 'Ce qu'a vu le Vent d'Ouest' his indication 'Revenir progressivement au mouv^t Animé' slipped from bar 17 in the autograph to bar 18 in the proofs and first edition; likewise, in 'Minstrels' 'un peu plus allant' inadvertently migrated from bar 9 to bar 5. While these are obvious instances of faulty proof annotations, a trickier case is the 'Cédez – – – // a Tempo' at bars 26–8 of 'Voiles', which makes little musical sense, yet whose autograph presence in both the composer's manuscript and the proof would seem doubly to authenticate it. Musical considerations suggest that the whole nuance properly belongs a bar earlier, and that the slip happened when Debussy perhaps absentmindedly added the indication to the autograph and then mechanically transcribed it onto the proof. The repeated lesson for editors and performers is that a composer's copying and revising processes mix improvements with inadvertent corruptions, sometimes making an earlier source more definitive in certain passages.

A subtler lesson from this is to read imaginatively backwards and solve illogicalities where no prior source remains, for example in the first movement of Mozart's Piano Concerto in C major K. 467 (Example 1.9a). Pianists occasionally fill in the overthin texture at bars 227–9, but I have not yet heard conductors more sensibly take the initiative by completing the violin parts as in Example 1.9b. In the autograph (see the facsimile in Mozart 1985: 24) Mozart left these bars blank but without rests, a piece of evidence masked by the Neue Mozart Ausgabe's well-meant policy of tacitly adding full-sized rests to empty bars.

This last case is supported by analogy with Debussy's Prelude 'Danseuses de Delphes', Debussy's piano-roll recording of which contains added left-hand offbeat notes in bars 8–9 (F and G, doubling the right-hand thumb; see Debussy 1985: 2). From comparison with a similar texture in bars 16–17, the added notes appear to correct an omission in the notated sources, and it is surprising that for seventy-five years neither pianists nor editors thought of this correction by simply relating the earlier passage to bars 16–17, even though the texture, like that in Mozart's Concerto K. 467, does not make proper sense without it. Better known examples in Mozart's piano concertos are the incompatible harmonies between piano and orchestra in bar 40 of the Larghetto of K. 491 and bars 58–60 of the finale of K. 503 – both amazingly left unsignalled in the Neue Mozart Ausgabe – where the piano part, obviously written in

Example 1.9  Mozart, Piano Concerto K. 467, I

a.  bars 222–6, piano and violins (other instruments *tacet*)

b.  bars 227–30, piano and hypothetical violin parts

relative haste, has to be reharmonised to fit with the orchestra. While most pianists
comply (otherwise it sounds like an embarrassing slip on their part), it is much rarer to
hear a retouching of bar 254 in the first movement of K. 491, where the piano's
dominant seventh chords and repeated left-hand A♭s, while not publicly disgracing the
pianist, swamp the orchestra's subtler quaver alternations of tonic and dominant.

Source work also engenders an awareness of the distortions perpetrated by well-
meant printing conventions. In preparing the Debussy complete edition, for instance,
numerous misplaced dynamics or inexact hairpins in earlier editions have been corrected (see Howat 1985: 102 and in press). The problem goes far beyond Debussy, of
course: we are all familiar with anomalies like hairpins climaxing on a trivial
accompanying quaver, or a crescendo going to the barline only to diminuendo onto
the first note of the ensuing bar. (Such sacrifices to the Great God Barline are a
particularly frequent engraver's ritual.) In isolation these may seem trivial, but together
they sap confidence in the composer's notation to the point where frustrated performers
just ignore the whole nuance, or start applying their own ideas instead. Publishers'
house rules of adding rests, inverting stemming and shifting notes across staves can
similarly obscure subtleties of voicing, hand layout and pedalling implicit from the

composer's notation. A more arcane engraving rule, formulated in the interests of visual grace, often limits the width of hairpin dynamics to a small fraction of their length (and in some contexts forbids their crossing the sacred barline). No doubt that rule lies behind the often insipid rendering of dynamics in performances of Fauré and Debussy, quite at variance with the many bold, wide hairpins visible in their manuscripts. This can make a big difference to works like *Dolly* as well as more obvious cases like *L'isle joyeuse*.

Although it was quickly agreed – on the strength of overwhelming evidence – to give priority in the Debussy *Oeuvres complètes* to the composer's manuscript logic in such respects, experience elsewhere shows that many publishers, even of self-styled *Urtext* editions, will not yet accept any such flouting of engraving or house conventions widely regarded as musical 'grammar' or 'laws'. When those conventions inadvertently distort or conceal a composer's indications, *Urtext* editing still has a major issue to confront. Meanwhile, as performers our task of interpreting notation often means quietly editing or re-editing it ourselves – a task far from wilful in intention, involving all our cognitive and musical faculties.

To conclude, the relationship between notation and music can be likened to the painter who works close to the canvas and then steps back: in the same manner, our reasoned, stylistic, analytical assimilation of a score is (ideally) followed by the lightning intuition that releases a performance into living sound. This relationship underlies Sir Thomas Beecham's observation that 'the function of music is to free us from the tyranny of conscious thought' (Atkins and Newman 1978: 80) – not, we may note, 'to free us from conscious thought', but merely from its tyranny. Beecham, one of the most careful preparers of scores and parts in the history of conducting, had every cause to understand the relationship, and his answer to an adolescent colleague's earnest question brings us back to where we began. 'What is music?', the young man asked. Beecham's response: 'The innumerable voices of eternity.'[32]

---

[32] Verbal information from the late Dennis Stoll, who as an adolescent posed the question to Beecham. Stoll knew Beecham through his father Sir Oswald Stoll, and was for some time an assistant and deputy conductor to Beecham.

REFERENCES

Atkins, H. and Newman, A., eds., 1978: *Beecham Stories* (London: Robson).
Boult, A., 1976: Letter to *The Musical Times* 117: 490.
Brendel, A., 1990: *Music Sounded Out* (London: Robson).
Debussy, C., 1970: *Prelude to 'The Afternoon of a Faune': An Authoritative Score*, ed. W. W. Austin (New York: Norton).
    1985: *Oeuvres complètes de Claude Debussy*, series 1, vol. V: *Préludes*, I and II, ed. R. Howat with C. Helffer (Paris: Costallat et Durand).
    1989: *Etudes pour le piano. Fac-similé des esquisses autographes (1915)*, with introduction by R. Howat (Geneva: Minkoff).

1991: *Oeuvres complètes de Claude Debussy*, series 1, vol. III: *Estampes*; *D'un cahier d'esquisses*; *Masques*; *L'isle joyeuse*; *Images*, I and II, ed. R. Howat (Paris: Costallat et Durand).

in press: *Oeuvres complètes de Claude Debussy*, series 1, vol. II: *Images* (1894); *Pour le piano*; *Children's Corner*, ed. R. Howat (Paris: Costallat et Durand).

Durand, J., ed., 1927: *Lettres de Claude Debussy à son éditeur, publiées par Jacques Durand* (Paris: Durand).

Eigeldinger, J.-J., 1986: *Chopin: Pianist and Teacher as Seen by His Pupils*, trans. N. Shohet with K. Osostowicz and R. Howat, ed. R. Howat (Cambridge: Cambridge University Press).

Elder, D., 1982: *Pianists at Play* (Evanston, Illinois: The Instrumentalist Company).

Ferguson, H., 1975: *Keyboard Interpretation from the 14th to the 19th Century* (London: Oxford University Press).

Howat, R., 1985: 'The New Debussy Edition: approaches and techniques', *Studies in Music* 19: 94–113.

1994: 'Debussy and Welte', *The Pianola Journal* 7: 3–18.

in press: 'Sources and performance: Debussy's piano music', in R. Langham Smith, ed., *Debussy Studies* (Cambridge: Cambridge University Press).

Long, M., 1960: *Au piano avec Claude Debussy* (Paris: Julliard). English translation: *At the Piano with Debussy*, trans. O. Senior-Ellis (London: Dent, 1972).

1971: *Au piano avec Maurice Ravel* (Paris: Julliard).

Mozart, W. A., 1985: *Piano Concerto No. 21 in C major, K. 467: The Autograph Score*, with introduction by J. LaRue (New York: Dover).

Nectoux, J.-M., [1990] 1991: *Gabriel Fauré, a Musical Life*, trans. R. Nichols (Cambridge: Cambridge University Press).

Nichols, R., 1992: *Debussy Remembered* (London: Faber).

Orenstein, A., 1990: *A Ravel Reader: Correspondence, Articles, Interviews* (New York: Columbia University Press).

Perlemuter, V. and Jourdan-Morhange, H., 1988: *Ravel according to Ravel* (London: Kahn and Averill).

Ravel, M., 1991: *Gaspard de la nuit*, ed. R. Nichols (Peters: London).

Saint-Saëns, C., 1910: 'Quelques mots sur l'exécution des œuvres de Chopin', *Le courrier musical* 13/10: 386–7.

Schubert, F., 1979: *The Complete Pianoforte Sonatas*, vol. III, ed. H. Ferguson (London: Associated Board of the Royal Schools of Music).

1987: *Drei große Klaviersonaten für das Pianoforte. Frühe Fassungen*, ed. E. Hilmar, 4 vols. in 1 (Tutzing: Hans Schneider).

Stravinsky, I. and Craft, R., 1962: *Expositions and Developments* (London: Faber).

Timbrell, C., 1982: *French Pianism: An Historical Perspective* (London: Kahn and Averill).

# CHAPTER TWO

# Expression in performance: generativity, perception and semiosis

ERIC CLARKE

## INTRODUCTION

Empirical and theoretical research during the last fifteen years has established a widely shared view of many of the principles involved in producing expressive musical performances, with a particular concentration on expressive timing properties (e.g. Clarke 1988; Sundberg 1988; Todd 1989). The paradoxical feature of this research is that while all authors recognise the subtlety and sophistication of skilled musical performance, their studies indicate that the principles governing expression in performance are comparatively simple. At the same time listeners appear to extract something from these expressive features which profoundly influences the overall effect of the performance: the simplicity of the general procedures that apply in performance expression seems to belie their communicative force. At the very beginning of empirical research into performance, Seashore (1938) pointed out the complex interaction between characteristics which are part of the performance (accentuations, lengthenings, shortenings, etc.) and properties which the listener may attribute to the performer but which are mental constructs resulting from the listener's own parsing of musical structures. The sense of accent on a metrically strong event, whatever its actual dynamic level, duration or style of articulation, is an example of this phenomenon. Seashore's observation, which has been largely ignored in subsequent research, raises the possibility of a somewhat different approach to understanding the meaning and force of expressive effects in performance – one which takes far more seriously the realities of performance features and the complex interdependence of intrinsic musical structure, stylistic norms and the expectations that they engender. This chapter surveys different approaches to expression in performance and develops a view, based on certain principles in semiotics, which recognises both the systematic simplicity of performance features and their rhetorical force.

Among the numerous studies of expression in performance and its relationship to structure, the majority have adopted an outlook influenced in some respect by Chomsky's generative linguistic theory. This is not the only approach, however, and it is important to consider at least two additional perspectives identifiable in recent writing on the subject: narrative/dramatic theories (e.g. Schmalfeldt 1985), and what may be termed the 'integrated energy flux' approach (Todd 1994). The first part of this chapter critically reviews all three perspectives before presenting an alternative, based on Peirce's semiotics, which seems to offer certain advantages over previous accounts.

## THREE PERSPECTIVES ON EXPRESSION

### Generative theory

If there is an orthodoxy in recent work on performance expression, it must be identified with the so-called generative approach. With its origins nominally rooted in generative linguistics, this influence often amounts to little more than the acknowledgement that a serially ordered temporal phenomenon (performance) is controlled by a hierarchically organised representation – an idea which can be traced at least as far back as Lashley ([1951] 1969). Sufficient literature exists for a full exposition of this theory to be unnecessary here (see e.g. Clarke 1988), but a re-examination of its core principles will be instructive. At its heart is the idea that expression comprises systematic patterns of deviation from the 'neutral' information given in a score, which take the form of rule-based transformations of canonical values originating in the performer's internal representation of the musical structure. There are problems with this definition, however. How does one distinguish between deliberate departures (or transformations) and mere accidents? What about unnotated music? And what about expressive markings already in the score (accelerandos and ritardandos, crescendos and decrescendos, etc.)? Must we regard corresponding tempo and dynamic changes in the performance as inexpressive simply because they follow such markings?

Other views of expression attempt to circumvent these problems while retaining the basic principle that expression is a departure from some norm. For instance Desain and Honing (1992: 175) suggest that 'Expression within a unit is defined as the deviations of its parts with respect to the norm set by the unit itself.' This definition is more generally applicable and can in principle deal with music for which there is no score, since 'the norm set by the unit itself' can be an emergent property of a given piece considered on its own (in the case of music which makes no recognisable stylistic references outside itself) or in a wider stylistic context. To make this more concrete, let us consider a hypothetical example – the analysis of expressive timing in a bebop jazz solo – and let us imagine that the melody of the jazz standard on which the solo is based contains a passage in even quavers. In jazz performance equal quavers tend to be played in an alternating long/short pattern (rather like the *notes inégales* of the French baroque) so that this pattern is a stylistic norm, rather than an expressive feature. An analysis of expressive timing based on Desain and Honing's definition will classify this underlying long/short alternation as part of the stylistic norm and identify as 'expressive' any deviations (intensifications or diminutions of the long/short ratio, or any other temporal features) which might be superimposed on it. The basic principle here is that global values for a parameter (e.g. tempo) at one hierarchical level become the norms against which smaller-scale features are assessed at a lower level: the overall tempo of a phrase defines the norm against which the tempos of two sub-phrases are expressively measured, and so on down the hierarchy.

Although the problems of a definition of expression which is too reliant on the authority of the score remain unresolved, the basic principle of deviation or transform-ation is still widely accepted. This suggests that expression is detectable only when a listener has sufficient stylistic knowledge to be aware of the norms against which the raw material of the performance is to be 'measured'. Although there is no systematic empirical evidence to refute or support such a proposal, it accords with intuition and anecdote: uninitiated listeners tend to be less sensitive to details of expression than their more sophisticated peers. Nevertheless, the very little empirical research related to this issue suggests virtually the opposite – but for interesting reasons. Repp (1992a) showed that highly trained listeners were least able to detect an intentionally introduced local timing perturbation in an otherwise metronomic rendering of a phrase from a Beethoven sonata at precisely those points where a performer would be expected to apply rubato – i.e. at phrase boundaries. Paradoxically, then, the very structural and stylistic expectations that are necessary for expression to be identifiable can make deviations *less* detectable due to the tendency for local details to become assimilated into the general expressive scheme.

A variant of the generative theory is Clynes's so-called 'composer's pulse' theory (Clynes 1983). This makes use of the same basic definition of expression but differs from the work discussed so far in its controversial claim that the expressive profile is generated from a particular 'pulse pattern' (a set of metrically related dynamic and timing values) which is characteristic of the composer. Clynes's theory by no means ignores musical structure – he proposes that the pulse pattern applies with variable strength at a number of structural levels – but the thrust of his model is the idea that performance expression is above all the articulation of a composer's personal blueprint. For Clynes, convincing performances of a work are attained only when a performer (or artificial performance system) respects the pulse pattern appropriate to its com-poser. At an intuitive/anecdotal level this is not wholly implausible: for the style of a particular composer to be identified, certain structural invariants must exist, and it is perhaps reasonable to claim that these invariants bring with them associated expressive performance invariants. However, the systematic empirical evidence for this claim is inconclusive at best: Repp (1990) did not find that listeners who heard artificially gen-erated performances of music by a number of composers consistently preferred them when they were generated with the pulse pattern specific to that composer versus another composer's. More recently Clynes (in press) has claimed that only the most expert musicians reliably show this differential response.

Whatever the conclusions of the empirical evidence, the idea hovering in the background of Clynes's theory – that a composer's work is necessarily and uniformly suffused with a particular expressive profile – does not stand scrutiny, unless hedged around with special conditions: there are too many composers for whom the degree of stylistic variation within their output is greater than the variation between them and their contemporaries, and unless a nominal or metaphysical case was made ('simply because the work is known to be by Haydn, it must be played with the Haydn pulse'), it seems impossible for a listener to prefer a composer-specific pulse pattern for a piece which cannot be distinguished from a work by another composer.

An alternative to this somewhat contradictory state of affairs is to dispense altogether with the notion of expression as deviation, which is precisely what Todd (1994) has done in recent work.

### Expression as integrated energy flux

Todd's research adopts the simple principle that expression can be identified with the continuously variable energy level of the performed music. This idea can be modelled as a filter which integrates energy over a time window with a constant decay function. Todd has developed the model with a series of filters operating at different time scales and producing a hierarchy of integrated energy profiles. An attractive feature of the model is the way in which it synthesises the various contributions of all components of expression (tempo, dynamics, articulation, timbre, vibrato) since each creates fluctuations in integrated energy. More significantly in the light of the previous discussion, it makes no distinction between energy changes caused by properties of the score and those brought about by performance features. Consider for instance Chopin's Prelude in E minor Op. 28 No. 4 (shown in Example 2.1 on p. 29). Irrespective of the way it is played, the integrated energy profile will rise in bar 9 as the right hand begins to move in quavers, simply because larger numbers of events result in higher levels of integrated energy. Similarly, changes in the marked dynamic level, chord density and tempo will result in corresponding increases and decreases in the energy over a series of time windows – as will changes in pitch and even timbre, since the integrated energy of a high frequency is greater than that for a low frequency. Todd has shown that the energy profile obtained from the model, from which a tree structure can be directly recovered, bears a very close relationship to a phrase-structure analysis arrived at by conventional musicological means.

The theory is, as is readily evident, an avowedly bottom-up, knowledge-free approach. It takes account of abstract structural characteristics (e.g. harmonic, melodic and metrical structures) only to the extent that these are expressed through changes in tempo and dynamics, and for that reason alone it cannot be a complete theory. Furthermore, it assumes as a principal starting point the idea that expressive properties are directly related to musical structure, so that changes in integrated energy which are brought about by expressive means (changes in dynamics and tempo primarily) have an essentially additive relationship with integrated energy changes resulting from properties of the score (such as changes in note density, register, notated dynamic level, etc.). This direct mapping of structure into expression is not shared by all writers on the subject: some have argued in particular for the importance of dramatic characterisation as a factor in expressive performance.

*Narration/Drama in performance expression*

One author who has claimed this is Schmalfeldt (1985). In considering the relationship between structural analysis and performance, Schmalfeldt observes that music can be analysed in innumerable ways, and that only a few of these might have bearing on, or value for, the act of performance. She conducts a dialogue between herself as analyst and as performer, and after an analytical discussion of Beethoven's Bagatelle Op. 126 No. 2, she summarises her position as follows:

> When the musician functions as analyst or listener, he has the opportunity simultaneously to enjoy several modes of perceiving the work of art. When the musician performs, his synoptic comprehension must be placed completely at the service of projecting the work through time – making moment-by-moment connections, holding the thread of musical logic at every point, living within and through the work until, and even after, its final tones have been achieved. The Analyst's interpretation of formal structure in terms of dramatic action [referring to the immediately preceding analysis of Op. 126 No. 2] attempts to capture the active, diachronic experience of the performer. And though the metaphor of the rivalry and ultimate confrontation of ideas may seem highly subjective, it speaks directly to *the need to find the character of the work* within its structure.
>
> (Schmalfeldt 1985: 17–18; emphasis added)

The significant feature here is Schmalfeldt's focus on characterisation and drama as primary considerations, which arises out of her acknowledgement that the temporal nature of performance creates priorities different from those of the analyst, for whom time becomes converted into space – or at least loses its dynamic and irreversible quality. While 'character' and 'drama' are both slippery terms and are also obviously related to more conventional structural categories (as Schmalfeldt's own analysis demonstrates), it is also clear that in some circumstances drama and structure in the more conventional sense may run into conflict. A case in point might be late Beethoven: despite a continuing adherence at a deep level to well-understood structural principles (especially the sonata principle), the musical surface often becomes highly disrupted and apparently discontinuous. In these circumstances a performer may be faced with a real dilemma: whether to try to glue together a structure threatening to come apart through the force of its own internal tensions, or to give prominence to the dramatic contrasts between sharply differentiated surface elements.

Shaffer (1992) has recently discussed performance expression in these terms, and it is perhaps no accident that the music he considers is late Beethoven – the posthumously published short piece known as WoO 60. The data of four pianists, each of whom performed the work several times, are analysed by Shaffer in terms of the unity or diversity of interpretation achieved by the individual performers and the range of interpretations discernible across all four. Focusing on the more contrasting performances, Shaffer suggests that it is not a difference in their structural implications which distinguishes them, but rather a difference of characterisation. He supports this interpretation by proposing that expression is used to convey mood and narrative in music and can only partially be reduced to a conventional notion of structure:

Expression, including the choice of tempo, seems relevant to conveying mood as an aspect of musical meaning. If we further suppose that music can convey an abstract narrative, then we can think of the musical structure as describing an implicit event, and the gestures of musical expression as corresponding to the emotional gestures of an implicit protagonist who witnesses or participates in the event. Thus, the performer's interpretation can be viewed as helping to define the character of the protagonist . . . Using this conception as a way of relating structure and mood in the music also allows us to see that, in principle, a performer can be faithful to its structure and at the same time have the freedom to shape its moods . . .

If the structures in the music, particularly those governing tension and relaxation, define the implicit event, then structure should be the primary determinant of the patterning of expressive gesture over the musical surface. On the other hand, the shaping of expression and the choice of expressive features – timing, dynamics, timbre, and articulation – is a function of the musical character, and is, at least partly, created by the performer. The concept of an underlying narrative takes the study of musical expression beyond recent studies that relate expression only to local properties of music structure . . .

(Shaffer 1992: 265)

As this extract makes clear, there is a tricky relationship between structure and character or narrative here, the latter category overlapping with, but not reducible to, the former. Shaffer himself justifies introducing the concept of musical narrative on three counts: first, it emphasises that expression cannot simply be mapped onto structure; secondly, it draws attention to the performer as a creator of musical character; and thirdly, it provides a link with the idea that performers unconsciously use the physical gestures associated with emotional states as a basis for shaping musical expression. There seems to be considerable agreement on at least the first of these points (that performance cannot be reduced to the articulation of structure) among commentators whose background is in both analysis and performance (e.g. Schmalfeldt 1985; Dunsby 1989; Rink 1990). Whether grafting on a component of mood, character, drama or narrative is the way to resolve this difficulty remains open to question, however, and it is with the aim of identifying a more inclusive framework within which to consider the issue that I now turn to semiotics.

## A SEMIOTIC VIEW OF PERFORMANCE EXPRESSION

One of the features of performance expression, and in a sense the rock on which all of the foregoing theories founder, is its diversity and multiplicity of function. All of the theories proposed above have something to offer, and yet each suffers from some serious limitation which renders it inadequate. It is not enough, furthermore, simply to combine these different approaches in the pluralistic hope that between them they will account for the various phenomena that seem important. What is needed is a more comprehensive means of explaining the relationship between the different components. I shall propose that semiotics is the discipline best able to achieve this, even though it is by no means a panacea for resolving all of the problems outlined earlier.

There are several semiotic traditions which might serve as the basis for a more inclusive theory of expression, but I shall draw primarily on the ideas of the American semiotician C. S. Peirce (1931–8). Peirce's work has been variously understood, the differences between interpretations fuelled by the difficulty and stylistic peculiarity of Peirce's writing. My aim is not to offer yet another commentary on Peirce, but to exploit a comparatively simple set of distinctions which he presents. I shall understand the three kinds of sign that Peirce terms Index, Icon and Symbol in the following way. For an Index, a *causal* relation exists between a sign and its object, as between smoke and fire or footprint and foot. For an Icon, a relation of *similarity* exists between a sign and its object, as between a map and the terrain it represents. Finally, for a Symbol, a purely *arbitrary* and *conventional* relation exists between a sign and its object, to be understood only by virtue of a system of signs of which it is a part, as in the relation between a word and its meaning.

In applying this classification to performance expression, I shall start with the Icon, since iconic signification is probably the most familiar mode of expression in performance for most listeners. It can be illustrated with a performer's use of tempo variation to convey phrase structure in music, the basic relationship being that phrase boundaries are marked by a decrease in tempo in proportion to the phrase boundary's structural importance. Thus, a large-scale sectional break will typically be approached with a greater degree of slowing than a small-scale group boundary, an effect which can be heard particularly in performances of nineteenth-century piano music (such as Chopin) and which has been observed and modelled in empirical studies of piano performance (e.g. Todd 1985; Clarke 1988). It is the direct relationship between the degree of slowing and the depth of hierarchical embedding that makes this aspect of performance expression iconic, and what is true of tempo in this case can also be observed to varying degrees in the control of other expressive parameters (dynamics, articulation, vibrato, etc.).

Indexical signification in performance can be observed in the way various aspects of the sound quality of a performance are causally related to the instrumental technique and physical effort required to produce the music. The sense of effort conveyed by a high note on the French horn or by triple stopping on the violin is a direct index of the physical/technical stress that the sound production requires. The effect of removing this aspect from performance can be heard in recent examples of synthesis which produce convincing versions of standard repertoire, but without any sense of actual physical production. The result is greatly to undermine the expressive quality of the performance, even if technical perfection is achieved. McAdams (1987) has strikingly illustrated this using the Chant system at IRCAM to synthesise a version of the Queen of the Night's second act aria from Mozart's *The Magic Flute*, which has a natural vocal sound and perfect timing and pitch, but lacks the sense of achievement and arrival on the top Fs that characterises a real performance.

Symbolic signification, which is arguably the most pervasive signifying process for musical structure, is a relatively minor feature of musical performance. Few situations can be imagined in which a listener would have to know a performance style in order to interpret the meaning or function of an expressive feature. It is true that different performance practices articulate the same essential functions in various ways (consider the contrasting uses of expressive timing variations in performing early-eighteenth-century and late-nineteenth-century repertoire), but the differences seem to be concerned with the specific physical realisation of functions which are essentially equivalent: whatever the precise trajectory of a tempo decrease, it still signifies the approach to a phrase or section boundary. Nevertheless, the hostility with which 'historical performance practice' was greeted for a long time by listeners and critics indicates the cultural specificity that applies. In truth, there is no hard-and-fast distinction between iconic and symbolic functions, only different degrees of arbitrariness or convention. Performance expression appears to lie towards the iconic end of this continuum, but it is not entirely devoid of a symbolic component. The very minor role of symbolic signification suggests that performance expression is a rather unsystematised semiotic domain in which the more primitive indexical and iconic functions are paramount, and in which much of its contribution to musical meaning must be understood with reference to the human body (see Lidov 1987).

A further semiotic distinction yielding important explanatory power for performance is that between denotation and connotation. Denotation can be defined as the primary relationship between a sign and its object, and connotation a secondary function in which the object of a sign in turn becomes the sign for a further object, such that the first sign, by a process of double denotation, acquires a signification at one remove.[1] This process is not confined to double denotations but can in principle extend to chains of denotations of any degree of remoteness. To give a concrete example of a relatively direct connotation, a decrease of tempo may denote a phrase boundary, and the phrase boundary itself might denote the completion of a section of music. A listener familiar with the musical style would almost certainly 'jump across' the double denotation and pick up the connotation (section completion) of the rallentando. A more remote connotation of the same kind would allow a similar rallentando in the appropriate context to connote 'recapitulation', in which case the listener jumps across a chain of intermediate denotations concerned with hierarchical phrase/section structure.

With a rather different effect, but nonetheless relying on the same principle of connotation, a whole performance ideology may be connoted by one or two local performance features. For example the characteristic patterns of vibrato/non-vibrato, timing (particularly at phrase boundaries and cadences) and dynamic change within a sonority that denote baroque performance practice connote the ideology of 'historically aware performance' (quite apart from their indexical and iconic denotations within that performance style) and all that it may be understood to stand for. This semiotic function is essentially orthogonal to that previously discussed, since the chain of connotations in this case extends away from the music itself towards aesthetics and social theory, while in the former example we remain in a more obviously musical domain. Once again this highlights the diversity of expressive signification, and the capacity of a semiotic approach to accommodate widely differing elements.

---

[1] Note that the concept of denotation presented here is not explicitly part of Peirce's theory, and that my use of Peirce's terminology is non-standard. Peirce, however, incorporates essentially the same idea into his theory using chains of objects and interpretants to give rise to more or less remote significations.

Example 2.1 Chopin, Prelude Op. 28 No. 4

Example 2.2    Voice-leading analysis of Chopin, Prelude Op. 28 No. 4

## TWO EXAMPLES: CHOPIN, OP. 28 NO. 4 AND BEETHOVEN, WoO 60

In order to show how the semiotic principles sketched here can be applied to concrete musical examples and empirical performance data, two short piano works and associated performance data are presented, illustrating in different ways how an accumulation of small-scale performance features can interact with the constraints of the musical structure itself to give rise to distinct global interpretations of the music.

### Chopin, Prelude Op. 28 No. 4

The score of this piece is shown in Example 2.1, and a voice-leading analysis in Example 2.2.[2] At first sight the Prelude's voice-leading structure seems straight-forward (a standard 'interruption form' with a $\hat{5}$–$\hat{2}$ ‖ $\hat{5}$–$\hat{1}$ descent in the top line over a i V ‖ i V i bass arpeggiation), until one realises that both structural descents apparently lack the necessary $\hat{3}$. In fact the top line has an almost pentatonic character which is particularly strong in bars 10–11 and 18–20.

The analysis in Example 2.2 shows that the initial right-hand B acts as head note for three linear structures: the quasi-pentatonic $\hat{5}$ $\hat{4}$ $\hat{2}$ ‖ $\hat{5}$ $\hat{4}$ $\hat{2}$ $\hat{1}$ of the main melodic material; a complete (diatonic) $\hat{5}$ $\hat{4}$ $\hat{3}$ $\hat{2}$ $\hat{1}$ spanning the whole Prelude but registrally trans-ferred into the left hand after the $\hat{4}$ has been reached (in bars 18–20); and a $\hat{5}$ $\hat{4}$ $\hat{3}$

---

[2]  I am indebted to Carl Schachter's analysis of the Prelude (1994) for many of the ideas presented here.

descent also involving downward registral transfer (in bar 9), which connects the two halves of the Prelude at precisely the point (bar 13) where the main melodic structure is resumed. One consequence of this interpretation is that the emphatic octave Bs in the left hand at the beginning of bar 17 (the lowest and loudest notes of the music so far, approached by a stretto and immediately followed by a jump to the work's melodic peak) are *not* understood as the primary structural dominant, contrary to the wealth of surface indications. The concealed melodic parallelism between bars 9 and 17–18 (see the lower part of Example 2.2) strongly suggests that the *subdominant* prevails until the structural dominant is reached on the downbeat of bar 19.

These observations lead to the following performance considerations:

(i) Pianists wishing to emphasise a conventional antecedent–consequent melodic structure in the piece might stress the subdivision at bars 12–13 and the parallelism between the two halves, which, because of their gapped, pentatonic melodic outline, results in a less unified interpretation of tonal structure, but one which highlights the similarity of surface melodic features between the two sections.

(ii) An interpretation placing primary emphasis on a unified fundamental structure requires the $\hat{5}\ \hat{4}\ \hat{3}$ connection between the first and second halves to be brought out. Similarly the melodic parallelism of the two halves must be under-played, and a strong sense of dominant/tonic relationship in the second half projected. In particular the melodic climax at bar 17 needs to be checked to allow the interrupted cadence at bar 21 and final cadential progression to become the more powerful centres of attraction.

*Performances of Chopin, Op. 28 No. 4*

This section assesses performance data in the light of the foregoing observations about structure and interpretation. I shall focus on two (of a total of six) performances of the Prelude given by a professional pianist, Robin Bowman (RB), on the same day at City University, London, on a Yamaha MIDI grand piano. The Yamaha allows digital performance data to be recorded directly from the instrument, providing detailed information about the expressive characteristics (timing, dynamics and articulation) of every note in a performance. In giving the six performances, the pianist was neither encouraged to vary his interpretation in a conscious or deliberate manner nor told to stick rigidly to a single way of playing the piece. It was apparent, however, from his wide-ranging spontaneous comments after each performance that he was himself aware of different properties in each one as his imagination was caught by varying technical and interpretative features of the music and different guiding images. None of his comments referred explicitly to the structural properties identified above.

Figures 2.1 to 2.3 show data for the two performances.[3] Figure 2.1 depicts the data of the right hand for the two halves of the Prelude (bars 1–12 and 13–25),

---

[3] The upper part of each graph shows dynamics and the lower part shows tempo. The vertical scales have arbitrary units for duration and dynamics but start from a true zero.

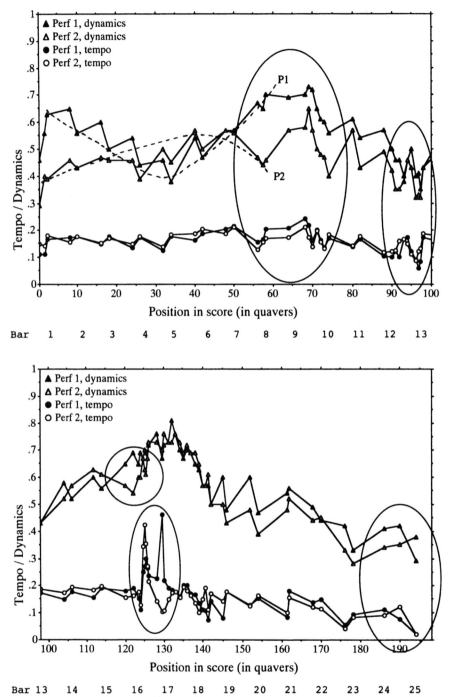

Figure 2.1   Data for RB's performances of Chopin, Op. 28 No. 4, divided into two halves, showing dynamic data and note-by-note tempo for the right hand alone

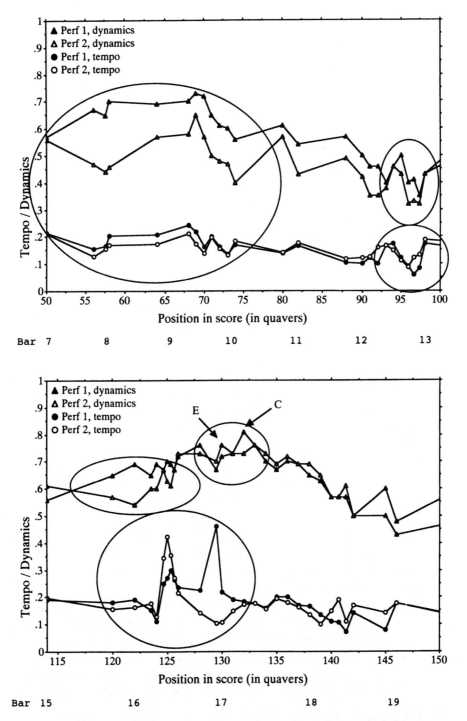

Figure 2.2   Detailed view of the right-hand dynamic and tempo data for RB's performances of Chopin, Op. 28 No. 4, focusing on bars 7–13 (upper graph) and 15–19 (lower graph)

while Figure 2.2 isolates the passages from bars 7–13 and 15–19. Together they illustrate four important differences between the two performances:

(i) The dynamic profiles for the first eight bars are almost the mirror image of one another. The first performance (P1) starts with a relatively high dynamic level after the initial upbeats, followed by a decrescendo to a local minimum at the start of bar 5, and a subsequent crescendo to the start of bar 8. The second performance (P2) starts with a much lower dynamic level which rises slowly to a (low) peak at bars 5–6, dropping again to a local minimum at the start of bar 8. As a consequence, P1 is considerably louder through bars 8 and 9, and remains louder throughout the rest of the first half – though the two performances converge to a point of dynamic identity at the start of the second half. P1 is also significantly faster in bars 8 and 9, so that tempo and dynamics together produce a definite climax (though not the main one) in bar 9.

(ii) P1 significantly decreases the tempo with the three triplets at the end of bar 12 (see Figure 2.2), while P2 slows much less in approaching the triplets and then accelerates through them into the start of bar 13. Taking into account the higher dynamic level of P1, the result is that P1 emphasises the Prelude's division into two halves at bar 12, while P2, with its generally low dynamic level throughout the first twelve bars, projects a sense of the first half leading inexorably into the second.

(iii) Bars 16–17, the Prelude's melodic climax, are treated in significantly different ways in the two performances (see Figures 2.1 and 2.2). P1 approaches the climax with a virtually continuous crescendo (from bar 13) while P2 brings the dynamic level down in bars 15–16, producing a steeper dynamic increase through the first half of bar 16 and a consequently greater sense of arrival when the dynamic peak is reached. As far as tempo is concerned, P1 obeys the stretto marking and accelerates through 16 and 17, while P2 does the opposite, slowing at the boundary between bars 16 and 17. This gives a sense of weighty (loud and slow) arrival at the start of bar 17, reinforced by the fact that the right-hand E there is the peak of the dynamic profile, whereas P2 continues to crescendo through to the high C on the third quaver, the Prelude's highest note.

(iv) In the perfect cadence concluding the work (Figure 2.1), P1 slows and becomes quieter through the three chords, while P2, starting from a considerably lower dynamic level than P1 at the start of bar 24, makes a continuous crescendo through the three chords, reaching a significantly higher dynamic level than P1 on the last chord. To emphasise this sense of impetus towards the final tonic, P2 actually accelerates through the cadential dominant.

Thus far, only the right-hand melody has been considered. Figure 2.3 shows comparable data for the left-hand chords, and it reveals little which has not already been observed. In both performances, a clear bar-by-bar rubato pattern arises in the

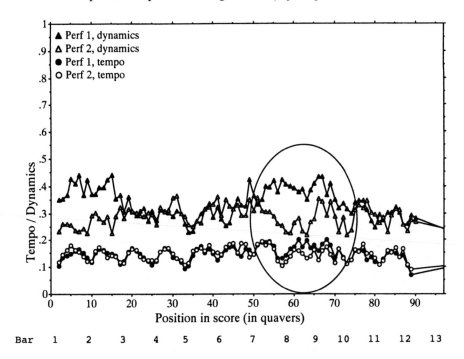

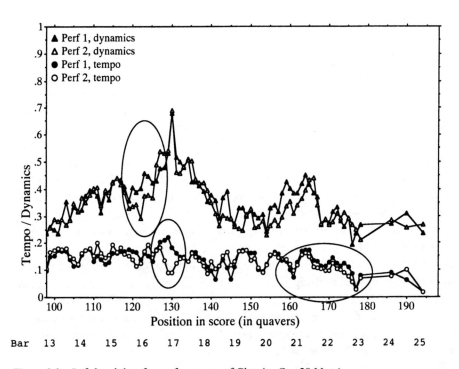

Figure 2.3   Left-hand data for performances of Chopin, Op. 28 No. 4

first seven bars and at the reprise. The distinctions of dynamics and tempo between the two performances in bars 1–9 and 15–17 are again evident in these data. Only one additional feature emerges, namely the treatment of the smorzando in bars 21–2: P2 produces a consistently slower tempo here and a more sustained and graded decelerando through to bar 23. The sense of winding-down that this engenders heightens the significant increase of dynamics and tempo through the final cadence (see above).

To summarise the preceding discussion, P1 stresses the more surface melodic structure of the music, while P2 places greater emphasis on the goal-orientated tonal unity that underpins the piece. This distinction is evident in three principal effects:

(i) P1 makes more of the division of the piece into two halves than does P2, cutting across the B–A–G third descent that links the two.

(ii) P1 aims for the melodic/registral peak (C) at bar 17, and by moving quickly through bars 16–18 makes less of the arrival at the dominant. P2 conversely places enormous weight on the arrival at V at bar 17, and then underplays the return to the introverted, captive music in the second half of bar 18.

(iii) P1 has a quiet, slow ending which produces a sense of resignation and hopelessness. P2, by contrast, moves in a purposeful and goal-orientated manner through the final three chords to create a feeling of arrival and conclusion on the cadential tonic, which is diametrically opposed to the effect produced by P1.

These observations, and the more detailed ones that precede them, illustrate the point made at the start of the chapter – that the force of musical expression must be gauged by interpreting the function of any expressive features within their specific structural context. What may appear to be the same expressive element (an acceleration, for instance) may have quite opposite functions depending on structural context (e.g. the acceleration through bars 24–5 in P2 which produces a sense of conclusion and goal orientation, in contrast with the acceleration through bars 16–17 in P1 which has the effect of deflecting a sense of arrival at the dominant). Equally, they illustrate the way in which an aggregation of local expressive details can have quite far-reaching effects in terms of the overall interpretation that is created. Each of these features has little or no impact in itself, but considered together, and in their specific contexts, they collectively point towards two distinct interpretations. This is something that none of the existing theories of expression can adequately handle: the small-scale changes have no systematic and pervasive relationship to the underlying structure, as a generative theory would predict, and they are too minimal in their energetic consequences to be able to change the global energy distribution, as the energy flux approach would require. Rather, they constitute a relatively sparse collection of indicators which function as the *clues* for two different conceptions of the piece, not as their empirical determinants. (This affinity between detecting clues and interpreting expression is explored in more depth in the final part of this chapter.)

Finally (and here we move beyond the performance data and discussion of musical structure offered so far), these observations illustrate the close interplay between musical structure, performance expression and human bodily movement (an issue given more systematic treatment in Shove and Repp's chapter in this volume): each of RB's six performances had a distinct somatic character to it, and it was this physical response to the music that informed much of his own spontaneous commentary on each of the performances, just as it is a language of emotion with a strongly physical component which Schachter (1994: 175, 178) uses when discussing the Prelude's melodic climax at bars 16–17: 'The sudden storm that builds up [here] . . . is all the more gripping in its contrast to the phrase's beginning, like a violent outburst of tears from a person not given to demonstrations of feeling . . . the music seems to have lost itself in an almost frenzied access of emotion'. None of these qualities individually demands a semiotic interpretation: each can be theorised in more familiar ways, but to do so results in a heterogeneous state of affairs where the different elements of the composite phenomenon employ different explanatory principles and as a result threaten to separate from one another. It is the sense of multiplicity in the concept of sign function (in terms of both the different varieties of sign function that can coexist and the potential for recursivity) that makes semiotics fruitful as an explanatory framework.

### Beethoven, WoO 60

If the Chopin Prelude shows how a single performer may explore different approaches to an ambiguous structure, WoO 60 demonstrates how two performers tackling the same piece can produce quite distinct interpretations of the music with little more than a scattering of differences in expressive surface detail. WoO 60 (shown in Example 2.3) bears clear traces of an oppositional structure derived, albeit unconventionally, from the sonata principle. The first section lasts just nine bars and contains contrasting material with a considerable degree of tonal instability, the first four bars being more dominant- than tonic-centred, while the following five bars veer unexpectedly away to the flattened mediant. In addition to this lack of tonal convention, the phrase structure is asymmetrical (4 + 5 bars) and ends with a series of three accented, syncopated chords culminating in a fermata. A more developmental sixteen-bar section (10–25) continues to introduce new thematic material, leading the music from D♭ major back to the tonic through an abrupt enharmonic change (bars 20–1). This section has a more regular 4 + 4 + 8 phrase structure, though the last phrase subdivides into an asymmetrical 3 + 5 bars on the basis of its harmonic structure. The reprise (bars 26–34) retains the asymmetrical phrasing of the opening section and, after a brief extension, incorporates a contracted version of the syncopated chords and fermata. The piece concludes with a five-bar coda,[4] the last beat of which contains virtually the only convincing root-position tonic chord in the work. (Two other root-position tonics, in bars 3 and 28, fall within dominant-orientated phrases and are rhythmically weak, while the potentially strong tonic at bar 30 is undermined by its reduction to a single pitch.)

---

[4] The analytical description here differs from that in Dunsby (1984), where the final bar alone is identified as the coda.

Example 2.3   Beethoven, WoO 60

The work has been analysed by Dunsby (1984), who describes it as a late master-piece roughly contemporaneous with the Bagatelles Op. 119 and having affinities with the last of these. His analysis falls into two parts. The first identifies motivic, rhythmic and harmonic features, and aims in particular 'to explore the sense of key in a piece where the reprise (bars 26ff.) is preceded by dominant, flat-mediant and mediant-major prolongations only' (: 57). The second and much briefer part portrays the reprise as a succession of reductions of the preceding music, so that in essence WoO 60 constitutes 'a projection of the paradigmatic axis onto the syntagmatic axis' (: 68).

Beethoven establishes a richness of connection throughout the piece in several ways. Much of the melody derives from motivic material in the first theme, which divides into antecedent and consequent halves, with the first motive repeated a fifth lower in the consequent beneath a second motive. In particular the fall of a fifth, G–C, in the opening motive (bar 1), plays a significant role by initiating a complete circle-of-fifths progression through the exposition and development sections which returns in the recapitulation to the fifth-motive's starting point. The recurrence of E♭ as a focal melodic note also maintains continuity.

At the same time, rhythmic variety is ensured by syncopation, the manipulation of phrase lengths, and rhythmic expansion and diminution of motivic material. All of these, together with the occasional creation of rhythmic ambiguity, serve to intensify important moments in the music, which tend to be points of significant harmonic change, often abrupt and radical in taking the music to remote harmonic regions. In a highly compact work, Beethoven thus achieves a continuity of motivic reference in the face of considerable rhythmic contrast and a tonal instability which persists from the opening bars until the final chord.

This brief synopsis of Dunsby's analysis will suffice as the background to a study of relevant performance data. It can already be seen that pianists may have to choose between emphasising either an essential unity (created by powerful linking references) or an apparent diversity (manifested in motivic contrast and tonal instability).

## Performances of WoO 60

Two expert pianists, Jonathan Dunsby (JD) and Vovka Ashkenazy (VA), performed the work:[5] JD (author of the analysis discussed above) played it four times, twice at each of two different tempos, while VA gave six performances, twice at each of three tempos. The repeat performances of each version allow one to estimate the consistency of expressive features. It is typically found that expert performers have precise control of expression and can accurately reproduce a prepared performance. This is true of JD and VA, as can be seen from the graphs shown in Figures 2.4 and 2.5, which depict the momentary performance tempo and the measured dynamic level for each crotchet beat, the latter represented by the most intensely played event in the beat. The graphs for each player are superimposed on the same scales to allow immediate comparison; by starting from a true zero, variation in relation to absolute values can also be seen.

---

[5]  Neither JD nor VA is included in Shaffer's (1992) discussion of WoO 60.

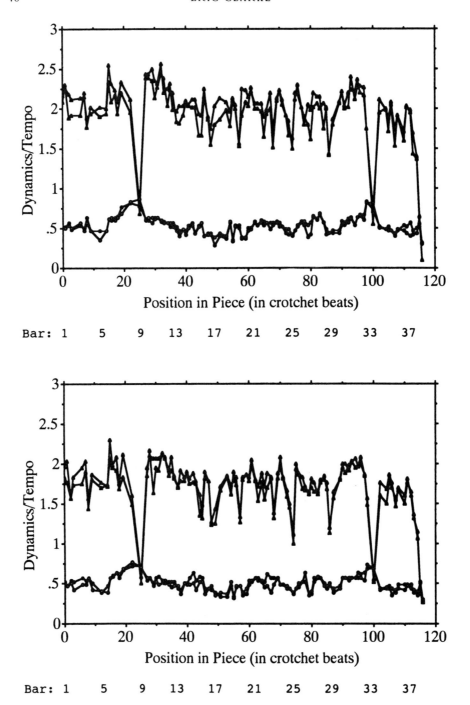

Figure 2.4   Tempo (upper part of each graph) and dynamic (lower part of each graph) data for two performances of WoO 60 by JD at each of two tempos. The upper graph shows data for the performances at 'normal' tempo, and the lower graph for the slower performances. Both dynamics and tempo are depicted in terms of arbitrary values starting from a true zero.

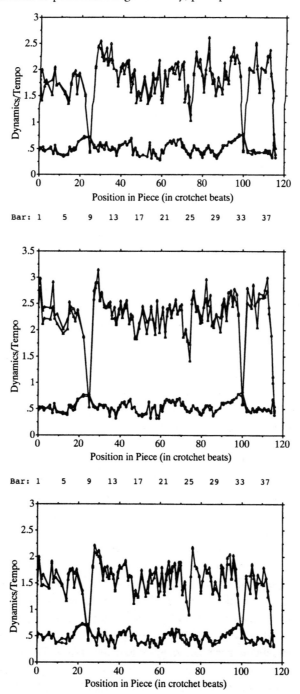

Figure 2.5   Tempo (upper part of each graph) and dynamic (lower part of each graph) data for two performances of WoO 60 by VA at each of three tempos. The top graph shows data for the performances at 'normal' tempo, the middle graph data for the faster performances, and the bottom graph data for the slower performances. Both dynamics and tempo are depicted in terms of arbitrary values starting from a true zero.

As with the Chopin analysis, the aim will be to identify differences in the performance data for the two pianists, to relate these to the structure of WoO 60 in order to understand the interpretative distinctions between them, and to show that these differences are best understood as sign functions. A superficial glance at Figures 2.4 and 2.5 might suggest that the players chose similar interpretations, but this would be only partly true: the differences between them are musically significant, as the following discussion will show. It might also appear that in order to change their interpretation the players did little more than alter the tempo. Certainly, changing tempo considerably affected the character of the music, but closer inspection reveals that the players did not merely scale time values up or down uniformly. Rather, the rubato used at slower tempos was often much reduced at faster tempos, and there were subtle shifts in local tempo relationships over the piece, some of which will be indicated.

Since tempo fluctuated continually over the music, nothing more than an approximate indicator is attempted here based on the total performance duration.[6] JD's spontaneously chosen and preferred tempo was about 111 crotchets per minute (cpm), with his alternative, slower version at about 94 cpm. The three tempos adopted by VA were about 99, 124 and 86 cpm. Thus his median tempo was similar to JD's slower performance, and although reluctant to express a clear preference among his performances he chose this one when asked to do so; it is reasonable to suppose that it therefore provided some sort of reference for the others. Thus, the players were in rough agreement over what constituted 'Ziemlich lebhaft' (fairly lively). However, it may be significant that JD seemed to feel more constrained than VA in adopting alternative tempos – a possible consequence of his analytical knowledge of the piece. As well as choosing a more restricted range of tempos, JD typically made much less use of rubato than VA. Maintaining a steady tempo enhances continuity in the music, which would be consistent with the findings of his analysis. By allowing tempo to fluctuate more, VA did less to convey such continuity, either because he did not perceive it or because he preferred to make more of the tonal ambiguity and abrupt shifts of tonal region and motivic material in the work. It should be mentioned that their performances became correspondingly more alike at the fastest tempos as both players made less use of rubato.

VA played the opening four-bar theme with greater fluctuation in tempo than JD, who kept the tempo constant through bar 5 – the start of the second theme. JD then accelerated through the semiquaver descent (dramatising the collapse of the opening's more contrapuntal texture into parallel octaves and rhythmic unisons), recovered tempo with the chords in bars 7 and 8, and then decelerated towards the pause in bar 9. VA slowed considerably in bar 5 and then pushed ahead on the downward run in bar 6, gradually recovering the original tempo thereafter. This more striking gesture achieved greater contrast between the two themes than JD attempted; VA also paused longer than JD on the chord in bar 9, further enhancing the dramatic treatment of this material.

---

6   This also reflects fundamental problems in estimating a performance's basic tempo – see Repp 1994.

In the following more developmental section, both players quickened the tempo in bar 10 and then slowed progressively over the four-bar phrase. However, JD accelerated only enough to resume the tempo attained briefly in bar 6 (thereby emphasising the rhythmic and tonal continuity with that bar), whereas VA adopted a faster tempo than hitherto, as though to effect a contrast with previous material. Similarly, JD maintained the gesture of slowing through the phrase ending in bar 17, thus forging a unity over the whole section in D♭, while VA accelerated and then slowed over this second phrase (bars 14–17), giving more distinctiveness to the two phrases as if in response to their textural difference.

Both players paused significantly at bar 17 to separate the two parts of the development, and again at bar 25 to mark the transition from development to reprise. JD treated the second half of the development section in a manner consistent with his written analysis. Since these eight bars and the reprise into which they lead form the crux and turning point of the piece, a more detailed analysis of their performance features will be presented below; I shall pass over them now. When the motive from bar 5 reappears in bar 30 in the tonic harmony, and thus with a fundamentally altered function and significance, JD responded with an immediate acceleration. VA, in contrast, held back here and established a motivic continuity with bar 5 by repeating an earlier pattern, extending the third beats in bars 30–2. Both players accelerated over the rest of the phrase, responding to the rising tension of the I–V/ii–ii–V⁷ progression, until arrested by the chords and the fermata. They were also in agreement in bringing the music to some kind of uneasy conclusion, giving more moderate emphasis to the sforzando and pause in bar 39 than to those in bars 9 and 34. JD slowed a little throughout this section, perhaps to underline its function as a summary of the whole piece; VA seems to have interpreted it differently, playing it more slowly in the slow version but actually going slightly faster in his fast version. If slowing confers a sense of repose and finality on the music, accelerating emphasises its eccentric, quirky character and the rhetorical nature of the final perfect cadence that has been expected, and withheld, for so long.

A more detailed discussion of bars 18–29 now follows, as these bars arguably contain the work's two crucial turning points: the enharmonic change at bars 20–1 and the reprise at bar 26. Three aspects of the performances will be examined – timing, dynamics and the synchronisation of notes in chords[7] – and data will be adduced from performances at different tempos by each pianist. Given the requisite level of detail the analysis is restricted to only one of the 'normal' tempo performances (in both cases the second of the two, which both performers considered better than the first) and one of the slower performances (in each case the first of the two).

Starting with the data for chord synchronisation, Figure 2.6 shows for both performers the amount of lag or lead between the top voice in the right hand and the next note to be depressed (in any voice) in each chord. A clear distinction can be seen between JD's and VA's chordal attacks. While VA tended in general to play right-hand melody notes first (positive values in the figure indicate by how much the melody note

---

[7]  Articulation, the fourth primary parameter of expression in piano performance, was examined but showed no interesting differences over the performances.

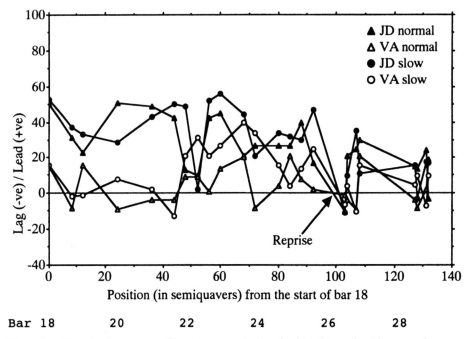

Figure 2.6   Data for the amount of lag (negative values) or lead (positive values) between the top voice and the next voice to be sounded in chords from bars 18–28 of Beethoven, WoO 60. The second 'normal' performance and the first slower performance are shown for both JD and VA. Values are in milliseconds.

led all other notes, negative values the equivalent in terms of lag), there was no systematic pattern to his asynchronies, which were all rather small. JD, in contrast, had a distinct tendency up to the reprise to lead the melody by around 40 milliseconds or more, followed by a much tighter coordination of attack from there on. This kind of asynchrony is a recognised means of separating the melody line from the chordal texture, and it gave JD's performances a stronger sense of linear connection during the crucial enharmonic link between D♭ major and D major in the eight bars before the reprise. Once the comparative tonal clarity of the reprise was reached, the asynchronies were reduced.

The dynamic shaping of the twelve-bar passage reveals further interesting features. Here VA showed the greater amount of dynamic shaping overall and a more faithful rendering of the indications in the score. Figures 2.7 and 2.8 depict the dynamic data for the normal tempo and slow performances by the two pianists. While JD established a voice separation by means of chord asynchrony, VA achieved something similar using dynamics, particularly in the slower performance: there was a clear and sustained dynamic separation between the soprano and tenor voices until the reprise was reached, bar 24 being the only exception, where the quaver movement in the tenor attracted a dynamic level equal to that of the top line.[8]

---

[8]   Interestingly, in his 1984 article Dunsby points out the motivic connection between this quaver passage and the semiquavers of bars 5–6, of which it is a rhythmically augmented inversion.

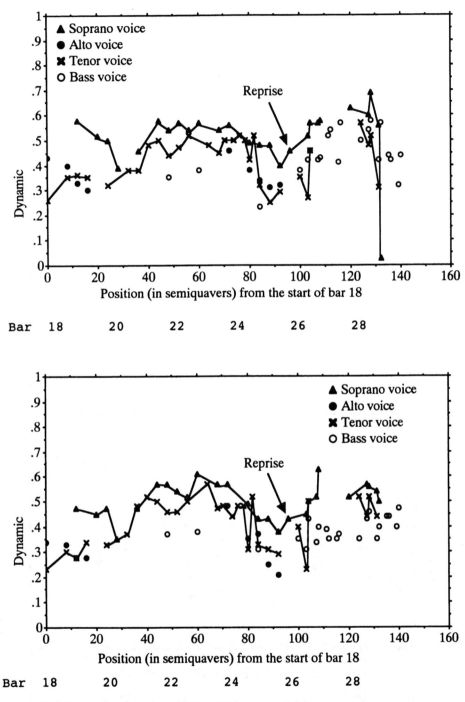

Figure 2.7   Note-by-note dynamic data for all four voices for the second 'normal' performance (upper graph) and first slower performance (lower graph) of bars 18–29 of WoO 60 played by JD

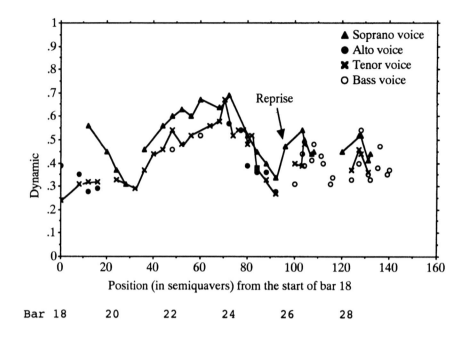

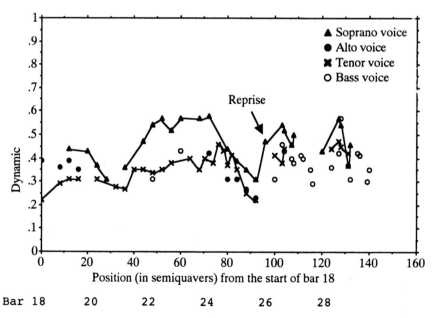

Figure 2.8 Note-by-note dynamic data for all four voices for the second 'normal' performance (upper graph) and first slower performance (lower graph) of bars 18–29 of WoO 60 played by VA. Note the clear voice separation, particularly in the slower performance, up to the point of reprise.

The dynamic data reveal three additional differences between the two performers. The first concerns the enharmonic change at bars 20–1, where in both performances JD maintained a steady crescendo in the tenor from the E♭ in bar 20 through the E♭♭ to the D of bar 21, helping the otherwise abrupt enharmonic shift to be anticipated somewhat, and allowing the left hand to push ahead towards the D major phrase and the cadence immediately preceding the reprise.[9] VA, by contrast, began his crescendo in bar 21 (where the marking appears in the score) and thus maintained more of a discontinuity between the two tonal regions.[10] The second distinction concerns the dynamic treatment of the moment of reprise. After a very considerable decrescendo in the latter half of bar 24 and through bar 25, VA introduced a marked increase in dynamic level as the reprise began. In conjunction with a definite ritardando on approaching the reprise (discussed below), this caused a clear discontinuity between the development and the reprise. JD, on the other hand, decrescendoed less through bars 24–5 and then only slightly increased dynamic level on starting the reprise. Coupled with a more modest ritardando than VA's (see below), this strategy again resulted in the projection of unity rather than discontinuity. Finally, there was an interesting contrast between the two players' dynamic treatment of bar 27. At both tempos, VA played the left-hand notes there as a quiet echo of the right hand in the preceding bar, leading to a sharp dynamic contrast when the right hand re-entered in bar 28. At his normal tempo, JD crescendoed through bar 27 in the left hand, reaching the dynamic level of the right hand in bar 26 and making a bridge to that of the new right-hand entry in bar 28. Once again this produced a continuity across sub-phrases which VA seemed to avoid. Interestingly, JD's slower performance adopted the same approach as did VA, with the left hand in bar 27 dropping to a dynamic level which contrasted with the right hand's in the adjacent bars; at the slower tempo he also seemed to favour the more discontinuous approach that characterised all of VA's performances.

Lastly we turn to the timing characteristics of this twelve-bar passage (see Figures 2.9 and 2.10). The general picture to emerge is that VA tended to slow towards the end of each bar – a pattern particularly evident in the slower performance, where there were decelerations at the ends of bars 18, 20, 21, 23, 24, 25, 27 and 29, while at the normal tempo the ritardandos were minimised or eliminated in bars 21, 23 and 27. JD's performances show a much flatter timing profile with only four points at either tempo revealing any significant slowing: the A♭ on the first beat of bar 20 (emphasising its function as a melodic appoggiatura) and the ends of bars 23, 25 and 29. At the slower tempo these ritardandos were somewhat more pronounced, and there was an additional slight slowing at the end of bar 27 – indicating a sub-phrase division which is consistent with the analysis of dynamics for the slower performance. In a similar vein, JD made a less emphatic ritardando than VA as he approached the reprise at the

---

9   When recording these performances, JD commented that one way to approach this enharmonic change is to hear the E♭ in bar 20 as connected to the true D♯ in bar 22, thereby anticipating the enharmonic alteration rather than stumbling on it out of the blue.

10   This is particularly evident in his slower performance.

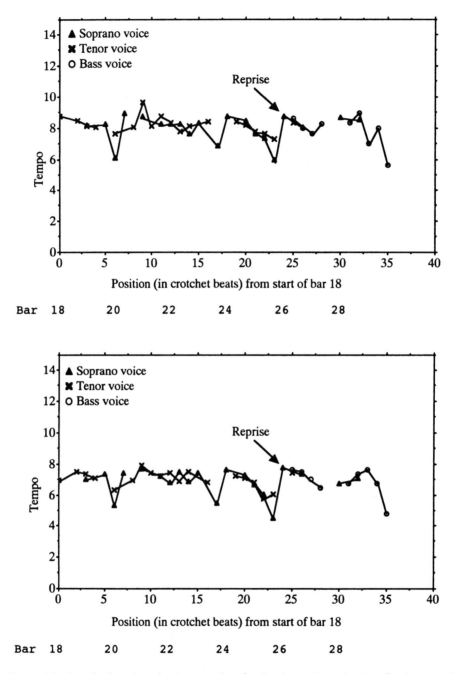

Figure 2.9   Beat-by-beat (crotchets) tempo data for the three principal voices for the second 'normal' performance (upper graph) and first slower performance (lower graph) of bars 18–29 of WoO 60 played by JD. Note the sparing use of local ritardandos.

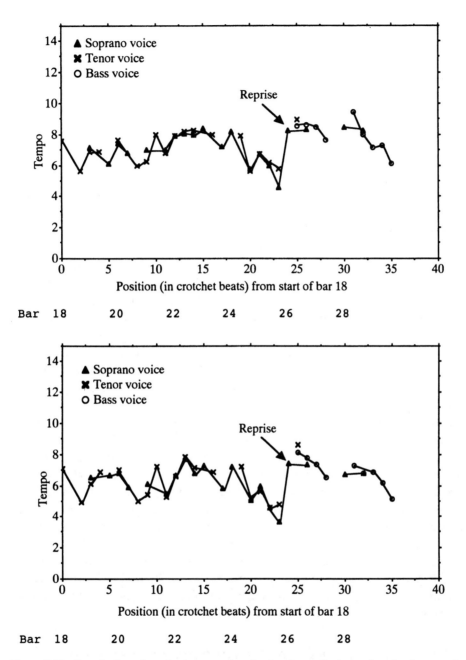

Figure 2.10   Beat-by-beat (crotchets) tempo data for the three principal voices for the second 'normal' performance (upper graph) and first slower performance (lower graph) of bars 18–29 of WoO 60 played by VA. Note the more widespread use of local ritardandos, used to mark the ends of successive bars.

normal tempo, though it was somewhat more pronounced at the slower tempo. The relative continuity of timing from development to reprise at normal tempo is consistent with the dynamic continuity noted above, as is the greater discontinuity in both timing and dynamics at the slower tempo: at his slower tempo JD's performances began to resemble those of VA at his normal tempo.

The summary picture that emerges from this discussion could be expressed rather baldly as the contrast between a more unified strategy (on the part of JD) and a more disjunct approach (on the part of VA) – a summary which does considerable injustice to the many details of the performances underlying this overall difference of characterisation, and the abundant contrasts manifested in the various player/tempo combinations. The problem with such a summary is twofold. First, it suggests a distinction between the two performers which is far too one-dimensional and categorical – the same problem of capturing a subtle and dynamically evolving qualitative feature that is encountered in (notoriously inept and unsatisfactory) attempts to describe listeners' affective responses to music with a crude vocabulary of emotional states. Secondly, the summary statement suggests that the interpretative difference is distributed throughout the data, and that it is an objective property of the data itself rather than a complex interaction between an unfolding structure with its own contours and landmarks and an associated set of continuously varying expressive features which both derive their significance from the structural context in which they occur and equally confer particularity upon the general field of possibilities afforded by the structure. Once again this argues against the positivism of prevailing views of expression, and emphasises the way in which surface features point well beyond their immediate context to fundamental differences of conception. It has been necessary to consider in some detail, and with a degree of atomism, the specific physical characteristics of the performances in order to demonstrate that there are real differences between them, and that these are not simply our own projections. However, a listener is almost entirely unaware of these differences at this level: what he or she hears in a far more direct and synoptic fashion is a particular interpretation which is both much greater than the simple sum of these disparate parts, and also considerably less than the barrage of detail that a veridical description invariably provides. It hardly needs emphasising that a semiotic perspective is required neither to observe and discuss performance data, nor to recognise that listeners hear differences of interpretation in performance. The approach is, however, a powerful way to understand the process that links the two – a far more interesting enterprise.

## CLUES, PARSERS AND THE SEMIOTICS OF EXPRESSION

In leading viewers to entertain particular hypotheses about the guilt or innocence of the characters in a detective film, the director will manipulate the clues made available, the context in which they occur and the rate at which they follow one another. He or she will also strike a balance between 'structural' clues in the unfolding narrative (the finding of a hidden diary, the disappearance of a vital witness) and 'expressive' clues (the confident tone of one character's voice, the shifty look of another and the jerky camerawork that follows a third). Although by their very nature certain events and expressions are heavily laden with an apparently incontrovertible meaning (the discovery of a murder weapon, a suspect's uncontrolled weeping), most of the information in such a film comes from a rich interaction between the particular content of an event, its narrative context and the intensity, clarity, brevity, tone of voice, camera angle, etc. with which it is portrayed. Whether the information reveals or misleads, there can be little doubt that to follow a detective film is an intensely semiotic process – a reading of signs in the most obvious fashion. The misleading nature of many such signs, far from being an impediment to this view, only confirms their semiotic status. Umberto Eco, whose fictional work (Eco 1983) is a virtuoso application of the issues under discussion here, goes so far as to define semiotics as 'in principle the discipline studying everything which can be used in order to lie' (Eco 1977: 7).

Musical performance is remarkably similar and can legitimately be viewed in the same semiotic fashion. Although the structure of a composition determines with greater or lesser constraint the semiotic field within which an interpreter can operate, the performer has the capacity within that field to manipulate the acoustical and temporal realisation of the music in order to lead (and mislead) the listener in an unlimited number of directions. These expressive features are 'clues' in precisely the sense used above, since they provide evidence and counter-evidence for an evolving interpretation of the music and for a host of extra-musical characterisations, including attributions of performer competence, a sense of physical motion (see Shove and Repp's essay in this book), extra-musical narrative and ideological allegiance (for instance to 'historically aware performance'). To take Eco's definition seriously, we must consider whether there are circumstances in which a performer can be said to lie – to which the answer is a definite 'yes'. An expressively convincing performance of a false recapitulation, for example, in which the performer intentionally misleads the listener into hearing it as a true return, is but one case in point: in effect the expressive treatment lies about the music's real function at that moment. There is a grey area too between unorthodoxy and lying: what should we make of a performer who, for intentionally humorous purposes, idiosyncrasy or simple lack of understanding, plays a composition in an utterly inappropriate manner – say, a bit of salon frippery rendered in the manner of a 'masterpiece'? In a sense it does not matter: the question exposes the crucial aspect of Eco's definition – the 'standing-for' relationship essential to all signs, which is clearly present in each of these imagined instances.

In contrast with the view proposed here (in which a degree of flexibility and even dislocation is allowed between expressive signs and their objects), both the kind of parsing involved in the generative approach and the direct registration of energy flux described by Todd (1994) depend on a directness between expressive sign and structural object which all but eliminates the fertile distance that semiotics celebrates. And yet one should not ignore the considerable evidence revealed by empirical performance research for a substrate of this directness. Repp (1992b), Todd (1985), Palmer (1989) and others have shown that there is a strong tendency for expressive timing and dynamics to follow phrase structure directly, a relationship which is easily confirmed by listening to innumerable recordings or performances of, say, much nineteenth-century piano repertoire. This directness presents no problem to a semiotic account, since both indexical and iconic signs themselves embody such a relationship. But this is only the substrate, and it ignores the less obvious but arguably more important expressive details that fall less neatly within this domain, and whose function and significance depend to a far greater extent on more arbitrary cultural codes. Repp (1992b) implicitly acknowledges this by demonstrating that the commonalities between many commercially recorded performances of Schumann's 'Träumerei' relate to the music's larger-scale features, and that increasing diversity is evident as one considers the detailed properties of the performances. One interpretation of this, which is consistent with a view of the directness of the relationship between structure and expression, is that performers substantially agree on the music's large-scale structure and expressive treatment, and differ only in the detail of expression. But this depends on equating small-scale expressive features with structural detail, which, as I have tried to show, may be misleading. The small differences between RB's various interpretations of the Chopin Prelude can be seen as projecting fundamentally different structural orientations, as can JD's and VA's disparate performances of WoO 60. The diversity of detail that Repp observes may actually be responsible for communicating a range of interpretations of the piece, while the commonalities may represent no more than underlying perceptuo-motor constants.

In a sense, this is where the psychology of music and critical analysis part company, the former being more interested in general mechanisms and the latter in the particular significance of individual manifestations. There is of course much fertile overlap between the two, but cognitive studies of music performance could legitimately be criticised for having revealed little or nothing about the specificities of interesting and exceptional performance. All of the performance models that have been proposed are (necessarily) extremely blunt tools when it comes to investigating individual performances, as they are built upon the premise of general mechanisms and specify the unremarkable background of commonality underlying a vast range of adequate or competent performances – an account of possible significance for those studying general cognitive processes, but surely less interesting to musicians. This does not mean that we should throw up our hands at the complexity and unrelenting specificity of performance, but it does strike a blow at naively empirical research on expression – leaving trenchant questions about how to do it better. The approach to a range of similarly complex cultural phenomena that is exemplified in Barthes (1972) and Williamson (1978) offers one possibility[11] – and, despite its radically different nature, a reason for continuing to capture the data of performance. The advantage of both Barthes' and Williamson's analyses is that they deal primarily with spatial rather than temporal phenomena, allowing reference to a relatively stable and public object. The perennial problem with the study of performance is its temporality and hence

[11]  The former deals with anything from soap powders to Hollywood films and the latter with the semiotics of advertising.

ephemerality, and if nothing else, concrete performance data at least give analysts and other parties the assurance that they are dealing with the same thing.

To finish, I return to the multiplicity of functions and diversity of significations that characterise expression in performance, at the same time acknowledging that this contribution has itself fallen into the trap of focusing too exclusively on the relationship between structure and expression. A host of equally significant perspectives warrants further investigation: the relationship between music and motion and the involvement of the human body (see Lidov 1987 and Shove and Repp in this volume); the social dynamics of performance, both between co-performers and between performers and audience; the visual component of expression in live performance, a field opened up by Davidson (1991, 1993); and much else. No doubt we will continue to obtain a variety of necessarily partial views of this rich and intriguing manifestation of human creativity, but, with increasing recognition of the possibilities of acquiring a more multi-dimensional perspective, perhaps progress can gradually be made towards a less fractured understanding.

### REFERENCES

Barthes, R., 1972: *Mythologies*, trans. A. Lavers (London: Jonathan Cape).

Clarke, E. F., 1988: 'Generative principles in music performance', in J. A. Sloboda, ed., *Generative Processes in Music* (Oxford: Clarendon), pp. 1–26.

Clynes, M., 1983: 'Expressive microstructure in music, linked to living qualities', in J. Sundberg, ed., *Studies of Music Performance* (Stockholm: Royal Swedish Academy of Music), pp. 76–181.

in press: 'Composers' pulses are liked most by the best musicians', *Cognition*.

Davidson, J. W., 1991: 'The perception of expressive movement in music performance' (Dissertation, City University, London).

1993: 'Visual perception of performance manner in the movements of solo musicians', *Psychology of Music* 21/2: 103–13.

Desain, P. and Honing, H., 1992: *Music, Mind and Machine* (Amsterdam: Thesis Publishers).

Dunsby, J., 1984: 'A bagatelle on Beethoven's WoO 60', *Music Analysis* 3/1: 57–68.

1989: 'Guest editorial: performance and analysis of music', *Music Analysis* 8/1–2: 5–20.

Eco, U., 1977: *A Theory of Semiotics* (London: Macmillan).

1983: *The Name of the Rose*, trans. W. Weaver (London: Secker and Warburg).

Lashley, K. S., [1951] 1969: 'The problem of serial order in behaviour', in K. Pribram, ed., *Penguin Modern Psychology. Brain and Behaviour 2. Perception and Action* (Harmondsworth: Penguin), pp. 515–40.

Lidov, D., 1987: 'Mind and body in music', *Semiotica* 66/1: 69–97.

McAdams, S., 1987: 'Organisational processes in music listening'. Paper presented at the Second Conference on Science and Music, City University, London.

Palmer, C., 1989: 'Mapping musical thought to musical performance', *Journal of Experimental Psychology: Human Perception and Performance* 15/12: 331–46.

Peirce, C. S., 1931–8: *Collected Papers of Charles Sanders Peirce*, ed. C. Hartshorne, P. Weiss and A. W. Burk, 8 vols. (Cambridge, Massachusetts: Harvard University Press).

Repp, B. H., 1990: 'Further perceptual evaluations of pulse microstructure in computer performances of classical piano music', *Music Perception* 8/1: 1–33.

1992a: 'Probing the cognitive representation of musical time: structural constraints on the perception of timing perturbations', *Cognition* 44/3: 241–81.

1992b: 'Diversity and commonality in music performance: an analysis of timing micro-structure in Schumann's "Träumerei"', *Journal of the Acoustical Society of America* 92/5: 2546–68.

1994: 'On determining the basic tempo of an expressive music performance', *Psychology of Music* 22/2: 157–67.

Rink, J., 1990: Review of W. Berry, *Musical Structure and Performance*, in *Music Analysis* 9/3: 319–39.

Schachter, C., 1994: 'The Prelude in E minor Op. 28 No. 4: autograph sources and interpretation', in J. Rink and J. Samson, eds., *Chopin Studies 2* (Cambridge: Cambridge University Press), pp. 161–82.

Schmalfeldt, J., 1985: 'On the relation of analysis to performance: Beethoven's Bagatelles Op. 126, Nos. 2 and 5', *Journal of Music Theory* 29/1: 1–31.

Seashore, C., 1938: *Psychology of Music* (New York: McGraw-Hill).

Shaffer, L. H., 1992: 'How to interpret music', in M. R. Jones and S. Holleran, eds., *Cognitive Bases of Musical Communication* (Washington: American Psychological Association), pp. 263-78.

Sundberg, J., 1988: 'Computer synthesis of music performance', in J. A. Sloboda, ed., *Generative Processes in Music* (Oxford: Clarendon), pp. 52–69.

Todd, N., 1985: 'A model of expressive timing in tonal music', *Music Perception* 3/1: 33–58.

1989: 'A computational model of rubato', *Contemporary Music Review* 3/1: 69–88.

1994: 'The auditory "primal sketch": a multiscale model of rhythmic grouping', *Journal of New Music Research* 23/1: 25–70.

Williamson, J., 1978: *Decoding Advertisements* (London: Marion Boyars).

# CHAPTER THREE

# Musical motion and performance: theoretical and empirical perspectives

## PATRICK SHOVE AND BRUNO H. REPP

▬

### THEORETICAL ISSUES

*Traditional perspectives*

Experiences of movement – of its character and expressiveness – are vitally important to composers, performers and listeners alike. This fact is borne out on several levels of discourse. As action plans, musical scores provide general instructions on how instrumentalists and singers may execute, control and coordinate their motor actions, the details of which are determined largely by the performers' musical sensibilities. Undergraduate harmony textbooks, theoretical treatises, analytical essays and historical studies all evoke images of movement presumably associated with the musical experience. 'Motion speak' may be as commonplace as the phrase 'C♯ moves to D', or as colourful as David Lewin's description (1982: 53) of a striking moment in Schubert's 'Auf dem Flusse', where the singer 'takes a sharp stone and scratches a G♯ on the icy surface of the [pianist's] right hand'. Do these expressions point to a genuine perceptual experience of movement or a propensity to speak in metaphor (or both)? If the former, then what is the nature of that experience?

In some form or another, these questions have occupied the minds of theorists and philosophers throughout the centuries, and more recently the minds of psychologists. Collectively, they have given us two basic categories with which to frame our understanding of musical motion: namely, *rhythmic motion* and *tonal motion* (the latter often being subdivided into melodic motion and harmonic motion). In the light of these categories, studies of musical motion tend to concentrate on one of four topics: (1) the source of motion; (2) the organisation of motion; (3) the character, or quality, of motion; and (4) the listener's perception and response to motion. In this part of our chapter, we focus on the first topic.

Identifying the source of movement has been of the utmost concern to music theorists. Phrases like 'arises from', 'basis of', 'result of' and 'product of' crop up in numerous discussions. Not all theorists, however, agree about the object of these phrases. Some see it as linked to the temporal patterning of sounds – to the rhythmic structure of music – and to the feeling of pulse and pulse-tempo. For many, rhythm in this more traditional (more restricted) sense is patterned movement. Esther Gatewood (1927) observed that listeners sense movement most strongly when a lively and distinct rhythmic pattern, rather than melodic contour or harmonic structure, predominates in the music. But some listeners, mostly analysts, have reported sensing movement across larger structural levels, as when successive rhythmic groups progressively increase or decrease in length, in effect producing large-scale deceleration or acceleration. The opening eight bars of Beethoven's Piano Sonata in F minor Op. 2 No. 1 are commonly cited to illustrate the latter effect.

Somewhat related to all of this is the more general idea that 'succession' itself is evidence of motion. This is the portrait Maury Yeston (1976) paints in his historical survey of musical rhythm (Chapter 1) and in his Schenker-influenced theory of rhythm. To be sure, the relationship between succession and motion has long been noted. As Jean de Muris ([1319] 1965: 172) put it, 'sound is generated by motion, since it belongs to the class of successive things . . . Succession does not exist without motion.'

More recently, Christopher Hasty (1981) has given careful attention to this relationship, particularly in terms of the continuity of succession in the face of discontinuous change. Bringing together the insights of the philosopher Errol Harris with the psychological notion of the 'perceived present' (a present in which events no longer sounding are nonetheless part of one's immediate consciousness), he concludes that 'motion arises . . . from the unification of events' (: 192). This unification is mainly temporal in origin, for it depends on the duration between successive events, although other structural factors may help to unify the events. Not surprisingly, de Muris also spoke on this subject: 'Time inseparably unites motion' ([1319] 1965: 172).

Looking beyond the succession of events, other theorists have pointed to the time-honoured qualities of tension and relaxation as sources of motion. These qualities manifest themselves melodically, harmonically and rhythmically.

Melodically, motion occurs when 'unstable tones' resolve to 'stable tones'. Victor Zuckerkandl ([1956] 1973) referred to these relative stabilities as the 'dynamic qualities' of tones. He averred that the experience of musical motion (specifically, tonal motion) is not based on the differences in pitch within a melody, or even on the melody's rhythmic structure, since, in his mind, rhythm is not a uniquely 'musical' phenomenon and, therefore, could not be the source of 'musical' motion (: 76). For motion to be musical it must be based on the qualitative differences in scale-degree position. He proposed that the diatonic scale, construed as a 'dynamic field', abstractly represents these differences as varying 'degrees of stability and instability' (: 98), the tonic being the most stable, the leading note the most unstable.[1] For Zuckerkandl, the

---

[1]  Zuckerkandl was not the first to observe these 'qualities'. Over a century earlier, Fétis ([1844] 1879) spoke of them as *affinités*. Kurth (1917), too, spoke of them, though in a seemingly impenetrable language. Beginning with the phrase 'Melodik ist Bewegung' (: 1), he set out to explain musical motion in terms of an 'absolute melody', an invisible stream of ebbing and flowing 'psychic forces'. Kurth believed that such 'forces' generated the transitions between discrete tones, which function 'only as markers along the path of a *Bewegungszug*' (Rothfarb 1988: 14). The main 'force' driving this motion is scale-degree $\hat{7}$ (: 9). It should be noted that Zuckerkandl ([1956] 1973) also applied the concept of 'dynamic quality' to the metrical order of pulses. Therefore, rhythm becomes motion only when it is in the dynamic field of metre (: 174).

dynamic field is imbued with a 'tonal force' with or against which the tones work. The natural state of this force is motion 'towards' a stable tone ($\hat{7}$ to $\hat{8}$, or $\hat{2}$ to $\hat{1}$), which acts as a centre of tonal gravity. Motion 'away from' this centre implies a succession of tones working against the natural state. In essence, dynamic qualities are directional qualities.

Harmonically, the sense of motion corresponds to the tension of dissonant intervals or chords resolving to consonant intervals and chords. As understood by some earlier writers, the primary aesthetic role of dissonance was to make the subsequent consonance 'sound more agreeable', providing 'great pleasure and delight' in its resolution (Zarlino [1558] 1983: 53). However, later writers such as Norman Cazden (1945: 5) came to view intervallic and harmonic dissonance as causing 'a restless expectation of resolution, of movement [to consonance]'. Walter Piston (1978: 7) is even more straightforward in this regard: 'The essential quality of dissonance is its sense of movement.'

Rhythmically, tension results from various forms of temporal 'conflict': local syncopation, complex polyrhythms ('rhythmic dissonance', according to Yeston (1976: 89–102)), rhythmic groupings 'out of phase' with metric groupings (another example of 'rhythmic dissonance'), metrically weak cadential endings and the like. But these conflicts, as well as the other tensional qualities of musical structure, are not so much sources of motion as they are sources of 'directionality'. In the words of David Epstein (1990: 198), 'Tension means energy unresolved and unresolved energy ultimately means forward motion.' Put differently, the tensional qualities of musical structure induce the expectation of resolution, in effect casting the listener forward in time. Nevertheless, Mari Riess Jones (1981: 37) characterises this future-orientated experience as 'psychological motion', which she attributes not merely to tension, but more generally to 'objective regularities in musical patterns' to which listeners of a given culture have become attuned and which they have learned to expect. The melodic and harmonic 'expectancies', as she calls them, induce motion-like percepts, i.e. subjective analogues of motion.

Looking more broadly at musical rhythm, some theorists have proposed that the changing properties of musical structure – pitch, duration, grouping, dynamics, timbre and texture – convey 'an analogical impression of motion' (Berry 1967: 8). Jan LaRue (1970) describes these parametric changes as 'sources of movement'; Bernard Vecchione (1987) calls them 'factors of mobility' (*facteurs de mobilité*); and a century earlier Eduard Hanslick ([1854] 1957) captured them in the well-known phrase 'tönend-bewegte Formen'.

One problem with this broad view of musical motion is that it can lead to the unfortunate conclusion that every kind of change on every level of musical structure is a potential source of motion. Indeed, Wallace Berry reaches precisely that conclusion (1967: 8): 'in music, change is motion'. But clearly this is an over-generalisation. We no more perceive a change in musical texture as an instance of *motion* than we do a change in physical texture, such as the surface of a car after a heavy hail storm. Both are significant events, to be sure, but not motion events, at least from the perspective of what James Gibson (1979) called the 'ecological level' of perception (the level situated between the microphysical and macrophysical extremes of reality). Although the perception of motion, musical or otherwise, is clearly linked to the perception of change (we shall reaffirm this point below), without proper constraint the idea that change in music induces an experience of motion has little explanatory power.

Countless others have spoken to these and similar ideas. Among the philosophers, Henri Bergson (1946) and Susanne Langer (1953) are perhaps the most influential. Psychologists other than Jones have also had their fair say, specifically, about melodic motion. For example, Roger Shepard (1981, 1984) suggests that melodic motion is the auditory equivalent of apparent motion, the experience of which 'seems to fall somewhere between perception and imagery' (1984: 423). This is different from the auditory illusions of locomotion observed by Harold Burtt (1917) or electronically simulated by John Chowning (1971) for compositional purposes. Rather, it is a mental image of a sonic object, a single tone, rising and falling in pitch space, in effect traversing an imagined path. Shepard has reason to believe that this 'auditory image' (to borrow from McAdams 1984) is evidence that 'the spatial apparatus of the brain, acquired through protracted interaction with concrete physical space [,] . . . has come – by extension or by preemption – to represent relations and transformations in spaces that are more abstract or metaphorical' (1981: 318). This explanation of melodic motion has much to commend it, especially since it sidesteps the problems inherent in the tension/relaxation theories noted above – problems such as mistaking the sources of 'directionality' for the sources of 'motion'. However, it accounts for only one part of the complex experience of musical motion. In the following section, we shall consider another part of the experience, though one rarely acknowledged by scholars.

### Different levels of musical awareness

Introspection, the heart of all phenomenological enquiry, has a way of obscuring one's vision of the obvious. Ludwig Wittgenstein (1953: 50) perhaps said it best: 'The aspects of things that are most important for us are hidden because of their simplicity and familiarity. (One is unable to notice something – because it is always before one's eyes.)' Traditionally, to explain the source of musical motion, theorists, philosophers and psychologists alike have turned to musical structure, which by most accounts is abstract. This has led some to believe that the motion heard is virtual, illusory or abstract. In the words of Roger Sessions (1950: 20), 'The gestures which music embodies are, after all, invisible gestures; one may almost define them as consisting of movement in the abstract, movement which exists in time but not in space, movement, in fact, which gives time its meaning and its significance for us.' Hidden from this view is perhaps the most obvious source of musical movement: the human performer. Why have so many theorists failed to acknowledge that musical movement is, among other things, *human* movement?[2]

---

[2] Pierce (1978: 24) is among the few who have acknowledged the crucial link between performance movement and musical movement: 'I recognized that a performer necessarily renders musical movement with

Despite the differences in focus, the explanations discussed in the previous section share an unnecessarily restrictive view of music's ontological status: that while performers must move to produce music, such movements exist 'outside the music proper' (Epstein 1981: 197 n. 5). But what is 'the music proper'?[3] A perusal of the analytical literature on Western music will reveal that 'the music proper' (or 'music as music') is invariably conceived in terms of such things as melodic contour, harmonic progression, phrase relations, structural function, affective content and the like. In short, 'the music proper' is inextricably linked to the structure of music.

Defined as such, however, music stands apart (presumably in cognition) from those who perform it. This is a peculiarly Western conception of music, emerging perhaps only within the last two or three centuries. It is our belief, however, that the idea of musical autonomy (as some call it) *reflects but one mode of musical awareness among several*. In this regard, we agree with John Baily (1985: 258) when he writes: 'Music may be as much a motor event as a sonic event, as well as, of course, a social fact.'

The idea of multiple modes, or levels, of musical awareness, which is implicit in Baily's statement, has found resonances in the work of several other researchers. For instance, Stephen Handel (1989: 181) identifies three 'levels' of event awareness, each representing a different, 'after-the-fact attempt to specify the characteristics of [the] event'. At one level, a listener may hear the physical characteristics of sound, its intensity, duration, pitch and so on. At another level, the listener may perceive other (perhaps subjective) qualities such as 'warmth', 'roughness' and 'hollowness'. (Although Handel does not say whether these are the qualities of sound itself or of the environmental objects involved in the event – the hollowness of a perfect fifth versus the hollowness of a tubular bell – what is important here is that the listener can attend to the qualities apart from their source.) At yet another level, what we call the 'ecological level', the listener may directly perceive the environmental objects, surfaces or substances involved in the event. In other words, the listener does not merely hear the *sound* of a galloping horse or bowing violinist: rather, the listener hears a *horse galloping* and a *violinist bowing*.

As regards the perception of music, Eric Clarke (1985) has proposed that a listener is apt to hear three different types of events based on the information in musical sound. The first type corresponds to Handel's third level: the musician playing an instrument or singing. We call this a *performance event*. The second type is abstract and is often described as a *structural event*. Hearing structural events means hearing the articulation of

the physical movements of playing: blowing, tonguing, breathing, fingering, foot pedaling and the manifold gestures which in playing encircle these elementary movements.'

3  On this matter, Clifton (1983: 2) argues that while a sound source, such as a piano, 'must be there if we are to experience music at all . . . it is precisely the knowledge that such and such an instrument is indeed the sound source which is not necessarily included in the experience itself'. There is nothing particularly problematic about this statement, given its context. However, what he says shortly thereafter is specious at best: 'I am constantly making an association between these sounds and the objects [pots and pans] which produce them. They are signs of something occurring in the factual world, and music, whatever else it is, is not factually in the world the way trees and mountains are' (: 3). But music *is* 'factually' in the world, inasmuch as the objects (the musicians–cum–instruments) that produce musical sounds are in the world. That one must transcend the physical aspect of the musical event in order to experience it 'as music' is a condition imposed by Western culture. It is not a universal condition of musical experience (see Baily 1985).

motives, phrases, durational patterns, cadential progressions and so on. The third type
of event is also abstract but corresponds to what Alf Gabrielsson (1973a, 1973b) calls
the 'emotion character' of music, patterns of movement whose general characteristics
are similar to bodily movement symptomatic of human emotions, moods or feelings.
We call this an *expressive event*. Although there may be several more ways of experiencing musical events, we shall limit our discussion to these three.

The common thread passing through each of these perspectives is the perception of
movement. On the ecological level, the source of this movement is the human
performer. In this regard, musical movement is human movement. To the listener
attending to music as a performance event, this fact is unmistakably clear, although the
advent of electronic and computer-generated music may confound the perceptual
experience. In those instances where the performer is indeed human, the listener may
hear any number of 'articulators' (lips, fingers, hands) or 'articulatory systems' (finger–
hand–arm units) moving rhythmically relative to the surface of an instrument
(including the mouth of a singer). Note that seeing these movements is not a
prerequisite to hearing them. By 'hearing' we do not mean that the listener must or
can identify the mechanical details of the 'articulatory movement' or even the continuity of movement between each discrete articulation.[4] Such an ability may come
with repeated aural experience, perhaps coupled with watching the performance, or it
may draw on one's personal experience as a performer. At some point in one's
experience, this ability will be no more necessary for the aural perception of performance movement than it is for the perception of someone walking in the dark. No
one needs to see how high the feet are being raised to hear someone walking or to
sense the continuity of the leg movements between the discrete footsteps. The series
of footsteps is a natural, lawful consequence of the continuous movements of the legs
(indeed, of the whole body). In this respect, their timing and amplitude 'specify' the
continuity of movement. The same, we submit, is true of performance movement:
the timing and amplitude of the sound-producing attacks lawfully specify the movement spanning a group of attacks, which one can hear as a unit of motion – as a
gesture. Some may object to this claim on the (false) assumption that all one hears are
the attacks, for they alone produce the sound. However, attacks are nested events,
constrained by, affected by and thus lawfully specific to the performer's actions. To
hear the attacks is to hear the performer move. That a listener fails to identify precisely
where a pianist's hand is at a given moment reflects his or her lack of experience, not
necessarily an inherent limitation of the auditory system.

It is instructive to note here that articulatory movements correspond more or less to
the so-called 'surface rhythm' of music. Put differently, the rhythmic motions of the
performer and of the 'musical object' are essentially one and the same. Of course, there
are many instances in Western and non-Western music where the movements of the
performer and the resultant auditory patterns do not correspond in a simple one-to-

---

4   Other types of performance movement include those that sustain sounds; those that modify sounds, either
    sustained or in a series; and those that are perhaps more visually than aurally interesting, but nonetheless affect
    the sound of the performance (for better or worse).

one fashion, if at all; the compound (or polyphonic) melodies of J. S. Bach's works for solo violin or solo cello are familiar examples.[5]

We readily acknowledge that the perception of musical movement is not limited to hearing the articulatory movements of a performer. In fact, from the other two perspectives, the performer quickly fades from view by most accounts. When attending to a sequence of sounds as a *structural* event, the listener is likely to attribute the motion heard to a 'musical object' – a melody, for example. By attending to the same sequence as an *expressive* event, the listener could hear it as an emotionally charged gesture, the source of which might remain indeterminate (Maus 1988). In either case, the experience of movement is undeniable.

Despite the obvious differences between these experiences of movement, we believe they have a common origin: the performer is the ultimate source of the movement perceived. True, the abstract image of a sonic object rising and falling in pitch space bears little, if any, resemblance to a pianist's fingers and hands moving across the surface of the keyboard. And if one takes into account the physical and mechanical differences between instruments, the resemblance becomes even more remote. Yet, without the performer's rhythmic movements (real, imagined or computer-simulated), the perception of melodic motion (for that matter, any motion) would be impossible. Simply put, patterned articulatory movements create patterned sequences of tones. In other words, articulatory movements are sound-structuring movements. The motion one attributes to a succession of tones – including its pacing, its character, even its directionality – belongs first and foremost to the performer. That a listener reports hearing a sonic object in motion, rather than a performer, reflects the listener's perceptual attitude towards the musical event.

## Gibson's theory of perception and information

To understand how the same acoustic signal can support at least three different perceptual experiences of motion, we turn to the theoretical insights of the American psychologist James Gibson (1966, 1979).[6] Despite the controversy surrounding Gibson's 'ecological approach' to perception (a controversy based largely on his out-of-hand rejection of many essential concepts underpinning the information-processing

---

[5]   Kubik made a similar observation about his encounter with African xylophone music: 'Our playing sounded much more complicated than it actually was, and I heard a number of rhythm patterns which I was sure that none of us had played, while on the other hand the rhythms which we had actually played were inaudible on the tape' (1962: 34). Although the primary function of the auditory system is to identify the location, source and nature of events, the human brain seems to have developed a 'mechanism' for detecting abstract pitch–time relations, independently of how well or poorly they match the spatio-temporal structure of the performer's articulatory actions. Bregman (1990) refers to this mechanism as 'auditory scene analysis', the principal effect of which he calls 'auditory stream segregation'. In most cases, however, the correspondence between what the performer does and what the listener hears on the musical surface is direct. Ecologically speaking, to hear a melody is to hear, among other things, a musician move relative to the surface of an instrument (and that includes the vocal apparatus).

[6]   Within recent years, several musicians and music psychologists have made significant contributions to what is called 'ecological acoustics' (complementing Gibson's work in 'ecological optics'). Most notable among them are Balzano (1986, 1987), Clarke (1987), Jones (1976, 1981, 1986, 1990a, 1990b), Jones and Hahn (1986), and Risset (1988).

approach, concepts like 'mental representation'), most psychologists acknowledge Gibson's contribution to the present understanding of perception. In particular, they cite his emphasis not only on the study of natural, or 'ecologically valid', encounters with one's environment, but also on the idea that the environment is rich in information about its structure and dynamics. Under favourable conditions, this information is sufficiently available to the perceptual systems, thus enabling the perceiver to tailor his or her actions to the environment.

During the mid to late 1950s, Gibson began to think that perception is based not upon discrete sensations, as commonly believed, but upon the 'pickup' of 'stimulus information', or simply 'information'. He had long since recognised, like many before him, that the environment both changes and persists. A child smiles, thus transforming the contours of his or her face, yet one continues to see the same face. Gibson proposed that the flowing pattern of light (the 'optic array', as he called it) must contain information 'specific' to both the changing and the persisting features of the face.

Interestingly, the information in light, sound, touch and so forth is not concrete like the objects and events it specifies. Rather, it is abstract and formless, consisting of relational invariants defined over a transformation – in other words, invariants of a higher, mathematical order. As Gibson understood it, the perception of a relatively permanent, yet ever-transforming environment may be as simple as extracting 'the invariants of structure from the flux of stimulation while still noticing the flux' (1979: 247), however complex the process of extraction may be.[7]

It is reasonable to assume that different aspects of the stimulus information correspond to different features of the event. For example, in listening to Kiri Te Kanawa sing 'O mio Babbino caro', one may identify at least three basic properties of the event: its *location* (on the concert stage), its *source* (Kiri Te Kanawa) and its *nature* (singing). Yet, which aspects of the acoustic information specify 'Kiri Te Kanawa' and which 'singing'? Do we assign only the invariant features of the sound pattern to the persistent sound source and the changing features to the transient nature of the event?

According to Robert Shaw and John Pittenger (1978), a working solution to this problem begins with the understanding that events are 'invariant patterns of change':

> For to the extent that change proceeds according to some style, then to that extent change can be specified by invariant perceptual information. A motor can run invariantly, a couple can waltz invariantly, or a flower can grow according to a natural rhythm – an invariant policy of growth. None of these are static phenomena, rather they are distinct *events* precisely because they do exhibit different patterns of change. (: 188)

---

[7]  Determining what remains invariant under transformation is by no means a simple task. Whereas change is usually easy to measure, isolating invariants is a perennial source of consternation. Handel (1989: 224) even goes so far as to suggest that 'it requires an act of faith to believe that a higher-order variable can be discovered'. Assuming, though, that Gibson's hypothesis is correct, the problem here may have more to do with the analytical method devised by the investigators than with the existence or nonexistence of such a variable. Balzano's (1987: 178–9) solution to this problem is to assume that perception itself is a 'species of measurement' and that what it measures need not 'show up' on a conventional measuring device. This is not a convenient sidestepping of the issue but rather an important acknowledgment that not all objective properties of our environment must be objectively measured to demonstrate their objective existence. Invariants, which one can model with the powerful tools of mathematical group theory, may have just such an existence, though forever eluding physical measure, save by the human observer.

With this novel understanding of change, it became necessary for Shaw and Pittenger to postulate two types of invariants: 'transformational' and 'structural'.

Transformational invariants are those relational aspects of the information that specify the identity of a particular pattern of change. Whenever Kiri Te Kanawa sings, she regulates the movements of her vocal tract in a manner distinguishable from most other forms of human activity, even speech. Consequently, her finely controlled vocal movements structure the surrounding air, distributing the initial energy of her actions through a sound field. The sound spectrum and temporal course of the resulting acoustic wave map onto the degree and rate at which she physically changes pitch and modulates the force of air through her vocal tract. Thus, one hears her *singing*.

Structural invariants, on the other hand, are relational properties specific to the structure of the source object undergoing a particular style of change. For the event 'Kiri Te Kanawa singing', these properties will correspond to the invariant structural features of her vocal tract and any other part of her body which may affect her production of sound. Her unique physical characteristics lawfully constrain the manner in which she sings and, consequently, the sound she produces, thereby allowing us to distinguish her from other singers. Presumably, the perception of a pianist's 'touch' also depends on the pick-up of structural invariants.

Though conceptually distinct, structural and transformational invariants are functionally interdependent. One perceives 'Kiri Te Kanawa' only as one encounters her singing, talking, laughing, walking and so on. Her identity is intertwined with what she does as a physical, dynamic being. And yet what she does – how she sings – is lawfully determined by the structure of her body.

The foregoing discussion exemplifies Sverker Runeson and Gunilla Frykholm's (1986: 262) claim that 'movements specify their causes', a claim theoretically supported by the Kinematic Specification of Dynamics (KSD) principle. Stated simply, the kinematic properties of an ambient array – the velocity profile of a sound sequence, for example – specify the dynamic factors of the source that generated the movement pattern, factors such as mass ratio and the effective damping characteristics of the source. We believe that the KSD principle, initially applied to visual perception, applies equally well to the auditory perception of events. Indeed, many analyses of musical sound are, in effect, analyses of the kinematic properties specific to the dynamics of a human performer. The difference here is that we are ascribing ecological values to traditional psychoacoustic variables.

Still, the problem remains: if acoustic information is lawfully specific to its environmental source, then why is the performer transparent to some listeners? In part, we have already answered this question. But as Clarke (1985) correctly notes, a perceiver can use perceptual information in various ways, especially when the experience entails looking at a painting or listening to music. The relational invariants in musical sound not only specify the structure and transformation of a performer, but also may constitute the structure and transformation of an imagined 'musical object', evident by such comments as 'the sound of a perfect fifth' and 'the transposition of the second theme into the tonic key'. Furthermore, it may be that both representational and non-representational (absolute) forms of music embody relational invariants specific to natural classes of movement, including those symptomatic of human emotional states.[8] Mari Riess Jones and June Hahn (1986) refer to these as 'prototypical invariants'. Having extracted these invariants, a listener may spontaneously structure his or her awareness of the musical event in terms of familiar motion patterns, such as galloping and breathing, or emotional behaviour, such as that associated with rage or joy. This level of awareness, we presume, relies heavily on the listener's imagination.

In analysing performance movement, one may refer to several interrelated factors: the mode of production (bowing, tonguing), the style of articulation (staccato, legato), the physical 'shaping' of a sustained sound (vibrato, lip trill), the rate of movement (tempo and timing, or agogics), the pattern of movement (rhythm, in the narrow sense), the force of movement (dynamics) and even the changes in pitch (musical space). All of these, some to a greater degree than others, are represented kinematically in the acoustic array and, upon their particular extraction, will shape the listener's perception of musical movement. We have suggested, relying on Gibson's theory, how the listener picks up and uses this information. In the second part of this chapter we present a selective review of empirical studies which specify in more detail the nature of motion information in the musical signal, and which demonstrate that listeners can indeed recover this information and convert it into overt body movement.

## EMPIRICAL APPROACHES

Music is made by moving hands, fingers or extensions thereof over an instrument, and the dynamic time course of these movements is reflected to some extent in the resulting stream of sounds. Conversely, people listening to music frequently perform coordinated movements ranging from foot tapping to elaborate dance. Although these movements on the listener's side are not the same as those of the performer, they are certainly not unrelated. At the very least, they share a rhythmic framework which is transmitted from player to listener via the sound structure.

In many cultures this close connection of music and body movement is so obvious as hardly to deserve comment. In Europe, however, the remarkable development of musical notation and of complex compositional techniques over the last few centuries has encouraged a focus on the structural rather than the kinematic properties of music, at least of so-called serious music. At the same time, as this music has been performed mainly in church, court or concert hall, a social proscription against overt movement by listeners has long been in effect. As a result of these practices, the close connection between music and motion has receded from people's consciousness, and twentieth-century aesthetic and technological developments have occasionally even severed that connection, with only few taking notice. There is a need today therefore to reassess the concept of musical motion and its role in performance and musical understanding.

---

[8]  Many writers have questioned the degree to which an emotion can be expressed in music, if at all (e.g. Hanslick [1854] 1957; Cone 1974; Newcomb 1984; Kivy 1989).

In this more empirical part of our chapter we briefly review the pioneering work of three largely forgotten individuals who were active in Germany during the early decades of this century. We then sample the work of two contemporary researchers who – knowingly in one case, unwittingly in the other – have elaborated upon the German pioneers' ideas and made them sufficiently precise that they can now be subjected to rigorous tests. We conclude with a very brief foray into the motor control literature, again focusing on a single researcher whose work seems to be particularly pertinent to the kinds of motion that music engenders. Space constraints do not allow us to do justice to the related work of others, but we hope to convey at least the flavour of past and current research on musical motion.

### Three German pioneers: Sievers, Becking and Truslit

Although no one doubts that there is visual information for motion, the concept of auditory motion information is less widely accepted among psychologists, especially since it involves an essentially stationary sound source – the musical instrument being played by a performer.[9] One reason for this scepticism may be that visual (spatial) motion information is generally continuous in time, whereas auditory (rhythmic) motion information, especially that in music, is often carried by discrete events (i.e. tone onsets) which only *sample* the time course of the underlying movement. The principal methodology for demonstrating that music does convey movement information is the reconstitution of an analogous spatial movement by a human listener. The listener's body thus acts as a *transducer*, a kind of filter for the often impulse-like coding of musical movement.

The first modern attempt to use such a technique in a systematic fashion must be credited to the German philologist Eduard Sievers, who applied it not to music but to literary works. Sievers called his method *Schallanalyse* ('sound analysis'), though it was concerned not with sound as such but rather with body posture and movement as a way of reconstructing and analysing the expressive sound shape of printed language, mostly poetry. Although he never published a complete account of his very complex methods, Sievers (1924) provides an overview, and Ungeheuer (1964) offers a more recent critical evaluation.

Sievers's initial impetus came from observations of a singing teacher, Joseph Rutz, published by his son Otmar Rutz (1911, 1922), about connections between body posture and voice quality. Certain body postures were said to inhibit vocal production, whereas others facilitated it and gave it a free, unconstrained quality. Sievers initially focused on these facilitating postures which he symbolised by means of 'optic signals' in the form of geometric shapes meant to cue different body postures in a speaker reciting a text. Subsequently, he elaborated this method into a system of dynamic

---

[9]   The pick-up of auditory information about the locomotion of a sound source is uncontroversial. Although such sound effects are occasionally used in music, both literally (by musicians walking across the stage, or by electronic simulation of sounds changing location – see Chowning 1971) and symbolically (e.g. by the extended crescendo–diminuendo pattern suggesting a passing procession in Albéniz's 'El Corpus en Sevilla' (*Suite Iberia*, I, 1906)), this is not the kind of motion with which we are concerned.

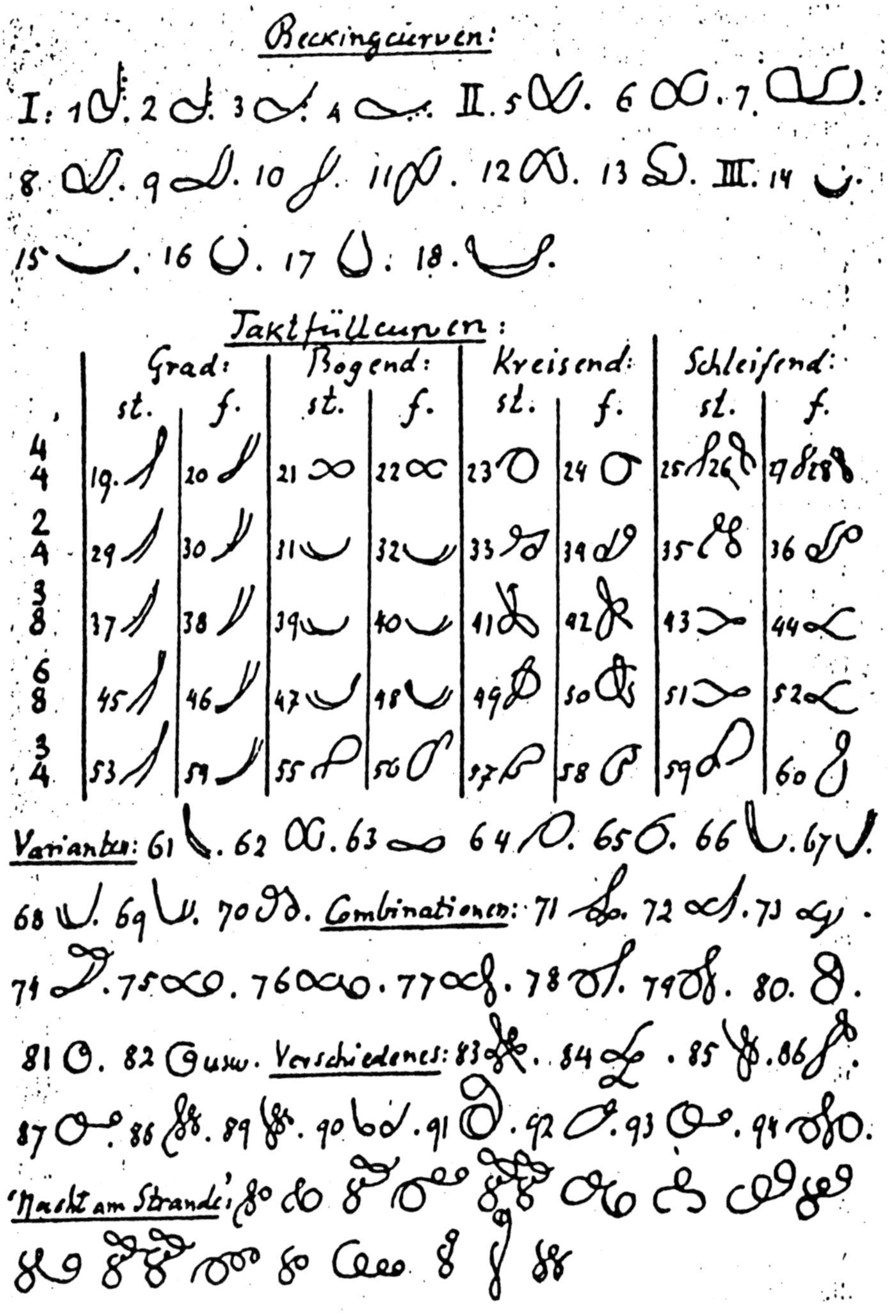

Figure 3.1 Examples of movement curves used by Eduard Sievers. Top: general curves. Centre: special curves (straight, curved, circular, looping). Bottom: variations, combinations, miscellaneous, and a kinematic interpretation of a text, 'Nacht am Strande'. (Reproduced from Sievers 1924: 73.)

movements to be carried out with a baton, with the index finger or even with both arms while speaking. The crucial criterion was the achievement of 'free and uninhibited articulation', and the goal of the analytical method was to find the accompanying movements that least interfered with (or most facilitated) the recitation of the text. The metric, prosodic and semantic characteristics of the text naturally varied with authors and their individual works, as did the accompanying movements considered optimal by Sievers. The movements were rhythmically coordinated with the speech and in general had a cyclic or looping character although a large number of their features were variable, such as the relative smoothness of turns, the tilt of the main axis, rising versus falling direction, etc.

Sievers distinguished two classes of curves, which are illustrated in Figure 3.1: general curves or so-called 'Becking curves' (to be discussed later), and specific or filler curves (*Taktfüllcurven*). The former, suggested to him by Gustav Becking, come in three types which in fact exhaust the possibilities for a cyclic movement with two turning points: pointed–round, round–round and pointed–pointed. Any individual speaker/writer was said to be characterised by one and only one of these types, if not as an obligatory then at least as a preferred mode of dynamic expression, and hence by a corresponding 'voice type'. However, many variations are possible within each type. The 'special curves', of which there is a bewildering variety, reflect the particular metric and sonic properties of a spoken text (or of music, as the case may be). It was to these special curves and their many variations that Sievers devoted most of his efforts.

Sievers was the only recognised master of the technique he had developed. He claimed to be in possession of an extraordinary 'motoric sensibility' which, combined with many years of self-training and observation, enabled him to find the accompanying movements for the most subtle variations in the sound shape of spoken texts. Although his dedication and expertise were never in doubt, the extreme subjectivity of his method obviously diminished its respectability as a scientific procedure. Nevertheless, its basic, underlying idea continues to be of value: rhythmic sound patterns have a dynamic time course which can be translated into accompanying body movements. Only the rules governing this translation remain somewhat obscure.

Sievers benefited from his interaction with Gustav Becking, a young musicologist who developed his own ideas in a monograph entitled *Der musikalische Rhythmus als Erkenntnisquelle* (Musical Rhythm as a Source of Insight) which appeared in 1928. Becking's pivotal assumption was that a *dynamic rhythmic flow* exists below the musical surface. This flow, a continuous up–down motion, connects points of metric gravity which vary in relative weight. Becking's important and original claim was that the distribution of these weights varies from composer to composer. The analytical technique for determining these weights was Sievers's method of accompanying movements, carried out with a light baton.[10] A downbeat always accompanies the

---

[10]  Even though Becking relied on and contributed to Sievers's system, he was in fact quite critical of the older scholar's methods. In particular, he criticised Sievers's movements as essentially passive, lacking pressure and dynamics, and hence devoid of musical content. According to Becking ([1923–4] 1975), the accompanying movements require an active attitude: one should not merely be moved by the music but should move as if one were the composer.

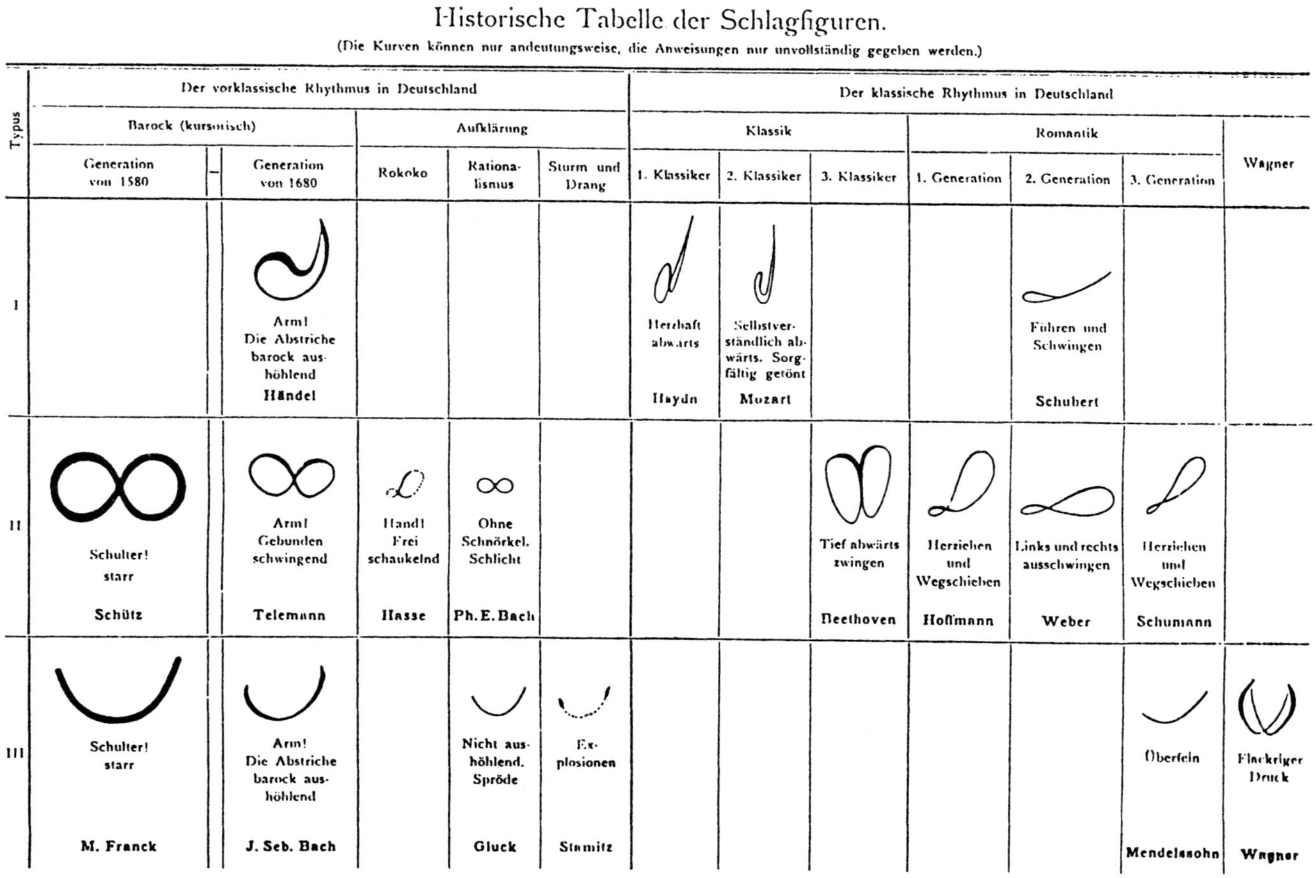

Historische Tabelle der Schlagfiguren.

(Die Kurven können nur andeutungsweise, die Anweisungen nur unvollständig gegeben werden.)

| | | Der vorklassische Rhythmus in Deutschland | | | | | Der klassische Rhythmus in Deutschland | | | | | | | |
|---|---|---|---|---|---|---|---|---|---|---|---|---|---|---|
| | | Barock (kursivisch) | | Aufklärung | | | | Klassik | | | Romantik | | | |
| Typus | | Generation von 1580 | Generation von 1680 | Rokoko | Rationalismus | Sturm und Drang | | 1. Klassiker | 2. Klassiker | 3. Klassiker | 1. Generation | 2. Generation | 3. Generation | Wagner |
| I | | Schulter! starr — Schütz | Arm! Die Abstriche barock aushöhlend — Händel | Arm! Gebunden schwingend — Hasse | Ohne Schnörkel. Schlicht — Ph.E.Bach | | | Herzhaft abwärts — Haydn | Selbstverständlich abwärts. Sorgfältig getönt — Mozart | Tief abwärts zwingen — Beethoven | Herziehen und Wegschieben — Hoffmann | Führen und Schwingen — Schubert | Herziehen und Wegschieben — Schumann | Oberfein — Mendelssohn |
| II | | M. Franck | J. Seb. Bach | | Gluck | Explosionen — Stamitz | | | | | | Links und rechts ausschwingen — Weber | Flackriger Druck — Wagner | |
| III | | Schulter! starr | Arm! Die Abstriche barock aushöhlend | Händl Frei schaukelnd — Hasse | Nicht aushöhlend. Spröde — Telemann | | | | | | | | | |

Figure 3.2 Becking's historical table of conducting curves for selected German composers. (Reproduced from the endplate in Becking 1928.)

heaviest metric accent; then an upward movement follows which leads into the next downbeat. The *dynamic shape* of this movement cycle is of interest. For example, the strongest pressure in the downbeat is never at the beginning but at varying delays; the movement may be deep and vertical or shallow and more nearly horizontal; and the connection of downward and upward movements may be smooth or abrupt.

Becking's primary interest was not in the differentiation and proliferation of movement curves for individual works of art but in the personal constants of individual composers – in other words, *invariance* rather than variability. He said that the personal curves reflect a composer's individual 'management of gravity'. Gravity being a physical given, different composers' solutions reflect different philosophical attitudes towards physical reality – as something to be overcome, to adapt to or to be denied, as the case may be. Becking's ultimate goal was thus a typology of personal constants linked to a typology of *Weltanschauungen* (world views) – a philosophical undertaking in which he was preceded by Nohl (1920), among others.

As already mentioned in connection with Sievers's 'Becking curves', Becking distinguished three types of 'personal curves', examples of which are illustrated in Figure 3.2. *Type I* has a sharp, pointed onset of the downbeat, which is straight and usually vertical but nevertheless actively guided rather than passively falling. At the bottom, there is a narrow but round loop ending in a small downward movement (a secondary accent between downbeats) before leading vertically upward, resulting in a figure somewhat like a golf club. This pattern, with its strong differentiation of rhythmic accents but nevertheless individual dynamic shape, is attributed to the 'Mozart family', which also includes Handel, Haydn, Schubert, Bruckner and most Italian composers. These composers are said to be monists (in that they largely obey the physical force of gravity) as well as idealists, because they actively impose a personal dynamic shape on the movement. *Type II* has a round, curving, inward-going (towards the body) onset of the downbeat and a similarly round, outward-going turn upwards, leading to a figure resembling a horizontal or tilted figure 8. Differences in accentuation among metric subdivisions tend to be reduced here. Composers characterised by this personal curve form the 'Beethoven family', including Weber, Schumann, Brahms, Richard Strauss and many other German masters. According to Becking, these composers aim to overcome gravity and force it into a winding path. Thus they are dualists (in that they oppose the material force with their own spiritual force or will) as well as idealists (in that they impose a personal dynamic shape on the raw pulse of the music). Finally, *Type III* is characterised by a pointed downbeat as well as a pointed return, resulting in a semicircular, pendulum-like curving motion from right to left and back. Consequently, the main accents on the downbeats and the secondary accents in between tend to be equally strong and to form a rigid rhythmic framework. This pattern Becking ascribes to the 'Bach family', among them Mendelssohn, Chopin, Wagner, Mahler and most French composers. These masters are said to be naturalists because they follow the force of gravity without opposing it or necessarily imposing a personal pulse on it. Yet there are numerous personal variants of the trajectory between the two rigid endpoints, resulting in more or less idealistic curves

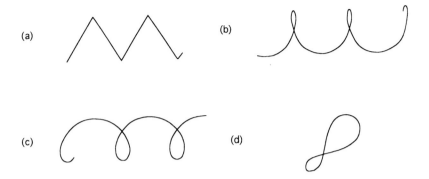

Figure 3.3   Truslit's movement types: a. straight (mechanical); b. open; c. closed; d. winding. (After Plate 2 in Truslit 1938; reproduced from Repp 1993: 54, with permission of the publisher.)

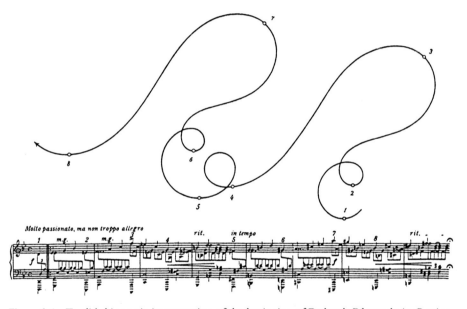

Figure 3.4   Truslit's kinematic interpretation of the beginning of Brahms's Rhapsody in G minor Op. 79 No. 2. Numbers along the movement curve correspond to numbered points in the score. (Reproduced from Truslit 1938: 144, with permission of the publisher.)

(as in the case of Wagner). Nevertheless, all these composers accept the objective, even pulse and hence are only minor idealists, with Bach being the least idealistic and most objective of all.

Becking's method of determining the personal curve of a composer was highly subjective. It required a thorough acquaintance with a composer's works as well as, presumably, performances by great interpreters and biographical details helping to elucidate the artist's personality. The personal curve is *not* derivable from the score, nor is its subjectively judged fit to a particular piece of music necessarily perfect, especially if that music is an early or otherwise atypical creation. Rather, knowledge of the personal curve, verified by the composer's most characteristic works, enables the scholar or performer to imbue even the less characteristic works with the composer's identity. Clearly, this method is somewhat circular and by no means scientifically rigorous; however, Becking's extraordinary perspicacity, well-chosen musical examples and eloquent verbal characterisations make his book a unique and fascinating document.

The third important person among the German pioneers is the least known today – Alexander Truslit, whose book *Gestaltung und Bewegung in der Musik* (Shaping and Motion in Music) appeared in 1938. Truslit's orientation is much closer to the natural sciences than that of his predecessors and in some ways presages Gibson's (1979) writings on ecological perception and action. Unlike Becking, who believed that composers' personal dynamics exist largely beneath the musical surface (i.e. in the listener's musical imagination), Truslit focused on the information in the sound pattern. He contended that the musical dynamics and agogics (timing variations) convey movement information directly to the sensitive listener, who can then instantiate these movements by acting them out, if necessary. For Truslit, the goal of music performance is to arrange the musical surface in accord with the appropriate underlying movement.

Like Becking, Truslit distinguished three basic types of movement curves: 'open', 'closed' and 'winding' (*gewunden*) – i.e. b–d in Figure 3.3, where they are contrasted with an unnatural linear motion path (a). Superficially, they resemble Becking's three types; in particular, the winding curve seems like Becking's Type II, and the open curve like his Type III. However, these similarities are more apparent than real. Truslit's curves are not conducting movements: they are to be carried out slowly and with outstretched parallel arms, so that the whole upper body is involved. Their height in space tends to follow the pitch contour of the melody; thus they often start at the bottom and move upwards rather than beginning with a 'downbeat'. They are a means of portraying the melodic dynamics in space, with the speed of movement and the consequent relative tension being governed mainly by the curvature of the motion path. That is, a slowing-down and commensurate increase in tension in the music is portrayed by a tight loop, whereas faster, more relaxed stretches correspond to relatively straight movements. The varied melodic structure of a composition elicits complex paths of various combinations of clockwise and anticlockwise turns, interpolated loops, etc. Even the type of movement may change within a composition. Figure 3.4 illustrates the combination of closed and winding movements that Truslit found most appropriate for the initial section of Brahms's Rhapsody in G minor Op. 79 No. 2.

Truslit's curves are not at all 'personal' and composer-specific; rather, they are work-specific. In that respect, he was somewhat closer to Sievers than to Becking. He explicitly assigned a secondary and subordinate role to rhythmic patterns: they should not be too pronounced, in order not to disrupt the smooth flow of the melody. Rhythmic patterns affect the limbs, he said (which is consistent with Becking's use of the hand to conduct), whereas the more global melodic patterns affect the large muscles of the back and hence the whole body. Thus Truslit's curves often extend over a number of bars, with the more detailed rhythmic structure marked by small local loops, if at all. Not surprisingly, Truslit seems most interested in music which exhibits a pronounced gestural character: many of his musical examples come from Wagner, while there are no Mozart or Bach examples in his book. His most intriguing speculation is that the perception and translation of musical movement at the scale he was interested in may be mediated by the vestibular organ (i.e. the labyrinth of the inner ear), which controls body orientation and equilibrium. In support of this claim he cited scientific evidence from early physiological experiments. Furthermore, to illustrate the concrete instantiation of different movement types in music performance, Truslit adduced recorded sound examples varying from scales and arpeggios to excerpts from commercial recordings of standard repertoire, as well as some measurements of the acoustic microstructure of the scales and arpeggios. Although his empirical contribution remains fairly negligible, the modernity of his theoretical ideas and the clarity and force with which they are presented must be greatly admired.[11]

### Two modern successors: Clynes and Todd

Despite the many interesting observations that these German authors, especially Becking and Truslit, have to offer the modern reader, their work has largely been forgotten. Although some of their ideas may be outmoded, others are clearly relevant to more recent research on musical expression and performance. Among the small group of researchers active in this area, two seem particularly close in spirit to the German pioneers: Manfred Clynes and Neil Todd. Clynes was acquainted with Becking's work as he began in the 1970s to develop further the concept of composers' 'personal curves', making ingenious use of computer technology. Todd independently formulated ideas resembling those of Truslit, without actually being aware of his work.

Over a number of years, Clynes (1977) developed the notion of *essentic forms*, dynamic time forms which characterise basic emotions. To measure them, he devised a simple apparatus called the sentograph, which consists of a button sensitive to finger pressure in vertical and horizontal directions and a computer registering the pressure over time and averaging successive pressure cycles. Subjects who imagine certain basic emotions (love, anger, grief, etc.) while pressing rhythmically on the sentograph produce very different pressure curves for different emotions.

Clynes argues that meaning in music derives from essentic forms, which are conveyed by the musical macrostructure (melody, rhythm) and microstructure (dynamics, agogics). The more closely an essentic form is approximated, the more beautiful and meaningful the music is perceived to be. This emotional 'story', however, unfolds against the background of a fixed, repetitive, dynamic rhythmic pattern which represents the composer's individuality and 'point of view'. This is the composer's 'inner pulse' – a concept clearly derived from Becking's theory of 'personal curves'. In

---

[11] See Repp 1993 for a synopsis of Truslit's book.

recent writing, Clynes (1992) has referred to this as his 'double stream theory' of musical expression.

The sentograph offered itself as a suitable instrument for measuring the essentic shapes of a musical work, as well as the composer's inner pulse. To assess the former, the (musically experienced) subject presses the button in synchrony with larger musical gestures or phrases while listening to or imagining a piece of music. To assess the latter, the subject presses more rapidly (about once per second) in synchrony with successive downbeats. These repeated pressure curves can then be averaged, yielding a stable average pulse shape. Such averaging cannot easily be achieved with the longer essentic shapes, which may be one reason why Clynes has not explored this aspect in any detail.[12]

To determine the shape of famous composers' inner pulses, Clynes used several outstanding musicians (including Pablo Casals and Rudolf Serkin) as subjects, as well as himself. They were asked to press rhythmically on the sentograph while imagining various works of Beethoven, Mozart, Schubert and others. It was not a counter-balanced experiment: not every subject produced every composer's pulse, while some produced several pulse shapes for different pieces by the same composer. In any case, as can be seen in Figure 3.5, the average vertical pressure curves (see Clynes 1977) show striking differences between these composers (i.e. Beethoven, Mozart and Schubert) and considerable agreement within composers across different subjects and different pieces. Clynes thus went one step beyond Becking by registering the 'conducting' movements that Becking represented only schematically by means of graphs. Even though the finger movements on the sentograph differ from the baton-aided hand movements Becking had in mind, they seem to capture some of the composer-specific characteristics that he talked about. The main analogy between Becking's and Clynes's curves seems to lie in the onset time, relative speed and depth of the downward movement.

Some years after his demonstration of composers' inner pulses on the sentograph, Clynes (1983) advanced towards an objectivisation of the pulse concept. Although Becking had provided some hints of the manner in which individual composers' pulses might be manifested on the musical surface of a performance, he basically thought of them as mental or 'inner' phenomena. Clynes pursued the idea that composers' personal pulses must somehow be manifested in the expressive microstructure of an expert performance. Rather than analysing the performances of great interpreters, he developed a computer program which enabled him to play back music with different agogic and dynamic patterns, repeated cyclically from bar to bar. Using himself as a listener and judge, he manipulated and refined these objective pulse patterns for various works of different composers, primarily Beethoven, Mozart and Schubert. He eventually arrived at settings which he considered optimally appropriate for each

---

[12]  Some interesting examples are presented in the appendix of his 1977 book, apparently representing his own responses to several musical excerpts. However, since the variety of dynamic shapes encountered in music is much greater than the small inventory of essentic forms, it is not clear what counts as an essentic shape and how the emotional meaning of a given dynamic shape is determined.

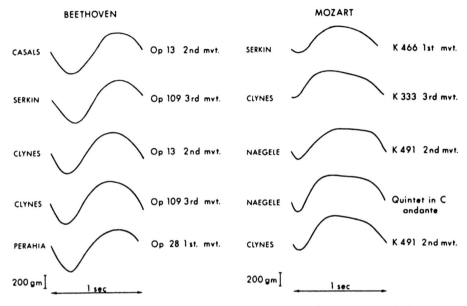

Figure 3.5    Average sentograph responses (vertical pressure curves) of several distinguished musicians during mental rehearsal of compositions by Beethoven and Mozart. (Reproduced from Clynes 1969: 200, with permission of the publisher.)

composer; these patterns were quite different between composers but seemed to fit various works by the same composer. They could be specified numerically in terms of the relative amplitudes and durations of the tones within a metric cycle. Subsequently, Clynes (1986) expanded his scheme to encompass one or two higher levels within which the basic pulse cycles are nested, and which in turn exhibit the temporal and dynamic relationships of the composer's inner pulse, so that the rhythmic surface pattern is a multiplicative combination of higher- and lower-level pulse parameters.

These pulse patterns, then, represent Clynes's subjective judgement, which identifies his enterprise as being partially in the intellectual tradition of Sievers and Becking. What distinguishes it from its historical precedents, however, is that the pulses are *quantified* and hence open to empirical testing. Several attempts have been made to test the effectiveness of Clynes's specifications in conveying the composer's individuality to unbiased listeners. The method was to generate computer performances of several composers' pieces with each composer's pulse, in a factorial design, and to see whether listeners prefer the performances with the 'appropriate' pulse over the others. Several experiments (Thompson 1989; Repp 1989, 1990a) have yielded mixed results, but the most recent study, conducted by Clynes himself (in press), provided unambiguous evidence that highly trained musicians prefer the appropriate composers' pulses over inappropriate pulses in computer-generated performances. Questions remain, however, about how a composer's inner pulse is manifested in human performances, where many factors besides the composer's individuality may affect the expressive microstructure (see Repp 1990b, 1992a).

In these studies, the emphasis was on the quantification and perceptual evaluation of cyclic pulse patterns, not so much on their relation to physical movement. Clynes and Walker (1982) addressed this latter point by investigating the biological 'transfer function' between rhythmic sound patterns and the rhythmic movement of a human listener. The subject pressed on a sentograph while listening to cyclic repetitions of two tones having variable onset times, durations and amplitudes. The resulting averaged pressure curves varied systematically with the sound patterns presented. For example, the downward movement of the finger, which usually accompanied the louder of the two tones, depended on the temporal separation of the softer tone from the louder tone. The timing of the upward movement depended on tone duration: patterns of long tones resulted in smooth, 'rounded' movements, whereas patterns of short tones (with long gaps in between) induced sharp, angular movements.

To relate these results, obtained with arbitrary rhythmic patterns, to the hypothesised pulse patterns of actual music, Clynes and Walker matched two-tone patterns to synchronously played music. They adjusted the physical parameters of the two tones until they perceived a congruence with the musical rhythm. Subsequently, they had subjects press the sentograph when listening to either the music or the matched two-tone 'sound pulse'. Figure 3.6 shows that there was a significant similarity between these motoric responses, indicating that the simple two-tone pulse patterns captured the rhythmic pulse of the acoustically much more complex music.

Clynes's theories and research (of which we have provided only a brief glimpse here) represent a highly original and important contribution to music psychology and to the understanding of music performance. However, his observations are in need of extension and replication in other laboratories, as they are often based on very limited data.

While Clynes was inspired by the ideas of Becking, Todd is in some ways the intellectual heir of Truslit. The most obvious coincidence is both authors' hypothesis that the perception of musical motion may be mediated somehow by the vestibular system (Todd 1992a, 1992b, 1992c, 1993). Although there is little evidence that vestibular stimulation actually occurs in ordinary music-listening conditions, we suspect that this is not really necessary: the sound patterns that characterise body movement could be recognised at an abstract auditory or cognitive level. They may be the very same as those that, under certain extreme conditions (e.g. in very loud music), can evoke vestibular sensations.

Like Truslit, Todd is concerned primarily with motion at the level of the whole body, rather than of the limbs or fingers. He appeals, as did Truslit before him, to physiological evidence concerning two distinct motor systems, the ventromedial and lateral systems (Todd 1992b). The former controls body posture and motion, and is closely linked with the vestibular system. Since larger masses are to be moved, the movements are slower than those possible with feet, hands and fingers, which are controlled by the lateral system. Typically their cycles extend over several seconds, whereas the pulse microstructure studied by Clynes (and executed by finger pressure on the sentograph) is contained within cycles roughly one second in duration which

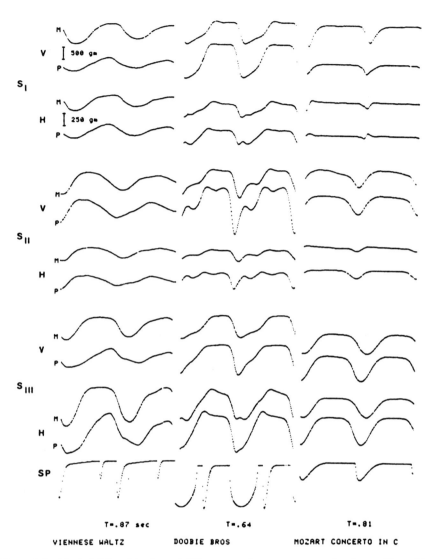

Figure 3.6   Vertical (V) and horizontal (H) sentograph pressure curves for three subjects ($S_I$, $S_{II}$, $S_{III}$) listening to music (M) or to a simple sound pulse (P) matched to the music. Each column represents a different piece of music. The amplitude envelope of the sound pulse (SP) is shown at the bottom. (Reproduced from Clynes and Walker 1982: 211, with permission of the publisher.)

may be nested within the larger cycles described by Truslit and Todd. Recently, Todd (1992b; Todd, Clarke and Davidson 1993) has undertaken to study the motoric instantiation of these larger cycles in the 'expressive body sway' of performers. His preliminary data indicate that pianists' head movements are synchronised with expressive tempo fluctuations in the music, such that tempo minima coincide with turning points in the head movement. Observations such as these have led Todd to propose that expressive variation in tempo and in the correlated dynamics may be a representation of self-motion. Clearly, such a representation has the potential of inducing actual or imaginary motion of a similar kind in a listener/observer.

Concerning the tempo variations in performances, Todd (1992a, 1995) has presented evidence that they are a linear function of real time. In other words, expressive timing consists of alternating phases of constant acceleration and deceleration, one cycle typically corresponding to a musical group or gesture. Listeners also seem to prefer performances whose timing follows this rule, although more extensive perceptual tests remain to be done. Constant acceleration or deceleration seems to characterise various forms of physical and biological motion, so that music having this property would seem an optimal stimulus for the perception and induction of motion. Todd (1992a) has also begun to investigate the way in which changes in musical dynamics accompany changes in timing and has devised a system for the automatic extraction of hierarchical rhythmic structure from the energy flux of the acoustic signal, be it music or speech (Todd 1994). His exciting work is at the cutting edge of research on music performance.

Other contemporary authors who have concerned themselves with problems of motion in music include: Gabrielsson (1973a, 1973b; Gabrielsson, Bengtsson and Gabrielsson 1983), who has done extensive work on the dimensions that underlie the subjective experience of different rhythms; Kronman and Sundberg (1987), who showed that the final ritardandos in performances of baroque music (Sundberg and Verrillo 1980) follow a function resembling the deceleration of physical motion, as in walking; Repp (1992a), who demonstrated that listeners prefer a particular, 'natural' timing pattern in a phrase; and Feldman, Epstein and Richards (1992), who examined examples of very slow tempo changes and concluded that they could be interpreted in terms of underlying force dynamics. These studies suggest that expert performers (and listeners) have a mental model of principles of natural movement which they apply to tempo changes in music. For a tempo change to 'sound natural', it must apparently conform to these principles.

*Research on biological motion*

As Feldman et al. (1992) point out, a performer who produces tempo changes is not under any physical constraint to follow a particular function; the constraint is a purely mental, aesthetic one. However, the finding that these mental constraints mimic aspects of human movement leads one to wonder whether additional, perhaps more intricate principles of physical motion have found their way into musical aesthetics. There have been few points of contact in the past between the study of kinematics and the study of music performance, and these have been restricted to the 'hard' physical constraints of playing an instrument.

Evidence for constraints on natural motion comes from research on human motor control. There is one body of research which seems particularly relevant, that of Paolo Viviani and his collaborators (for overviews, see Viviani 1990, and Viviani and Laissard 1991). Over the last decade, they have investigated the constraints that link the geometry and the kinematics of guided hand movements. The movements in question involved the drawing or tracking of ellipses or of more complex curvilinear paths. The consistent finding has been that, within a single coherent movement, velocity varies as a power function of trajectory curvature (Viviani and Terzuolo 1982; Viviani and Cenzato 1985; Viviani and Schneider 1991). In other words, the greater the local curvature, the slower the movement.[13] Viviani, Campadelli and Mounoud (1987) have demonstrated that subjects are unable accurately to track a light point moving at a constant velocity around an elliptical path, whereas the task is easy when the target velocity changes with curvature according to the power function. It has also been shown that dynamic visual stimuli of the latter kind are judged by observers to represent constant velocity, whereas elliptical stimuli exhibiting constant velocity seem to vary in speed (Viviani and Stucchi 1992; see also Derwort 1938 and Runeson 1974).

The *spatio-temporal coupling* described in this research on biological movement enhances considerably the scientific respectability of the technique of 'accompanying movements' developed by Sievers, Becking and (particularly) Truslit. If spatial trajectory determines the velocity profile, then a given velocity profile also implies a spatial trajectory of a particular kind. What Truslit evidently did was to convert the velocity information available in the temporal and dynamic microstructure of music into arm movements with a matching spatial trajectory whose direction also took the melodic pitch contour into account. In his book he describes how, with practice, a close subjective match between the spatial trajectory and the auditory information can be achieved. What at first seems like a highly idiosyncratic method may in fact have a solid foundation in the constraints of biological motion.

*Conclusions*

We conclude from this very limited survey of empirical studies that performed music, by virtue of its temporal and dynamic microstructure, has the potential to represent forms of natural motion and to elicit corresponding movements in a human listener. While a rigid rhythm may inspire only foot tapping or finger snapping, an expressively modulated structure can specify movements with complex spatial trajectories which, for the purpose of demonstration and analysis, can be realised as guided movements of the limbs or the whole body. However, execution of such movements is not necessary to appreciate the motion information: experienced listeners, at least, can judge by ear whether the musical motion is natural or awkward, and they can move along with the music inwardly, as it were. An aesthetically satisfying performance is presumably one whose expressive microstructure satisfies basic constraints of biological motion while also being responsive to the structural and stylistic requirements of the composition.

---

13   In particular, the angular velocity is equal to the 2/3 power of the curvature times a constant. The exponent of this function increases with age; that is, children slow down more as a function of curvature than adults do (Viviani and Schneider 1991). The constant is different for different movement segments (Viviani and Cenzato 1985) and represents a velocity gain factor which depends on the linear extent of the movement: the larger the extent, the faster the movement.

Much music composed in this century encourages only primitive forms of motion or inhibits natural motion altogether. Many twentieth-century composers focus on sound qualities or on abstract tonal patterns, and performers of their compositions often neglect whatever kinematic potential the music may have. The absence of natural motion information may be a significant factor limiting the appreciation of such music by audiences. While compositional techniques and sound materials are subject to continuous change and exploration, though not without perceptual and cognitive constraints of their own (Lerdahl 1988; McAdams 1989), the laws of biological motion can only be accepted, negated or violated. If more new music and its performers took these laws into account, the size of audiences might increase correspondingly.

### REFERENCES

Baily, J., 1985: 'Music structure and human movement', in P. Howell, I. Cross and R. West, eds., *Musical Structure and Cognition* (London: Academic Press), pp. 237–58.

Balzano, G. J., 1986: 'Music perception as detection of pitch-time constraint', in V. McCabe and G. J. Balzano, eds., *Event Cognition: An Ecological Perspective* (Hillsdale, New Jersey: Erlbaum), pp. 217–33.

1987: 'Measuring music', in A. Gabrielsson, ed., *Action and Perception in Rhythm and Music* (Stockholm: Royal Swedish Academy of Music), pp. 177–99.

Becking, G., [1923–4] 1975: 'Über ein dänisches Schul-Liederbuch, über Mitbewegungen und Gehaltsanalyse', originally in *Zeitschrift für Musikwissenschaft*, reprinted in Kramolisch 1975: 191–218.

1928: *Der musikalische Rhythmus als Erkenntnisquelle* (Augsburg: Benno Filser).

Bergson, H., 1946: *The Creative Mind*, trans. M. L. Andison (New York: Philosophical Library).

Berry, W., 1967: *Structural Functions in Music* (Englewood Cliffs, New Jersey: Prentice-Hall).

Bregman, A. S., 1990: *Auditory Scene Analysis: The Perceptual Organization of Sound* (Cambridge, Massachusetts: MIT Press).

Burtt, H. E., 1917: 'Auditory illusions of movement – a preliminary study', *Journal of Experimental Psychology* 2/1: 63–75.

Cazden, N., 1945: 'Musical consonance and dissonance: a cultural criterion', *Journal of Aesthetics* 4/1: 3–11.

Chowning, J. M., 1971: 'The simulation of moving sound sources', *Journal of the Audio Engineering Society* 19: 2–6.

Clarke, E. F., 1985: 'Structure and expression in rhythmic performance', in P. Howell, I. Cross and R. West, eds., *Musical Structure and Cognition* (London: Academic Press), pp. 209–36.

1987: 'Categorical rhythm perception: an ecological perspective', in A. Gabrielsson, ed., *Action and Perception in Rhythm and Music* (Stockholm: Royal Swedish Academy of Music), pp. 19–33.

Clifton, T., 1983: *Music as Heard* (New Haven: Yale University Press).

Clynes, M., 1969: 'Toward a theory of man: precision of essentic form in living communication', in K. Leibovic, ed., *Information Processing in the Nervous System* (New York: Springer-Verlag), pp. 177–206.

1977: *Sentics: The Touch of the Emotions* (New York: Doubleday).

1983: 'Expressive microstructure in music, linked to living qualities', in J. Sundberg, ed., *Studies of Music Performance* (Stockholm: Royal Swedish Academy of Music), pp. 76–181.

1986: 'Generative principles of musical thought: integration of micro-structure with structure', *Communication and Cognition (CC-AI)* 3/3: 185–223.

1992: 'Time-forms, Nature's generators and communicators of emotion', in *Proceedings of the IEEE International Workshop on Robot and Human Communication, Tokyo* (Tokyo: IEEE), pp. 1–14.

in press: 'Composers' pulses are liked most by the best musicians', *Cognition*.

Clynes, M. and Walker, J., 1982: 'Neurobiologic functions of rhythm, time, and pulse in music', in M. Clynes, ed., *Music, Mind, and Brain* (New York: Plenum Press), pp. 171–216.

Cone, E. T., 1974: *The Composer's Voice* (Berkeley and Los Angeles: University of California Press).

Derwort, A., 1938: 'Untersuchungen über den Zeitablauf figurierter Bewegungen beim Menschen', *Pflügers Archiv für die gesamte Physiologie des Menschen und der Tiere* 240: 661–75.

Epstein, D., 1981: 'On musical continuity', in J. T. Fraser and N. Lawrence, eds., *The Study of Time*, vol. IV (New York: Springer-Verlag), pp. 180–97.

1990: 'Brahms and the mechanisms of motion: the composition of performance', in G. Bozarth, ed., *Brahms Studies: Analytical and Historical Perspectives* (Oxford: Clarendon), pp. 191–226.

Feldman, J., Epstein, D. and Richards, W., 1992: 'Force dynamics of tempo change in music', *Music Perception* 10/2: 185–204.

Fétis, F.-J., [1844] 1879: *Traité complet de la théorie et de la pratique de l'harmonie contenant la doctrine de la science et de l'art*, 12th edn (Paris: Brandus).

Gabrielsson, A., 1973a: 'Similarity ratings and dimension analyses of auditory rhythm patterns, I and II', *Scandinavian Journal of Psychology* 14: 138–76.

1973b: 'Adjective ratings and dimension analyses of auditory rhythm patterns', *Scandinavian Journal of Psychology* 14: 244–60.

Gabrielsson, A., Bengtsson, I. and Gabrielsson, B., 1983: 'Performance of musical rhythm in 3/4 and 6/8 meter', *Scandinavian Journal of Psychology* 24: 193–213.

Gatewood, E. L., 1927: 'An experimental study of the nature of musical enjoyment', in M. Schoen, ed., *The Effects of Music* (London: Kagan), pp. 78–120.

Gibson, J. J., 1966: *The Senses Considered as Perceptual Systems* (Boston: Houghton Mifflin).

1979: *The Ecological Approach to Visual Perception* (Boston: Houghton Mifflin).

Handel, S., 1989: *Listening: An Introduction to the Perception of Auditory Events* (Cambridge, Massachusetts: MIT Press).

Hanslick, E., [1854] 1957: *The Beautiful in Music*, trans. G. Cohen (London: Novello).

Hasty, C. F., 1981: 'Rhythm in post-tonal music: preliminary questions of duration and motion', *Journal of Music Theory* 25/2: 183–216.

Jones, M. R., 1976: 'Time, our lost dimension: toward a new theory of perception, attention, and memory', *Psychological Review* 83/5: 323–55.

1981: 'Music as a stimulus for psychological motion: part I. Some determinants of expectancies', *Psychomusicology* 1/2: 34–51.

1986: 'Attentional rhythmicity in human perception', in J. R. Evans and M. Clynes, eds., *Rhythm in Psychological, Linguistic, and Musical Processes* (Springfield, Illinois: Charles C. Thomas), pp. 13–40.

1990a: 'Learning and the development of expectancies: an interactionist approach', *Psychomusicology* 9: 193–228.

1990b: 'Musical events and models of musical time', in R. A. Block, ed., *Cognitive Models of Psychological Time* (Hillsdale, New Jersey: Erlbaum), pp. 207–40.

Jones, M. R. and Hahn, J., 1986: 'Invariants in sound', in V. McCabe and G. J. Balzano, eds., *Event Cognition: An Ecological Perspective* (Hillsdale, New Jersey: Erlbaum), pp. 197–215.

Kivy, P., 1989: *Sound Sentiment: An Essay on the Musical Emotions, including the Complete Text of 'The Corded Shell'* (Philadelphia: Temple University Press).

Kramolisch, W., ed., 1975: *Gustav Becking zum Gedächtnis. Eine Auswahl seiner Schriften und Beiträge seiner Schüler* (Tutzing: Hans Schneider).

Kronman, U. and Sundberg, J., 1987: 'Is the musical ritard an allusion to physical motion?', in A. Gabrielsson, ed., *Action and Perception in Rhythm and Music* (Stockholm: Royal Swedish Academy of Music), pp. 57–68.

Kubik, G., 1962: 'The phenomenon of inherent rhythms in East and Central African instrumental music', *African Music* 3/1: 33–42.

Kurth, E., 1917: *Grundlagen des linearen Kontrapunkts: Einführung in Stil und Technik von Bachs melodischer Polyphonie* (Bern: Drechsel).

Langer, S. K., 1953: *Feeling and Form* (New York: Scribner).

LaRue, J., 1970: *Guidelines for Style Analysis* (New York: Norton).

Lerdahl, F., 1988: 'Cognitive constraints on compositional systems', in J. A. Sloboda, ed., *Generative Processes in Music* (Oxford: Clarendon), pp. 231–59.

Lewin, D., 1982: '*Auf dem Flusse*: image and background in a Schubert song', *19th-Century Music* 6/1: 47–59.

Maus, F. E., 1988: 'Music as drama', *Music Theory Spectrum* 10: 56–73.

McAdams, S., 1984: 'The auditory image: a metaphor for musical and psychological research on auditory organization', in W. R. Crazier and A. J. Chapman, eds., *Cognitive Processes in the Perception of Art* (Amsterdam: Elsevier), pp. 289–324.

1989: 'Psychological constraints on form-bearing dimensions in music', *Contemporary Music Review* 4: 181–98.

Muris, J. de, [1319] 1965: *Ars novae musicae, Book II*, trans. O. Strunk, in O. Strunk, ed., *Source Readings in Music History: Antiquity and the Middle Ages* (New York: Norton), pp. 172–9.

Newcomb, A., 1984: 'Sound and feeling', *Critical Inquiry* 10/4: 614–43.

Nohl, H., 1920: *Stil und Weltanschauung* (Jena: Eugen Diederichs).

Pierce, A., 1978: 'Structure and phrase, part I', *In Theory Only* 4/5: 22–35.

Piston, W., 1978: *Harmony*, 3rd edn (New York: Norton).

Repp, B. H., 1989: 'Expressive microstructure in music: a preliminary perceptual assessment of four composers' "pulses"', *Music Perception* 6/3: 243–74.

1990a: 'Further perceptual evaluations of pulse microstructure in computer performances of classical piano music', *Music Perception* 8/1: 1–33.

1990b: 'Patterns of expressive timing in performances of a Beethoven minuet by nineteen famous pianists', *Journal of the Acoustical Society of America* 88/2: 622–41.

1992a: 'Diversity and commonality in music performance: an analysis of timing microstructure in Schumann's "Träumerei"', *Journal of the Acoustical Society of America* 92/5: 2546–68.

1992b: 'A constraint on the expressive timing of a melodic gesture: evidence from performance and aesthetic judgment', *Music Perception* 10/2: 221–42.

1993: 'Music as motion: a synopsis of Alexander Truslit's (1938) "Gestaltung und Bewegung in der Musik"', *Psychology of Music* 21/1: 48–72.

Risset, J.-C., 1988: 'Perception, environnement, musique', *Inharmoniques* 3: 10–43.

Rothfarb, L. A., 1988: *Ernst Kurth as Theorist and Analyst* (Philadelphia: University of Pennsylvania Press).

Runeson, S., 1974: 'Constant velocity – not perceived as such', *Psychological Research* 37/1: 3–23.

Runeson, S. and Frykholm, G., 1986: 'Kinematic specification of gender and gender expression', in V. McCabe and G. J. Balzano, eds., *Event Cognition: An Ecological Perspective* (Hillsdale, New Jersey: Erlbaum), pp. 259–73.

Rutz, O., 1911: *Musik, Wort und Körper als Gemütsausdruck* (Leipzig: Breitkopf & Härtel).

1922: *Sprache, Gesang und Körperhaltung*, 2nd edn (Munich: C. H. Beck).

Sessions, R., 1950: *The Musical Experience of Composer, Performer, Listener* (Princeton: Princeton University Press).

Shaw, R. and Pittenger, J., 1978: 'On perceiving change', in H. Pick and E. Saltzman, eds., *Modes of Perceiving and Processing Information* (Hillsdale, New Jersey: Erlbaum), pp. 187–204.

Shepard, R. N., 1981: 'Psychophysical complementarity', in M. Kubovy and J. R. Pomerantz, eds., *Perceptual Organization* (Hillsdale, New Jersey: Erlbaum), pp. 279–341.

1984: 'Ecological constraints on internal representation: resonant kinematics of perceiving, imagining, thinking, and dreaming', *Psychological Review* 91/4: 417–47.

Sievers, E., 1924: *Ziele und Wege der Schallanalyse* (Heidelberg: Carl Winter's Universitätsbuchhandlung).

Sundberg, J. and Verrillo, V., 1980: 'On the anatomy of the retard: a study of timing in music', *Journal of the Acoustical Society of America* 68/3: 772–9.

Thompson, W. F., 1989: 'Composer-specific aspects of musical performance: an evaluation of Clynes's theory of pulse for performances of Mozart and Beethoven', *Music Perception* 7/1: 15–42.

Todd, N., 1992a: 'The dynamics of dynamics: a model of musical expression', *Journal of the Acoustical Society of America* 91/6: 3540–50.

1992b: ' Music and motion: a personal view', in C. Auxiette, C. Drake and C. Gérard, eds., *Proceedings of the Fourth Rhythm Workshop: Rhythm Perception and Production* (Bourges: Imprimerie Municipale), pp. 123–8.

1992c: 'The communication of self-motion in musical expression', *Proceedings of the International Workshop on Man-Machine Studies in Live Performance* (Pisa: CNUCE/CNR), pp. 151–62.

1993: 'Vestibular feedback in musical performance: response to *Somatosensory Feedback in Musical Performance* (edited by Sundberg and Verrillo)', *Music Perception* 10/3: 379–82.

1994: 'The auditory "primal sketch": a multiscale model of rhythm grouping', *Journal of New Music Research* 23/1: 25–70.

1995: 'The kinematics of musical expression', *Journal of the Acoustical Society of America* 97/3: 1940–9.

Todd, N., Clarke, E. F. and Davidson, J., 1993: 'The representation of self-motion in expressive performance'. Paper presented at the Annual Conference of the Society for Music Perception and Cognition, 16–19 June 1993, University of Pennsylvania, Philadelphia.

Truslit, A., 1938: *Gestaltung und Bewegung in der Musik* (Berlin-Lichterfelde: Chr. Friedrich Vieweg).

Ungeheuer, G., 1964: 'Die Schallanalyse von Sievers', *Zeitschrift für Mundartenforschung* 31/2–3: 97–124.

Vecchione, B., 1987: 'Eléments d'analyse du mouvement musical', *Analyse musicale* 8: 17–23.

Viviani, P., 1990: 'Common factors in the control of free and constrained movements', in M. Jeannerod, ed., *Attention and Performance XIII* (Hillsdale, New Jersey: Erlbaum), pp. 345–73.

Viviani, P., Campadelli, P. and Mounoud, P., 1987: 'Visuo-manual pursuit tracking of human two-dimensional movements', *Journal of Experimental Psychology: Human Perception and Performance* 13/1: 62–78.

Viviani, P. and Cenzato, M., 1985: 'Segmentation and coupling in complex movements', *Journal of Experimental Psychology: Human Perception and Performance* 11/6: 828–45.

Viviani, P. and Laissard, G., 1991: 'Timing control in motor sequences', in J. Fagard and P. H. Wolff, eds., *The Development of Timing Control and Temporal Organization in Coordinated Action* (Amsterdam: Elsevier), pp. 1–36.

Viviani, P. and Schneider, R., 1991: 'A developmental study of the relationship between geometry and kinematics in drawing movements', *Journal of Experimental Psychology: Human Perception and Performance* 17/1: 198–218.

Viviani, P. and Stucchi, N., 1992: 'Biological movements look uniform: evidence of motor-perceptual interactions', *Journal of Experimental Psychology: Human Perception and Performance* 18/3: 603–23.

Viviani, P. and Terzuolo, C., 1982: 'Trajectory determines movement dynamics', *Neuroscience* 7/2: 431–7.

Wittgenstein, L., 1953: *Philosophical Investigations*, trans. G. E. M. Anscombe (New York: Macmillan).

Yeston, M., 1976: *The Stratification of Musical Rhythm* (New Haven: Yale University Press).

Zarlino, G., [1558] 1983: *The Art of Counterpoint*, trans. G. A. Marco and C. V. Palisca (New York: DaCapo Press).

Zuckerkandl, V., [1956] 1973: *Sound and Symbol: Music and the External World*, trans. W. R. Trask (Princeton: Princeton University Press).

# CHAPTER FOUR

# Deliberate practice and elite musical performance

## RALF TH. KRAMPE AND K. ANDERS ERICSSON

Although millions of people learn to play musical instruments, relatively few succeed in reaching the standard of excellence that we call elite performance.[1] The definition of elite performance proposed in this chapter radically differs from received opinion, which typically attributes the skills and accomplishments of a first-class performer to ostensible talents or 'gifts'. The notion of talent is also invoked to explain 'child prodigies', the idiosyncratic interpretative styles and technical prowess of outstanding adult players, and the levels of performance sustained by excellent older musicians seemingly able to defy the effects of ageing. Most people would dismiss any claim that these various phenomena primarily reflect the result of *acquired* skills and training, for the idea that natural, innate constraints (i.e. talents) determine the level of performance that individuals can achieve is widely accepted.

Nevertheless, this flies in the face of compelling evidence both within and outside the realm of music. In athletics, for instance, the best performances have been improved upon throughout history (see Schulz and Curnow 1988), reflecting structural refinements and increases in the duration and intensity of training. Musical performance has seen similar developments. Tchaikovsky's Violin Concerto was deemed unplayable in his day (Platt 1966), whereas elite violinists now consider it a standard part of their repertoire. And according to Roth (1982: 23), the virtuoso Paganini would 'cut a sorry figure if placed upon the modern concert stage': his legendary technique was 'superhuman' only until appropriate systems of training were devised to acquire it more generally. As musical technique and training methods have become increasingly refined, the standards required for elite performance have risen commensurately.

Two abilities often encountered in highly skilled musicians have been cited as evidence for innate talent: absolute (perfect) pitch and exceptional musical memory. But several empirical studies (for reviews, see Sloboda 1985; Ericsson et al. 1993;

---

[1] In the theoretical framework outlined in this study, elite performance encompasses both *expert* (i.e. professional) and *eminent* performance, the ultimate level of musical achievement. We consider expert-level performance the prerequisite for the latter; to achieve eminence, experts must make new and innovative contributions to their domain. The distinctions between these terms will be fully elaborated below.

Takeuchi and Hulse 1993) argue that perfect pitch – the ability to name isolated tones – is an acquired rather than inborn skill. Musicians with perfect pitch tend to respond better when the tones to be judged are played on their instrument rather than produced by sound generators (Oakes 1955), indicating an acquired, specific skill as opposed to a general, innate ability. Adults can develop perfect pitch through training (Brady 1970), although it is probably more easily acquired by children under the age of five or six (Cohen and Baird 1990; Takeuchi and Hulse 1993), who are not distracted by contextual considerations in attending to individual sounds. (See Costall 1985 for discussion.) Exceptional musical memory, a rarer phenomenon occasionally found in so-called *idiots savants* (individuals with very low general IQ but outstanding specific skills), tends to be restricted to familiar harmonic structures and does not transfer to the memorisation of atonal music (Sloboda et al. 1985) – again, evidence for an acquired skill rather than an inborn memory capacity. In fact, most *idiots savants* with exceptional musical memory are blind (Judd 1988), and it is likely that the development of specific memory skills compensated for their inability to acquire music in the same way as sighted individuals. Furthermore, Wolf (1976) notes that exceptional sight-reading ability and outstanding musical memory rarely occur together in accomplished musicians, which suggests that acquiring either of these skills partly compensates for weaknesses in the other.

Scientific attention to musical talent originated with studies of well-known musical families such as the Bachs (Scheinfeld 1939; see also Rowley 1988), but the idea that musical talent runs in the family has not been supported in recent investigations (Sosniak 1985; Sloboda and Howe 1991). Outstanding performers are more likely to come from a general musical background than from families of professional musicians. The notion of innate musical ability is also disputed in behavioural genetics research: a recent study (Coon and Carey 1989) found similar correlations of musical abilities in identical and fraternal twins, illustrating the effect of environmental factors on the development of musical skills. Interestingly, the environmental impact was stronger in the group with higher involvement in music than in the less accomplished one, which supports the hypothesis that inborn ability accounts for differences between untrained individuals but that its effect becomes increasingly smaller when specific skills have been acquired (Ackerman 1988). When musical talent tests were administered to highly skilled professional musicians in earlier studies (reviewed in Sloboda 1985), unexpected results emerged: correlations between musical accomplishment and performance in a pitch discrimination exercise like that in the Seashore Musical Abilities Test were moderate (for violinists) or zero (for clarinet or trombone players), indicating that the test scores did not reflect the ability that the test was supposed to measure – in other words, the test was invalid. It appears that the tasks in musical talent tests are most sensitive to specific skills (like pitch discrimination) fostered by playing particular instruments, rather than reflecting general abilities which could predict later musical accomplishment.

This survey of empirical evidence suggests that belief in the existence of musical talent might be widespread simply because of a lack of plausible alternatives. In this chapter we propose an altogether different framework which perceives elite performance as the extreme of a continuum in acquired ability and achievement. Having defined the concept of deliberate practice, we shall investigate the daily activities and past experiences of elite performers, revealing the means by which prolonged application can lead to an exceptional standard of performance maintained throughout the elite performer's lifetime. The findings of three recent studies on violinists and pianists will illustrate our model, focusing respectively on the acquisition of elite performance levels, the transition towards public recognition or professional distinction in middle years, and the maintenance of high-level skills in late adulthood. Finally, we shall show how the career paths of certain modern performers of international renown support our framework.

## DELIBERATE PRACTICE

We define deliberate practice as a highly structured activity with the explicit goal of improving some aspect of performance. In deliberate practice, the performance is carefully monitored for weaknesses and specific tasks are devised to combat them. Elite performers try to maximise the amount and outcome of their practice activities at every developmental stage, subject to three major constraints: the resource constraint, the motivational constraint and the optimal intensity constraint (see Ericsson et al. 1993).

The *resource constraint* concerns the availability of instructors, training materials and facilities (e.g. instruments, practice rooms, concert opportunities). Methods of deliberate practice are taught by teachers who usually are experienced performers themselves. The earlier musicians find appropriate coaching, the more considerable the benefits for their development. Financial support and encouragement from parents ensure the provision of proper instruction and instruments as well as the necessary time to engage in deliberate practice, which inevitably consumes energy and time otherwise allocated to socialising or schoolwork. In adult life, grants and professional positions allow the further development of abilities.

The *motivational constraint* acknowledges that deliberate practice is not intrinsically motivating or enjoyable, but is undertaken to achieve specific goals, principally improved performance. Deliberate practice must be distinguished from both recreational music-making and certain unavoidable professional duties, neither of which directly encourages the further development of skills.

The *optimal intensity constraint* or effort constraint is based on the assumption that deliberate practice is effortful and can be maintained for only a limited period. The renowned violin teacher Auer (1921), for example, recommended practice sessions of less than an hour with ample rest in between. According to him, the individual's full attention is required to spot areas needing improvement and to avoid errors; lack of concentration may even be detrimental to the improvement of performance. There is also evidence that the time of day affects one's efficiency. Simple perceptual-motor performance is maximised in the afternoon and early evening, whereas intellectually demanding tasks are enhanced in the morning (Folkard and Monk 1985).[2]

---

[2] This is reflected respectively in the performance of elite athletes (Winget et al. 1985) and in the working practices of such authors as Thomas Mann (Schröter 1964; see also Cowley 1959 and Plimpton 1977).

Amateur music-making tends to involve practice just before lessons and playing through pieces for fun, rather than deliberate practice. Gruson's (1988) analysis of video-taped practice sessions by amateurs and accomplished musicians working on the same composition revealed that in general the former tried to 'get through' the piece despite making the same mistakes over and over, whereas accomplished players worked on difficult passages until they had mastered them before continuing their performance. A detailed study of an advanced pianist learning a piece by Debussy supports this (Miklaszewski 1989): technical problems were successively mastered by means of technical exercises specifically designed to achieve the desired performance.

Various studies have revealed greater efficiency of cognitive-motor processes in skilled musicians than in less accomplished individuals, such as a higher rate (Telford and Spangler 1935; Krampe 1994) and more exact timing (Keele et al. 1985) of repetitive simple finger movements. Of greater significance, however, are qualitative differences between the two groups. These include the ability of skilled musicians to vary dynamic characteristics of expressive musical performance in a consistent – presumably controlled – manner across repeated performances (Shaffer 1982; Sloboda 1983; Palmer 1989; Krampe 1994); to memorise music while visually inspecting a score (Halpern and Bower 1982; Sloboda 1985); to vary tempo and dynamics independently (Clarke 1982); to achieve hand independence in expressive rubato (Shaffer 1981); and to coordinate both hands in contrary motion (Krampe 1994) or in polyrhythmic structures (Ibbotson and Morton 1981; Summers et al. 1993; Krampe et al. 1993). These differences appear to result from a prolonged and focused regimen of deliberate practice, which alone enables individuals to master the technical and musical skills necessary for expert performance.

## STAGES OF SKILL DEVELOPMENT

The theoretical framework described in this chapter employs the monotonic benefits assumption derived from skill acquisition research (Anderson 1982), according to which the performance level achieved continually increases in a power function relation with the amount of deliberate practice at each stage of development, subject to the law of diminishing returns – in other words, the relative gains get smaller as skill and effort increase. The early phases of development in elite performers have been described in a model by Bloom (1985) which has greatly influenced our framework, as has Manturzewska's (1990) more recent model of skill development in musicians, with six phases covering the whole life-span. A novel aspect of our framework, however, is that the specific effects of the three constraints described above change as a function of age and level of skill (see Figure 4.1).

At early stages the individual is extremely dependent on a supportive environment. Initial involvement (Phase I) often takes the form of exploratory play, and parents are instrumental in enabling and encouraging the start of systematic practice, which marks the beginning of Phase II. If the child shows promise during this stage, practice intensity increases. According to our framework, early success in competitions – of

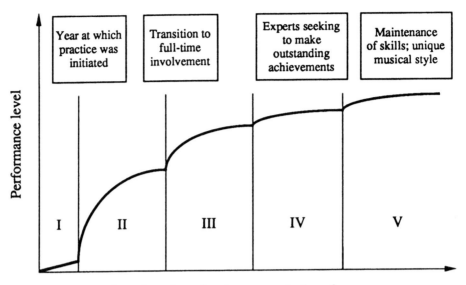

Figure 4.1   Stages in the development of elite performance

vital significance in attracting the attention of renowned teachers and gaining funding – can be attributed to differences in the amount of practice that the young musicians have accumulated at any given point, and this underscores the critical nature of the starting age. Given the non-linear (albeit monotonic) relation between the amount of practice and the level of performance, slight differences in the former due to younger or older starting ages can cause relatively large disparities in performance level in the early phases of skill acquisition.

The transition to full-time commitment, which normally occurs upon entry to a music school, marks the end of Phase II. Individuals at the third stage are taught by acknowledged experts and have few other constraints on their time. Financial support takes the form of loans or stipends, and the allocation of time and energy is under the individual's control.

Phase IV is the first phase of full professional status and commences with the end of formal training. The challenges encountered in this phase are new. After graduation, financial subvention is no longer available and the individual has to earn a living from public performances, teaching or orchestral work. Full-time employment as a solo performer optimally promotes further development, while teaching and playing in an orchestra divert time from deliberate practice activities which would increase the level of musical performance. The highest degree of musical success for instrumentalists generally belongs to this phase (Lehman 1953; Roth 1987; Manturzewska 1990), which represents the turning point of most careers. To reach and maintain maximum public recognition, the musician must consistently offer outstanding, unique interpretations, and if successful, he or she can support a career on the basis of public performance alone; if not, alternative careers normally include teaching or joining an orchestra.

The last phase in our framework denotes the years prior to retirement. It might be expected that older experts practise at a level sufficient to maintain skills of professional utility, but again, career status is crucial: if performers manage to survive by concert work alone, they gain greater independence than less successful performers. Our sample discovered that recurrent problems had driven some experts from the stage: limited freedom in choosing repertoire, difficulties in making practical arrangements and unfavourable reviews were reasons for giving up public performance and pursuing a teaching career.

## MEASUREMENT OF THE AMOUNT OF DELIBERATE PRACTICE

Several factors facilitate the study of skill development in performing musicians. First, a sizeable number of people of different ages and levels of proficiency play a musical instrument, and public recognition, success in competitions, financial reward and professional appointments make it possible to identify relative degrees of accomplishment. Secondly, our notion of deliberate practice can easily be communicated to musicians who by definition practise in a concentrated way in order to achieve expertise. Thirdly, because deliberate practice involves time at the instrument, it is possible to obtain reliable information from subjects simply by asking them when and for how long they practise.[3]

In our studies we used two different methods to measure past and current amounts of deliberate practice. (More detailed descriptions can be found in Ericsson et al. 1993 and Krampe 1994.) Past levels were assessed from subjects' retrospective estimates for each year of their lives. Following a brief biographical report, we asked standard questions related to the commencement of practice activities, length of study with different teachers, age of deciding to become a professional and so forth. Participants then used the derived biographical data as cues for estimating the weekly amount of practice throughout their lifetime. Figure 4.2 is an example from an expert pianist born in 1936.

The second method used diaries to assess the current level of deliberate practice and the allocation of time to other pursuits. This involved a taxonomy of twelve musical activities (e.g. public performance, taking lessons, playing for fun) and ten non-musical ones (e.g. sleep, recreation) which we devised in order to distinguish deliberate practice from other pursuits. Participants kept a record of daily activities over one week and then classified their records according to the different categories in the taxonomy. Based on the coded diaries we could assess each participant's allocation of time for each activity during that week. Figure 4.3 shows a segment of the diary form-sheet from the same expert pianist.

## THE ACQUISITION PHASE: A STUDY OF YOUNG VIOLINISTS

Our first study (Ericsson et al. 1993) focused on the skill acquisition phase. Three groups of young violinists of differing abilities were recruited. The *best* group consisted

---

[3] By comparison it is far more difficult to study the role of practice in chess or language acquisition.

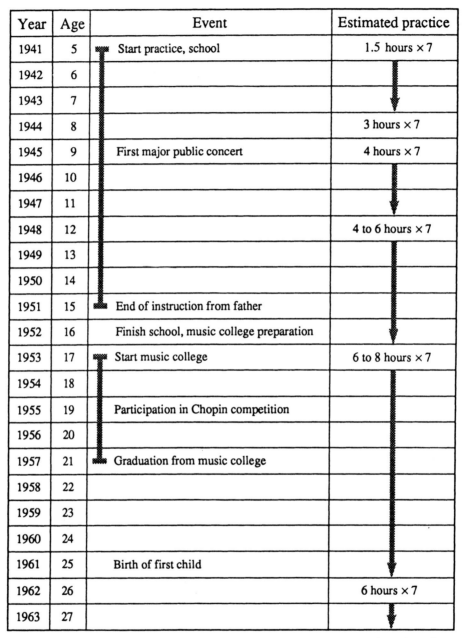

| Year | Age | Event | Estimated practice |
|------|-----|-------|--------------------|
| 1941 | 5 | Start practice, school | 1.5 hours × 7 |
| 1942 | 6 | | |
| 1943 | 7 | | |
| 1944 | 8 | | 3 hours × 7 |
| 1945 | 9 | First major public concert | 4 hours × 7 |
| 1946 | 10 | | |
| 1947 | 11 | | |
| 1948 | 12 | | 4 to 6 hours × 7 |
| 1949 | 13 | | |
| 1950 | 14 | | |
| 1951 | 15 | End of instruction from father | |
| 1952 | 16 | Finish school, music college preparation | |
| 1953 | 17 | Start music college | 6 to 8 hours × 7 |
| 1954 | 18 | | |
| 1955 | 19 | Participation in Chopin competition | |
| 1956 | 20 | | |
| 1957 | 21 | Graduation from music college | |
| 1958 | 22 | | |
| 1959 | 23 | | |
| 1960 | 24 | | |
| 1961 | 25 | Birth of first child | |
| 1962 | 26 | | 6 hours × 7 |
| 1963 | 27 | | |

Figure 4.2  Retrospective estimates of deliberate practice. Segment from a form-sheet for an expert pianist (b. 1936).

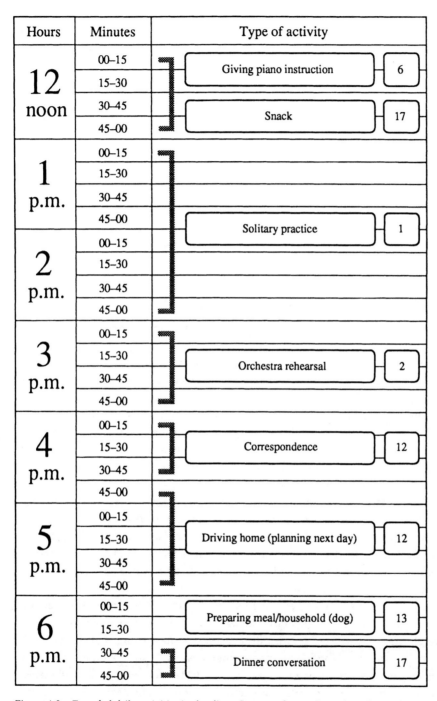

| Hours | Minutes | Type of activity | |
|---|---|---|---|
| **12 noon** | 00–15 | Giving piano instruction | 6 |
| | 15–30 | | |
| | 30–45 | Snack | 17 |
| | 45–00 | | |
| **1 p.m.** | 00–15 | | |
| | 15–30 | | |
| | 30–45 | | |
| | 45–00 | Solitary practice | 1 |
| **2 p.m.** | 00–15 | | |
| | 15–30 | | |
| | 30–45 | | |
| | 45–00 | | |
| **3 p.m.** | 00–15 | | |
| | 15–30 | Orchestra rehearsal | 2 |
| | 30–45 | | |
| | 45–00 | | |
| **4 p.m.** | 00–15 | | |
| | 15–30 | Correspondence | 12 |
| | 30–45 | | |
| | 45–00 | | |
| **5 p.m.** | 00–15 | | |
| | 15–30 | Driving home (planning next day) | 12 |
| | 30–45 | | |
| | 45–00 | | |
| **6 p.m.** | 00–15 | Preparing meal/household (dog) | 13 |
| | 15–30 | | |
| | 30–45 | Dinner conversation | 17 |
| | 45–00 | | |

Figure 4.3   Encoded daily activities in the diary. Segment from a form-sheet for an expert pianist (b. 1936). The numbers on the right refer to codes in the taxonomy of activities.

Table 4.1   *Characteristics of a typical practice session*

|  | Best students | Good students | Potential music teachers |
|---|---|---|---|
| Average duration (minutes) | 105.3 | 108.0 | 103.5 |
| Number of daily sessions | 3.6 | 2.7 | 1.4 |
| Maximum duration of efficient practice (minutes) | 132.8 | 174.0 | 192.0 |
| Minimum duration of efficient practice (minutes) | 29.3 | 49.8 | 30.5 |
| Duration until first break (minutes) | 51.9 | 66.0 | 47.1 |
| Number of breaks per session | 2.0 | 1.3 | 1.1 |
| Maximum duration of single practice activities (minutes) | 65.0 | 88.3 | 76.7 |

of students who, according to their teachers, had the potential for a solo career, whereas the *good* students (in the same course of study at music college) showed only 'average' promise. The third group intended to become music *teachers*, and although in the same conservatory (with violin as their main instrument), their course had lower admission criteria. (We were able to validate our distinction between skill levels by comparing the number and standard of competitions in which the violinists had participated.) Diaries and measures of past amounts of deliberate practice were collected from these subjects as described above.

We shall focus in this discussion on three questions: (1) How do subjects' conceptions of practice activities relate to our definition of deliberate practice, and what kind of knowledge do subjects possess to optimise the outcome of their practice efforts? (2) Is this knowledge reflected in their actual allocation of time to practice? (3) Can past and current amounts of deliberate practice be related to current level of performance?

To answer the first question, we had subjects rate each activity from the taxonomy in three respects: effort, inherent enjoyment and relevance to improving performance. Almost all subjects gave solo practice the highest relevance rating, and this was also judged to be especially effortful. As for inherent enjoyment, subjects found pleasure in listening to music and group performance, but not deliberate practice, which illustrates that practice activities are motivated by a desire to improve rather than being a source of fun or relaxation.

In conducting detailed interviews about practice habits, we asked participants questions related to the optimal duration of practice sessions. Table 4.1 gives the mean

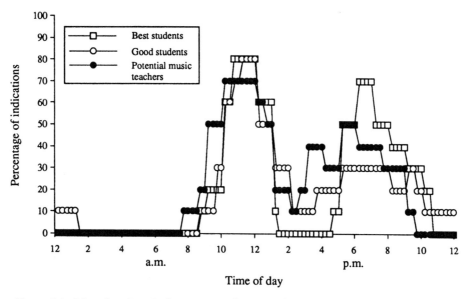

Figure 4.4   Most alert times in three groups of young violinists. Percentage of subjects indicating a given time, as a function of time of day.

estimates for various activities. The only consistent difference between the three groups concerned the number of practice sessions; in accordance with our findings from the diary procedure, the best and the good students estimated a higher number of daily sessions than the potential music teachers. The estimates are informative in two other ways: the subjects seemed to recognise that optimal practice was of limited duration, and the three groups did not differ in their knowledge of how best to organise practice activities. We also asked participants when they felt most alert (Figure 4.4). The patterns are similar for the three groups, with peaks from 10 a.m. to 1 p.m. and in the late afternoon. Note that the peaks as well as the early afternoon dip are more pronounced for the best students.

According to the diary data, the best and the good students engaged in more deliberate practice (on average 24.3 hours a week) than the potential music teachers (9.3 hours per week). The mean duration of practice was 80 minutes, which is closer to the optimal durations recommended by respected pedagogues than the estimates shown in Table 4.1. Best and good students had 19.5 practice sessions during the week in question compared with only 7.1 sessions per week for the prospective music teachers. Practice in all three groups was evenly distributed throughout the seven days, with no drop at the weekend (as is typical of music professionals generally). The frequency distribution showed a preference for the hours between 10 a.m. and 2 p.m. in the two more accomplished groups, whereas practice activities for the potential music teachers filled the entire day. While all groups agreed about the times they felt most alert, only the best and the good students made optimal use of this knowledge in scheduling practice sessions.

Interestingly, many violinists in the more accomplished groups used the early afternoon for a nap. Sleep was the only non-musical activity which our musicians judged especially relevant to improving violin performance. The afternoon nap led to significantly more weekly sleep among the best and the good students than the prospective music teachers, and this can be construed as additional evidence for their need to recuperate from strenuous practice activities.

Although at first glance the similar practice habits of the best and the good students seem to support the talent hypothesis, these results do not acknowledge potential differences in their earlier development and practice history. To estimate the amount of past practice, we totalled the hours spent practising until subjects entered music college at the age of eighteen. The best students had accumulated 7,410 hours of practice on average, considerably more than the average for both the good students (5,301 hours) and the potential music teachers (3,420 hours). Although subjects in the two better groups practised at the same maximal level at the time of the investigation, evidence suggests that differentials in past practice accounted for disparities in skill prior to entry to music school. The differences in weekly practice intensity between the best and the good students were largest at the age of fifteen, the height of adolescence, when social pressures are most likely to impinge on deliberate practice.

## MIDDLE AGE IN EXPERT PERFORMERS

In a recent investigation by Heizmann, Krampe and Ericsson (described in Ericsson et al. 1993), the procedures outlined above were applied to a group of distinguished professional violinists in two internationally renowned Berlin orchestras, the Radio Symphony Orchestra (RSO) and the Berlin Philharmonic Orchestra (BPO). On average, our ten male subjects were fifty years old. The main goal of this investigation was to compare our earlier findings to a group (henceforth called the middle-aged professionals) which represented the most likely future of the best young violinists from the first study.

The relevance that the middle-aged professionals attributed to the different activities for improving musical skill showed essentially the same pattern as in the younger sample. Solo practice was deemed the most important activity, and the only marked difference concerned the attitude to lessons, which professionals considered far less important to current development than young subjects. In general, it seems that knowledge of how to improve and the basic perception of the role of practice do not differ between age-groups.

Diary analysis showed that the middle-aged professionals spent 45 hours during the week in question on music-related activities, which was not statistically different from our best group of young violinists. The professionals practised alone for 7 hours that week, which was markedly less than the 24 hours we had observed in the best young violinists. Three other musical pursuits exceeded 5 hours: practice with others (14.7 hours), group performance (7 hours) and administrative duties (10.9 hours). Note that only the first of these was judged especially relevant to improvement. While the mean for practice with others was substantially higher than in the best young violinists

(7.8 hours), the difference was not statistically reliable due to large disparities between individuals.

In comparing the average duration of practice sessions we found that middle-aged professionals had considerably shorter sessions (48 minutes) than the best young violinists (73 minutes). This might suggest that experience allows subjects to optimise practice efficiency even further and to compensate for a lack of time. Alternatively, the effect of ageing might reduce the length of time that subjects can sustain optimal concentration without rest.

We also discovered that the middle-aged professionals sleep as much as the best young violinists and more than the prospective music teachers. As before, sleep was the only non-musical activity deemed particularly important for improvement, as it allowed the expert violinists to recuperate from demanding professional activities. An afternoon nap prior to public performance was especially common.

Are the middle-aged professionals really the most likely future of our best young subjects? A comparison of the amount of weekly practice derived from retrospective estimates shows a strikingly similar development for the two groups. In fact, the average accumulated practice at the age of eighteen was virtually identical for the middle-aged and best young violinists. After the age of twenty-three, we see a decline in the amount of solo practice in the middle-aged subjects, and our model suggests that this might be accounted for by motivational shifts and changes in time and energy constraints related to professional development. Indeed, the middle-aged subjects reported that they attained their first orchestral job on average at the age of twenty-three; at twenty-seven they became members of the RSO or the BPO; and they felt they had reached their best occupational position at twenty-nine. The requirements of a prestigious orchestral appointment seem to limit available time and energy for individual practice, and the professional security for members of German orchestras might also decrease the motivation to excel individually. Note, however, that the middle-aged professionals dated their best musical success at the age of thirty-three on average, which is in line with estimates from the literature on the age of peak performance (Lehman 1953; Roth 1987; Manturzewska 1990). Thus we can assume that most musicians felt their skills were still improving after they had joined an orchestra. During middle age, having already carved out a professional niche, several musicians reported increasing solo or small ensemble activities outside the orchestra, partly reviving solo ambitions from earlier in their careers.

## MAINTAINING SKILL IN LATER ADULTHOOD

Our third study (Krampe 1994; Krampe and Ericsson 1994) focused on the maintenance of pianistic skill in later adulthood. Participants were professional pianists in their fifties and sixties who were compared to an amateur sample from the same age range; two groups of expert and amateur pianists in their twenties allowed a further comparison based on age difference. In addition to biographical variables, retrospective estimates of past practice intensity and current time allocation to musical and everyday activities (discerned from diaries), we collected performance measures in experimental tasks. The main questions in this study were: (1) How do older experts organise their daily lives? (2) Do they maintain skill-relevant abilities at the level of young expert performers or do their professional skills undergo age-related decline? (3) Does the degree to which they maintain their skills depend on the amount of deliberate practice at a given phase of their lives? The last question was intended to clarify which of the following alternatives is correct: on the one hand, older experts might preserve their skills due to high investments in practice during acquisition at younger ages, which is plausible if one assumes that high-level skills, once acquired, require only minimal amounts of training to be retained; on the other hand, it is possible that high-level skills must be actively maintained by deliberate practice efforts, in which case one would expect practice intensity during later years of life to be the critical factor.

The experimental tasks comprised measures of (1) biomechanical efficiency (i.e. speed of repetitive tapping for the two index fingers and alternate index finger tapping); (2) bimanual coordination of complex finger movements; and (3) memorisation of complex bimanual movement sequences. In addition subjects were asked to perform J. S. Bach's Prelude in C major (*WTC*, I), for which a Yamaha Clavinova with a weighted action mimicking the performance of a 'real' piano was used. Two tests of general cognitive-motor efficiency which are frequently applied as markers of age-related slowing in speeded performance were also administered to investigate whether our musicians were similar to the normal population.[4]

The number of professional musicians among the parents of our participants was slightly higher in the amateur sample than the expert group. Expert pianists (young and old combined) had started to practise the piano at a younger age (6.8 years) than amateurs (9.3 years) and had also chosen their profession earlier (on average at 14) than amateurs (at 18). Diaries revealed that expert pianists spent about fifty-six hours a week on music-related activities, which considerably surpasses the normal forty-hour professional week. Average practice by the amateurs was less than two hours during the diary week, whereas young experts had twenty-six hours of solo practice compared with eleven hours in the older expert group. The scheduling of practice activities with preferences for certain times of day in young experts was similar to what we found in the groups of accomplished violinists described above, and this was also true for the older experts; however, the effect was less pronounced due to their overall lower level of practice and a decrease in practice activities over the weekend.

Participants' retrospective estimates indicated that old and young experts had similar weekly practice regimens up to their mid-twenties. Following the end of formal instruction, older experts tended to decrease deliberate practice activities. That this drop indicated a retreat from the profession was clearly not the case: a comparison of the amount of time spent on professional activities showed, if anything, a slightly

---

4   Experimental research suggests grim prospects for the effect of ageing on mental and physical abilities. Speeded processes tend to decline until the age of sixty and more rapidly thereafter (for overviews see Kausler 1982 and Salthouse 1985), and this is also true of motoric processes, including the rate of repetitive movements (Salthouse 1985), synchronisation of movements to an external pulse (Nagasaki et al. 1989) and coordination of bimanual movements (Stelmach et al. 1988).

higher value for the older experts (who were working a sixty-hour week) compared with the younger pianists, although the older experts did change the focus towards teaching. This finding was independently supported by the analysis of leisure time: while young experts and amateurs did not differ in the time allocated to relaxation, older experts had consistently less opportunity for recreation than any other group, their extensive professional commitments making it necessary to sacrifice leisure pursuits in order to practise.

How did our four groups differ in the experimental tasks? The older expert pianists showed the predicted age-related decline in the two general measures of cognitive-motor performance; however, in all skill-related measures our older experts performed as well or nearly as well as the young experts and better than both amateur groups. At the same time, older amateurs showed the typical decline of skills in speeded tasks which required complex coordination of movements, but not in simple tapping and musical interpretation exercises. Most important, we found that the amount of deliberate practice during the previous ten years was a predictor of the current level of performance. This was especially pronounced in the older expert group, where the pianists who had maintained a higher degree of deliberate practice in recent years performed better in the most challenging tasks. This finding indicates that high-level musical skills acquired in younger years are not automatically preserved, but must be actively maintained through deliberate practice.

## EXTENSION OF THE FRAMEWORK TOWARDS EMINENT PERFORMANCE

The three studies described above support our model of the development of expert performance, which we define in terms of deliberate practice. However, although all of our subjects were highly accomplished musicians, their level of skill did not reach that of world-class performance: none of the older or middle-aged professionals could support themselves by solo performance alone, and only very few of the best young violinists might eventually be successful as international soloists.

In our model eminent performance is the highest level of achievement: whereas expert performance involves mastery of established techniques and polished inter-pretations of musical works, eminent performance transcends the expert level by offering a unique and valued contribution in terms of a new style, technique or interpretation. While expert performance can be attained through instruction and prolonged deliberate practice, eminent performance differs in one crucial respect: by definition, an eminent performer irrevocably changes and expands the known possi-bilities for a given instrument or repertoire, and this involves something which cannot be taught, something beyond the mere acquisition of skills and interpretative tech-niques necessary to the particular performance domain. One important factor enabling the musician to move beyond what has already been attained may be a comprehensive knowledge of prior eminent achievements, and for this reason the limited societal resources dedicated to music performance imply that only a very small number of individuals will be able to undertake such a rigorous investigation of innovative aspects of solo performance. The selection of these individuals often occurs early on, for instance by winning a major international competition, which is generally viewed as a prerequisite for a solo career (Roth 1987). Successful participants in such competitions exhibit very high levels of expert performance, but the innovations required to achieve a standard of eminence normally occur later.

Our theory allows us to predict that the early commencement of deliberate practice will lead to a standard of expert performance at a relatively young age, and this in turn will provide access to professional opportunities and contacts which could facilitate the achievement of eminence (Ericsson et al. 1993). Although it is likely that various factors such as the amount of deliberate practice will influence the development of eminent performance, we shall focus here on biographical factors leading to this end, in a comparison of certain twentieth-century virtuosos with our middle-aged professional violinists and the group of older expert pianists from our third study.

The middle-aged violinists started systematic practice at the age of 8.2 years on average, the older professional pianists at 7.8 years. Starting ages in the virtuoso samples were significantly earlier, namely 5.0 years for violinists and 5.8 years for pianists. Virtuoso soloists had worked with fewer teachers (the mean for violinists was 2.1, that for pianists 2.4) than expert musicians in our studies (4.0 for violinists, 4.4 for pianists), a finding which suggests that internationally renowned soloists encountered their most influential teachers early on in their careers and did not need to change mentors as often in their search for optimal instruction. Indeed, the starting age for working with a recognised master was 11.5 for the virtuoso violinists. Two other biographical variables are illustrative: outstanding virtuosos in our sample dated their professional debut to the age of 11.5 (violinists) and 13.2 (pianists), and first participation in a major international competition was at the age of 18 for violinists and 19 for pianists.

Unfortunately, the most exalted musicians rarely specify past amounts of practice. The testimony of Claudio Arrau, however, provides some support for our ideas. In an interview (Horowitz [1982] 1984) the celebrated pianist reported a daily practice regimen of eight to ten hours and up to fourteen hours a day when he was 18 or 19; at the time of the interview (when he was approaching the age of 80!), he claimed to practise two to three hours regularly, and five to six hours when he was learning an unfamiliar piece. These estimates place Arrau far above the professional pianists in our study, especially compared with older subjects between 53 and 68. They also explain Arrau's reputation as both a 'Wunderkind' and a workhorse.

Examining the biographical variables shows that the development of eminent performers systematically differs from that of the adult expert performers in our studies. At consistently much earlier ages than the experts, the eminent performers commenced deliberate practice, had access to master teachers, made their first public appearance and won international contests. Our proposition concerning the simple availability of opportunities for intensive study and solo performance as adults appears to explain these differences, but future research will permit a more detailed description of both necessary and sufficient factors accounting for the rare occurrence of eminent performance.

## CONCLUSION

We have described a framework for the development of elite performance centred on the notion of deliberate practice. The amount of deliberate practice invested in skill acquisition is related to different levels of accomplishment in young instrumentalists. Furthermore, the amount of practice in later adulthood determines the degree to which older expert musicians can maintain their skills. None of these observations follows from a view of elite performance based on the notion of talent. The values for weekly amounts of practice that we derived from the retrospective estimates of our most accomplished group of young violinists approximate those obtained with diary methods in two German studies on young award-winning musicians (Ruoff 1981; Kaminski et al. 1984), and this agreement and the close correspondence between the middle-aged professionals and the best group of young violinists speak for the validity of our findings, despite the somewhat contradictory results of Sloboda and Howe (1991), who discovered no differences in weekly and accumulated amounts of practice when they interviewed over forty students (aged from ten to eighteen) divided into two skill levels in a music school. However, practice intensity for a given age-range in Sloboda's and Howe's sample was much lower than in our investigations or the two German studies cited above, and in any case, only a fraction of students at that music school were actually working towards becoming professional musicians, so we may attribute the absence of differences to the selection of their samples.[5]

Our proposition that the amount of deliberate practice determines one's degree of success at each stage of development implies that the age at which practice starts plays a crucial role. We have shown that expert performers began earlier than amateurs and that eminent soloists started even before the professionals in our samples. In Manturzewska's larger-scale study of Polish musicians (1990), the overwhelming majority of subjects had commenced musical training between the ages of five and six, and Manturzewska concludes that latecomers can reach international levels of artistic competence only as conductors or composers: it is virtually impossible for pianists and violinists with such late starting ages to succeed.

We have illustrated how the effort, motivational and optimal intensity constraints implicit in the notion of deliberate practice can affect musicians' scheduling of practice activities, the intentionally limited durations of practice sessions and the greater need for rest and recuperation. Weekly amounts of practice gradually increased after the start of systematic training in our expert subjects, and in young adulthood practice intensity is highest. Motivational as well as time constraints related to career decisions explain changes in the amount of practice, and here our findings are similar to those of Kaminski et al. (1984): that is, many elite performers who stop participating in competitions remain active performers but virtually give up practising.

The role of teachers in defining appropriate motivational constraints can hardly be overemphasised. The study by Heizmann, Krampe and Ericsson (described in Ericsson

---

[5] Sloboda's recent follow-up study (described in a personal communication) of similar subjects who, in contrast, had been screened for specific levels of professional aspiration in music found a strong correlation between accomplishment and accumulated amounts of practice. This accords well with our results.

et al. 1993) has revealed important differences in this regard between the professionals in our study and internationally recognised soloists. Teachers of the virtuoso violinists in Heizmann's study gave their students the feeling of being exceptional, and David Oistrakh's teacher Stolyarsky offers a good example: 'One of the fundamentals of [Stolyarsky's] method was to instill confidence in the young pupil by assuring him that he had extraordinary talent. The child worked with enthusiasm' (Schwarz 1983: 458). Manturzewska (1990) points to the special nature of the master–student relationship as a feature distinguishing her group of renowned virtuosos from less successful professionals, and Sosniak (1985) also emphasises the sense of 'being exceptional' as an important motivation to sustained practice. Along these lines, we have suggested (Ericsson et al. 1993) that although 'talent' might not be the direct cause of ability, it is at the very least a socially validated label encouraging the individual to maintain a high level of practice at the expense of social or recreational activities. Of course, while the belief that one is destined for eventual success can be motivating, the talent notion might also backfire: a lack of talent cannot be compensated for, and performers who after a failure start to consider themselves without talent might well give up altogether.

Furthermore, pushing practice beyond the limits of individual resources poses serious risks. Injuries and motivational burnouts due to overpractice are frequent phenomena in music as well as sports (Caldron et al. 1986; Fry 1986; Newmark and Lederman 1987), and preventing such negative consequences is an important task for teachers during early development. From this perspective, the development of expertise resembles a long-distance race in which each individual has to find his or her optimal pace at different stages.

## REFERENCES

Ackerman, P. L., 1988: 'Determinants of individual differences during skill acquisition: cognitive abilities and information processing', *Journal of Experimental Psychology* 117/3: 288–318.

Anderson, J. R., 1982: 'Acquisition of cognitive skill', *Psychological Review* 89/4: 369–406.

Auer, L., 1921: *Violin Playing as I Teach It* (New York: Frederick A. Stokes).

Bloom, B. S., 1985: 'Generalizations about talent development', in B. S. Bloom, ed., *Developing Talent in Young People* (New York: Ballantine), pp. 507–49.

Brady, P. T., 1970: 'The genesis of absolute pitch', *Journal of the Acoustical Society of America* 48/4: 883–7.

Caldron, P. H., Calabrese, L. H., Clough, J. D., Lederman, R. J. and Lederman, J., 1986: 'A survey of musculoskeletal problems encountered in high-level musicians', *Medical Problems of Performing Artists* 1/4: 136–9.

Clarke, E. F., 1982: 'Timing in the performance of Erik Satie's "Vexations"', *Acta psychologica* 50/1: 1–19.

Cohen, A. J. and Baird, K., 1990: 'Acquisition of absolute pitch: the question of critical periods', *Psychomusicology* 9/1: 31–7.

Coon, H. and Carey, G., 1989: 'Genetic and environmental determinants of musical abilities in twins', *Behavior Genetics* 19/2: 183–93.

Costall, A., 1985: 'The relativity of absolute pitch', in P. Howell, I. Cross and R. West, eds., *Musical Structure and Cognition* (London: Academic Press), pp. 189–208.

Cowley, M., ed., 1959: *Writers at Work: The Paris Review Interviews* (New York: Viking Press).

Ericsson, K. A., Krampe, R. Th. and Tesch-Römer, C., 1993: 'The role of deliberate practice in the acquisition of expert performance', *Psychological Review* 100/3: 363–406.

Folkard, S. and Monk, T. H., 1985: 'Circadian performance rhythms', in S. Folkard and T. H. Monk, eds., *Hours of Work* (Chichester: Wiley), pp. 37–52.

Fry, H. J. H., 1986: 'Incidence of overuse syndrome in symphony orchestras', *Medical Problems of Performing Artists* 1/2: 51–5.

Gruson, L. M., 1988: 'Rehearsal skill and musical competence: does practice make perfect?', in J. A. Sloboda, ed., *Generative Processes in Music* (Oxford: Clarendon), pp. 91–112.

Halpern, A. R. and Bower, G. H., 1982: 'Musical expertise and melodic structure in memory for musical notation', *American Journal of Psychology* 95/1: 31–50.

Horowitz, J., 1984: *Leben mit der Musik: Gespräche mit Arrau* (Bern: Scherz Verlag). English original: *Conversations with Arrau* (1982).

Ibbotson, N. R. and Morton, J., 1981: 'Rhythm and dominance', *Cognition* 9: 125–38.

Judd, T., 1988: 'The varieties of musical talent', in L. K. Obler and D. Fein, eds., *The Exceptional Brain: Neuropsychology of Talent and Special Abilities* (New York: Guilford Press), pp. 127–55.

Kaminski, G., Mayer, R. and Ruoff, B. A., 1984: *Kinder und Jugendliche im Leistungssport* (Schorndorf: Hofmann).

Kausler, D. H., 1982: *Experimental Psychology and Human Aging* (New York: Wiley).

Keele, S. W., Pokorny, R. A., Corcos, D. M. and Ivry, R., 1985: 'Do perception and motor production share common timing mechanisms: a correlational analysis', *Acta psychologica* 60/2–3: 173–91.

Krampe, R. Th., 1994: *Maintaining Excellence: Cognitive-Motor Performance in Pianists Differing in Age and Skill Level* (Berlin: Edition Sigma).

Krampe, R. Th. and Ericsson, K. A., 1994: 'Maintaining excellence: deliberate practice and cognitive-motor performance in young and older pianists' (manuscript submitted for publication).

Krampe, R. Th., Kliegl, R. and Mayr, U., 1993: 'The fast and the slow of skilled bimanual movement timing' (unpublished manuscript).

Lehman, H. C., 1953: *Age and Achievement* (Princeton: Princeton University Press).

Manturzewska, M., 1990: 'A biographical study of the life-span development of professional musicians', *Psychology of Music* 18/2: 112–39.

Miklaszewski, K., 1989: 'A case study of a pianist preparing a musical performance', *Psychology of Music* 17/2: 95–109.

Nagasaki, H., Itoh, H., Maruyama, H. and Hashizume, K., 1989: 'Characteristic difficulty in rhythmic movement with aging and its relation to Parkinson's disease', *Experimental Aging Research* 14/4: 171–6.

Newmark, J. and Lederman, R. J., 1987: 'Practice doesn't necessarily make perfect: incidence of overuse syndromes in amateur instrumentalists', *Medical Problems of Performing Artists* 2/4: 142–4.

Oakes, W. F., 1955: 'An experimental study of pitch naming and pitch discrimination reaction', *Journal of Genetic Psychology* 86/2: 237–59.

Palmer, C., 1989: 'Mapping musical thought to musical performance', *Journal of Experimental Psychology: Human Perception and Performance* 15/12: 331–46.

Platt, R., 1966: 'General introduction', in J. E. Meade and A. S. Parkes, eds., *Genetic and Environmental Factors in Human Ability* (Edinburgh: Oliver and Boyd), pp. ix–xi.

Plimpton, G., ed., 1977: *Writers at Work: The Paris Review Interviews*, series 2 (New York: Penguin).

Roth, H., 1982: *Master Violinists in Performance* (Neptune City, New Jersey: Paganinia).

1987: *Great Violinists in Performance: Critical Evaluations of over 100 Twentieth-Century Virtuosi* (Los Angeles: Panjandrum).

Rowley, P. T., 1988: 'Identifying genetic factors affecting musical ability', *Psychomusicology* 7/2: 195–200.

Ruoff, B. A., 1981: *Psychologische Analysen zum Alltag jugendlicher Leistungssportler. Eine empirische Untersuchung (Kognitiver Repräsentationen) von Tagesabläufen* (Munich: Minerva).

Salthouse, T. A., 1985: *A Theory of Cognitive Aging* (Amsterdam: North Holland Press).

Scheinfeld, A., 1939: *You and Heredity* (New York: Frederick A. Stokes).

Schröter, K., 1964: *Thomas Mann* (Hamburg: Rowohlt Monographs).

Schulz, R. and Curnow, C., 1988: 'Peak performance and age among superathletes: track and field, swimming, baseball, tennis and golf', *Journal of Gerontology: Psychological Sciences* 43/5: 113–20.

Schwarz, B., 1983: *Great Masters of the Violin* (New York: Simon and Schuster).

Shaffer, L. H., 1981: 'Performances of Chopin, Bach, and Bartók: studies in motor programming', *Cognitive Psychology* 13/3: 326–76.

1982: 'Rhythm and timing in skill', *Psychological Review* 89/2: 109–22.

Sloboda, J. A., 1983: 'The communication of musical metre in piano performance', *Quarterly Journal of Experimental Psychology* 35A/2: 377–96.

1985: *The Musical Mind: A Cognitive Psychology of Music* (Oxford: Oxford University Press).

Sloboda, J. A., Hermelin, B. and O'Connor, N., 1985: 'An exceptional musical memory', *Music Perception* 3/2: 155–70.

Sloboda, J. A. and Howe, M. J. A., 1991: 'Biographical precursors of musical excellence: an interview study', *Psychology of Music* 19/1: 3–21.

Sosniak, L. A., 1985: 'Learning to be a concert pianist', in B. S. Bloom, ed., *Developing Talent in Young People* (New York: Ballantine), pp. 19–67.

Stelmach, G. E., Amrhein, P. C. and Goggin, N. L., 1988: 'Age differences in bimanual coordination', *Journal of Gerontology: Psychological Sciences* 43/1: 18–23.

Summers, J. J., Rosenbaum, D. A., Burns, B. D. and Ford, S. K., 1993: 'Production of polyrhythms', *Journal of Experimental Psychology: Human Perception and Performance* 19/2: 416–28.

Takeuchi, A. H. and Hulse, S. H., 1993: 'Absolute pitch', *Psychological Bulletin* 113/2: 345–61.

Telford, C. W. and Spangler, H., 1935: 'Training effects in motor skills', *Journal of Experimental Psychology* 18: 141–7.

Winget, C. M., DeRoshia, C. W. and Holley, D. C., 1985: 'Circadian rhythms and athletic performance', *Medicine and Science in Sports and Exercise* 17/5: 498–516.

Wolf, T., 1976: 'A cognitive model of musical sight-reading', *Journal of Psycholinguistic Research* 5/2: 143–71.

# PART TWO

# Structure and meaning in performance

# CHAPTER FIVE

# The conductor and the theorist: Furtwängler, Schenker and the first movement of Beethoven's Ninth Symphony

## NICHOLAS COOK

### I

Among the many hats worn by Paul Henry Lang was that of record critic for *High Fidelity* magazine.[1] Writing in the late 1960s, Lang was an early proponent of what might nowadays be called modernist performance. So it is not surprising that he reserved some of his most vitriolic comments for Wilhelm Furtwängler, the great exponent of the Wagnerian tradition of conducting, who had died in 1954 but whose recordings were still available at the time. According to Lang (1978: 17), Furtwängler was 'a dyed-in-the-wool romantic, favoring arbitrary and highly subjective procedures in tempo, dynamics and phrasing'. And he wrote of the most famous of all Furtwängler's interpretations, the 1951 recording of Beethoven's Ninth Symphony, that it is a 'stereo "reconstruction also playable on mono", but it does not make any difference how you play it. This recording, with the Bayreuth Festspielhaus forces, is something of a treasured antique, though I can't see the reason for the admiration' (: 24). At best, Lang concluded, Furtwängler's recordings of Beethoven were 'for collectors and historians, not for enjoyment' (: 17).

As might be expected, Lang's characterisation of Furtwängler is blatantly contradicted by enthusiasts like Peter Pirie, the author of a book on Furtwängler's recordings. For Pirie, the way Furtwängler performed Beethoven was anything but arbitrary; on the contrary, says Pirie (referring specifically to the first movement of the Ninth Symphony), 'his interpretation analyzed the structure' (1980: 49). He continues: 'The mystery of the hollow fifth implied the tremendous unison first subject, and the misty procession of fragments that is the second subject; and all these things implied the mighty conflagration of the recapitulation – how meaningless the precise articulation of the sextuplet seems in this searing sheet of flame!' (This is a dig at Toscanini, who insisted on 'precise articulation' of the rustling tremolandos that open the movement, much to Furtwängler's disgust.) Pirie concludes: 'Such points were not lost on Furtwängler, whose natural style is fulfilled by this movement, in which

---

[1]  My thanks to William Drabkin for his comments on a draft of this chapter.

Beethoven left behind the classical allegro with its fixed tempo in favour of a flexible declamation' (: 49).

What Pirie calls 'flexible declamation' lies at the heart of the Furtwängler style. In an important article on performing the Ninth Symphony, Richard Taruskin characterised this style as follows: 'his tempos are eternally in flux, accelerating and decelerating in great waves' (1989: 244). Lang thought – or affected to think – that these great waves were the consequence of Furtwängler's incompetence as a conductor; speaking this time of the Seventh Symphony, he refers to 'Furtwängler's inability to keep to a steady tempo . . . This is not always the result of deliberate intention; it is due rather to a certain lack of the sort of orchestral discipline we expect from our conductors' (1978: 22). The disagreement between Lang and Pirie, then, can be focused on Furtwängler's modifications of tempo: were they arbitrary and uncontrolled, as Lang maintained, or a response to structure, as Pirie asserts? The problem, of course, is that assertion is not enough. What is needed is evidence, and Pirie's descriptive commentary does not provide it.

Evidence of one sort is provided by Furtwängler himself. In his extensive writings on music, most of which date from the inter-war period, Furtwängler went out of his way to condemn the arbitrary and subjective interpretations of what Weingartner used to call 'rubato conductors'; Furtwängler's equally disparaging term for them is 'virtuosi' ([1948] 1977: 54). What characterises such conductors, Furtwängler writes, is a 'tendentious preference for individualistic emotionalism and vague, colouristic self-indulgence at the expense of formal structural values' (1991: 9). Such 'creative interpretation' (he is using the phrase pejoratively) goes hand in hand with 'literal performance', that is, 'the sterile worship of the literal text'; they are 'the two sides of a coin' (: 11, 10). This, Furtwängler explains, is because they both result from a lack of musical understanding, and this in turn is the result of the severing of the traditional continuity between composer and performer.

The precondition of adequate performance, says Furtwängler, is that 'the work in question, its vital form and structure, is fully and properly understood, i.e. that we are fully capable of "reading" it' (: 14). In order to acquire this sort of understanding, the performer 'has to laboriously reconstruct' the composer's 'overriding vision' of the work as 'an artistic entity' (: 12), working from the visible parts to the whole that unites them. The payoff is that, once such a vision has been achieved, performance becomes in essence a 'process of re-creation' (: 13); the essence of adequate performance is that the performer should 're-experience and re-live the music each time anew' (: 36). And because of this, Furtwängler disparaged conductors who prepared everything in advance:

> A well-known conductor is supposed to have said: one should rehearse until the conductor appears superfluous. This is a fundamental mistake, born of a misconception . . . of the essence and purpose of making music. A conductor's anxiety to determine everything beforehand down to the smallest detail is caused by his fear of having to rely too much on the inspiration of the moment . . . This attitude is wrong because it cannot possibly do justice to living masterpieces. The great masterpieces of music are subject to the law of improvisation to a far higher degree than is commonly realized. ([1948] 1977: 47)

Here, and in Furtwängler's writings in general, there are unmistakable echoes of Heinrich Schenker. Most obvious among these is the basic idea that the composer has a vision of the work as an organic whole, and that the performer's primary duty is to recreate it; hence the disparagement of the virtuoso as someone who fails in this duty and merely trades in superficial effects.[2] Again, Furtwängler attacks the traditional, textbook conception of sonata and other forms as surface patterns; when he says that these forms should instead be understood as 'the natural precipitate from a process of improvisation' (: 48), he is in effect paraphrasing Schenker's statement ([1926] 1977: 53) that 'improvisation . . . alone creates the organic structure of sonata form'. And when it comes to the specific application of such ideas to performance, the echoes are closer still. Furtwängler argues that 'a score cannot give the slightest clue as to the intensity of a forte or a piano or exactly how fast a tempo should be . . . The dynamics are quite deliberately not literal but symbolic, not with a practical meaning for each individual instrument but of a broad significance, added with the sense of the work as a whole in mind' (1991: 8–9). In other words, such markings are not instructions for immediate execution; they are a specification of content, to be realised in terms of the particular musical context, and perhaps even in terms of the specific occasion of performance. Or as Schenker put it in his 1912 monograph on the Ninth Symphony,

> it is not the task of orthography, as is generally believed and taught, to provide the player with perfectly definite means for achieving effects allegedly specified and attainable only through precisely these means, but rather to arouse in his mind, in an a priori manner, specific effects, leaving it up to him to choose freely the appropriate means for their attainment. ([1912] 1992: 9)

By this Schenker does not, of course, mean to endorse the 'arbitrary and highly subjective procedures in tempo, dynamics and phrasing' of which Lang accused Furtwängler. On the contrary, such markings

> do not represent a perhaps arbitrary determination by the masters, which ultimately could have been made differently for the same content, but rather signify, like the content itself, a definite immutability! If the Ninth Symphony . . . had, like most of the works of J. S. Bach, come down to us without explicit indications, a capable hand would have had to enter the dynamic markings exactly as Beethoven himself did. (: 10)

And this is echoed by Furtwängler's equally trenchant statement that 'for every musical work – and the greater, the more complex the work, the truer this is – there is only one approach, one manner of interpretation, that consistently proves to make the deepest impression, precisely because it is the "correct" interpretation' (1991: 12).

Such echoes of Schenker in general, and of the Ninth Symphony monograph in particular, are not surprising. As is well known, Furtwängler encountered the monograph shortly after it was published, and was so impressed by it that he arranged to visit Schenker in person. This gave rise to a long-term relationship, with Furtwängler frequently consulting Schenker about the scores he was preparing for performance.[3]

---

[2]  For a discussion of Schenker's views on this, see Cook 1991.
[3]  For details see Federhofer 1985.

Furtwängler felt that in his later theories 'Schenker . . . let himself be carried away too far in his quest for the absolute' ([1954] 1985: 3); he was not prepared to follow Schenker all the way to the ultimate background. But his musical thinking was permanently affected by what he described as Schenker's concept of *'long-range hearing, i.e. hearing applied over great spans to fundamental relationships that often spread across many pages'* (: 3). He is referring to what we might call the remote middle-ground, and this is the level of structure with which Schenker was principally grappling in his Ninth Symphony monograph. 'With the idea of advancing *long-range hearing*', Furtwängler wrote, 'Schenker forged a platform, revealed a condition, that is objectively present, beyond all historical tests, beyond all simple subjective preferences, and which, properly grasped, will be just as demonstrably certain as other contemporary scientific judgments' (: 3–4).

In this chapter I shall argue that Furtwängler's modifications of tempo are no more (and, if you like, no less) arbitrary and subjective than Schenker's theories of musical structure. And I shall put forward the account of Beethoven's music that Schenker offers in his monograph as a basis for understanding those modifications. Schenker works through the Ninth Symphony section by section, and within each section he first gives a structural description and then draws conclusions for performance. This is the standard format for much of his writing from the *Erläuterungsausgabe* of J. S. Bach's *Chromatic Fantasy and Fugue* (1910) to the *Meisterwerk* essays of the 1920s. In view of the high profile of Schenkerian studies and the growing interest in relating analysis to performance, the performance indications that Schenker offers in these works might be expected to represent a thriving area of research. But this is not really the case; there has been little in the way of follow-up to William Rothstein's highly suggestive introductory study (Rothstein 1984). The reason, I suspect, is that Schenker's performance indications relate to a style of interpretation which is neither current nor adequately understood today. And tempo modification is an essential element of this style. Indeed Schenker's very first performance direction in the Ninth Symphony monograph is concerned with it: 'the selection by Beethoven of a particular tempo at the beginning of a piece', he says, 'which is precisely what the metronome marking represents, by no means ruled out possible tempo modifications . . . The master himself always preferred a free manner of playing to a rigid one' ([1912] 1992: 40–1).

If the sort of performance Schenker had in mind is to be heard anywhere, it should be in Furtwängler's recordings – even when they date from forty years after the publication of Schenker's monograph. This is for two reasons which are rather contradictory, but probably incapable of being disentangled. In the first place, Furtwängler's performance style retained many (though we cannot be sure exactly how many) of the features of late-nineteenth-century performance; as Taruskin puts it, referring specifically to the Bayreuth recording of the Ninth, his conducting 'preserved in aspic a century-old tradition of Beethoven interpretation that went back precisely to the great figure that the Bayreuth Festival worships' (1989: 244). In the second place, Furtwängler's recordings undoubtedly reflect his studies with Schenker, although there is again no way in which we can know how direct or distorted this reflection may be. And this means that exploring the relationship between Schenker's analysis and Furtwängler's performance of the Ninth Symphony may contribute to our understanding not just of Furtwängler, but of Schenker too.

## II

Two of Furtwängler's recordings of the Ninth Symphony are currently available on general release; both are taken from live performances, and both date from when Furtwängler was in his mid-sixties, not long before his death in 1954. (The current catalogue numbers may be found in the discography.)[4] The first of these recordings dates from 29 July 1951; this is the famous Bayreuth Festival performance held to mark the reopening of the theatre after the war. It was a highly symbolic occasion presided over by the spirit of Wagner; in his book on Furtwängler, Sam Shirikawa describes it as 'the litmus test of whether German culture had indeed survived what Nazis and Allies both had literally hammered into the ground' (1992: 482). Since its first release, this recording has appeared on forty labels throughout the world (: 485). The second recording dates from 31 May 1953 and was made at a Vienna Festival concert; this was the last of Furtwängler's fifty-two performances of the Ninth Symphony with the Vienna Philharmonic Orchestra. The concert was broadcast live, and the recording is taken from the archive of the 'Rot–Weiss–Rot' radio station which was run under the auspices of the American authorities in the post-war period.

It would certainly not be adequate to consider these performances as simply illustrating what Schenker said in his Ninth Symphony monograph. There are many occasions when Furtwängler puts in rallentandos which Schenker proscribes, or omits dynamic shading which Schenker insists on as indispensable. On the other hand, time and again Furtwängler shapes his phrases, balances the instrumentation or articulates formal junctures in ways which do match what Schenker says, or which at least seem to belong within the same language of performance that Schenker is talking. But judgements of this sort are inevitably vague and impressionistic, especially in view of the limited sound quality and control over balance that was possible in live recordings around 1950. And close listening, by itself, is even more inadequate when it comes to large-scale tempo modifications; Taruskin's great waves of accelerando and decelerando are clearly audible, but it can be difficult to disentangle them from dynamics, articulation, tonal quality and all the other dimensions that contribute to the energy or tension level of the music. Unlike these other dimensions, however, tempo relationships can easily be measured in an empirical and reasonably accurate manner.

The method used in this chapter is based on a computer equipped with a CD-ROM player; that is why the data I shall offer are limited to recordings available on CD. It involves listening to the recording and tapping to mark where each bar begins;[5]

---

[4] Since this chapter was written, a further recording has become available on Music and Arts CD-2002. Another live performance, it features the Stockholm Konsertförenings Orkester and was recorded in 1943.

[5] Occasionally it is impossible to establish where a bar begins as nothing happens on the downbeat, for instance in bar 2. In such cases an average value is taken, with bars 1 and 2 each being assigned half the duration between the onset of bar 1 and that of bar 3. The selection of the bar as the primary measure (rather than the beat or half-beat) is dictated both by practicality and by the fact that this study is directed specifically towards what I earlier referred to as the remote middleground.

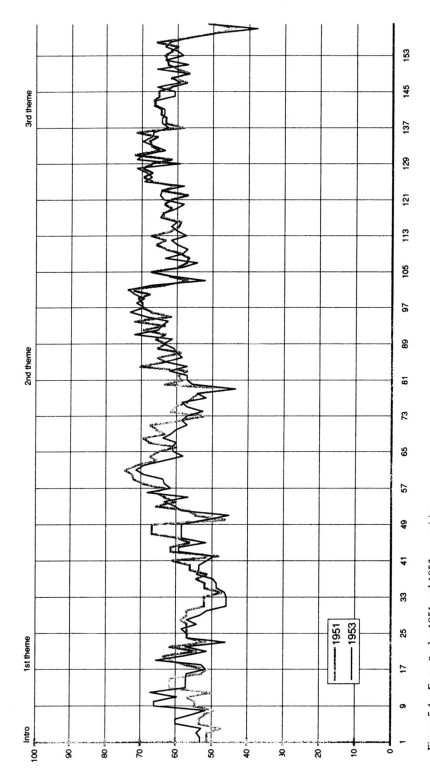

Figure 5.1  Furtwängler 1951 and 1953, exposition

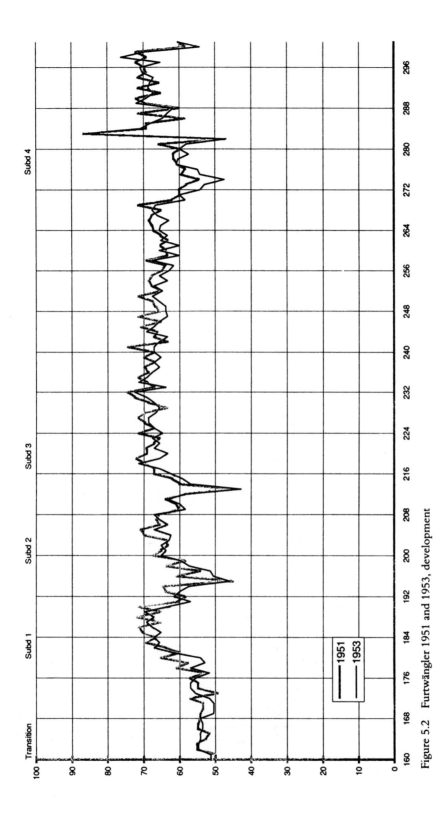

Figure 5.2  Furtwängler 1951 and 1953, development

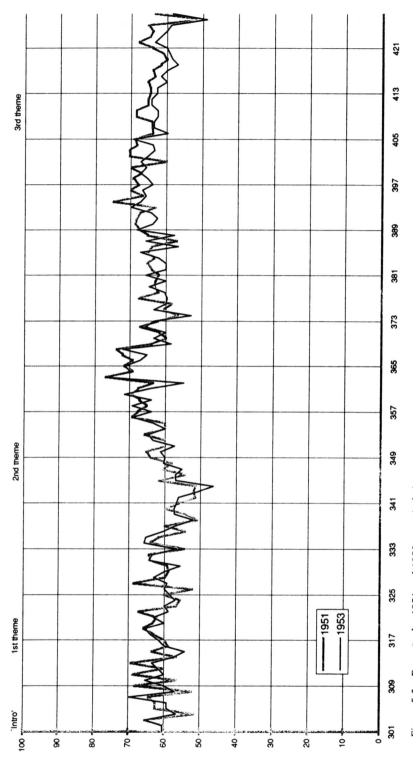

Figure 5.3　Furtwängler 1951 and 1953, recapitulation

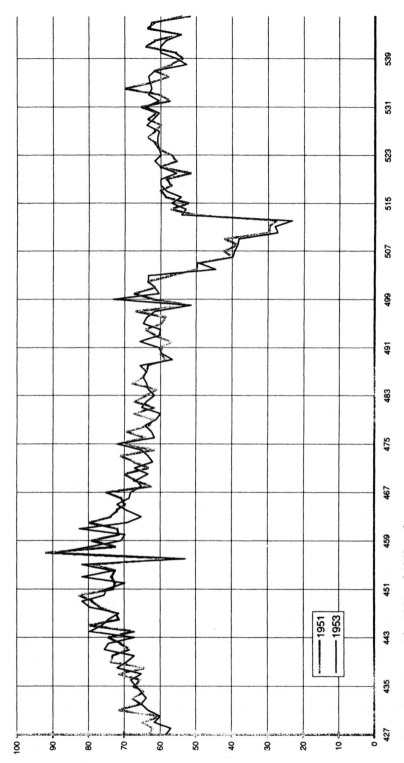

Figure 5.4　Furtwängler 1951 and 1953, coda

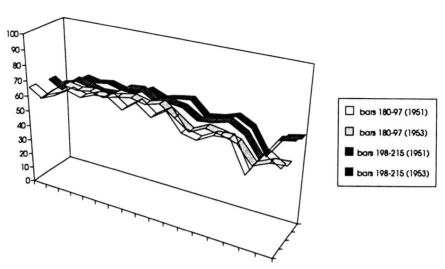

Figure 5.5    Comparison of bars 180–97 and 198–215 in Furtwängler 1951 and 1953

the computer logs the times at which each tap occurs. The result is a chart which
shows the length of each bar. Because it is sometimes difficult to decide exactly where
the downbeat falls, and because of factors of motor control, this process is not entirely
reliable. In repeated tests based on the same passage of music, my responses varied by an
average of 60 milliseconds, which is around 3 per cent of the total duration of each bar;
deviations of 100 milliseconds (5 per cent) were quite frequent. For this reason it would
be foolish to make too much of small transitions which appear on the bar-to-bar level;
the data are not sufficiently accurate. But the discrepancies are not cumulative, and this
means that inferences regarding the broad shaping of tempo (which is what this chapter
is about) are robust. And indeed this is obvious from the graphs of the four main sections
of the movement, shown in Figures 5.1–5.4;[6] the profiles of the 1951 and 1953 performances show a high degree of correlation throughout.

   These data allow us to dispose quickly of some of Lang's criticisms. To be sure,
they show that Furtwängler did not often adhere to metronomic tempos. But they
also show how consistent he was in deviating from them. For instance, as Figure 5.5
makes clear, there is a high degree of correlation between the parallel passages at bars
180–97 and 198–215 within each recording, as well as between the recordings. Such
data do not set a limit on the degree to which Furtwängler was able to control his
tempos; he may not have been *trying* to make each of these passages identical.[7] But
they should remove any lingering doubts about whether or not his tempo modifications were the result of 'deliberate intention', as Lang put it. Indeed, the degree of
correlation between the 1951 and 1953 performances as a whole demonstrates how far

---

[6]  In these figures, the vertical axis shows metronome markings (in crotchet beats), and the horizontal axis
      bar numbers. For convenience, I have also shown the principal sections into which Schenker divides the
      movement.
[7]  See Clarke 1985: 210 for a general discussion of the problem of replication.

Furtwängler had, by the end of his life, forged a consistent interpretation of the first movement of the Ninth Symphony. The question that remains is what this interpretation owed to the structural understanding that Furtwängler considered the only basis of adequate performance.

## III

We can stay with the development section, since of the four principal sections of the movement it presents the most familiar picture. I shall argue that Furtwängler's interpretation is highly compatible with the structural description in Schenker's monograph. As Figure 5.2 indicates, Schenker describes bars 160–79 as a transitional passage, leading to four principal subdivisions: bars 180–97, 198–217, 218–74 and 275–300.

Furtwängler's interpretation of bars 160–79 fits well with Schenker's description of it as a transition. He plays it at a tempo which is rather variable (and the two recordings are quite dissimilar at this point), but in any event slower than the majority of the development section. In each performance Furtwängler prolongs bar 177 and abbreviates bar 178, and then accelerates over the next four or so bars until he reaches something like ♩ = 68; the effect is to project the G minor cadence at bar 178 as the beginning of a directed motion leading into the main part of the development (everything up to that point seeming in retrospect to have lacked direction). Furtwängler's interpretation here could possibly be said to contradict Schenker's insistence that the D major of bars 170–8 should be understood as functioning throughout as V of G minor ([1912] 1992: 90). But then Schenker does not put this forward as a performance instruction. His argument here, and even more so a few pages later where he turns it against Riemann, has more to do with theoretical propriety than practical application; in fact it seems primarily polemical in motivation. This is a side of Schenker which disturbed Furtwängler; 'in many instances', he wrote of the Ninth Symphony monograph, 'the author's polemic attitude went too far for me' ([1954] 1985: 2).

Schenker comments that 'the performance of the Development will be the better the more its subdivisions . . . are given clear expression as such' ([1912] 1992: 97). The segmentation he offers is based partly on the fact that 'at the end of each subdivision [Beethoven] always uses – fully with the effect of a refrain – only bar 3 of the first theme [i.e. bar 19]' (: 90). In both recordings, Furtwängler brings out each of these refrains with a strongly marked ritenuto (bars 195, 213, 274, 300). But the first two of these ritenutos are specified by Beethoven, while the third announces the second subject and the last marks the end of the development, so this is hardly strong evidence of a Schenker connection. However, Schenker has in mind the need to integrate each section as well as to distinguish it from its neighbours. So he continues:

> To achieve the effect of clarity, one must . . . summon all powers to direct one's consciousness immediately, exactly upon entering the first subdivision – thus as early as bars 180–181! –, toward the cadence of bar 192ff., which awaits beyond the 'mountain pass' of bars 188–194; that is, one must organize the performance of the subdivision according to a kind of bird's-eye view, a premonition of the overall course of the subdivision from

its first tonic up to the last cadence. Only then will the cadence be performed as a cadence to the whole subdivision and not, as we unfortunately hear all too often, as a new unit in itself. (: 97)

Furtwängler shapes the tempo of the first subdivision (bars 180–97), and also of its modified repetition in the second subdivision (198–217), in such a way as to achieve precisely this. He brings out the beginning of the cadential phrases at bars 192 and 210, either by lengthening the beginning of the phrase (this is what Riemann called an 'agogic accent') or by slowing down or inserting a caesura in the preceding bar;[8] this can be seen in the change of direction towards the end of each subdivision in Figure 5.2. However, as the figure also shows, the beginning of the cadential phrase is clearly subordinated to the boundary that follows it. In this way Furtwängler projects bars 192–7 and 210–17 as integrated within their respective subdivisions, just as Schenker stipulates. The contrast with some of the other performers of the period is very obvious; in his 1940 recording, Mengelberg, for instance, drops speed substantially at bars 192 and 210, giving these points as much structural weight as bars 197 and 217. In this way he creates just the bitty effect that Schenker disparages.

Schenker makes the same point regarding the much longer third subdivision (bars 218–74). 'The essential thing again', he says, 'is to attain that view into the distance that allows us to see already at the first entrances of the fugal section . . . the syncopes of bar 236ff., the modulations and finally the broadly relaxing cadence in A minor (bar 259[ff.])!' (: 98). And he censures Sir George Grove, who in his well-known book on the Beethoven symphonies described bar 253 as the beginning of a new section: 'such hearing!', Schenker snorts. Furtwängler's hard-driven, rhythmic performance of the fugato section can be matched in other performances of the period, including Mengelberg's (though Mengelberg does not bring out the second violin sextuplets from bar 240 in the same steely manner that Furtwängler does, particularly in the 1953 recording). But whereas Mengelberg brakes sharply at bar 253 in order to bring out the *piano* and the gentler quality of the refrain, Furtwängler barely lets up until the *a cappella*-style chords (as Schenker calls them) of bars 267ff. Contrary to his general reputation, then, Furtwängler assures the integrity of this subdivision by maintaining a more or less steady tempo.

Of Schenker's four subdivisions, it is the final one (bars 275–300) which looks least like an integrated unit in Figure 5.2. This is principally a consequence of the way in which Furtwängler postpones the downbeat at bar 283; that is, he lengthens bar 282 but compensates by abbreviating bar 283. In doing this, he throws great emphasis on the modulation to F major that occurs at this point. Now this has no special significance in terms of large-scale tonal design,[9] and Schenker does not comment on it in

---

8    These apparently contrary procedures – lengthening the first bar of a phrase as against the previous bar, and lengthening the previous bar – achieve the same result, that is, to mark the beginning of the phrase. This is analogous to Caroline Palmer's observation that 'the amount of change (rather than the direction of change) may signal a new musical phrase or idea' (1989: 345). See also Clarke 1985: 213.

9    The F major can be seen as a neighbour-note harmony, resulting from a middleground E–F motion over the A and C that are sustained throughout in the horns and timpani (bars 279–93). In other words, it is enclosed within the progression from A minor to A major$^{\flat 9}$ which is completed with the bass motion to C♯ at bar 295.

his performance directions. To this extent, Furtwängler is performing *against* the structure rather than with it at this point (an effect heightened by bars 269–73, where the tone of his strings and the use of portamento create the effect of having somehow blundered into the sound-world of Mahler). Why does Furtwängler do this? Part of the answer may lie in tradition; precisely the same emphasis on bar 283 may be found in many other contemporary performances, including those of Mengelberg, Weingartner and Walter. But in any case, the coherence of this subdivision as a whole is so obvious, both in thematic terms and as an approach to the D major explosion at bar 301, that further projection on the performer's part is superfluous; under such circumstances, performing against the structure becomes as valid an option as performing with it.

## IV

Furtwängler's modifications of tempo in the development section are nicely judged in terms of musical structure, but there is nothing very unusual about this kind of nuance. The use of rallentandos, caesuras and agogic accents to mark structural points is still a commonplace of performance practice, although today's performers avoid the extremes to which Furtwängler and other conductors of the inter-war period routinely went. There is a basic principle underlying this practice, which is that the caesura or rallentando will be longer or shorter according to the importance of the structural division.[10] This is the principle according to which I explained Furtwängler's tempos in the development section, and it might also be invoked to account for his stupendous rallentando at bar 512, which in effect upgrades the closing function of Schenker's refrain phrase from that of a subdivision, as at bars 195 and 213, to that of the entire coda or even perhaps of the whole movement. We could express this principle in psychological terms by saying that any given tempo creates an expectation of continuation; the caesura or rallentando temporarily contradicts this expectation, and in so doing marks this point in the music for consciousness (to borrow Cooper and Meyer's phrase).[11] And the greater the contradiction of expectation, the greater the resulting emphasis.

This psychological formulation is useful because it allows us to generalise the principle. For if a fixed tempo can create an expectation of continuation, so can a changing one. And, for Furtwängler, changing tempos – and specifically what I shall call tempo gradients – are just as important as fixed tempos. For instance, he accelerates throughout the second subject in both the exposition and the recapitulation (Figures 5.1 and 5.3, bars 80ff. and 345ff.). This might be called nuance expanded to the level of a complete thematic statement. The effect is to underline what Furtwängler himself called the process of musical growth, creating a kind of transition from the intimate style of the second subject to the orchestral tutti of its continuation; Furtwängler's

---

[10]   The general correlation between prolongation and hierarchical depth has been confirmed in empirical studies of expert performance by Neil Todd (1985, 1989), who draws a parallel between this phenomenon and the phrase-final lengthening model of motor control.

[11]   Their description of an accent (1960: 8).

swaying tempos reveal the ancestry of the Viennese symphonic style in solo versus ripieno textures in a way present-day performances do not. Because a sustained accelerando of this kind creates the same expectation of continuation as a fixed tempo, it can accommodate nuance in the same way; this explains Furtwängler's approach to bars 275–96 (the second-subject material near the end of the development), where a profile similar to that of bars 80ff. and 345ff. is temporarily interrupted as a result of the emphasis on F major that I discussed earlier. The continuity of the tempo gradient helps tie the section together despite this massive nuance.

Furtwängler's sustained accelerandos were by no means just a personal quirk; Weingartner, the self-appointed scourge of 'rubato conductors', wrote of bar 345 that 'at the beginning of this section the conductor has an opportunity of gradually animating the time so that by about bar 359 the original time is reached again' (1969: 194). And accelerandos can be heard at this point not just in Weingartner's recordings, but also in those of Mengelberg and even Toscanini – though in no case is the accelerando either as sustained or as marked as Furtwängler's. But sustained accelerandos have not been part of accepted performance practice for many years. As early as 1938, Eric Blom likened music to elastic in order to advance what has since become an orthodoxy:

> elastic will stretch, but cannot be pushed together. In other words, and words applied to Beethoven, the pace of any movement of his, slow or fast, can often be slightly spread out with advantage, whereas it can scarcely ever be tightened or hurried with anything but an untidy, scatter-brained effect.                              (quoted in Philip 1992: 15)

Such a thing as a structural accelerando should, therefore, be a contradiction in terms. But no other term will describe bars 427–53 as Furtwängler performed them, a dramatically perceptible accelerando which starts at the very beginning of the coda – long before Beethoven's crescendo marking and stretto (bars 439, 447) – and builds right through to what Schenker calls 'the first $f\!f$ catharsis' at bar 453 ([1912] 1992: 130). Schenker asks for a stringendo from bar 449, resulting in a local reinforcement of the climax at bar 453. What Furtwängler provides is on a different order of structural significance.

As Figure 5.4 makes clear, Furtwängler shapes both his performances in a very similar manner. He embraces the whole of bars 427–512 within a single, arch-shaped profile. The tempo is at no point static; to use Taruskin's words, it is eternally in flux. The initial accelerando peaks at bar 453; averaged over a number of bars, this passage represents the fastest sustained tempo of either recording at around $\downarrow$ = 75. It continues in a smooth curve through the equally sustained decelerando, levelling out at around bar 480; then there is a tumultuous fall after bar 502, which leads to a virtual standstill at bar 512, the second of Beethoven's written-out rallentandos. ('Furtwängler insists on giant fermatas', writes Lang with some justice, 'and the pauses after them are so long that the unwary may think that the end of the side has been reached' (1978: 24).) This smooth, highly controlled profile is punctuated by a few individual features, notably the prolonged offbeat chords at bars 456 and 498; each of these prolongations is partly compensated through the abbreviation of the following bar. But they do not affect the overall profile of the tempo, which continues uninterrupted throughout; they are purely rhetorical features, not structural ones.

In using these terms I mean to imply that dynamically changing tempos open up structural possibilities which do not exist with fixed tempos, or even with continuous accelerandos or decelerandos. Furtwängler's arch-shaped tempo profiles have something which neither a fixed tempo nor an accelerando has: the implication of closure. They create the sense of a final destination, because they embody directions and rates of tempo change. They embrace extended passages of music within a single span, and give rise to structural divisions when one arch succeeds another. And these structural properties function quite independently of local rallentandos or caesuras. If the caesuras at bars 456 and 498 had been located in a passage at a fixed tempo, they would have implied a structural division proportional to their length; that, as I said, is a basic principle of today's performance practice. But in Furtwängler's performance they carry no such implications, because the tempo profile continues uninterrupted; that is why I called them rhetorical and not structural. In other words, Furtwängler's dynamically changing tempos mean that rhetorical effects are mapped onto a different dimension from the projection of structure. This is something which cannot be achieved through the use of fixed tempos, where rhetorical features are categorically indistinguishable from structural ones.

If this account of the structure-building properties of dynamic tempo profiles seems excessively abstract, then consider the D major horn passage at bar 469, which Tovey described as 'a moment of distant happiness [which] has never been surpassed for tragic irony' (1935: 21). Perhaps surprisingly, Schenker offers no advice on what to do at this point, but other commentators have expressed contradictory views. In his book on the performance of Beethoven's symphonies, Weingartner writes: 'An ideal execution of this horn solo demands a somewhat more moderate speed than that of the preceding bars, and this must be maintained if [i.e. when] the strings, henceforth in a minor key, take over the theme (bar 477)' (1969: 201). By contrast, Norman Del Mar, in *his* book on the performance of Beethoven's symphonies, claims that 'here continuity is of the essence, the poetry of the horn solo emerging in strict tempo from the previous period of protest' (1992: 180). Weingartner's and Del Mar's injunctions are diametrically opposed, and yet Furtwängler complies with both. With Weingartner, he drops his speed at or around bar 469, giving the horns room to speak and accentuating the sharp contrast of mode and mood. In doing so, he maintains the curve of the now falling tempo profile, and so realises the continuity that Del Mar demands. In this way, the use of dynamically changing tempos allows Furtwängler to have his cake and eat it.

If bars 456, 469 and 498 are all passing events, mere nuances, then what occurs at bar 104 is quite different. In each performance, there is a rallentando over the two preceding bars together with a caesura; these bring out the change of texture and mood. And the effect is reproduced at the modified repetition four bars later. The difference between what happens here and what happened at bars 456 and 498 is that the tempo profile continues at the new, lower level rather than returning to the previous one; to this extent, the tempo change is structural, not rhetorical. But the tempo gradient, that is, the direction and rate of tempo change, remains the same; the result is still an arch-shaped profile between bars 80 and 159, but a stepped one. In this way, discontinuity of tempo is encompassed within continuity of gradient; Furtwängler is structuring tempo hierarchically. And as might be expected, he reproduces this profile in the corresponding passage of the recapitulation (bars 369ff.), though this time the effect is not quite so clearly defined.

Even in an age of tempo modification, Furtwängler's treatment of such passages seems to have been exceptional. In a purely quantitative sense, the extreme of tempo modification is Mengelberg's 1940 recording, which crashes from $\downarrow$ = 72 to $\downarrow$ = 52 at bar 104, returns to the original tempo at 106 and does the same each time this figure appears subsequently. As is generally the case in Mengelberg's performance, there is little or nothing in the way of tempo transition; he simply butt-joins his tempos. Mengelberg's approach works for some music, but not for the first movement of the Ninth Symphony. It reduces Beethoven's vast spans to a series of episodes; it is hard to quarrel with Pirie's harsh judgement that 'whereas in every Furtwängler modification of phrasing or tempo there was a purpose, in Mengelberg's they seemed often to be merely ornamental or even pointless'[12] (1980: 10). Mengelberg, in short, comes across as a rubato conductor, a virtuoso; he treats tempo modification as principally a means of creating nuance. Such a term is altogether inadequate when applied to Furtwängler, for whom tempo modification was the primary means for creating what are, in effect, analyses in sound.

## V

Because they create the sense of a destination, because of their gestural coherence, Furtwängler's dynamic tempo profiles convey the same organisation of the music into large spans that Schenker strove to express in his analyses. In fact, Furtwängler sometimes seems more successful in his articulation of these spans than Schenker managed to be at the relatively early stage of his career when he wrote the Ninth Symphony monograph. Perhaps the best illustration of this is the exposition, which Furtwängler performed as three spans of increasing clarity and size (bars 1–35, 35–79 and 80–159).

Schenker begins his account of the first movement with an analytical chart, which governs the formal labels that he adopts in his commentary ([1912] 1992: 30). He divides bars 1–35 into two sections, an introduction (bars 1–16) and an antecedent (bars 17–35). This is not really a very lucid way of seeing the music, because it gets the various hierarchical levels tangled up. The problem is that Schenker's consequent (bars 35–79) includes a repeat of the introduction, and as if to make up for this confusion of levels Schenker insists in his commentary on the inseparability of the intro-duction and the main theme proper (: 35). Furtwängler's interpretation of bars 1–35

---

12  But also refreshingly playful, I would add, precisely because of the way they contradict expectations.

avoids strong segmentation of any kind; overall it could be described as neutral. By broadening the multiple-stop chords at bars 21 and 23, he emphasises the ♭II–V–i cadential progression that begins at bar 24 and concludes the opening span. He also gives some emphasis to the main theme at bar 17, but much less than at the corresponding point of the second span (bar 53); this is perhaps because the more distinct arch-shaped profile of bars 35–79, with its apex at bar 61, makes a higher degree of rhetorical emphasis possible without compromising the perceived integrity of the span.

Schenker also divides bars 35–79 into two sections (he calls bars 35–70 a consequent and bars 71–9 a modulation passage), but backtracks on this division in his commentary. The modulation passage, he says, must not be projected as a unit in its own right; it is necessary to

> keep our gaze directed toward the coming second theme and, while giving proper attention to the modulation-theme [i.e. bars 74–9], nevertheless at the same time preserve in the performance a quality of scouting ahead. Thus all that would suggest lingering or retardation should be excluded from the passage; not until bar 79 should a *ritenuto* be applied, to signal the approach of the second theme. ([1912] 1992: 45)

Schenker is in effect warning against a performance like Mengelberg's, where the drastic decrease of tempo at bar 74 in effect turns the modulation theme into a true second subject. (The result is that bar 80 becomes altogether incoherent.) As Figure 5.1 shows, Furtwängler does not follow Schenker's advice in a literal sense. He slackens the tempo to mark the beginning of the modulation theme; it is hardly possible otherwise to do justice to Beethoven's 'dolce' marking. But by clearly subsuming this within the arched profile of the span as a whole, Furtwängler simultaneously fulfils the demands of immediate expression and overall structure.

Yet again, at bars 80–159, Furtwängler integrates within one span what Schenker analyses as two sections: the second theme (bars 80–137) and the third theme (bars 138–59, subdivided at bar 150). And once more Schenker's commentary insists on the need to bring out in performance the unity that his formal labels and diagram deny:

> just as in harmonic terms only the one scale degree, the V, literally seems to lie in wait from bar 120 for the tonic (which, however, does not arrive until bar 138), so too all melodic content, as a great, careening mass that gives the impression of being under a single slur encompassing eighteen bars, must likewise obey only the one driving force – the force that drives toward the future, embodied by the closing theme! (: 64)

Furtwängler's arch-shaped tempo profile encompasses all this, subsuming a slight quickening of the pulse in line with the crescendo of bars 124–31 and holding back a little for the intricate closing theme at bar 138. In this way he avoids swallowing the notes at bar 138 through the adoption of too fast a tempo (like Mengelberg's or Toscanini's), while at the same time achieving the integration that Schenker asks for – unlike Weingartner, whose rallentando at bar 138 makes this sound like the beginning of a new section.

Again and again, Furtwängler creates a correlate in performance of the 'long-range hearing' he so admired in Schenker's approach. If Furtwängler's performance style could be summarised in just two words, they would be 'long-range conducting': he outlines the spans of Schenkerian theory, while still giving close attention to the expressive detail of the musical surface. Where other conductors have to choose between bringing out structure and doing justice to details, Furtwängler consistently manages to do both. And if my analysis is correct, it is the use of dynamically changing tempo profiles that is the key to his success. In view of this, it is hardly surprising that Furtwängler was reluctant to record the Ninth Symphony under studio conditions; the fragmentation involved in multiple takes would have been inimical to such control of tempos. All nine of Furtwängler's currently known recordings of the work are taken from live performances.[13]

## VI

In a programme note to the recent reissue of Oskar Fried's 1928 recording of the Ninth Symphony, Julian Haylock writes that between the wars

> attitudes towards performance were entirely different from those accepted today . . . The world of music was still dominated by the last flowerings of nineteenth-century Romanticism . . . Most music was viewed in terms of its poetic expression, and inter-preters invariably sought to project music as a succession of moods or pictorial images. The current obsession with structure and formal design was very much a thing of the future. This meant that even an extended work, such as Beethoven's Ninth, might find itself subjected to quite marked fluctuations in tempo in the interests of seeking out the 'message' behind the score.

To the extent that Furtwängler is representative of this period, the truth seems to be exactly the opposite of what Haylock says. Conductors in the Wagner tradition used tempo modification precisely as a means of projecting structure and formal design as they understood it; when he says of Furtwängler that 'his interpretation analyzed the structure', Pirie is making a simple statement of fact. But that does not mean such conductors had no regard for music's poetic or spiritual qualities; Haylock's antithesis is a false one. On the contrary, Furtwängler believed that 'with Beethoven, pure com-poser that he was, the structure of the work is identical with the spiritual message. That is the key to all Beethoven interpretation' (1991: 35).

This sounds like a typically grandiose, which is to say vacuous, statement of romantic ideology. But Furtwängler has something very specific in mind. His next words are:

> Wagner was the first to point out the practical implications of this organic experience of the structure of Beethoven's works. Foremost among them is the use of rubato, that almost imperceptible yet constant variation of tempo which turns a piece of music played rigidly according to the notes on the printed page into what it really is – an experience of conception and growth, of a living organic process.[14] (: 35–6)

---

13   Shirikawa 1992: 482. According to Shirikawa, a studio recording was planned as part of Furtwängler's 1952 contract with HMV/EMI but was never realised. Further discographic details may be found in Pirie 1980.

14   It is striking that Furtwängler sees Wagner as a founding figure in structurally aware performance, whereas for Schenker he was the exact opposite. I have suggested elsewhere (Cook 1993: 59) the extent to which Schenker's theoretical thinking echoes Wagner's; it seems as if Schenker's increasingly virulent anti-Wagnerian stance may have disguised a degree of indebtedness he was not prepared to admit. For further discussion see Cook 1995.

And yet we are singularly ill equipped to understand this phenomenon. Furtwängler's very terminology betrays this. Etymologically the term *tempo rubato* derives from the idea of 'robbing' time by prolonging a note or a passage, and then 'paying it back' through a compensating abbreviation; as practised in the baroque period, when the term originated, the premise of the rubato concept is therefore a steady, underlying pulse. But this does not offer a good description of nineteenth-century or later practice, in which no steady, underlying pulse is generally perceptible during rubato passages; it is always possible to calculate the average tempo of any such passage as a whole, of course, but there is no compelling reason for ascribing psychological reality to it.[15] And much the same applies to 'tempo modification', which has been a standard term ever since Wagner announced that 'the rendering of our classical music depends . . . vastly on modifications of tempo' (Wagner [1869] 1966: 324); after all, there has to be a tempo before it can be modified. In this way, the available terminologies lead us to think of what we hear in Furtwängler's recordings as distortions or deviations from norms of metronomic regularity.[16] On the other hand, one could equally well turn the logic around, and view a fixed tempo as an arch-shaped tempo profile of zero gradient! I do not think either interpretation is profitable. If instead we approach the issue from a psychological angle, we can attribute the same kind of significance to *any* tempo profile which implies a specific continuation; this applies equally to fixed tempos, constant accelerandos or decelerandos, and the arch-shaped tempo profiles so characteristic of Furtwängler.

Neither Furtwängler nor any other exponent of the tradition of tempo modification left a rationale of the practice; they merely asserted its indispensability. But it is possible to hazard how Furtwängler might have formulated such a rationale in terms of the Schenkerian principles he espoused. What a Schenkerian theory of tempo would *not* involve would be looking for rules governing the correlation of tempo with other surface features such as dynamics, strength of articulation and so forth; as one might expect, general correlations can be found between such features and Furtwängler's tempos (thus faster means louder means more strongly articulated), but it is a matter of observation that these correlations are neither close nor invariable. Instead of looking for direct correlations between surface features, a Schenkerian approach would mean relating each such feature to the totality of the musical structure; the tempo profile would represent, so to speak, the shadow cast by that totality on a particular dimension of musical measurement. If for Schenker (or at least for the Schenker of 1912) the span is the summarising representation of musical structure, then the arch-shaped tempo profile is its correlate in Furtwängler's performance. It encompasses everything.

Whether or not Furtwängler would have agreed with this rationale, he seems to have viewed tempo modification as a kind of window opening directly on musical

---

[15]  This is the problem with hierarchical models of rubato based on tempos averaged over phrases, sections or structural spans, as in Cook 1987 or Gottschewski 1992.

[16]  This dualistic paradigm is built into the standard vocabulary for all forms of 'expressive performance', where 'expression' is used (as in much contemporary music-psychological writing) as the antonym of 'structure'.

structure. He regarded it as the litmus test of authenticity in performance: 'it is possible to tell from the treatment of the so-called *rubato*, as from a barometer reading, whether or not the impulses provoking it are in accordance with the real feeling of the passage or not, whether they are genuine or not' ([1948] 1977: 52). And I would suggest that this quotation offers an essential clue to the special quality of Furtwängler's recordings that makes them so vividly *audible* against the background of the dozens of competent and well-engineered recordings of the Ninth Symphony available today. For according to Furtwängler, authentic performance is subject to 'the law of improvisation, which . . . demands that the artist should identify himself completely with a work and its growth' (: 51). We do not have to believe that Furtwängler's way of performing Beethoven is the only correct one in order to recognise the exceptional identification of artist and work that distinguishes his recordings of the Ninth Symphony. To listen to them is to witness a process of improvisation which somehow, as if by happy accident, coincides with the notes of Beethoven's score.

REFERENCES

Clarke, E. F., 1985: 'Structure and expression in rhythmic performance', in P. Howell, I. Cross and R. West, eds., *Musical Structure and Cognition* (London: Academic Press), pp. 209–36.

Cook, N., 1987: 'Structure and performance timing in Bach's C major Prelude (WTC I): an empirical study', *Music Analysis* 6/3: 257–72.

1991: 'The editor and the virtuoso, or Schenker versus Bülow', *Journal of the Royal Musical Association* 116/1: 78–95.

1993: *Beethoven: Symphony No. 9* (Cambridge: Cambridge University Press).

1995: 'Heinrich Schenker, polemicist: a reading of the Ninth Symphony monograph', *Music Analysis* 14/1: 89–105.

Cooper, G. and Meyer, L., 1960: *The Rhythmic Structure of Music* (Chicago: University of Chicago Press).

Del Mar, N., 1992: *Conducting Beethoven, vol. I: The Symphonies* (Oxford: Clarendon).

Federhofer, H., 1985: *Heinrich Schenker nach Tagebüchern und Briefen in der Oswald Jonas Memorial Collection* (Hildesheim: Georg Olms).

Furtwängler, W., [1948] 1977: *Concerning Music*, trans. L. J. Lawrence (Westport, Connecticut: Greenwood Press).

[1954] 1985: 'Heinrich Schenker: a contemporary problem', *Sonus* 6: 1–5.

1991: *Furtwängler on Music*, ed. and trans. R. Taylor (Aldershot: Scolar Press).

Gottschewski, H., 1992: 'Graphic analysis of recorded interpretations', in W. Hewlett and E. Selfridge-Field, eds., *Computing in Musicology: An International Directory of Applications*, vol. VIII (Menlo Park, California: Center for Computer-Assisted Research in the Humanities), pp. 93–6.

Lang, P. H., 1978: 'The symphonies', in *The Recordings of Beethoven as Viewed by the Critics from High Fidelity* (Westport, Connecticut: Greenwood Press), pp. 1–25.

Palmer, C., 1989: 'Mapping musical thought to musical performance', *Journal of Experimental Psychology: Human Perception and Performance* 15/12: 331–46.

Philip, R., 1992: *Early Recordings and Musical Style: Changing Tastes in Instrumental Performance 1900–1950* (Cambridge: Cambridge University Press).

Pirie, P., 1980: *Furtwängler and the Art of Conducting* (London: Duckworth).

Rothstein, W., 1984: 'Heinrich Schenker as an interpreter of Beethoven's piano sonatas', *19th-Century Music* 8/1: 3–28.

Schenker, H., [1912] 1992: *Beethoven's Ninth Symphony. A Portrayal of its Musical Content, with Running Commentary on Performance and Literature As Well*, trans. J. Rothgeb (New Haven: Yale University Press).

    [1926] 1977: 'Organic structure in sonata form', trans. O. Grossman, in M. Yeston, ed., *Readings in Schenker Analysis and Other Approaches* (New Haven: Yale University Press), pp. 38–53.

Shirikawa, S., 1992: *The Devil's Music Master: The Controversial Life and Career of Wilhelm Furtwängler* (New York: Oxford University Press).

Taruskin, R., 1989: 'Resisting the Ninth', *19th-Century Music* 12/3: 241–56.

Todd, N., 1985: 'A model of expressive timing in tonal music', *Music Perception* 3/1: 33–58.

    1989: 'A computational model of rubato', *Contemporary Music Review* 3/1: 69–88.

Tovey, D. F., 1935: *Essays in Musical Analysis, II: Symphonies (II), Variations and Orchestral Polyphony* (London: Oxford University Press).

Wagner, R., [1869] 1966: 'About conducting', in *Richard Wagner's Prose Works, IV: Art and Politics*, ed. and trans. W. A. Ellis (New York: Broude Brothers), pp. 289–364.

Weingartner, F., 1969: *Weingartner on Music and Conducting: Three Essays* (New York: Dover).

## DISCOGRAPHY

Fried, O., [1928] 1989: Berlin State Opera Orchestra, Bruno Kittel Choir (GEMM CD 9372).

Furtwängler, W., [1951] 1984: Chor und Orchester der Festspiele Bayreuth (EMI CDH 7 69801 2).

    [1953] 1991: Wiener Philharmoniker, Wiener Singakademie (DG 435 325-2).

Mengelberg, W., 1940: Concertgebouw Orchestra. (Not on current release. My thanks to Robin Holloway for making a copy available to me.)

Toscanini, A., [1952] 1990: NBC Symphony Orchestra, Robert Shaw Chorale (RCA GD60256).

Walter, B., [1949 (I–III), 1953 (IV)] 1989: New York Philharmonic Orchestra, Westminster Choir (CBS MPK 45552).

Weingartner, F., [1935] 1990: Vienna Philharmonic Orchestra, Vienna State Opera Chorus (GEMM CD 9407).

# CHAPTER SIX

# A curious moment in Schumann's Fourth Symphony: structure as the fusion of affect and intuition

## DAVID EPSTEIN

■

How musicians conceptualise music, particularly in preparing it for performance, is a murky issue, despite the copious discussion and research that have been devoted to the matter.[1] Ultimately, it would seem, musical concepts are a synthesis of structure and intuition – of rational views of organisation and construct; of felt entities; of an affective sense of the rightness of these perceptions.

The rational/structural is the easiest of these perspectives to deal with, which may in part explain why analytical studies in our century, influenced as that century has been by the positivistic aspect of scientific research, have gravitated towards the musical version of structuralism. Structure can be seen, heard, demonstrated. It is tangible and specific.[2]

Intuition, of which affect is a major component, is by contrast 'messy'. Like structure, it is experienced – perceived, specific, tangible (felt). Unlike structure, it is difficult to communicate through words and discourse – the major means by which human beings exchange ideas and concepts. As Langer has pointed out (1948, 1953, 1967), language and rational discourse are not the currency of affective communication. The materials of the modes are not only different, but essentially incompatible.[3]

---

[1] The origin of this chapter was a talk presented in 1988 at the Internationale Robert-Schumann-Tage in Zwickau and subsequently published in condensed form (Epstein 1989). The present essay is an expansion of that paper, drawing upon evidence concerning neurophysiology and additional musical manuscript sources. I am grateful to Dr Gerd Nauhaus and Dr Martin Schoppe of the Zwickau Robert-Schumann-Gesellschaft for the opportunity to explore these ideas at a developmental stage.

[2] Structural materials, however, come to us by way of sensory input, and are to that extent prone to the uncertainties of perception. This is an inescapable condition of all study, whether in the arts or the sciences, and thus a condition with which all investigators must contend.

[3] Intuition is among the least defined, though much applied, terms in current parlance. Its usage largely implies knowledge arrived at by means other than 'intellection', i.e. rational, possibly computational, modes of thought, thus knowledge acquired essentially through some affective mode. Other usages suggest that this knowledge indeed involves 'ratiocination', but that the thinking is executed so quickly as to happen 'in a flash'.

Very likely both aspects of the term are applicable. Intuition does seem to resolve matters in a flash of 'rightful recognition', so to speak. The judgement(s) that inform such recognition, however, would seem to involve an assay of data which must to some degree be analytical.

Mozart's process of composition, which, as he described it, often involved the conception of works in something of a visionary flash, seems a case in point – for instance, the overture to *Don Giovanni*, hastily written the night before the opera's premiere, or the 'Linz' Symphony, composed during a few days' sojourn in that city. Clearly, composition at such speed had to involve musical aspects quickly conceptualised. The

As a consequence, in our time at least, we have tended to eschew the issue. Not dealing with affect is more comfortable than dealing with it inadequately. We deal thereby with but half an artistic loaf, however; what we ignore is critical to the artistic process. Lying behind all judgements which pertain to performance, to the shaping of artistic concepts, are criteria of 'rightness' whose roots are intuitive, essentially affective – seemingly, though not definitively, beyond the grasp of discourse and reason.[4]

These issues are central to the discussion of Schumann in this study. The musical incident that evokes them precipitates one of those unusual moments where the perceptions of numerous performing artists – many of them major interpreters of Schumann – seem at variance with the composer's indication in the score. This is not an issue of tempo, which at best is a relative matter, nor of notes, rhythms, accents and other seeming certainties. The debatable moment focuses elsewhere; it involves a detail which quickly passes, though its consequences affect much that precedes and follows it. The event is thereby something of a juncture in the score. As such it constitutes an interesting view of the melding of affect and structure, and the means by which analytical perspectives may resolve a significant performance enigma.

The moment lies in the opening movement of Schumann's Fourth Symphony. Its discussion here is something of a symposium, in some respects speculative, concerned with matters of structure as they bear upon a critical arrival point in the score. At issue is a dynamic marking of *sfp* which appears inadequate; the moment seems to call for a *forte* dynamic instead.

This is no pedantic matter of an insular dynamic. The passage in question is, if one agrees with the structural perspective offered here, a high point of the movement, if not *the* high point – namely, the recapitulation. What happens here with regard to dynamics thus shapes the sense of the entire movement. The resolution of this matter brings into play issues of articulation, intensity, indeed the very essence of musical motion, and the effect upon all of these of rhythm-in-the-large, of harmony and of tonality, as components of rhythmic delineation.

---

sheer quantity of notes, rhythms, tonal structures, dynamics and the like, given these time frames, could permit no longer deliberation. Yet the 'rightness' of these structures, as sensed by Mozart during the compositional act, suggests that judgements had to have been made, however quickly.

Thus the intuitive, as this example indicates, seems to be a melding of thought and feeling, of intellection and affect, all of which operate at high speed.

[4] Though we may speak of affects or emotions as abstractions, they are in reality linked to specific, demonstrable objects or events. Love, a powerful emotion in human experience, is a case in point. In the abstract, the term is a useful concept for certain levels of discourse. Love as experience, however, is anything but abstract: it is tied specifically to a recipient – a lover, child, parent, friend – and to events connected with that recipient. The nature of love will thus vary in each case.

The argument is no different with respect to the arts. Consider the notion of expressiveness, for example, connoted by the indication *espressivo* in musical scores. Though capable of abstract discussion, expressiveness inheres in the structural details of a given passage – melodic contours, dynamics, articulations, sense of motion and so on. It is thus specific in each instance, embodied in the elements of a particular piece.

'Affect' is used here in discussing these matters not to denote moods or emotions in themselves, as, for example, 'love' in its specific aspects seen above, but to convey on a more abstract plane the symbolised and often formalised representations of emotion with which works of art are generally concerned, representations which deal with feeling and emotion in terms of their morphology and structure. These aspects of affect – of art as symbolic representation, as structured insight into the nature of affective experience – are discussed in detail by Langer (1948). See in particular Chapter 8, 'On significance in music', pp. 165–99.

Prior to studying this passage in detail, it would be well to elaborate on the earlier discussion of matters affective. Current knowledge indicates that structure and affect may in fact be two sides of the same coin – in effect, different modes of knowledge by which we comprehend phenomena. This is borne out by evidence from numerous quarters, not least the findings of neurophysiology with respect to laterality of brain function. It is by now common knowledge that the left and right sides of the brain deal with information in different modes, analytical aspects of cognition lying mainly within the left hemisphere, whereas the right hemisphere operates in a largely holistic manner. Less widely known is the fact that a vast number of fibres (on the order of some 200 million) interconnect the two hemispheres. While the hemispheres are thus spatially separate, their functions are to a large degree interdependent. Indeed, current neural theory views the brain as a complex of interconnected networks, whereby specificity of function is both attenuated and enriched by the intercommunication among subcomponents.

The interconnectedness of brain laterality with respect to music was demonstrated by Petsche et al. (1985, 1989) and Mazziotta et al. (1982) in experimental studies of brain activity among people with various backgrounds and levels of musical training as they listened to music.[5] All participants in Petsche's studies revealed neural response in both halves of the brain as they listened to African drum music, a Mozart string quartet, etc. Non-professional music lovers showed differing (largely greater) degrees of right-lobe activity than did professionally trained musicians, with whom right/left hemispheric response was more equally balanced. This result is perhaps not surprising, for music lovers, in the main unconcerned with the technicalities of music-making, probably approach the listening of music with expectations and needs which lie more in the domain of affective response than is the case with professional performers. Performance seems to generate listening habits which divide attention between matters of performance control, hence analytical observation of structure and heard musical detail, and an affective sense of how a performance, as it progresses, may feel.

In general, the world with which we deal comes to us as a mixture of the affective/sensual and the cognitive/computational. Information with respect to the external world arrives through the sensory system and must go either to the brain stem or, if the data are complex, to higher levels of the brain which deal with cognitive functions, where the information is treated analytically, computationally.[6]

Processing of the physical materials of music – sound, pulse, timbre, etc. – involves affective as well as cognitive transformation of percepts. Musicians think in terms of pitch, for example. Pitch, however, is itself a mental transformation, in effect a cognitive interpretation, of frequency – the quantity of sound waves per second. Likewise our sense of loud/soft is a transformation, one with significant sensory/affective aspects, of amplitude, as timbre is a transformation of relative overtone strength. In a similar sense stereophony, a commonplace in electronic music systems, transforms the 'raw' data of

---

[5]  The experiments respectively used EEG (electroencephalogram) recordings and PET (positron emission tomography) scanning as the means of illuminating this activity. A detailed review and critique of brain scanning and brain mapping in connection with musical perception and performance is given by Sergent (1993).

[6]  This process is described in detail by Shepherd (1983).

sound *vis-à-vis* its spatial location into an affective sense of sound 'richer' in quality than that provided by monophonic presentation. Physiologically, the 'richness' stems from the brain's comparison of the sound in terms of the spatial location of its various components – a comparison made possible by stimulation in the inner ear of cilia attuned to directionality, thereby registering time differences among the received sonic elements.

The terminology, often approximate or even elliptical in meaning and implication, by which performing musicians refer to these various qualities of sound attests to the essential inadequacy of words as purveyors of sensory affects. Thus pitches are heard as 'in' or 'out' of tune, high or low, sharp or flat; tone colours are described as 'dark', 'clear'; sound has 'presence', 'fullness', etc.

Commonplace experience reinforces this analytical/sensory, cognitive/affective response to phenomena. Consider, for example, a geometrical figure such as a sphere. Mathematics provides us with the analytical means to determine numerous of its properties – volume, circumference, diameter, surface area, curvature and the like. 'Sphericality' as a concept, however, has affective aspects as well as computational properties. Think of the sensuous roundedness of flesh, for instance, so common with the cherubs and nudes found in paintings of the Italian baroque period; by contrast, recall the hard roundedness of musculature in the upper arm and shoulder of Moses, seen in the famous statue by Michelangelo. These figures impact forcefully upon our senses; it is clear, however, from the sketches of Michelangelo, and from the drawings and other studies of Leonardo, that the sensual qualities found in the paintings and statuary of these artists demanded preparatory work which was analytical in nature.

Relatively recent research has shed further light upon the neurophysiological and biochemical bases upon which emotions are structured, and by which they function. Knowledge of neurotransmitters, now commonplace, is only decades old. The subclass of neurotransmitters known as endorphins, which are involved in the transmission of neural signals interpreted by the brain as pleasure or pain, is yet newer information. Catecholamine chemical structures (dopamine, norepinephrine, serotonin) may constitute the underlying neuropharmacological aspects of depression and its inverse affect, elation, even mania. How precise their association with these aspects of emotional life may be is not fully clear. For instance, various factors which seem to play a role in the pathogenesis of depression – the inadequate binding of transmitters to receptors at special sites in the brain, deficient quantities of these neurotransmitters themselves, insufficient quantities of transmitter or receptor cells within nerve synapses – may, when present in excess, conversely be associated with elation and mania. (See Restak 1979: 166ff. and Gazzaniga 1992: 169ff.) Gazzaniga's study, though largely concerned with selection theory and evolution, devotes much space to the physiological basis of emotion, and of affective disorders as well – further evidence (though this is not the central focus of the study) of the structural bases of affect, of affective functions and malfunctions.[7]

These views of emotion, of affective function – limited excerpts though they are from a vast contemporary literature – are relevant to discussions about music: they

---

[7]  I am grateful to Dr Harald Hefter (Medical School of the University of Düsseldorf) for discussions about these neurobiological and neuropharmacological matters.

reveal affects as structured phenomena. The findings, in tandem with Langer's explication (1948, Chapter 8) of the precision with which affect is delineated in works of art, move feeling, emotion, affect some distance beyond the 'messy' category referred to earlier. The major problem in dealing with affect is not its ostensible imprecision as phenomenon, but its incompatibility with language. We would be wise to avoid describing, much less 'translating', affective qualities into language, certainly to the extensive degree that preoccupied nineteenth-century philosophers and aestheticians such as Schopenhauer ([1818] 1947) and Hanslick (1854).

Affect speaks its own language, one readily perceived, precisely delineated, though in non-lexical modes. Admittedly, the inadequate matching of word and feeling is inescapable in a world where language is a prime means of discourse.

More important than describing affect is to seek the mechanisms by which it is structured. Those mechanisms, perceived and understood, offer the key to the shaping of affect, indeed its modulation as part of the performing process. That affect partakes of structure, that it is the Janus face, so to speak, of musical constructs, is significant. For as we interpret structures, reveal them within the time processes by which music flows, we deal simultaneously with affect. As we shape structures, modulating the intensities that demarcate them, we likewise shape affect. And shaping, as every musician knows, is the essence of interpretative performance.

Discussion of the performance issue in the Schumann Fourth Symphony profits from this perspective. What is involved here is in essence a matter of affect as it pertains to structure: the critical *sfp* marking identified earlier. What makes this moment particularly fascinating is its ambiguity as a focal point in the movement. The moment can be seen as the high point that we have suggested. Alternatively, it can be seen as a way station, a point within a trajectory of movement and intensities whose goal lies farther on. To some extent the latter view creates a dissynchrony between the affective pulls of the music and the structures within which these pulls inhere. How the moment is perceived thus relates to the performance of the entire movement. The coming discussion indicates a role which analysis can play not only in revealing structural anomaly and ambiguity, but also in handling this moment as it devolves upon affect and interpretation.

Two major criteria for this discussion must be clarified at the outset. One concerns the form of this movement; the second, the nature of Schumann's thematic construction. As is well known, Schumann wrote two versions of the Symphony, the first in 1841, the second, which is the one generally performed today, in 1851.[8] Both versions make clear that the Symphony is conceived and should be heard as one movement. Schumann's four-hand version of the work, as well as an early copy of the orchestral score, note this specifically, as did the programme of a concert in Düsseldorf on 3 March 1853, in which a subtitle stated: 'Introduction [*sic*], Allegro, Romanze, Scherzo

---

[8]   Brahms, that tireless friend and advocate of Schumann, was so impressed by features of the first version, which by the mid nineteenth century had already fallen into disuse, that he persuaded Breitkopf & Härtel to publish it. It appeared in 1891 and remained in print for some years in Breitkopf's Partitur-Bibliothek as a pocket score (No. 3662) under the title 'Erste Bearbeitung aus dem Jahre 1841'.

Example 6.1   Fourth Symphony, I, bars 29–33: opening theme of the Lebhaft section

Example 6.2   Fourth Symphony, I, bars 59–63: second thematic group

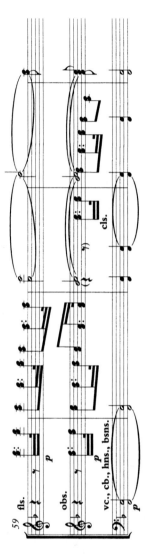

Example 6.3   Fourth Symphony, I, bars 76–80: closing theme

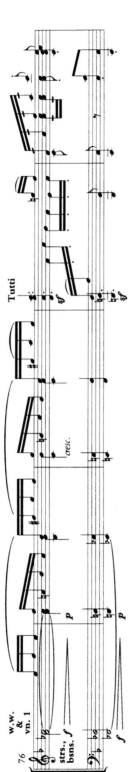

Example 6.4   Fourth Symphony, I, bars 265–80: approach to the dominant preparation for the recapitulation

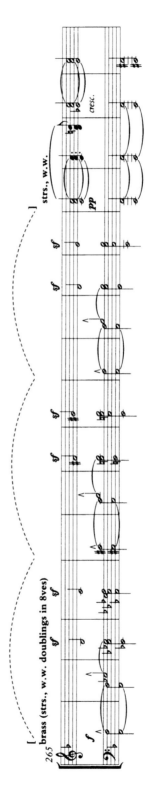

und Finale in einem Satz'.[9] Schumann makes this *segue* character even clearer in the 1851 version by using thin double lines to separate the sections (movements).

Though Schumann's conception of continuity is amply evident, the Symphony is nonetheless divided into four movements, though they are fused in performance. The first movement, which largely, if anomalously, follows many of the principles of sonata form, begins with a slow introduction, as the Düsseldorf programme subtitle suggests. The fact that there is a first movement, in the sense delineated above, is critical to our discussion, for the place in question, with its soft dynamic marking, serves as the point of return of this movement – in essence, its recapitulation.

To speak of this place (bar 297) as the point of recapitulation is to denote the high point of an inspired though idiosyncratic form. The anomaly of form from this point onwards – so striking, and so critical to the argument of this article – demands discussion of what precisely recapitulation entails. It suffices for the moment to note that the 'Lebhaft' portion of the movement follows the norms of sonata form throughout the exposition and development. An opening theme in the tonic key of D minor (bar 29, Example 6.1) is followed by a transition (bars 43–59) to the relative major, F, at which point the second thematic group appears (bars 59ff., Example 6.2). A closing theme follows (bars 76ff., Example 6.3), as well as a codetta to the exposition (bar 83).

So far the flow of events seems straightforward enough, and so does the development section (bars 87–296) – a sequential structure stated on three tonal levels a minor third or equivalent apart (E♭, bar 101; F♯, bar 175; A, bar 249). (It is notable that these tonal levels reflect the principal motivic structure of the movement, and indeed the entire Symphony – the interval of a third, as will be seen shortly.) Following a brief foray of clashing suspensions and temporary modulations, notably, again, on levels a third apart (this time in descending order: F–C♯–A, bars 265–76, Example 6.4), the music returns to F, though the upper melodic voice in bar 277 retains the presence of the dominant, A.

The structure reverts to the dominant at bar 285 after a slow, incremental chromatic ascent in the bass. It is at this point that that most common and necessary feature of tonal form takes place – the retransition, i.e. the build-up of tension upon the dominant harmony, which prepares the return to the tonic. That return marks what in essence, though in an idiosyncratic manner, serves as the recapitulation (Example 6.5).

Return, whether in sonata form, ABA form or other formal procedures, is not only a staple feature of tonal music but an important moment of delineation as well. It would be virtually derelict not to underline such a place by some special nuance, whether of high drama (think of Beethoven's Eighth Symphony, first movement), motivic by-play ('Eroica' Symphony, first movement), subtle musical disguise (the Brahms symphonies) or gentle flow of the music (Mozart, Piano Sonata in F major K. 332, second movement). Schumann does not fail in this regard. The intense

---

[9]  Marc Andreae's article (1984) contains much interesting information on the origins of the Symphony, as does the commentary by Egon Voss (1980) in the Goldmann/Schott edition of the score.

Example 6.5 Fourth Symphony, I, bars 285–338: dominant preparation (bars 285ff.), return to the tonic region (bar 297), 'angular' treatment of the theme (bars 313ff.) and initiation of the coda (bars 337ff.)

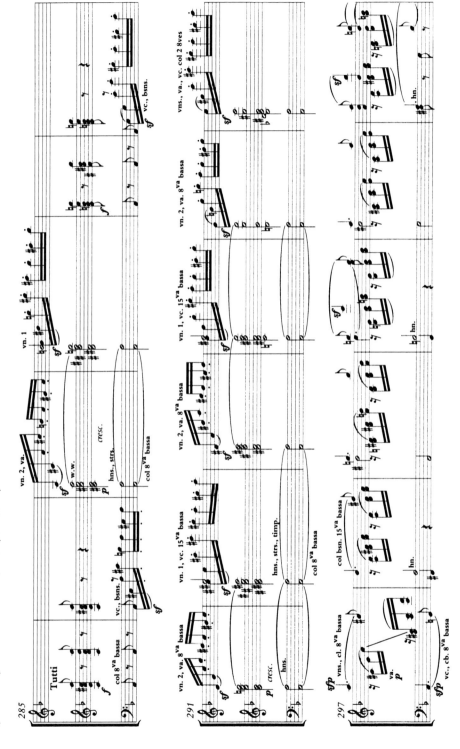

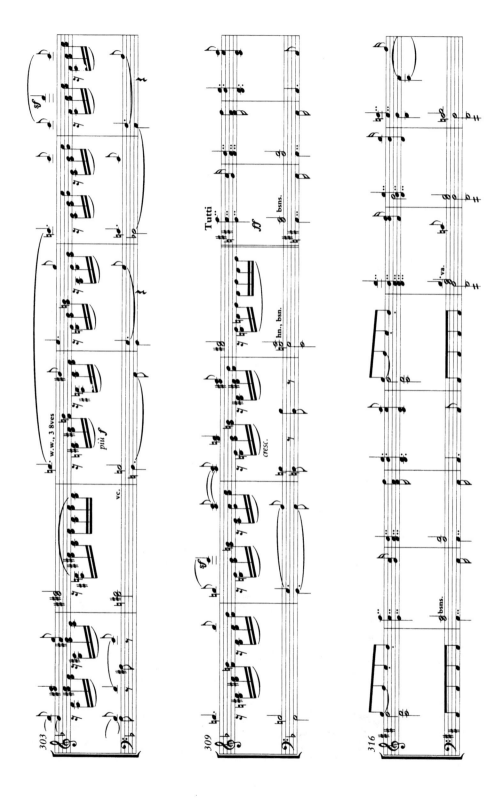

crescendo over the dominant pedal point that these twelve bars embody makes powerful and inevitable the return to the tonic at bar 297.

That return is curious in two respects. For one, we do not find the initial theme of the exposition at this place, a procedure which by and large is *de rigueur* for recapitulation. What we do hear is a largely new theme – strange indeed at this most important of moments, a moment which so often in the great literature is one of recognition. Secondly, what follows this point of return bears little relation to the norms of recapitulation, for no second thematic group arrives, nor does a closing group. Instead the music expands upon the new theme, driving it to a more angular and marked character (bar 313). The movement then closes with a coda based on the opening theme of the Lebhaft (bar 337). (See again Example 6.5.)

The form is thus idiosyncratic, though anomaly with respect to form is itself not infrequently something of a norm. High-level creativity hardly follows rulebooks; intuition, much along the lines discussed earlier in these pages, is the guiding force in shaping the music.[10] The formal logic would seem to stem from some element of the work which is sensed as unique and significant, the consequent musical path dictated by properties intrinsic to that element itself.[11]

[10]   The intuition that seems to have inspired not only the anomalous properties of return in the first movement of this Symphony, but also the key schemes found in its development, appears to have been characterised by fantasy, in the sense of 'imagination', which informs the German equivalent of that word. Though the key schemes arise from the core motivic interval of the first movement, a practice which is hardly unprecedented in tonal music (I discuss this matter extensively in Epstein 1979), the manner by which tonal levels are distributed and established reflects an imaginative embodiment of this motivic aspect of structure. Certainly the idiosyncratic way in which tonal return and 'recapitulation' are effected is an imaginative extension of the principles inherent in sonata form as an earlier generation of composers embraced this concept. Could, in fact, this imaginative transformation of the recapitulation principle have stimulated the thinking of the then young Brahms, with his close ties to the Schumann family, who would later develop his own original, indeed idiosyncratic, usage of recapitulation as a 'disguised' moment of return, a point of beclouded demarcation?
        The role of fantasy is made explicit on the title page of the 1851 revision of the Schumann score, which bears the description 'Symphonistische Phantasie für grosses Orchester. Skizzirt im J. 1841. Neu instrumentirt 1851.' (See Voss 1980: 143.)

[11]   Compare Haydn's Symphony No. 104, the slow movement of which would be difficult to classify: its tight construction is self-evident, but its mode of organisation fits no conventional pattern, though elements of sonata form, also of ternary form, are present. Similarly, the final movement of Beethoven's 'Eroica' Symphony finds its own formal path. The causative factor in this case – increasing rhythmic activity in the initial three, classically orientated variations – pushes the music towards a degree of rhythmic complexity which cannot continue indefinitely. The solution that Beethoven finds heads the music in new directions which, though they retain compositional premises, engender formal structures seemingly without precedent. (See Epstein 1979: 188–91 for a detailed discussion of this aspect of the movement.)
        Two examples of this same tendency towards formal uniqueness, the initial movements of Schubert's Symphony No. 5 and Mozart's Piano Sonata in C major K. 545, ply their way within the confines of conventional sonata form. In each case, however, the recapitulation breaks with standard practice by eschewing the return to the tonic, settling instead in the subdominant. Formal logic, indeed formal parallelism, seems to lie behind this scheme. By retaining in the recapitulation the conventional tonal practice of exposition sections, i.e. the second thematic group's move to a key centre lying a fifth above the first group, the music in both works thereby returns to the tonic.
        Tchaikovsky, in the initial movement of his Fourth Symphony in F minor, follows a somewhat similar path. The second group in the exposition, as per convention, lies in the tonal region of the relative major (A♭), though, unconventionally, in its minor mode. A similar scheme, with similar adjustments of mode, is followed in the recapitulation. This section arrives in the natural submediant (D minor – anomalously, the submediant of F *major*, despite the fact that the tonic is F *minor*). Via a parallelism of tonal design to that of the exposition, the second group of the recapitulation reestablishes the tonic. The generative factor here seems to be the interval of a minor third. Thus the second group of the exposition is in A♭, a minor third above the tonic, while the

Example 6.6    Fourth Symphony, I: antecedent version (bars 147–50) of the melody heard at the recapitulation in bars 297ff.

What is not idiosyncratic about Schumann's Symphony, and what is most important about recapitulation, as Heinrich Schenker with his insight into tonal music pointed out numerous times, is the return of the music to the tonic. Tension, generated by a musical voyage through distant tonal realms, is resolved at this moment of reprise by reunion with the central reference frame of tonality. This aspect of tonal return is indeed part of Schumann's Fourth Symphony. That powerful return, above all else, suggests that bar 297 is the movement's recapitulation.

Schumann's return is not unequivocal, however. It is, if anything, paradoxical. Though the tonal framework embraces the tonic, the resolution of tension that this moment normally embodied in the tonal music of earlier eras is absent. Foreground harmonies in the passage are unstable, moving through secondary regions of the key (itself now changed to the major mode) and going so far afield at one point (bars 307–8) as to strain matters tonal to some degree. The dominant pedal point underlying the theme in its 'angular' version (bar 313) further denies resolution. Nor does the tonic pedal (bars 321ff.) that grounds the extension of this angular theme allow the music to relax, for over it there is a complex and dissonant play of harmonies. It is not until the coda (bar 337) that a 'true', or full, sense of tonal resolution arrives.

Ambiguity of perception is thus forced upon us by Schumann's musical language. We hear the moment of return as rooted in the tonic, yet that very tonic remains unresolved. As a consequence, the music pushes ever forward, its impulse, indeed its musical feeling, essentially controlled by this sophisticated harmonic scheme.

The 'largely new theme' occurring at bar 297 (see again Example 6.5) further clouds the matter of recapitulation. Return, so characteristic a feature of recapitulation, is found here only in a *tonal* sense, albeit not definitively. If *thematic* return is not to be found, however, is our expectation of recapitulation, indeed its perception, thereby diminished?

There is in fact a return of thematic material, though it is cast in the context of Schumann's idiosyncratic form. The melody at bar 297 is an extended variant of a theme encountered more than once in the development (bars 147 and 221; see Example 6.6). In a deeper sense we have been hearing these and all other themes continually, for they are an outgrowth of the central motivic shape of the movement – in fact, of the entire Symphony: the interval of a third, and its complementary shape, a

closing group and beginning of the development lie in B major, yet a minor third higher. The recapitulation in D minor carries this scheme a step further, as does the ultimate return to F. The minor third is structurally significant from the outset of the Symphony: it is the first interval defined by the opening horn call. I discuss this structure, as well as the tempo relations that bind together the entire Symphony, in Chapter 8 of Epstein 1995.

sixth. Schumann presents this shape in numerous ways, some of them shown in Example 6.7. The intervals are heard directly in some instances, elsewhere as filled in with passing and neighbour notes, as the brackets in Example 6.7 indicate. Occasionally the melodies are harmonised by their own motivic interval, the patterns constituting a distinctive part of the setting – hence the parallel sixths in the introduction, the parallel thirds in the folk-like second theme of the Lebhaft. The characteristic sound of the ubiquitous third/sixth interval – the work's primary motif – imparts to the 'new' theme at the recapitulation a sense that it is new only superficially, that it has been heard before.

The passage beginning at bar 297, despite its quirky characteristics, fulfils basic demands of return in music: the primary tonal region (the tonic) is once again established; the thematic material, though 'new', shares salient motivic properties with the central themes of the movement. It makes musical sense to hear this moment as that most central feature of tonal forms: return – indeed, return on a hierarchically significant level. Whether this return constitutes *bona fide* 'recapitulation' depends on one's view of how closely the form of the movement embraces – or must embrace – sonata form. Certainly the sonata *principle* is integral to the music, though invoked in unique fashion.

Viewed in terms of another criterion, that of full tonal resolution, the focal arrival point is postponed beyond bar 297. How distant is it? Does bar 313 serve the matter adequately? In some senses, yes. The reversion from 'wandering' harmonies to the unclouded perspective of D as tonic occurs here, further delineated by the 'angular' quality of the rhythm, the full orchestration, the *ff* dynamic. The pedal point on the dominant, however, robs these bars of true stability, thus enervating the sense of tonal closure, which does not arrive until bar 337, the coda. To feel *that* moment as the culminating point of the score, however, seems to fight nature; arrival is delayed too long.

The entire passage from bar 297 on can be seen in yet another context, one inherent in the ambiguous casting of its elements. It can be understood as an extension, a developmental culmination, of what has gone before. To wit: the earlier statements of the melody heard at the return, those segments lying at bars 147ff./159ff. and 221ff./233ff., are different in three critical respects: they form part of a *descending* sequence; they are registrally constrained; and they exist as four-bar melodic 'fragments', rather than fully treated melodies or themes. What happens at 297ff. creates a very different sense, one of aspiration, caused by the breaking-out and expansion of register, by the ascending progression and by the long-breathed, more lyrical treatment of the theme, its span increased to a full *sixteen*-bar period. This transformation of the material gives to 297ff. the sense of a new and exciting play on familiar materials, indeed a *reversal* of expectations which, along with the strong sense of aspiration, builds the intensity of this climactic passage.[12]

---

[12] I am indebted to John Rink for the insights contained in this paragraph, which were generously shared during the editing of this article.

Example 6.7  Fourth Symphony, I: opening theme from the introduction (bars 1–2), initial theme of the Lebhaft (bars 29ff.) and of the second thematic group (bars 60ff. and 73ff.), and initial theme of the closing group (bars 77ff.). Brackets designate structural intervals of thirds and sixths.

We are forced by the brilliance of Schumann's harmonic structure to feel the entire passage after bar 297 in all the perspectives seen above. Each phrase in this passage fulfils certain, but not all, degrees of expectation and closure associated with recapitulation and return. The power of tonal reprise at bar 297, however, lends this moment special force, particularly as it emerges from the strong crescendo on the dominant.

This discussion forms a backdrop for the issue at hand. If we hear bar 297 as the focal point of return, the *piano* character at that point, and in the fifteen bars that follow, can strike the listener as unsatisfying – and has done so with many musicians. There is an exhilaration felt at bar 297, for it serves as the climax of the twelve-bar retransition that crescendos to it. That exhilaration is further bound up with the moment that the bar in question demarcates – those qualities of return that we have just considered. The buoyancy of this moment extends beyond the arrival on the first beat of bar 297: it seems to fill the following sixteen bars as well – songful bars, of a youthful and joyous nature typical of Schumann the romantic in characteristic exuberance.

All of this argues against the *piano* dynamic that the composer indicates should prevail for the first phrase of the recapitulation. The ebullience here seems to cry out for a more intense, indeed louder level. Many conductors have in fact interpreted this passage as *forte*, among them George Szell, a leading Schumann interpreter.[13] Szell went further than this, intensifying the melody of the second phrase (bar 305) by having the cellos and first bassoon complete the melody (as opposed to Schumann's orchestration; see Example 6.8), and reinforcing the cello line by adding a few violas in unison, carefully blended in sonority.[14]

The fact that a conductor of Szell's stature viewed the recapitulation as an intense *forte*, as have other major maestros, does not make this interpretation 'right'. It does indicate, however, that distinguished musicians have felt a quality in the music which seems in contradiction to the score. That fact leads to the central questions of this enquiry. Why the soft dynamic in this passage? Was this the true character Schumann meant to convey? Or could there have been other reasons, possibly technical ones, which suggested this marking?

---

[13] Others include Krips (London Symphony – London CM 9211), Barenboim (Chicago Symphony – DG 2709-075), Furtwängler (Berlin Philharmonic – DG KL 27/31 and MGM/Heliodor H 25073), Klemperer (New Philharmonia – EMI CMS 7/636132) and Haitink (Amsterdam Concertgebouw – Philips 416 126-2). In the latter two performances, the conductors seem uncertain whether to play *forte* or only *poco forte*.

[14] As a young conductor working under Szell with the Cleveland Orchestra, I was privileged to have access to his scores and thus found these markings. Following Szell's practice, but extending it further, I have at times taken some second violins from their accompanying line at bars 297ff. and added them in unison with the first violins, thus making this passage sing all the more by its greater intensity. This is in keeping with Schumann's implicit indication that the melody at the reprise needs intensity: although in the 1841 version the second violins begin the melody at the reprise (bar 564 in Breitkopf & Härtel's 1891 edition – see note 8 above), they are doubled in the upper octave five notes later – at the B♮ – by the first violins.

It is interesting to compare Szell's emendations with Mahler's retouchings of the Schumann symphonies. (I have often wondered to what extent the markings in Szell's scores reflected those of Mahler; the opportunity to discuss this with him did not arise.) In his study of Mahler's re-scoring of these symphonies, Carner (1941: 105) points out that one of Mahler's devices for augmenting intensity in the strings was to transfer accompaniment figures to other string sections *divisi*, and to use the original section to support a melodic line in the higher strings.

Example 6.8 Fourth Symphony, I, bars 305–12, showing George Szell's changes in Schumann's orchestration at the recapitulation

Plate 6.1 Fourth Symphony, I: photographic reproduction of p. 71 of the autograph of the 1841 version, showing the recapitulation (fourth bar from the right). Note the dynamic markings of *mf* in the lower strings and *mf* altered by the composer to *f* in the second violins (the melody).

Plate 6.2   Fourth Symphony, I: enlargement of Plate 6.1, right-hand bars, string parts. Schumann's crossed-out 'm' (from the original 'mf') can be discerned, as can the darker, more intense character of these letters compared with other dynamic markings in the excerpt. Note also the word *divisi* in the second violins and the faint outlines of 'sf', possibly 'sfp', traceable under the first violin's high A.

The autograph of the first version of the Symphony (1841) reveals a very different view of the passage at bar 297, one which indicates that the composer, in his earlier view of the work, unequivocally wished the passage to be intense in its dynamics. Where Schumann placed a *sfp* under the violins and clarinets (the carriers of the melody) in the later version, he marked a *mf* in the second violins (which alone play the melody – the firsts and clarinets have rests) in the first version. (See the photograph of the 1841 score in Plate 6.1.)[15] The *mf*, moreover, also appears in the

15   The autograph of the first version of the score (1841) is in the Nachlaß von Johannes Brahms at the Gesellschaft der Musikfreunde in Vienna. I am indebted to the Robert-Schumann-Gesellschaft of Düsseldorf

lower strings, which bear the bulk of sound in the passage, suggesting that the *p*, found only in sparsely scored winds, may pertain to balance and/or timbre, not to the fundamental intensity of the phrase. Yet more interesting is the fact that at the *mf* of the second violins, the *m* is crossed out, leaving the *f* clearly in view.

Some further points bear on this matter. Immediately following the *mf*-turned-*f* in the second violin line is a word which at first glance appears to be 'dim', though in handwriting somewhat obscure. Were this the case, the direction would seem contradictory, an impediment to a phrase to be played with intensity. An enlargement of the score puts this matter to rest. As seen in Plate 6.2, the word, in Schumann's hand, is '*divisi*', which makes sense, as the violins here play in octaves. Equally interesting is the rather obscure indication lying under the first violins at this place. The writing is very light, possibly in pencil, seemingly partly erased. Two letters in this marking are clear, namely '*sf*'. Following them is a yet fainter indication, which appears to be the outward curve of the letter '*p*', with the vertical stroke of the letter missing.

'*Sf*', possibly '*sfp*'. Could this be the origin of the marking found at this juncture in the 1851 version of the score? As for the earlier version, the context of this indication, under a single note which ends a previous line, suggests that the composer wished a certain articulation, possibly an expressive one, as *sfp* (or even *sf*, the unequivocally clear letters here) often connotes. As such the high A of the first violins, eliding with the downbeat of the new phrase, would reinforce that downbeat, thereby helping to launch the romantic, singing melody of the second violins.

The intensity of the handwriting at this place is three-tiered, possibly indicating successive considerations of the phrase, if not, in fact, the evolution of a concept. The dynamic markings for the lower strings and the winds appear to have been made with normal pressure, consistent with the appearance of all else on the page. The *mf*-turned-*f* is notably darker, suggesting not only a revised view that the melody must be more intense but, further, that this view itself may have been felt with some intensity (conviction?), leading to an entry made via more pressure on the pen. The '*sf* [*p*?]' may have been entered and then erased. An afterthought? A fillip later considered unnecessary, excessive?

Whatever the history of these markings, it is clear that Schumann initially felt this passage as we have suggested it − a singing melody at *forte* level.[16] The 1851 version further indicates that a growing intensity is part of the long-range character of the passage, for the second phrase is marked '*più f*' (bar 305), and six bars later, at bar 311, a two-bar crescendo leads to the *ff* of the angular version of the theme found at bar 313.

for making a photograph of this part of the 1841 score available to me, including an enlargement of the page of the score containing the earlier counterpart of bar 297. My particular thanks to Dr Bernhard Appel for his help and interest in this matter, and for his illuminating observations about Schumann's handwriting in the dynamic markings in this bar, which are discussed below. The Gesellschaft der Musikfreunde, Vienna, kindly gave permission to reproduce the excerpt in Plate 6.1.

16   The published score of the 1841 version did not observe Schumann's revised manuscript marking of *f* for the second violins at the reprise (bar 564, p. 35), nor did it include the *divisi* specified in the same bar. Instead, the dynamic indication in the second violin part remained *mf*, and the entire section played only the upper line of the octave *divisi* found in the autograph.

Schumann's initial sense of how the recapitulation should go (whatever the reasoning that led to the *sfp* marking in the later version), considered together with the large-scale growth in dynamics over the two phrases that precede the *ff* at bar 313, suggests an alternative view of this passage – which occurs at so critical a juncture in the score. They imply that the entire segment from bars 297 to 313 may have been felt with the intense, singing *forte* character discussed above. If, however, there was to be a clearly marked crescendo towards the climactic *ff* of bar 313, common musical practice would dictate that the players start 'softer' in order to have room to swell to a true *fortissimo*. Hence the element of *piano* in the indication at bar 297 (if, that is, it was not intended simply as an *espressivo* nuance).

If this view is convincing, it yields a yet broader picture of the music, one which supports the case for playing the full passage from bars 297 to 313 in the *forte* manner suggested above. The critical issue here is what a crescendo, in its deepest sense, truly means. Interpreted narrowly, it obviously indicates an increase in loudness. In a broader sense, however, it connotes more than just a growth in dynamics, or levels of soft and loud. Rather it suggests what German musicians would term a *Steigerung*, a continually mounting sense of overall intensity. Such a *Steigerung* would involve every element of the music – sound, timbre, dynamics, registration, instrumental doublings and other features of orchestration, and, far from least, the affective sense of the music, to which all elements contribute.

This sense of *Steigerung* fits the Schumann score, reflecting both the growth in dynamics, indicated by the *più f* of bars 305ff. (the second phrase of the recapitulation) and the ultimate *ff* at bar 313, and the exploitation of the full orchestra's power (see again bar 313), including brass and timpani which have not been heard since the arrival at the recapitulation in bar 297. Furthermore, and this perhaps is the central point of our discussion, the wandering harmonies, the destabilising pedal points, the clear but unresolved sense of the tonic that underlies the broad swathe of the music from recapitulation to coda – all these elements contribute to the powerful mounting of intensity that finds its fullest resolve, its high point, at bar 337, the start of the coda.

Seen in this perspective, the passage at bar 297 (the recapitulation) seems to call for a *forte* level. The need for the music to have room to grow in intensity has been accommodated by the composer not in terms of dynamics alone, but through the total language of the music, which makes inevitable this mounting pressure so often associated with dynamics and crescendos in their narrow sense. The *Steigerung* is thus the result of all elements of the music, which drive it ever forward.

The *sfp* plays a still greater role, if the music is viewed in this light: it becomes an expressive accent which serves two functions. One of these is to demarcate the peak of the crescendo, a crescendo which extends over the entire dominant preparation. The arrival at this peak is a moment of excitement, the summit of the retransition, as well as the critical point of return.

This climactic point, moreover, is structurally an elision – a melding of the incremental crescendo that precedes it with the inception of the intense, singing melody that begins on this note. The *sfp* thus fulfils a second function, that of an impulse to set the new songful phrase on its way. Such an impulse, or expressive accent, is not only reasonable at this point but almost a necessity. Not to designate the moment in this way would risk its being passed by, performed as 'just another' phrase.

Upon reflection, the predicament (if such it was) that faced Schumann and that may have engendered the *sfp* in 1851 seems palpable. Given contemporary conventions for expressive markings, how indeed could one mark this moment? A *f* or *ff* alone would be misleading; either would connote climax, but not necessarily a sense of accent-as-impetus, thereby beginning the new phrase. *Forte espressivo* might do, as could *espressivo* alone, though neither fully covers the implications of this complex nuance. *Cantando* would be inadequate to convey the multiple connotations of the phrase. *Passionato* might be excessive and would, like *cantando*, fail to purvey the multiple facets of this moment. No one marking would be adequate.[17]

This discussion touches upon some of the deepest implications of compositional craft – and some of its more elusive dilemmas. Craft viewed on this level, a level of manifest control at the service of musical expression, with all the complexities and perplexities that this involves, is both the seedbed and the progenitor of significant composition.

The discussion has also portrayed the close link between structure and affect. The initial sense that the passage at the reprise should be played *forte* was an *emotional* response, which suggests that affects may have their own sense of logic, that they may be bound to each other by 'rules', ordering, relationship – by some mode (non-lexical, probably non-linguistic) of syntax. Is this the domain of intuition?

Analytical logic was called upon secondarily in this process; how the passage might go, how one's sense of it might be justified, were examined in terms of structure. The exercise revealed further complexities – the ambiguous, multi-tiered treatment of material in the reprise, which cast the music in varying states of tension and resolution. That ambiguity yields different perceptions, thereby different ways to shape the phrases. Interpretative choice is demanded.

In these manifold ways the intuitive feeling of the music, indissolubly tied to the formal embodiment of structural detail, causes the shaping of structure concurrently to shape the affective sense of the music's flow. Perceiving that flow, understanding the structural forces allied with it, seem elemental preconditions for interpretation.

---

[17]   A later generation – Mahler, Strauss – might have appended detailed notes to the score.

### REFERENCES

Andreae, M., 1984: 'Die vierte Symphonie Robert Schumanns, ihre Fassungen, ihre Interpretationsprobleme', in *Robert Schumann – Ein romantisches Erbe in neuer Forschung*, ed. Robert-Schumann-Gesellschaft Düsseldorf [*sic*] (Mainz: Schott), pp. 35–41.

Carner, M., 1941: 'Mahler's re-scoring of the Schumann symphonies', *The Music Review* 2/2: 97–110.

Epstein, D., 1979: *Beyond Orpheus: Studies in Musical Structure* (Cambridge, Massachusetts: MIT Press).

1989: 'Ein Problem in Schumanns 4. Sinfonie d–Moll und Perspektiven zu einer Lösung', in G. Nauhaus, ed., *Schumann-Studien 2* (Zwickau: Rat der Stadt Zwickau), pp. 32–7.

1995: *Shaping Time: Music, the Brain, and Performance* (New York: Schirmer Books/ Macmillan).

Gazzaniga, M. S., 1992: *Nature's Mind* (New York: Basic Books).

Hanslick, E., 1854: *Vom Musikalisch-Schönen* (Leipzig: R. Weigel).

Langer, S. K., 1948: *Philosophy in a New Key* (New York: Mentor).

1953: *Feeling and Form* (New York: Scribner).

1967: *Mind: An Essay on Human Feeling*, 3 vols. (Baltimore: Johns Hopkins Press).

Mazziotta, J. C., Phelps, M. E., Carson, R. E. and Kuhl, D. E., 1982: 'Tomographic mapping of human cerebral metabolism: auditory stimulation', *Neurology* 32/9: 921–37.

Petsche, H., Lindner, K., Rappelsberger, P. and Gruber, G., 1989: 'Die Bedeutung des EEG für die Musikpsychologie', in H. Petsche, ed., *Musik-Gehirn-Spiel* (Basel: Birkhäuser Verlag), pp. 111–34.

Petsche, H., Rappelsberger, P. and Pockberger, H., 1985: 'Musikrezeption, EEG und musikalische Vorbildung', *Zeitschrift für EEG-EMG* 16/4: 183–90.

Restak, R. M., 1979: *The Brain* (New York: Warner Books).

Schopenhauer, A., [1818] 1947: 'Platonic idea and the object of art', trans. Y. H. Krikorian, in D. J. Bronstein, Y. H. Krikorian and P. P. Wiener, eds., *Basic Problems of Philosophy* (New York: Prentice Hall), pp. 439–51.

Sergent, J., 1993: 'Mapping the musician's brain', *Human Brain Mapping* 1: 20–38.

Shepherd, G. M., 1983: *Neurobiology* (New York: Oxford University Press).

Voss, E., 1980: 'Einführung und Analyse', in R. Schumann, *Symphony Nr. 4* (Munich and Mainz: Goldmann/Schott), pp. 131–208.

# CHAPTER SEVEN

# Beginning–ending ambiguity: consequences of performance choices

JANET M. LEVY

∎

## I

I begin with the premise that there can be no performance without some inter-pretation. In other words, except for wholly recorded compositions (e.g. computer-generated music) or improvisations unconstrained by tradition, every performance *is* an interpretation. Indeed we often use the words interchangeably.[1] For, however much a performer seeks to understand and convey what a composer intended, music – including the eighteenth- and nineteenth-century music to be the focus of this study – cannot be said entirely to 'speak for itself'.[2] Obvious behavioural evidence of this is that we might choose to listen to 'Norrington's Ninth' (read: Roger Norrington's interpretation of Beethoven's Ninth Symphony) rather than Leonard Bernstein's, Arturo Toscanini's and so on.

Just as every performance is an interpretation, every interpretation is either a performance or, when written as analysis and criticism, construable as a set of 'instruc-tions' for a performance, though seldom explicitly so. As Leonard Meyer (1973: 29) has written: 'The performance of a piece of music is . . . the actualization of an analytic act – even though such analysis may have been intuitive and unsystematic. For what a performer *does* is to make the relationships and patterns potential in the composer's score clear to the mind and ear of the experienced listener.' But which of the myriad 'relationships and patterns' (surely never all in a single performance), on what basis and to what degree? Most importantly, with what consequences for the way in which experienced listeners apprehend a musical work or part of a work?

My general concern in this essay is with two kinds of consequentiality which exist symbiotically: consequences of interpretation for performance, and consequences of performers' choices – whether made intuitively or deliberately – for experienced

---

[1]  We commonly say things like 'in X's interpretation' but mean 'in X's performance', and vice versa.

[2]  The ongoing aesthetic debate as to whether music can and does speak for itself or whether some kind of interpretation is always involved dates back to the early nineteenth century, when the roles of the performer and the composer became separated (see Taruskin 1982: 338–49). Here I can simply position myself in the debate rather than enter into it.

listeners' understanding.[3] My specific concern is with the performer's power to communicate those functional ambiguities that arise when a passage in music could be a
beginning or an ending – whether the very beginning or the very ending (themselves of course often elusive moments), or one or the other along the way, that is,
of a section of a composition, at some structural level.

For most of us, the fascination of beginnings and endings needs no justification:
how, when and where they take place have been and continue to be deeply compelling subjects – in religion, science, psychology, aesthetics and so on. But there seems
to be less agreement about the subject of ambiguity, especially about whether
ambiguity can be aesthetically valuable.[4] Indeed, except for the realm of harmonic
function, it is only recently that musical ambiguity might, colloquially, be said to have
'come out of the closet' as a subject.[5] When Leonard Bernstein (1976) boldly entitled
one of his Charles Eliot Norton lectures 'The delights and dangers of ambiguity', he
doubtless knew he would sound iconoclastic. In general much music theory and
analysis has concerned itself with attempts to 'disambiguate' ambiguous meanings of
musical events or passages in which one or more alternative interpretations appear
possible. This is especially true in harmonic analysis, where the graphing and charting
of harmonic progressions and voice-leading are aided by arriving at a single unequivocal reading.

Often the concept of ambiguity itself seems ambiguous, partly because the term
tends to be loosely applied to anything 'susceptible of multiple interpretations',[6] as
some dictionaries have it. And though it is fashionable these days to make the critical
act somehow mirror the attributes of the art work(s) being studied – e.g. an essay
about fragments in painting and sculpture may self-reflectively assume a fragmentary
character – my aim is quite the opposite. I mean to use the notion of ambiguity
unambiguously, and, in distinguishing several kinds of beginning–ending ambiguities,
I hope to call attention to the performer's power to shape the listener's experience.

I shall use the notion of ambiguity not as synonymous or interchangeable with
uncertainty or vagueness, as many do, but as a *sub*class of uncertainty, and diametrically

---

[3]  By 'experienced listener' I mean one who has internalised the constraints of the style. Hereafter 'listener'
     means an experienced one.

[4]  For example, in a largely sympathetic review of my 1982 monograph *Beethoven's Compositional Choices*, Bruce
     Campbell (1985: 193) objects to my suggestion that certain passages are rich in ambiguity:

     > Of course, ambiguity in music does not really exist. Some musical phenomena can be understood in
     > several ways . . . but surely one of the functions of analytical insight is to show how all but one of the
     > apparent or 'theoretical' possibilities are artistically untenable in a given context . . . Certainly, the
     > performers have to decide where the music is going (how does one perform ambiguously?), and the
     > composer *had* to know where he was going.

     Responding to Campbell, Carolyn Abbate and Roger Parker write: 'the reviewer's implication is that
     Beethoven wrote music that is unambiguous (and therefore good)' (1989: 3).

[5]  To my knowledge, there has been no sustained critical discussion of ambiguity in music comparable, say, to
     William Empson's ([1930] 1947) pioneering study of ambiguity in literature. With the exception of Meyer
     (1956), the subject barely surfaces in discussions of music until the 1970s, and then it is largely centred on
     metric/rhythmic ambiguity. For relatively recent attention to the subject of musical ambiguity treated more
     broadly, see, for instance, Bernstein 1976, Berry 1976, Epstein 1979, Lerdahl and Jackendoff 1983, Thomson
     1983, Kramer 1988 and Agawu 1994.

[6]  Since this might be said of any non-absolutist position in aesthetic theory – and perhaps none more so than
     deconstructive literary theory – it is clearly too broad and, to my mind, too imprecise a definition to be useful.

opposed to vagueness. In his *Dictionary of Philosophy* ([1979] 1985: 11), Anthony Flew broadly defines ambiguity as 'the existence of two or more clearly different senses in the meaning of a word or expression', and he goes on to say: 'anyone claiming that a word or expression is ambiguous must, therefore, be ready to specify the senses that they wish to distinguish'.[7] To this we must add the dimension of time: a musical situation is ambiguous if at the same time, or very close in time, it gives rise to two or more specifiable meanings. The definitional requirement of at least two specifiable possibilities is necessary if we are to distinguish ambiguity from uncertainty, in which the multitude of conceivable meanings is so great that we are forced, as it were, to suspend grappling with them – we have to wait and see (hear!) which of an indeterminate number of meanings is or are primary.


## II

Example 7.1 shows the end of the Adagio introduction from the first movement of Haydn's Symphony No. 94 in G major ('Surprise'), and what we read as the beginning of the movement proper, marked 'Vivace assai' by Haydn in bar 17. Few who look at the score would question that this is where the main part of the movement – the expected exposition of a sonata form – begins, despite the fact that 'the join is blurred' (Webster 1991: 163) by open sequential harmonies and the absence of a fermata at the end of the introduction. If, however, one listens to the 1951 recording by Wilhelm Furtwängler and the Vienna Philharmonic, there is some ambiguity as to where the Vivace assai does begin: instead of a decisive tempo change in bar 17, Furtwängler makes an accelerando from bar 17 to bar 21, emphasising the 'through-composed', 'run-on' character (Webster 1991: 163–4) of the composer's open treatment of harmony, rhythm and sound rather than his designated tempo boundary. The gradual acceleration to the new tempo (established with the *forte* tutti) makes bar 21 sound as though *it* may be the beginning of the exposition. One significant consequence of this local performance choice is to call into question the large-scale structural boundaries of the movement. Rather than *being* the beginning of the Vivace, in Furtwängler's performance the first four bars (starting with the second half of bar 17) are in some sense *becoming* the Vivace – a difference which of course reflects a nineteenth- rather than eighteenth-century attitude towards the world.

In addition to generating structural ambiguity, Furtwängler's interpretation – pushing forward, flowing through – has the perhaps paradoxical effect of weakening the *composed* openness of bars 17–21. That is, the conductor's progressive tempo change (his well-known 'tempo modification') tends to focus attention on the goal (the tutti harmonic arrival at bar 21) and to distract attention from what is happening in the process of getting there. As a result, the force of the contrast at bar 21 is

---

[7]   I thank Kofi Agawu for calling Flew's definition of 'ambiguity' to my attention.

   In this context 'be ready to specify' means only that if the listener is articulate about such matters he or she will be able to specify the alternative meanings involved in an ambiguity. Such specification is not literally required; rather, the several 'senses' must in some experiential way be distinguish*able*, specifi*able*.

Example 7.1   Haydn, Symphony No. 94 in G major, I, bars 16–24

undermined. This interpretation of Haydn's beginning as emergent has consequences, too, for our apprehension of certain formal relationships, simply because the identity of bars 17–21 is not marked as an entity as it would be in a single tempo (e.g. in the 1981 recording by Colin Davis and the Concertgebouw Orchestra).

Another paradoxical consequence of Furtwängler's accelerando at the 'beginning' of the Vivace is that on the one hand he introduces ambiguity with respect to a large-scale structural boundary where presumably none is called for, and on the other he reduces, if not obliterates, the possibility that listeners will experience conflict between metric organisation and melodic structure. The passage might be heard as if it began on a downbeat rather than an upbeat and ended with a rhythmic stretch of one beat before the cadence at the tutti (see the alternative readings of the metric structure below the score). But the experience of metric/melodic conflict requires a reasonable regularity of pulse, and a performance such as Furtwängler's greatly reduces the possibility of that experience.

Although in this performance it is the conductor who creates ambiguity, the kind of musical ambiguity on which I shall now focus – ambiguity about whether a musical gesture or phrase unit is a beginning or an ending – can be regarded as part of the *composer's* plan. And in the performer's interpretation of that plan, often the simplest local details have enormous capacity for affecting the 'life' of the ambiguity. Again and again the most fundamental aspects of performance (slower/faster, louder/softer – either suddenly or gradually; tiny hesitations versus rushings forward; agogic or dynamic stresses; points of attack and so on) are involved in conveying separation versus connection, event versus process. There is little new here. What I hope is new and provocative are the reasons for the immense communicative power of such performance details in the realisation of functional ambiguities.

### III

One class of composed functional ambiguities whose realisation is contingent on performance is that of witty *double entendres*. The listener's apprehending of, and delight in, *double entendres* depends not only on the recognition of certain elements of conventional succession – their 'proper' or normal arrangement – but also on their precise timing, which can transform an otherwise ordinary passage into subtle and witty play. To take a highly instructive example: imagine what would happen to the famous 'joke' at the end of Haydn's Quartet Op. 33 No. 2, fourth movement, if the performers held back in any way in the very last phrase (see Example 7.2).[8] There have already been several playfully thwarted attempts to close the movement. After a four-bar silence, the opening two-bar phrase makes yet another appearance at bars 171–2. The preceding play with what will follow – and when – has made a game of predicting the next musical event. Will the piece close *this* time? Given the immediate context, 'the joke of Haydn's departing gesture is . . . not simply that the opening phrase

---

8   So far, I have found only one recorded performance which tampers with Haydn's ultimate joke: the 1964 recording by the Janáček Quartet introduces a ritenuto on the final upbeat to downbeat in the last phrase.

Example 7.2    Haydn, String Quartet in E♭ major Op. 33 No. 2 ('Joke'), IV, bars 1–8 and 148–72

contradicts presumed closure, but that this beginning implies a continuation of even more outrageous manipulation than those heard previously' (Wheelock 1992: 12).[9]

Obviously, if we interpret the final gesture this way, the joke will be spoilt by holding back and concomitantly emphasising the last beat, for, as a natural sign of closure, any slowing will weaken the implied continuation.[10] In a similar vein, if the expressive character to be communicated at the very end of Beethoven's Bagatelle in C major Op. 33 No. 2 is excessive mechanical continuation (as I believe it is), then the humour so created will depend significantly on a straightforward, uninflected performance, with no hint of braking.[11]

The witty play on beginning–ending ambiguity in the trio of Mozart's 'Jupiter' Symphony (Example 7.3) is surely at the heart of the musical discourse of this movement and may be the quintessential example of 'an ambiguity between closing profile and opening process' (Kramer 1988: 146).[12] To varying degrees, the functional ambiguity can be made manifest or obscured in performance; that is, performance nuances can be crucial in the communication – or not – of the movement's syntactic ambiguities.

As Leonard Ratner (1980: 39) neatly puts it, 'the cadence [at the beginning of the trio] never seems to find its proper place; it is used for everything *but* a point of arrival, and this seems to be the point of the trio – to put the cadence out of countenance'. In performance there are several critical moments for conveying Mozart's play on 'normal' syntactic relationships. The first and most obvious involves the temporal relation between the end of the minuet and the beginning of the trio.[13] For if one of the ambiguous elements – the possibility that the trio's opening cadence is an echo of the minuet's close[14] – is to be realised, then even a single beat's delay between the

---

9   See also Wheelock 1992: 10–13 and Levy 1992: 232–4.

10  After formulating these ideas about the end of the 'Joke' Quartet, I was surprised – but, obviously, unpersuaded – to find a diametrically opposite viewpoint in Keller 1986: 71. About the performance of the last phrase, Keller writes that 'a subtle combination of a *ritardando* and a *ritenuto* makes perfect sense: it does define the end and, at the same time, points to the fact that this needn't have been the end . . .' I am not sure how disagreements of this sort can be readily resolved since they rest on differences in critical interpretation. I have gone even further (Levy 1992: 239) in the interpretative stance I take here by noting that the performers may continue Haydn's game by delaying putting their bows down.

11  As I suggest in Levy 1992: 233–4, my view in cases such as this regarding the relationship of interpretation to performance goes against the grain of most training. That is, being 'expressive' in this context entails being deliberately rigid – inexpressive, as it were.

12  There are of course numerous instances of archetypal closing gestures used to open movements (e.g. in Haydn's string quartets, the second movement of Brahms's Sonata in G major Op. 78 for Violin and Piano, and so on) but usually they are not ambiguous, either because they do not fully close until late in the movement, or, more to the point in the context of the 'Jupiter' trio, they are unequivocal beginnings and listeners will suspend disbelief: if the piece is just beginning it cannot be ending. The more archetypal the closing shape, the more playful – or tensional – the out-of-place uses may be, and perhaps the more 'ambivalence' generated. See, among others, Rosen 1971: 78 and passim; Meyer 1973: 214–17; Levy 1981; Wheelock 1992: 98–110 and passim.

13  Elaine Sisman (1993: 66) makes the interesting point that the trio's opening cadence figure 'resolves, in register and instrumentation, the chromatic wind passage in the minuet, in which the leading tone in bar 51 never went to the tonic'. If apprehended as such, the cadential aspect of the opening of the trio is enhanced. In discussing the use of the 'inverted ending–beginning order' as a rhetorical device (: 67), she points out that this cadence figure is 'like a cart' (as in the proverbial 'cart before the horse') in having 'no power to move by itself'.

14  See also Ratner 1970: 359–60.

two sections (as in Nikolaus Harnoncourt's recording with the Concertgebouw Orchestra) can weaken, if not virtually destroy, this meaning.[15]

The second critical moment occurs at the phrase beginning with the upbeat to bar 3 of the trio. This is of course a more 'normal' opening gesture. The fourfold occurrence of the cadence figure (bars 1–2 and 5–6, and their repeat), with the more normal antecedent phrase (bars 3–4, with upbeat) in second rather than first place, creates a continuous tape-loop effect. The resulting ambiguity – whether the cadence figure is the end and/or the beginning of a phrase-group (see the brackets in Example 7.3) – will surely be affected if one of the functions is emphasised at the other's expense. This happens in the recording by Franzjosef Maier and the Collegium Aureum: a slight delay between the upbeat to bar 3 and the following downbeat, a slurring of the two-note upbeat and a light stress on the F♯ make bar 3 seem like a beginning. Such a performance obscures one of the conflicting meanings: namely, the possibility that the cadence figure will be heard not merely as an echo, i.e. an ending, but also as a beginning. That is, in this performance the cadence figure tends to sound only like a close. Yet the recurrence of highly conventionalised functions in displaced order would seem to invite a revelling in the ambiguity. Indeed, the ambiguity intensifies as we go round and round, uncertain whether the cadence gesture is ending or beginning a phrase (especially in bars 3–6, and bar 7 through the repeated bar 2).

In the second part of the trio, the moment of return (bar 21) might lead the connoisseur listener to do a double take, at least in retrospect. This third critical moment, too, is a structural juncture which can be made more or less ambiguous in performance, for the return 'comes as a circle-of-fifths sequential outgrowth' (Kramer 1988: 146) of a process begun in bar 17. In other words, the return is at once a regular continuation and final stage of a process *and* the beginning of restatement. A ritardando taken as the sequence approaches the return will weaken the effect of the overlap of continuity and articulation; so too, of course, will any articulative break. The experience of the cadence figure's double function at bar 21 is easily undermined in performance since, after all, Mozart articulates the return here by the block change in instrumentation (strings to woodwinds) and by the abrupt halt (removal) of the oom-pah-pah accompaniment pattern of the retransition.[16] This composed articulation itself places a stark spotlight on the perversity of the cadence figure.[17]

A surprising performance – surprising, that is, compared with his reading of the rest of this movement, which does realise other playful functional ambiguities – is that of Fritz Reiner and the Chicago Symphony Orchestra, in which a ritardando at bars

[15]    Among fifteen performances sampled, however, only Harnoncourt's noticeably delays the beginning of the trio in this way. The recording by Fritz Reiner and the Chicago Symphony Orchestra is a good example of a performance which does realise the beginning–ending ambiguity at the juncture.

[16]    This is also a witty inversion of more normal textural functions. Typically, an oom-pah-pah accompaniment is a sign of presentation, not transition. (See Levy 1982: 489–97.) In addition, one might consider Mozart's treatment of texture here a kind of textural-rhetorical conceit of the 'cart before the horse' type (see note 13).

[17]    'Perverse' not only in its functionally inverted position but also in its internal counter-cumulative durational relationships, which are unusual for such a cadence.

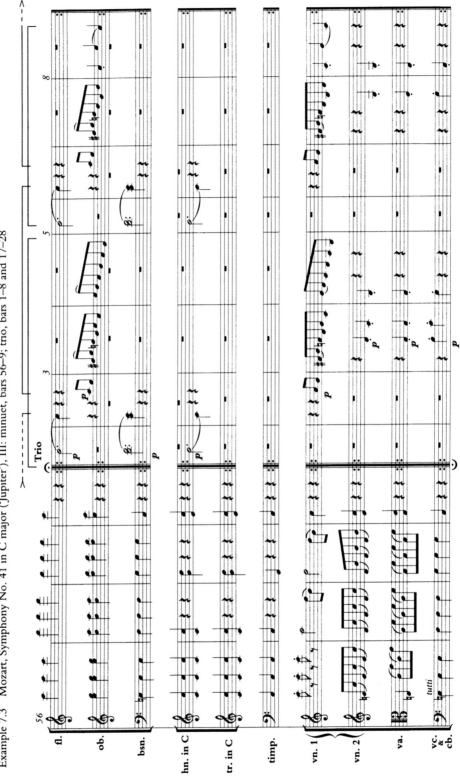

Example 7.3   Mozart, Symphony No. 41 in C major ('Jupiter'), III: minuet, bars 56–9; trio, bars 1–8 and 17–28

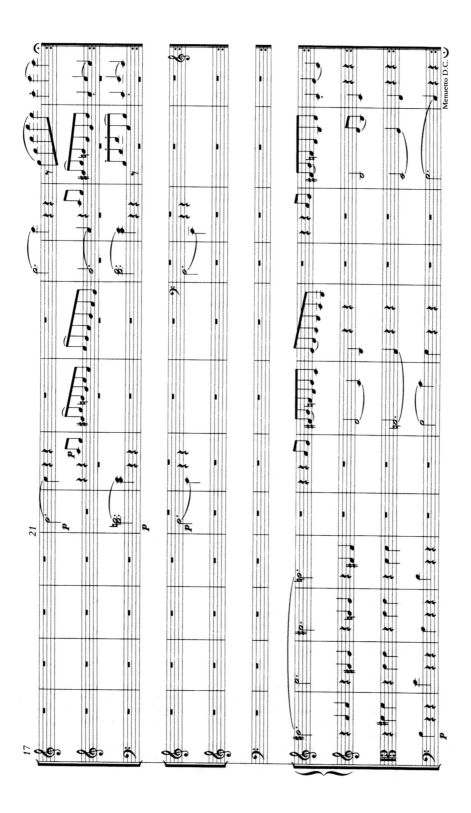

Menuetto D.C.

19–20 privileges the impending articulation (the return at bar 21) over the processive sequential continuity into the return. The result is that the effect of return as outgrowth is partly lost. Once again, the simplest of performance nuances has a higher-level consequence: it weakens the *double entendre* at a nodal moment – return – in Mozart's play. What is critical in letting such an ambiguity 'live' in performance is to recognise *both* functions so that *both* can be communicated.[18]

IV

In the 'Jupiter' trio, beginning–ending ambiguity arises from a playful permutation of musical events which normally follow one another in immediate succession. Sometimes, however, such ambiguity – and its full realisation in performance – involves the recognition of relationships separated in time. This is the case in the first movement of Beethoven's Eighth Symphony. In his commentary on the movement, Sir George Grove ([1898] 1962: 291) writes that 'after a few bars of alternate strings and wind, the end is reached, with great point, by the soft repetition of the identical six notes with which it started', but with *what* point he never says. Donald Tovey (1935: 64), another of the few critics I have found who remarks on the meaning of this close, refers to it simply as a 'comic quiet ending'. Surely, however, an important part of the point here is that the ending is a musical pun on the beginning.

A pun, as defined by Mahadev Apte (1985: 179), is 'a play on words [which] involves the use of homonyms in a single context in which only one meaning is appropriate, while the other meaning may appear so only by extension or by association and in some instances may seem incongruent'. The *sine qua non* is that the words or, in this context, musical events resemble one another in sound but differ in meaning. Of course this is easier when semantic meaning is present. In the absence of semantic reference – as in musical puns like Mozart's at the beginning of the 'Jupiter' trio – the double meaning must be based on discrepancy between function and placement. Thus musical puns are closely bound to syntax: the meaning created by conventionalised syntactic order must in some way be understood if a listener is to savour a musical pun.

---

[18]    George Szell's recording with the Cleveland Orchestra comes closer to communicating both functions.
     The double meaning of bars 21–2 – outgrowth as well as beginning of return – suggests a useful comparison with linkage technique, where a beginning evolves from or grows out of an end, sometimes in a quite explicit manner. Brahms's music has numerous instances of such connections. Walter Frisch (1984: 15) describes linkage as the technique 'by which a "new" idea evolves spontaneously from a preceding one'. We are led in stages, so to speak, through the change in meaning of a musical gesture or event – first end, then beginning – as in the juncture between the end of the Allegretto quasi Menuetto and the beginning of the trio in the Sonata in E minor Op. 38 for Cello and Piano. In this example of linkage Brahms isolates the link, a quasi non-metric repeated motive, as a clear transition between the movement's two segments. (And, as always, differences in performance reflect different interpretations of the 'process and product' of the linkage.)
     While there is uncertainty as to when and how the new idea will appear, it would be difficult to speak of ambiguity in such a passage because the identity of the link – what its single function is – is clear, and a listener is not involved in choosing between a finite number of specifiable alternative continuations since there are in effect too many possible ones. This comparison helps, I think, to illuminate the difference between the experience of musical uncertainty and that of ambiguity.

The appropriate meaning of the motive in Beethoven's last two bars (see Example 7.4) is of course that of ending; everything immediately preceding has told us that the piece is closing. But, improbably, the phrase that ends the movement is the one that, from the very start, has functioned as a beginning (or else reiteratively, in a tensional process, as in the development). That it has the capacity for closure is something that has not yet been made manifest in the movement.[19] The unexpectedness is compounded because the continuation of the theme is *not* forthcoming. The ambiguity of the end of the movement, however, lies not only in the pun per se – for, on the basis of preceding events, hardly anyone could doubt that the movement is ending – but also in the sudden reappearance of the first phrase of the piece and its aborted continuation.

What sort of performance will best realise this interpretation? First, and very basically, to the extent that context and the change of dynamic level do not deny it, the sameness of the opening and closing motives must be clear if the pun is to be realised. This is not solely a matter of pitch and rhythm but significantly one of the identity of tempo and character. To capture most fully the wit of this ending pun, the gesture must seem offhand and understated – almost like a whispered aside. Such is the case, for example, in Arturo Toscanini's performance with the NBC Symphony Orchestra. Of course, the phrase is so well shaped and by now so familiar that, even somewhat transformed, it will still be recognisable, and for this reason the pun cannot be completely spoilt in performance.

But the degree of its realisation can vary enormously. In Leonard Bernstein's performance with the Vienna Philharmonic a sense of closure predominates because of the noticeable ritardando in the last two bars of the movement. The slowing, not indicated by Beethoven, intensifies the closural effect created by the decreasing dynamic level (which *is* notated), especially when combined with Bernstein's very clear realisation of the upward tonic triad in the flutes. Closure is underscored because, in a slower performance, the internal rhythmic structure of the motive is apprehended as directed to the downbeat's arrival in the last bar. The emphasis is on arrival, rather than the open-ended incompleteness of the statement.

By comparison, the faster the tempo – as in Toscanini's performance – the more the weak beats at the end of the penultimate bar will be tied to the accents that *precede* them, and will sound less like upbeats leading to the downbeat in the last bar. The tempo modifications also alter the degree of similarity and thus the clarity of the dual function and meaning. If the pun is to be most vividly projected, then the end must seem somewhat open, as if stopped in its tracks halfway through a complete sentence – something less possible in Bernstein's performance than in Toscanini's.[20]

[19] It is interesting to compare this with, say, the opening gesture of Haydn's String Quartet in G major Op. 33 No. 5 and what happens to that gesture in the course of the first movement. From the outset, we know, on stylistic grounds, that the beginning is a closing gesture. So, when the gesture is used for closure as early as the end of the first phrase and as late as the end of the movement, it is a pun but not a surprise. At the end of the first movement of Beethoven's Eighth Symphony, in contrast, the pun is indeed a surprise.

[20] This is not to denigrate Bernstein's performance: it is affecting in its own – closural – way, as though the opening motive had finally given out.

Example 7.4    Beethoven, Symphony No. 8 in F major, I: bars 1–4; bars 362–73

V

The beginning–ending ambiguities considered thus far have been rooted in *successive* events in a composition – whether proximate, as in the 'Jupiter' trio, or remote, as in Beethoven's Eighth Symphony. That is, the elements that generate ambiguity have followed one another, and ambiguity occurs because their contextual (syntactic) functions seem noncongruent with their identity. At the moment the ambiguity is experienced, however, some kind of cognitive cotemporality of the alternative meanings must occur since memory is necessarily involved.[21] One musical event occupies one temporal moment, and although we know that it is impossible to be at the beginning and ending at once, we somehow override this knowledge to experience a single pattern in two (or more) functions at the same time.[22]

But some ambiguities arise not in successive relationships but in compositionally simultaneous ones – overlaps – where the cotemporality is written into the score. The ambiguity is a result of functions which normally occur successively but now occur simultaneously. In such cases, apprehending ambiguity depends on our being able cognitively to separate the alternative functions concurrent in a single sound complex. It seems probable that the experience of ambiguity takes place in that process of separation.

Issues related to the performance of overlapping syntactic functions which create ambiguity arise at a high-tension point in the first movement of Mozart's Symphony No. 40 in G minor (shown bracketed in the excerpt in Example 7.5). The clear overlap of functions here is between the completion of a process of retransition (at the end of the development) and the beginning of the recapitulation – prospectively a moment of ambiguity, retrospectively recognised as having occurred in two stages. Fourth-species contrapuntal descending motion in the woodwinds, over a dominant pedal, is dovetailed with the beginning of *thematic* return in the violins (upbeat to bar 165) before the developmental process has reached its full close (on the downbeat of bar 166).

The two basic functional events can be comprehended and 'processed' simultaneously, and yet, because the full join of ending (retransition) and beginning (recapitulation) comes only at the point of harmonic-cum-textural arrival (bar 166), there is some ambiguity at bar 165 (with upbeat). This results because the harmony has not yet stabilised (there is even the possibility of a non-tonic resolution at bar 166) and because we have, after all, heard the first part of the opening motive in the immediately preceding context, especially bars 159–60 – and although it signalled a return in those earlier passages, it was not itself a return.

If a conductor wishes to convey the ambiguous elements in the overlap – the sense that in one dimension (melody) the recapitulation has already begun by the time we catch up with it at its full realisation in bar 166 – how should this moment be handled? Consider two performances, one by Fritz Reiner and the Chicago Symphony

---

[21]  Inter- as well as intra-opus memory. That is, if we hear 'closing gesture' as the function, it may be on the basis of either stylistic knowledge of other works or experience of this work's closes.

[22]  In this sense ambiguities based on successive compositional events may be analogous to certain ambiguities in visual perception. Consider for instance the Necker cube: because we know that both possible representations cannot occupy the same physical space we see the ambiguity of identity by means of very rapid cognitive oscillations between the two.

Example 7.5   Mozart, Symphony No. 40 in G minor, I, bars 158–66

Orchestra, the other by George Szell and the Cleveland Orchestra. In Reiner's performance the overlap is handled without much 'articulative intervention';[23] it is, in other words, rather 'straight'. The second, by George Szell, makes a noticeable ritenuto within bar 165, just before the fourth beat of the bar, as well as an articulative break or pause before the downbeat of bar 166.

One might say that in Reiner's performance the listener is allowed the pleasure of experiencing the ambiguity as it unfolds, as well as the sense that he or she has discovered it. In contrast, by signalling and articulating the moment of harmonic resolution (lest we miss it?), Szell seems to privilege the moment of arrival – the harmonic and textural resolution and the end of the melody's first phrase – rather than the overlap, thus detracting from listeners' perception of the double strand of action at bar 165.

An interpretation like Szell's is didactic: marking the join, the full return, underlines the change of meaning that has taken place gradually, but in so doing it tends to make the event of return more significant than the dovetailed *processes* that give rise to the experience of ambiguity. In calling attention to what a listener has been in the process of discovering, Szell's type of interpretation may deprive some listeners of the pleasure of their 'discovery'.

In Beethoven's Bagatelle in G major Op. 126 No. 1, the ambiguities stemming from compositional overlap at a principal structural juncture – the ending of a harmonically unstable process and the beginning of return in the second part (Example 7.6b, bars 30–5) – are, so to speak, raised to a higher power than those at the analogous moment in Mozart's Symphony in G minor. And the consequences of performance choices for the life of the ambiguity become even weightier in the Bagatelle.

Beethoven primes us for ambiguity with overlapping phrase ends and beginnings from the very first juncture at bar 4 (Example 7.6a), where, in this style, a clear break might normally have occurred. But, as Edward Cone writes (1977: 94), 'it is difficult to determine exactly where, or whether, phrase-division occurs'.[24] And the considerable range of difference in recorded performances of bar 4 might be taken as an index of this difficulty.[25]

The *molto tenuto* trill on $V^7$ (bar 30), followed by the cadenza, signals closure, so when this cadenza opens out unexpectedly and dramatically to prolong *non*-resolution – i.e. when it moves on the last beat of bar 30 not to the implied tonic but rather to a diminished seventh of the dominant followed by a dominant seventh – both the route and the anticipated timing of closure are disrupted. The repetitions of the harmony and melodic/rhythmic pattern in the top voice, first across bars 30–1 and then 31–2 (bracketed in Example 7.6b), will, by virtue of their similarity, tend to be heard as a reiterative instability, a continuity. Indeed, the harmony remains open, unresolved, pushing on until at least the third beat of bar 32, where the $V^7$ of bar 30 is resolved in

---

[23]   My use of the expression 'articulative intervention' in characterising certain kinds of performance choices is indebted to Wallace Berry (1989).

[24]   About the opening Cone asks (1977: 94): 'Does the first phrase . . . conclude with the arrival of the bass at the tonic on the first beat of bar 4, before the melody has had a chance to complete its feminine afterbeat? Or with the completion of the melody, at which point the bass has already moved away?'

[25]   Compare, for example, performances by Stephen Bishop, Alfred Brendel, Jörg Demus and Artur Schnabel.

Example 7.6   Beethoven, Bagatelle in G major Op. 126 No. 1

a. bars 1–8

b. bars 25–39

the soprano. Meanwhile, outlined in bare octaves, the Bagatelle's opening theme has entered on the tonic in the bass, below the repetitive unstable pattern of continuity. At what point will the bass melody be apprehended as a return?

A comparison of performances of this passage by Jörg Demus and Artur Schnabel suggests the range of possibility within the pianist/interpreter's power to communicate the ambiguity generated by this wide dovetailing of functions – functions normally separated but here conjoined, if uneasily, in a single sound complex. Among the per-formances studied,[26] Schnabel's is unusual in regaining his opening tempo by the end of the second beat of bar 32. Surely a return to tempo is fundamental to conveying the sense of thematic/harmonic return, for it is not a matter of tempo per se but of tempo *relationships*: the opening and its return must be matchable. Schnabel subtly manoeu-vres this return: even though he lingers and hesitates on the first diminished seventh chord to the dominant, he matches the two occurrences of the diminished seventh melodic outline at their beginnings, so that the conformance of the harmonic/rhythmic/melodic gesture from bars 30–1 with that from bars 31–2 is evident. To push through to an *a tempo* return, Schnabel enters the diminished seventh gesture one way and leaves it in another – i.e. the second time, the E–E♭–D part of the gesture is enmeshed in a forward process. Despite the fact that the left hand is not strongly projected (dynamically) in this recording, the return in Schnabel's performance is perceptible almost from the second beat of the bar.

Demus, in an altogether more rubato-laden and introspective performance (especially from early in the second reprise), lingers markedly on the diminished seventh to domi-nant seventh both times (i.e. across bars 30–1 and 31–2). He seems reluctant to leave the world of improvisatory fantasy that has characterised his performance from bar 20 and especially in the composed accelerando within the L'istesso tempo. At the same time, by so lingering – slackening the pace within the gesture – his performance brakes (and breaks), strongly indicating the coming closure that he seems disinclined to reach. By prolonging – almost brooding on – the repeated gesture, as if it were something separate, his interpretation works against the projection of ambiguity. And once again, tempo is crucial: strikingly, Demus's tempo at bar 32 is roughly thirty metronome notches slower than his opening tempo. As a result, it is difficult for him to make the returning melody coalesce and be identified with the shape of the opening of the Bagatelle.[27]

With this kind of ambiguity, created by the overlap of distinguishable functions usually presented successively but now sounded simultaneously (see above, p. 163), it is likely that part of the affective experience for an engaged listener resides in the attempt cognitively to separate out the overlapped meanings or functions. If a listener is to be enabled to experience the pleasurable tensions of such ambiguities, the performer must convey both functions as fully as possible. As Wayne Booth (1974: 128) writes about the ambiguity of the famous rabbit–duck figure, once it is understood as an optical illusion, 'our *chief* pleasure now becomes our awareness of the duplicity'.

---

[26]    See note 25.

[27]    A comparison of Schnabel's and Demus's performances of the cadenza also raises interesting issues of consequentiality for what follows in bars 30–2. Schnabel's performance is a dazzling, single-breathed sweep as compared with Demus's internally patterned treatment of the cadenza. Almost vaporising the sense of metre, first with an unusually long *molto tenuto* trill, and then by the sweep of the cadenza, Schnabel directs us towards the goal of *resolution* of the trilled $V^7$ chord, which is about to be denied by the deflection to the inverted vii°$^7$/V. Thus, too, the differentiation created by the resumption of patterning on the last beat of bar 30 is emphasised; it is further enhanced by Schnabel's performance of the crescendo on the diminished seventh.

Demus's considerable internal patterning, or shaping, of the cadenza creates a more *grazioso* character (compare Beethoven's marking), but it weakens the full drama of the resumption of patterned (after relatively non-patterned) action when the jarringly unexpected diminished seventh chord breaks in.

Ambiguities in music might be thought of as artistic counterparts to identity crises in life. In both cases identity – 'whatness' – is being grappled with. But while conflicts and contradictions in our personal lives tend to torment us and even to make us feel powerless, the contradictions and conflicts of meaning that occur as ambiguities in music, once they have been recognised and understood, are empowering for performers and listeners. They need not – indeed should not – be resolved. The choice of the performer to let ambiguity 'live' releases the power to shape and enrich musical experience.

### REFERENCES

Abbate, C. and Parker, R., 1989: 'Introduction: on analyzing opera', in C. Abbate and R. Parker, eds., *Analyzing Opera: Verdi and Wagner* (Berkeley and Los Angeles: University of California Press), pp. 1–24.

Agawu, K., 1994: 'Ambiguity in tonal music: a preliminary study', in A. Pople, ed., *Theory, Analysis and Meaning in Music* (Cambridge: Cambridge University Press), pp. 86–107.

Apte, M., 1985: *Humor and Laughter* (Ithaca: Cornell University Press).

Bernstein, L., 1976: *The Unanswered Question: Six Talks at Harvard* (Cambridge, Massachusetts: Harvard University Press).

Berry, W., 1976: *Structural Functions in Music* (Englewood Cliffs, New Jersey: Prentice-Hall).

1989: *Musical Structure and Performance* (New Haven: Yale University Press).

Booth, W., 1974: *A Rhetoric of Irony* (Chicago: University of Chicago Press).

Campbell, B. B., 1985: Review of J. M. Levy, *Beethoven's Compositional Choices: The Two Versions of Opus 18, No. 1, First Movement*, in *Journal of Music Theory* 29/1: 187–97.

Cone, E. T., 1977: 'Beethoven's experiments in composition: the late Bagatelles', in A. Tyson, ed., *Beethoven Studies 2* (London: Oxford University Press), pp. 84–105.

Empson, W., [1930] 1947: *Seven Types of Ambiguity* (New York: New Directions).

Epstein, D., 1979: *Beyond Orpheus: Studies in Musical Structure* (Cambridge, Massachusetts: MIT Press).

Flew, A., [1979] 1985: *A Dictionary of Philosophy*, 2nd rev. edn (London: Pan Books and Macmillan Press).

Frisch, W., 1984: *Brahms and the Principle of Developing Variation* (Berkeley and Los Angeles: University of California Press).

Grove, G., [1898] 1962: *Beethoven and His Nine Symphonies* (New York: Dover).

Keller, H., 1986: *The Great Haydn Quartets: Their Interpretation* (New York: George Braziller).

Kramer, J. D., 1988: *The Time of Music: New Meanings, New Temporalities, New Listening Strategies* (New York: Schirmer Books).

Lerdahl, F. and Jackendoff, R., 1983: *A Generative Theory of Tonal Music* (Cambridge, Massachusetts: MIT Press).

Levy, J. M., 1981: 'Gesture, form, and syntax in Haydn's music', in J. P. Larsen, H. Serwer and J. Webster, eds., *Haydn Studies: Proceedings of the International Haydn Conference, Washington, D.C. 1975* (New York: Norton), pp. 355–62.

1982: 'Texture as a sign in classic and early romantic music', *Journal of the American Musicological Society* 35/3: 482–531.

1992: '"Something mechanical encrusted on the living": a source of musical wit and humor', in W. J. Allanbrook, J. M. Levy and W. P. Mahrt, eds., *Convention in Eighteenth- and Nineteenth-Century Music: Essays in Honor of Leonard G. Ratner* (Stuyvesant, New York: Pendragon Press), pp. 225–56.

Meyer, L. B., 1956: *Emotion and Meaning in Music* (Chicago: University of Chicago Press).

    1973: *Explaining Music: Essays and Explorations* (Berkeley and Los Angeles: University of California Press).

Ratner, L. G., 1970: '*Ars combinatoria*: chance and choice in eighteenth-century music', in H. C. Robbins Landon and R. E. Chapman, eds., *Studies in Eighteenth-Century Music: A Tribute to Karl Geiringer on His Seventieth Birthday* (London: George Allen and Unwin), pp. 343–63.

    1980: *Classic Music: Expression, Form, and Style* (New York: Schirmer Books).

Rosen, C., 1971: *The Classical Style: Haydn, Mozart, Beethoven* (New York: Viking Press).

Sisman, E. R., 1993: *Mozart: The 'Jupiter' Symphony* (Cambridge: Cambridge University Press).

Taruskin, R., 1982: 'On letting the music speak for itself: some reflections on musicology and performance', *Journal of Musicology* 1: 338–49.

Thomson, W., 1983: 'Functional ambiguity in musical structures', *Music Perception* 1/1: 3–27.

Tovey, D. F., 1935: *Essays in Musical Analysis, I: Symphonies* (London: Oxford University Press).

Webster, J., 1991: *Haydn's 'Farewell' Symphony and the Idea of Classical Style: Through-Composition and Cyclic Integration in His Instrumental Music* (Cambridge: Cambridge University Press).

Wheelock, G. A., 1992: *Haydn's Ingenious Jesting with Art: Contexts of Musical Wit and Humor* (New York: Schirmer Books).

## DISCOGRAPHY

L. van Beethoven, Bagatelle in G major Op. 126 No. 1:
    S. Bishop (Philips 6500 930)
    A. Brendel (Turnabout KTVC 34077)
    J. Demus (Westminster WST 17066)
    A. Schnabel (Seraphim mono IC-6067)

L. van Beethoven, Symphony No. 8 in F major Op. 93:
    L. Bernstein and the Vienna Philharmonic (DG 2740 216-10)
    A. Toscanini and the NBC Symphony Orchestra (Vic 8000)

J. Haydn, String Quartet in E♭ major Op. 33 No. 2 ('Joke'):
    Janáček Quartet (London CS 6385)

J. Haydn, Symphony No. 94 in G major ('Surprise'):
    C. Davis and the Concertgebouw Orchestra (Philips 412871-2)
    W. Furtwängler and the Vienna Philharmonic, 1951 (Angel EMI WF-60034)

W. A. Mozart, Symphony No. 40 in G minor:
    F. Reiner and the Chicago Symphony Orchestra, 1956 (RCA LM 6035)
    G. Szell and the Cleveland Orchestra (Col MG 30368)

W. A. Mozart, Symphony No. 41 in C major ('Jupiter'):
    N. Harnoncourt and the Concertgebouw Orchestra (Telefunken 6.42846)
    F. Maier and the Collegium Aureum (Pro Arte PAL 1009)
    F. Reiner and the Chicago Symphony Orchestra, 1956 (RCA LM 6035)
    G. Szell and the Cleveland Orchestra (Col MG 30368)

# CHAPTER EIGHT

# Strategies of irony in Prokofiev's Violin Sonata in F minor Op. 80

## RONALD WOODLEY

—

> The kings of Siam, it is said, had a way of punishing nobles by honouring them with a
> gift of a sacred white elephant, a gift they were unable to decline but obliged to maintain
> at ruinous expense. (Muecke 1982: 9)

Irony can be seen as one of the central (if intrinsically slippery) turns of thought in the critical and artistic discourses of the twentieth century. We live in a generation particularly, peculiarly sensitised to those facets of the ironic that have become dominant modes within a postmodernist aesthetic; it is also a generation for which those ironies are redoubled through the disjunctions created between a critical-theoretical stance demanding radical undermining of presumed categories and identities, and an emergent global, political condition in which new nationalisms and ethnic/religious identities are attempting to recategorise the world and the individual subject within an increasing number of less negotiable boundaries. The substitution of political diffraction for postmodern pluralism – further ironised by the new global networking and transnational economic dependencies – is nowhere seen more clearly than in the former Soviet Union and Eastern Bloc, and it seems a particularly appropriate time to reinvestigate the music of Prokofiev within such a context, especially since the composer has been curiously neglected in the musicological and analytical literature, by comparison, say, with his near-contemporary Shostakovich.

In music, notions of the ironic – though still lamentably under-researched – are of long standing and diverse manifestation. Most of us can point to our favourite twist in a Mozart opera; but it is also possible to trace instances of irony, broadly conceived, in such diverse sources as the allegorical figure of Faux-Semblant in Machaut (see Bent 1991), or the aestheticisation of incongruity in the word–music relationships of Schumann's Lieder, or indeed the use of the Barber Adagio to accompany scenes of violent destruction in the Vietnam War film *Platoon*. In such instances, the 'purely' musical text is commonly being confronted with other images and meanings – verbal, visual or intellectual – against which it is heard to rub. But how is one to construe the notion of the ironic in instrumental music, where the 'meaning' of the text, and of the experience, is already problematic? More to the point, how should performers approach the difficult task of transmitting such ironic layers of meaning where these seem to be intrinsic to the music? What effect can their interpretative decisions have on the perceived structure and sense of the work? This chapter examines Prokofiev's Violin Sonata in F minor Op. 80 (completed in 1946, though sketches date back to 1938) as an exemplification of some of these issues, drawing upon the present author's performing experience of the Sonata and comparing various recorded interpretations to investigate how performers can/should locate themselves, in a creative or interventionist role, in relation both to the compositional structure and to the listener's experience. The intention is not to attempt a 'decoding' of the piece in order to achieve a critically 'correct' performance attitude and practice, but rather to demonstrate how the multiple processes of contradiction and congruence, frustration and satisfaction, and degrees of partiality in the sense of closure can be dynamically exploited by the performers to different expressive and structural ends.

The central premise of this study – unashamedly subjective in origin – is that the dark and semantically dense struggle that permeates Op. 80 can be read as a modernist reworking of transcendental romantic irony as defined by Schlegel, mediated by something akin to Bakhtin's dialogistic conception of the novel as 'a self-conscious genre that dramatizes the gap between what is told and the telling of it' (Bishop 1989: 205). The struggle of Op. 80 is not that of the work against something outside itself: it is rather the struggle of something within, unmanifested, yearning to break out, and constantly finding its attempts at emergence blocked by the very material, outward form and language that have enabled its presence to be identified. Though extremely difficult to pin down in words, this blocking of 'something within' concerns the frustration of a desire for cathartic release into some supremely positive state of being, where meaning – musical and supra-musical – is transparent and unironisable: in short, a domain of spiritual 'purity'. It is a domain infinitely unattainable, only distantly glimpsed, yet at once inseparable from one's corporeal humanity. In such a reading of the Sonata we find, re-energised in the artistic and political climate of Stalin's Soviet Union, characteristic traces of Schlegel's *Welt-Ironie*: recognition of the irredeemably flawed and incongruous nature of the phenomenal world, and the function of the artist to engage in an inexhaustible process of regeneration and transcendence through the process of ironisation. Schlegel's anticipation of Bakhtin – and, indeed, elements of post-structuralist thought – can be seen here. For Schlegel, 'irony . . . contains and arouses a feeling of indissoluble antagonism between the absolute and the relative, between the impossibility and the necessity of complete communication' (Muecke 1982: 24); for Bakhtin, a 'true novel is always criticizing itself, questioning its own language and form, and always finding them wanting. It is conscious of the impossibility of achieving full meaning and ironically exploits this lack' (Bishop 1989: 205–6).

We are clearly in territory far removed from the expectations that the title of this chapter may have evoked in the minds of some readers. For the juxtaposition of Prokofiev and irony has in the past tended to be circumscribed by the altogether looser near-equation of the term with such notions as the 'grotesque', 'sardonic' or 'sarcastic'. While these notions are often encompassed within the greater depth of field that irony commands, they are relatively surface-level and unidimensional, whereas post-Schlegelian irony depends at its very heart on the essential multivocality of artistic utterance. Again, the concept of the ironic as promoted in this reading of Op. 80 is not bounded simply by the kind of 'aestheticisation of incongruity' encountered above in relation to Schumann's Lieder – though both of these strategies certainly participate in the same romantic project, sharing with the 'annihilating' tendency of humour (Bonds 1991: 63–4) and Bakhtin's notion of the carnivalesque (Holquist 1990) the necessity to decentre the subject, even if the longer-term strategy of irony is to liberate, transform and re-poeticise that subject at a higher, more 'sublime' level.

Furthermore, it will be clear by now that the conditions required for an exploration of the ironic, as outlined here, are not necessarily predicated on the medium of language: although a large proportion of scholarly work on irony has tended to focus on its poetic-literary and philosophical-literary manifestations, there is no intrinsic reason why music, including textless music, should not be readable within the same parameters. Indeed tonality itself, as surviving in the first half of the twentieth century, can be understood as a powerful narrative medium for the ironic tendency. In much of Prokofiev's music, for instance, tonality, rather than acting as a metacritical principle, is partially contingent – but only partially, so that it just manages to sustain a residue of idealistic, transcendental function against which the competing foreground material can struggle. The idealism may already be chronically compromised by history, but it is still – crucially for Prokofiev – not entirely beyond reach. Of course, the fact that such an apparently transcendental function is indeed (*pace* Schenkerian metaphysics) largely historically contingent and socially constructed adds a further level of irony to its deployment in the idealistic struggle. In this sense it may enrich our reading of Prokofiev's ironising tendency to draw into the picture Kierkegaard's critical reorientation of romantic irony ([1841] 1968). For Kierkegaard the proper, ethically justifiable function of irony lies in its corrective, ultimately stabilising value: the romantic ironist is reprehensible because 'dwelling in a self-imposed exile, frenetically poeticizing each moment into an aesthetically pleasing experience, he knows no continuity but "boredom: this eternity void of content, this bliss without enjoyment, this superficial profundity, this hungry satiety"' (Lang 1988: 28). The irony of Schlegel and Tieck, for Kierkegaard, is 'a disgusting self-titillation, an unnatural activity intended to compensate for the subject's frustrating failure to relate "naturally" (directly) to the Other' (: 3). Here, though, both the extent and the limit of the Kierkegaardian analogy are evident: the residual metaphysical aura of tonality is sufficiently present for Prokofiev to sense and explore its stabilising, potentially reconciliatory function; but Kierkegaard's de-aestheticisation of the ironic, his disgust for its erotic exploitation, can hardly be claimed to hold sway for Prokofiev, at least in Op. 80, whose eroticisation of the ironic, with its longings, frustrations and (temporary) satisfactions, form the basis of the work's aesthetic trajectory. Tonality, then, and in particular the dialectic between diatonicism and chromaticism, plays a crucial double role in the ironising process here: it provides a metaphor for the unattainable sublime, as well as the medium through which, in association with other musical parameters, the process of growth and revelation is channelled. In addition, the tonal and motivic dynamic of the work, and its evolving, internal structural relationships, can be read as participating in the processes of *ostrananie* (defamiliarisation) and *zatrudnenie* (problematisation) coined by the Russian Formalist theorist Viktor Shklovsky in his 1917 essay 'Art as technique' (see Selden and Widdowson 1993: 30–3 and Eagle 1981: 4–5; partial text in Rylance 1987: 48–56). Here Shklovsky was elucidating both his belief in the necessary transformational process to be applied to 'life' by 'art', since 'the essence of art lay in *renewing* percepts about "reality" which daily life tended to *automatize*, to make mechanical, perfunctory, and therefore, imperceptible', and his theory that art forms die out because they 'lose their ability to *defamiliarize* experience' (Eagle 1981: 4). Transferred to Prokofiev's musical domain, the defamiliarisation and problematisation of tonality are explored both at a local level, in the displacement of individual tones within an underlying, normative tonal vocabulary (see Bass 1988), and in the larger-scale, strategically placed dissolutions of diatonicism into a temporarily disorientated chromatic dialect.

Still more cogently, in the context of a specifically Russian/Soviet musical criticism, the nexus of contentions emerging here surrounding the ironic finds fascinating parallels in the writings of the theorist Boris Vladimirovich Asafiev (1884–1949), friend and one-time student colleague of Prokofiev. For Asafiev, through training more Hegelian than Marxist, the conception of form as process is central, as is that of musical motion characterised by a dialectical conflict between the tendency towards equilibrium and the 'no less strong impulse toward postponement of the achievement of equilibrium' (Carpenter 1988: 817; see also Tull 1976: II, 257). His complex notions of *intonatsiia* (intonation) and *melos* can be read as contributing quite specifically to the kind of modernist, ironising tendency in Prokofiev that we have been trying to contextualise. *Intonatsiia*, though characteristically evolving in meaning during the course of Asafiev's major work *Musical Form as Process* (1930–47), might be reasonably depicted as the inner psychological and emotional life of the musical gesture, as well as the formal embodiment of that gesture in its technical properties and its interpretation in sound; *melos* encompasses the whole linear and spatial dimension of the music's inner relationships, its 'linkages, cohesion, and dynamics' (Carpenter 1988: 852; see also McQuere 1983: 224), of which 'melody' is only one (limited) constituent part. The invocation of Asafiev in this study seems apposite, too, given his passionately held belief in the importance of performance and of the physical act of interpretation in working out the music's structural energies, and his consequent rejection of what he perceived as the sterile, predetermined formal schemata of conservative German theorists such as Riemann (see McQuere 1983: 237).

Words, then, are no more necessary for the conveyance of irony than they were for those kings of Siam; and music, perhaps especially the highly wrought, extended tonal music represented in Prokofiev's Op. 80, provides a narrative medium through which the ironic can be explored with potency. It is an irony of 'progress', however, rather than 'suspension' (see Wilde 1981), though the two are in a dynamic relationship, and the frictions in operation within Prokofiev's tonal world already betray the conflict between a need for organicist connection and the historical impossibility at this stage of the modernist enterprise for the musical language to yield any such connections 'naturally'. It is of such tensions, such ironies, that some neo-classicisms, even some postmodernisms are born; yet Prokofiev ultimately rejects the historical short-circuiting, the freezing of human evolution, the artistic insincerity, that he perceived lying down that path for the intellectually lazy or the spiritually submissive. Significantly, the composer's preliminary work on Op. 80, in the late 1930s and early 1940s, coincided with his growing awareness of the strains of cultural and ideological acceptability under Stalin, an awareness that the verbal frankness for which he was notorious was now more a political liability than an asset, that meanings in art were ideologically volatile, infinitely re-readable and (by author or reader) ironisable.[1] Rather than allow himself to be defeated, however, Prokofiev seems in Op. 80 to have actively chosen – at some level of consciousness – to harness the inescapable ironies of his historical location and redirect them to, as he saw it, more spiritually fulfilling ends which at times cohabit uncomfortably with the epic spirit of national pride emphasised by Prokofiev's Soviet commentators both prior and subsequent to Zhdanov's renewed cultural clampdown of the later 1940s. It is surely no coincidence that, even in his earlier years in Paris, he became sufficiently involved with the Christian Science Movement to copy into his personal notebook a list of twenty central tenets, invoking the power and vigour of Mind and Spirit to transcend the material world of tribulation (see Samuel 1971: 122–3).

In order to observe more clearly how the composer's harnessing of the ironising process manifests itself in the music and, importantly for this study, how performers and listeners can engage with that process, we must now look at some of the internal workings of the Sonata in F minor, along with a number of recorded interpretations.[2]

The music's process of self-exploration – self-ironisation in the wider sense – is clearly articulated over the span of the first movement (Andante assai), though its structure is only partially closed, to allow the implications of the material to be worked out further in subsequent movements. How the performers respond to this process, in terms of large-scale overview but also at the level of individual note-relationship and nuance, contributes significantly to the way in which their performance maps on to the available ironic readings. For example, the articulation of the octave descent outlined in the piano's opening gesture, followed by the violin's initial response (Example 8.1), is of the greatest long-term importance to the narrative evolution of the work. Both tonal and rhythmical/metrical factors are involved here. The unfolding of the octave

---

[1]  Compare the onset of the New Criticism in the West at exactly this time, and in particular Cleanth Brooks's influential essay 'Irony as a principle of structure' (1949; for the 1951 version, see Rylance 1987: 37–47).

[2]  The five recorded performances of Op. 80 considered here are as follows:
David Oistrakh and Frida Bauer (Harmonia Mundi PR 250 041; 1969, reissued 1993); Itzhak Perlman and Vladimir Ashkenazy (RCA LSB 4084; 1969); Shlomo Mintz and Yefim Bronfman (DG 423 575-2; 1988); Mayumi Fujikawa and Craig Sheppard (Academy Sound and Vision CD DCA 667; 1989); Gidon Kremer and Martha Argerich (DG 431 803-2; 1992).

In the examples below, extracts from the score are reproduced with permission of Boosey & Hawkes Music Publishers Ltd.

Fs through i–VI–iv–[V]–i – notionally 'strong' but destabilised by its asymmetrical positioning within the alternations between 3/4 and 4/4 – lends a searching, unsettled quality to this first 'impetus' (Asafiev's term).[3] In the course of the movement this initial *intonatsiia* achieves only incomplete resolution, as will be seen, through the background, arpeggiated bass structure (Example 8.2) and the final triadic descent in the treble of bars 103–7, paced as a more stabilised written-out ritardando (Example 8.3). The subtlety of Prokofiev's notation at the opening lies in the progressive weakening of the structurally significant pitches F–D♭–B♭–F within the local metrical scheme. But in some of the recordings considered here, other more superficial strategies, such as equalising the upper-note stresses of the four falling fifths or stressing each structural pitch as if it were the first beat of the bar, conspire to strengthen artificially the downward motion, to give it a sense of conventional integrity which closes off rather than opens out the music's potential (Example 8.4). Most of the representations in Example 8.4 are rather cruder than the actual performances concerned. Nevertheless, of the five versions, only Craig Sheppard comes close to transmitting the nuances of Prokofiev's notation, though even here the first C and final F are stronger than their metrical position seems to warrant (see the alternative version in brackets). To take a different case, Frida Bauer's playing, by its tendency to stress the upper note of all but one of the fifths as well as the final low F, has the effect of emphasising the tonicity of the pitches C–A♭–F–F, in addition to regularising the overall shape into a more consistent triple metre. In both respects this restabilisation of the notation seems inappropriate to the music's longer-term ends.[4]

The apparently trivial nature of the metrical relationship between the G and A♭ at the beginning of bar 2 has an additional, medium-term function, for there is a clear linkage with both the pitch content and the articulation of the violin's first entry. This quaver figure in bar 4 is notationally and quantitatively long–short, and hence congruent, in a sense, with the piano part in bar 2. But in performance the tendency towards unstressed–stressed articulation, emphasised by the relatively dead sound of the open G string and the subsequent accented trill on A♭, has the effect of reversing this congruence; and the new highlighting of $\hat{3}$ provides the preparation, via the G♯s of the Poco più animato (e.g. bars 17 and 21–2) and the piano's descent to V/iii (bars 17–27), for the reworking of the opening material in A♭ minor (bars 28ff.). Here we have the first of three such reworkings before the return of something closely related to the opening at bar 89 and finally bar 98. It is insufficient, however, within the ironising reading suggested here, to regard the relationship of these three reprises – bars 28ff., 51ff.

[3]  Upper- and lower-case Roman numerals are used to depict major and minor harmonies respectively. For the sake of notational clarity such harmonies are shown in the text and examples without super- or subscript Arabic numerals to depict their constituent intervals in relation to the prevailing key signature. Thus, in the key of F minor, '♮iv' (which properly should be notated '♮iv₅⁶') stands for a B minor chord.

I should like to express my gratitude to Deborah Mawer for her invaluable advice on some of the analytical examples presented in this chapter.

[4]  This may not have troubled Bauer's partner here, David Oistrakh (who worked extensively with the composer on the Sonata – see Schlifstein [1961]: 242–3), even though he later expressed the (rather naive) view that the 'best performance of Prokofiev's music, or of any other good music for that matter, is one in which the personality of the performer does not intrude in any way' (cited in ibid., 240).

Example 8.1    Op. 80, I, bars 1–5

Example 8.2    Op. 80, I: bass structure

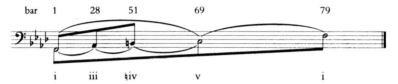

Example 8.3    Op. 80, I, bars 102–7

Example 8.4    Comparative stress patterns in five recorded versions of Op. 80, I, bars 1–4

Example 8.5   Op. 80, I, bars 28–33

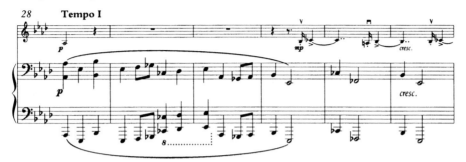

(especially 57ff.) and 69ff. – as a purely formalist one. Particularly in the light of the 'metaphysics' of tonality speculated upon earlier, it is significant that Prokofiev places each stage of this process of growth-through-irony precisely at those structural points of the movement that articulate the background triadic bass arpeggiation i–iii–v–i, the middle areas being linked by ♮iv (B minor), whose voice-leading function is both as a leading note to the minor dominant and a continuation of an ascent in minor thirds (i–iii–iii/iii), and perhaps as a quasi-passing motion between iii and v (see Example 8.2). At each of these points the tonal/modal language clears into audibly more transparent, diatonic structures, as though the music, through its intermediary, chromaticised struggles (the poeticised description is unavoidable), is periodically managing to achieve some kind of temporary enlightenment through an altered (ironised) consciousness of the basic material. Returning, then, to the A♭ minor of bars 28ff. (Example 8.5), the growth-through-irony is achieved in the piano part by the extension of the octave descent one stage further to E♭ (bar 31), which not only picks up the E♭ pedal from bars 24–7, but provides forward momentum for the bass (after the false return to i in bars 37–8) to continue its descent by step to the new ♮iv (B minor) reprise of the material at the next point of stable, diatonic emergence in bar 51. In addition, the slightly greater degree of quaver movement at bar 29 appears inconsequential compared with the opening; but this is clearly another level of linkage between the more chromaticised movement of the previous Poco più animato, the more heightened version of this at bars 39ff. and the eventual arrival of bar 51, which presents the most tonally distanced and fragmented version of the material, though with a strangely resolute, 'aspirational' eloquence. In the violin part, too, the re-exploitation of bars 4–5 in bars 31ff. is more than a formulaic variation of its source material: it represents an ironised self-examination of its previous metrical/articulational bivalence, clarifying the local $\hat{3}$ as stressed, even though – again ironically – the tonal environment of this $\hat{3}$ has already been compromised by the extension of the piano's descent beyond the tonic A♭ to its quasi-dominant (bar 31).

Though consequential, at least in voice-leading terms, to the B minor (♮iv) section in bars 51–68, the arrival of v at bar 69 represents a significant turning point in the movement's psychological contour. From here to the end (save for the chromaticised link in bars 74–8), the overpowering sense is of tonal/modal suspension – an almost painful inability to achieve full closure and the longed-for, unironisable transparency of spirit. For Prokofiev, the tensions here between a romantic quest for full, organic connectivity and a Bakhtinian resistance to any such univocality are essentially the tensions of the ironic-dialogic condition. This 'suspensive' quality in the music is in part due to the avoidance of leading-note motions, which – interestingly in view of previous observations – Asafiev regarded as 'the chief motive force of European music' (see Carpenter 1988: 876–8). Prefigured by the ambivalence in the quality of the sevenths in bars 67–8, this leading note avoidance is virtually complete: the only, very fleeting, instance of an E♮ between the tonic return at bar 79 and the end nearly thirty bars later occurs in the desperate reconfiguring of the violin's first utterance at bars 89–90 (Example 8.6), where it signally fails to lead anywhere at all. In the minor dominant area from bar 69, the flattening tendency is further enhanced by the contour and pitch content of the ascending triadic interpolations in the piano part (Example 8.7), which can perhaps be read as a compression and assimilation of the previous, larger-scale iii–♮iv–v movement into the local C minor modality. At a more distant relational level, too, these interpolations seem to refer back to the A♭–B♭–C quaver movement of the very opening (bars 3–4; Example 8.1), and later, transposed, they are tonicised as the final cadential bass progression D♭–E♭–F (bars 103–7; Example 8.3) – though this tonicisation is ironically uncompleted (note the middle harmonies in Example 8.8, orientated towards the mediant A♭ major), despite the convergence of treble and bass to $\hat{1}$. The emptiness of the final, open fifth sonority at bar 107 is also doubly significant in the ironising process, especially following the harmonic content of bars 103–6, since it not only subverts the initial attempt of the music to highlight $\hat{3}$ (bars 4ff.), but, as will be seen below, also provides a temporary void into which an even more ironic highlighting of the *major* $\hat{3}$ can be introduced in the second movement.

The performance implications of all this are quite fascinating. To take even the small example of the violin's first entry at bars 4ff. and the manner in which the interpretation is related to its reworking at bars 31ff., the variation in approach is astonishing. In particular, Gidon Kremer, whose performance of the Sonata is characterised by a wildness and abandon at times brilliant, at times perverse, calculates these opening bars in such a way as to anticipate the reversal of bar 31. The open Gs of bars 4, 6 and 8 are progressively shorter and the A♭s thrown away with increasingly greater menace as the notated dynamic level rises from *p* through *mp* to *mf*, so that the quaver figure spills into the three-note *Vorschlag* at bars 11 and 12. This gradual evolution of long–short into short–long accomplishes, in a sense, the ironising reading suggested above, though brought forward in such a way that the next stage of the process is already in place for the return of the opening material at bars 28ff. In fact, Kremer's Poco più animato at bars 17ff. is so powerfully presented that the Tempo I at bar 28 actually seems anticlimactic, and the notated prefiguring of bar 31 at bars 22–3 – *mp* in the score but here significantly louder – pushes bar 31 into a more secondary relationship than the movement's structure would appear to warrant. Of course, this could itself be heard as adding a further layer of irony to the reading, so it is extremely difficult to talk of greater and lesser degrees of 'correctness' in such an instance.

Example 8.6    Op. 80, I, bars 89–92

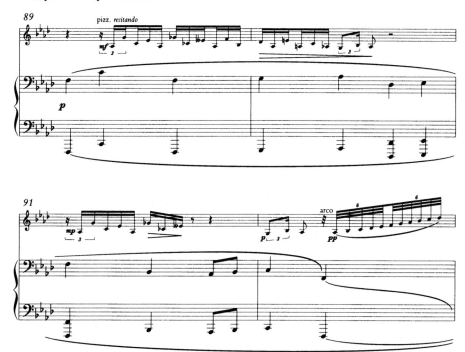

Example 8.7    Op. 80, I, bars 69–73

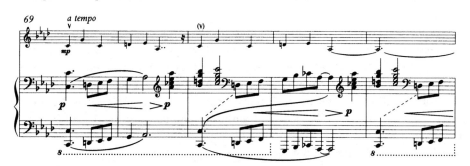

Example 8.8    Op. 80, I, bars 103–7: final cadential structure

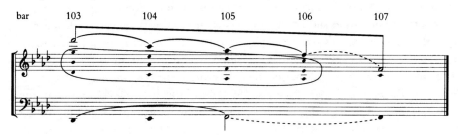

By contrast with Kremer's interpretation (shared to a more refined extent by
Perlman), the work's dedicatee David Oistrakh prefers his opening utterance long and
lyrical. The staccato A♭s are not at all staccato, and there is a strongly vocal sense of
connection between the G and A♭ quavers. Then, when the material returns at bar 31,
its short–long reversal is greatly exaggerated, the initial semiquaver becoming virtually
halved in value to a demisemiquaver. Because this over-shortening has not been
anticipated in Oistrakh's playing of bars 22–3, where the semiquavers are in time but
still lyrical, the Poco più animato section successfully links the material on either side
into a slowly unfolding, evolutionary process. The unfortunate corollary, though, is
that the opening has not been dangerous enough to alert the listener to the troubles in
store, and this in turn conspires with the artificially stabilised nature of Bauer's initial
piano statement, already discussed, so that the searching quality played up by Kremer
is here over-refined, even defused. Another interesting point of interpretative divergence comes at bar 69 and then (especially) bars 79ff., where the music reaches the
inconclusive v–i motion outlined earlier. At bars 79ff. (Example 8.9) the performers
must decide whether to try to homogenise the very different sound-worlds of the two
instruments, or convey an internal textural and timbral irony between the translucent,
bell-like quality of the piano's crotchet progression – the emergent but only partially
achieved transfiguration – and the *freddo* demisemiquaver sussurations of the violin,
famously described by the composer to Oistrakh as 'like the wind in a graveyard'
(Schlifstein [1961]: 242). The reading of the movement suggested here would strongly
support the latter interpretation, and this is indeed taken up by, in particular, Kremer
and Martha Argerich, and to a lesser extent by Mayumi Fujikawa and Craig Sheppard.
One of the violinist's key decisions in these notoriously awkward *pianissimo* scales is
how much *sul ponticello*, if any, to employ in addition to the indicated *con sordino*, even
though neither Prokofiev himself nor Szigeti – editor of the most commonly used
Anglo-Soviet edition – chooses to specify the effect. Kremer opts for a great deal,
rejoicing in the eerie, flickering harmonics that result, especially down on the G string
(e.g. in bar 88). Argerich accompanies this with a very straight, clear-toned voicing of
her chords, with only slight treble dominance, allowing the subtleties of the inner
voice-leading to be heard, but warmed with some judicious through-pedalling to
enable the listener to savour the discreetly erotic sevenths and ninths in which is
embedded a veiled image of the work's opening. In contrast, the performance by
Shlomo Mintz and Yefim Bronfman brings together the two instruments, homogenising the music and, to a large extent, neutralising the multi-dimensional qualities
that Kremer and Argerich explore. As with the earlier discussion of the beginning of
the Sonata, though, one should not dismiss their reading as 'wrong'. While it is
debatable whether Mintz's demisemiquaver scales are thus really *freddo*, their more
neutral rendering certainly emphasises the 'suspensive' nature of this section, outlined
above from a more analytical perspective. The most curious reading, however, is
Oistrakh's. Taken from a live concert in 1969, it is difficult to tell how much of the
eventual recorded balance is due to microphone placement, engineering or projection
to the audience; but he seems to play these scales remarkably forward, full-toned and

Example 8.9    Op. 80, I, bars 79–84

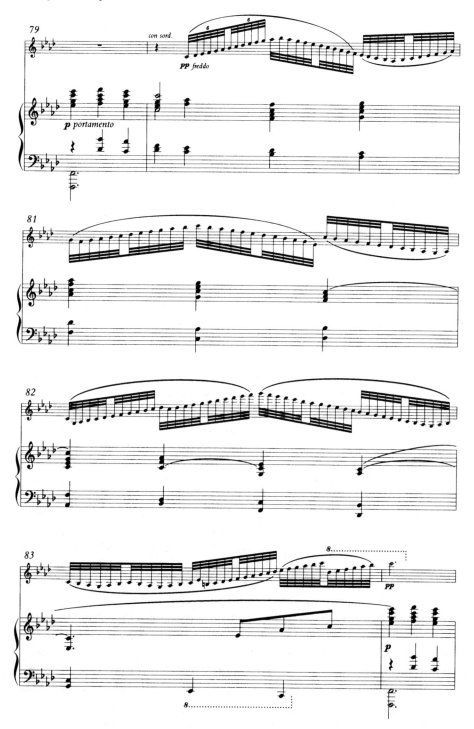

strangely (ironically?) incongruent with the composer's own graveyard imagery, as suggested to him over twenty years previously.

The final cadential gesture of this first movement provides a further example of how the performers' reading of the music's meaning can affect quite directly their relationship to one another. Earlier in this discussion it was suggested that the relatively unstable piano descent in bars 1–4 becomes, at least partially, restabilised by the tonic triadic descent in the treble of bars 103–7. From a quasi-Bakhtinian perspective, a significant factor in this process is the move from monologue to dialogue – in other words, the shared nature of the relative closure emerging from the 'pre-socialised' opening soliloquy. All players who have seriously rehearsed Op. 80 will have spent considerable time working out how to match, or deliberately mis-match, the timbres of pizzicato violin and pedalled grand piano in these alternating, arpeggiated chords (Example 8.3). The violin arpeggiations, especially the first one in bar 103 with its high F, are extremely difficult to make 'ring'. By contrast, the piano chords are straightforward, though the duplicated pitches between right and left hands in bar 104 (but not bar 106) may indicate that here, too, Prokofiev wishes the cadential process to wind down in relative complexity, along with the paced diminuendo and the written-out ritardando, over the five bars. To what extent should the two players adapt the 'natural' sound of their respective instruments with a view to homogenising the dialogue?[5] The various performances under consideration again vary widely in their answer to this question. Kremer and Argerich, as might be expected, emphasise the ironic disjunction of timbre and hence minimise the closure, in preparation for the second movement. Mintz and Bronfman adopt precisely the opposite solution, attempting to match their speed of arpeggiation and articulation, at least within the limits of their instruments' capabilities. (And this qualification itself exposes an ironic connotation – of a different kind – in *their* reading.) In both of these performances, then, there is a sense of continuity with their respective interpretations of bars 79ff. Perlman and Ashkenazy follow the same homogenising solution as Mintz and Bronfman, with all the arpeggiations taken very slowly and deliberately, so that the sense of closure is relatively strong. (In a live concert performance, the degree of closure will also be partially determined by the violinist's purely physical motion in 'placing' (or not) the final pizzicato dyad.) Oistrakh and Bauer are noticeably subtle at this point, apparently commencing the cadence at bar 103 with deliberate timbral disjunction, but gradually bringing the dialogue together as the outer voices converge to the final bar. Because the music is so fragmented, however, there can be no possibility of really convincing reconciliation, and just sufficient openness remains at the end of the movement to carry the listener beyond the double bar to the Allegro brusco.

As regards this second movement and the remainder of the Sonata, selected pointers will have to suffice to suggest some of the ways in which the ironising process is continued and worked through to its incomplete conclusion. The focal points of the process in the Allegro brusco are the second subject (bars 50ff. and 257ff.) and the coda

[5] It is not especially significant, I think, that the arpeggiations are notated with a wavy line in the violin and as grace notes in the piano; the latter simply clarifies the position of the simultaneities between the hands.

Example 8.10    Complementary scalic inflections in Op. 80, II, bars 1–7

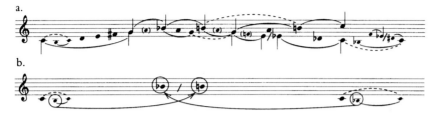

Example 8.11    Op. 80, II, bars 295–300

(bars 271–300). But even at the opening, the surface-level *brusco* affect conceals an internal structure of scalic inflections which can be read as complementary and self-ironising. The principal ascending configuration C–C has an 'aspirational' thrust in its direction and sharpened fourth but is blocked in its initial segmentation (bars 1–4) by the more depressive flattened leading note B♭; the system bifurcates at this point, one fork continuing upward through a newly sharpened leading note to the octave, the other descending, this time through both natural and flattened third degrees (E♮ and E♭) and the especially depressive flattened supertonic (D♭), to the starting point (bars 4–8: Example 8.10a). In addition, a kind of self-cancelling chiasmus involving the undecided quality of the leading note can be traced between neighbour-note functions at the outer points of the eight-bar phrase and the central point of bifurcation in the thematic material just discussed (Example 8.10b). Over the course of the movement, and indeed the whole work, these ironically interlocked expressive tendencies – presented in a particularly concise form here, but already signalled, as we have seen, in the first movement – are in constant, almost Manichean-dualist struggle. Just as the first movement was concerned both structurally and expressively with partial closure and incomplete tonicisation, so the coda to this second movement, while able to start in the brightest C major (for reasons which will shortly become apparent), is forced back into a more compromised position at the end (Example 8.11), where the abruptly paced (and deliberately 'unsatisfactory'?) cadential gestures (bars 298–300) are underpinned by a bald, descending third motion undeniably related to the intervallic infrastructure of the first movement.

But the most telling focus for the ironic unfolding in this movement is certainly the second subject, marked *f* and *eroico* in the exposition and, crucially, *mp* without the *eroico* marking in the recapitulation. Oistrakh's view of the entire work, doubtless exemplified by this second subject, is as a grand, patriotic narrative: 'S. Prokofiev's F minor Sonata is a tremendous epic in which the picture of the past of our great country lives again and in which the composer's thoughts about his people's fate take form' (quoted in Jusefovich 1979: 166). The cinematic tableau is extended by Oistrakh's son Igor:

> I must say that my own opinion of the first Sonata comes very close to that of my father. The Sonata also arouses thoughts in me, which are connected with the Russian past. In the first movement I even imagine quite concrete pictures and figures: the Russians under the yoke of the Tartars (remember the heart-moving violin passage in the pianissimo, which Prokofiev at the time explained to father as the howling of the wind in a cemetery); in the second movement, a bloody battle; in the third, the picture of a Russian woman which reminds me of Jaroslawna, a figure in Borodin's opera *Prince Igor*, and finally in the finale, with its changing rhythm which reminds one of the finale of *Alexander Newski* (in my opinion, the Sonata has altogether the same atmosphere as Prokofiev's Oratorium, Alexander Newski's arrival at Pskow). All this is of course very relative, but I am talking of subjective impressions; I am trying to clothe my associations with words, which is not easy. (: 166)

However difficult Igor Oistrakh found his verbalisation of the work's impact, his sense is clear if not quite sufficient. As suggested earlier, the emergence of the F major second subject, with prominent local $\hat{3}$s at both the beginning and the end of the theme (Example 8.12), is less a subdominant move within the movement's overall C major than a belated and cathartic release from the end of the first movement. But the point is surely that, even here, the catharsis is incomplete, being still subject to subversion from ♭VII – a tonicisation of the ♭$\hat{7}$ that was a principal vehicle for the previous blockage (Example 8.13a). It can be no coincidence that in the violin part Prokofiev marks this temporary sinking to ♭VII *espressivo* and clearly desires a further screwing-up of intensity here, heightened by the quite specific *tenuto* marking on the last quaver of bar 55 *et seq*. Whether or not one accepts the *eroico* as intrinsically ironic, the passage seems nevertheless to be self-ironis*ing*, both at a local level and in relation to the first movement. The C major return of this material in the compressed recapitulation (bars 257ff.), soon after a further battering of the *eroico* in E♭ major at bars 196ff., can then be read as an attempt to de-ironise the subject and transfigure it into a higher domain: not only is the violin tessitura allowed to spread its wings, compared

Example 8.12    Op. 80, II, bars 50–72

Example 8.13   Bass structures in Op. 80, II, second subject

a. exposition (bars 50–66)

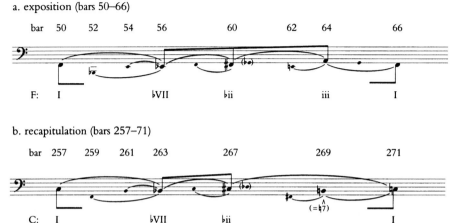

b. recapitulation (bars 257–71)

with its curiously cramped ambitus in the exposition, but the medial plunge to ♭VII is itself regenerated by a new chromatic rise through a 'real' bass leading note B♮ (bars 269–70) to allow a 'proper' release of the tonic at least at the start of the coda (Example 8.13b).[6]

In a strange way, the reading of this second subject material depends more on the pianist's than the violinist's contribution. Of the five recordings, there is little significant difference in the violinists' approach to their part (except, perhaps, for Oistrakh's characteristically 'straighter' playing), and they all share a certain reluctance to differentiate the *espressivo* of bars 55ff. from the previous *eroico*. But it is impossible to detect whether in any given version the violinist is imagining the *eroico* as intrinsically ironic or not, unless, for example, the vibrato, portamentos, etc. were so ludicrously hammed up as to destroy the credibility of the performance altogether. But the pianists' contributions are more telling. The most successful of these in enriching the possible ironic layers of meaning in the music – however they are conceived – are those which show an awareness of the underlying bass structure (Example 8.13) and also give sufficient weight to the off-beat, slurred right-hand groupings, which often anticipate or otherwise distort the notional implications of that bass structure underneath the violin theme. Argerich is particularly good in this respect, as is, to a slightly lesser extent, Ashkenazy. But both Bauer and, especially, Bronfman seriously underplay these subtleties and drain the music of any possible deeper significance. As a consequence, the (at least partially) de-ironised presentation of the material in the

---

6   According to his biographer Nestyev, Prokofiev described this second subject simply as 'broad', though this can scarcely be taken as the final critical word on the music. In any case, it occurs in a synoptic description of the Sonata which is concise to the point of dissimulation: 'The first movement, Andante assai, is severe in character and is a kind of extended introduction to the second movement, a sonata allegro, which is vigorous and turbulent, but has a broad second theme. The third movement is slow, gentle and tender. The finale is fast and written in complicated rhythms' (quoted in Nestyev 1960: 385–6). Nestyev, who adopts the cinematic-epic view of the work embodied in Igor Oistrakh's description (see above), himself goes on to depict this second subject as 'rich' and 'soaring' (: 387).

Example 8.14    Op. 80, III, bars 1–8

recapitulation has nothing to which it can relate back, emerging as rather banal in its own right, as well as insufficiently supported, semantically, to provide the necessary impetus to the coda.

In the exquisite F major slow movement (Andante), a higher degree of ironic transfiguration is accomplished than anywhere else so far in the Sonata. This is signalled right at the opening (Example 8.14), where the 'aspirational' significance of the sharpened fourth, already explored in the first and second movements, evolves several stages further: not only the $\natural\hat{4}$ (B$\natural$), but also, as a kind of natural corollary, $\sharp\hat{2}$ (G$\sharp$) and $\natural\hat{7}$ (E$\natural$) emerge from their decorative function in relation to I, to form a triadic constellation of E major. This new triad on the real leading note of F seems to pick up deliberately the three pre-tonic octave sonorities at the 'unsatisfactory' end of the second movement (Example 8.11), but is in turn subjected to infiltration by the $\hat{7}$ in E major (D$\sharp$), the resultant sense of G$\sharp$ minor (bars 6–7, prefigured in bars 2–3) enabling A$\flat$ major (= $\flat$III) to function as the next significant structural point at the reprise of the main subject in bar 18. This relationship with the tonal workings of the first movement does not stop here, for the large-scale motion of the third movement evolves as a further ironisation of the former's i–iii–$\natural$iv–v–i structure. The ironic content of the process here lies in a twofold presentation of the tonal arch. The initial presentation is transformed for the first time in the work into an almost normalised I–IV–V–I motion (bars 1/8–56ff.: Example 8.15), allowing at least a degree of C major radiance to emerge at the first physical high point of the movement (bar 38), though even this is ironised by chromatic encirclements persisting from the movement's opening, and by $\natural/\flat\hat{3}$ and $\natural/\flat\hat{7}$ interference at the next attempt (bars 54–5: Example 8.16). The second presentation (bars 58/63–96) is not only more compressed, starting close to the primary Golden Section of the movement, but so deeply reinflected by the old $\natural$IV (see especially bars 84ff.) that the V (C$\natural$) of the potential I–$\natural$IV–V–I motion is suppressed into an unresolved I$^6_4$ sonority (bars 93–5, prefigured in 85 and 87: Examples 8.15 and 8.17), still chromatically encircled and once more 'unsatisfactorily' closed by the final root position I (bar 96).

In performance, the extent to which the transfigurative nature of the central C major is achieved or marred depends largely upon how the move from 4/4 to 12/8 at bar 29 is envisaged. The interpretation of the movement offered here suggests that the almost mythological, pastoral-idyllic connotations of the gently swaying triple submetre in this section can be exploited to induce an image of Apollonian yearning which lies beyond the surface chromaticism. None of the other recordings considered in this study comes close to Perlman and Ashkenazy in this regard: the ethereal but quietly searching quality that they achieve and their exceptionally well judged tempo are in marked contrast, for example, to the strangely stilted, halting and hard-edged qualities that Kremer brings to the music at this point. And, at the other extreme, the over-relaxed, undifferentiated character projected by Mintz and Bronfman compromises their performance to an equal degree, though for opposite reasons. Again, the process of ironic transfiguration followed by de-transfiguration outlined here as a metaphorical/metaphysical model for the music's tonal structure suggests that the latter

Example 8.15   Bass structure of Op. 80, III (registers chosen in order to highlight relationship with I)

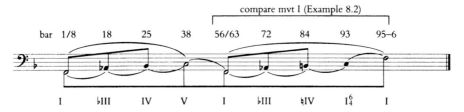

Example 8.16   Op. 80, III

a. bars 38–9

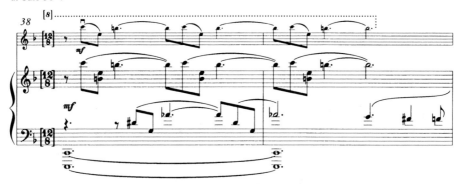

b. bars 54–5

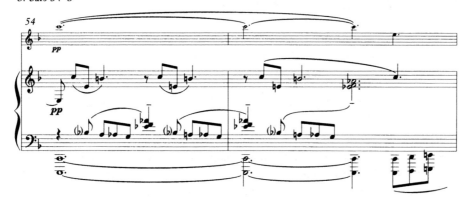

part of the movement, from the arrival of ♮IV at bar 84 to the end, should sound relatively unsettling and non-final. Even the *tranquillo* at bars 86ff. provides only an illusory expectation of serene closure in the tonic minor, since its ostensible third degree (A♭) is soon revealed as a bivalent G♯ in F major, and hence collusive with the other chromatic encirclements, B♮ and D♭, that undermine the ending. Taken in isolation, then, Kremer's performance at bars 84ff., characterised by a sense of desperate wandering, seems appropriate, but it has already failed to make the necessary

Example 8.17    Op. 80, III

a. bars 84–5

b. bars 92–6

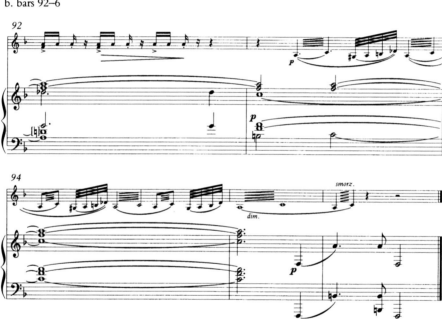

expressive transformation earlier in the movement, which this (non-)closure might act
to subvert. Mintz's playing, while very 'beautiful', is simply too under-characterised
for this medium-term relational point to be made; Fujikawa is better, and Sheppard's
version of bar 84 certainly brings the listener up short more than most. But once again
Perlman and Ashkenazy are the most successful, and the latter's unexpected through-
pedalling of bars 84 and 86 – emphasising the initial Bs rather than the D-dominated
second half of each bar (Example 8.17a) – helps to heighten the $\natural\hat{4}$–$\hat{5}$ motions, as do
the foregrounded left-hand B♮s at bars 93 and 96 (Example 8.17b).

   The final movement of the Sonata (Allegrissimo) brings more corporeal struggles;
indeed the initial tripartite statement (bars 1–12) can be read as a desperately ironic
attempt to normalise and root the music into a conventional I–IV–V–I schema in

Example 8.18    Op. 80, IV, bars 226–33

F major, which has hitherto proved impossible, though, as we have seen, partial 'success' has been achieved in the first section of the preceding movement. (Not only do the furious polymetres in the finale subvert this attempt, but they may also be ironising those unstable metrical/tonal motions at the opening of the first movement.) As one approaches the end of the Sonata, it becomes clear that the conflict between a belief in the possibility of resolution and the worldly experience of its impossibility itself remains unresolved at the work's ironic core. The enormity of the arrival at bar 195 lies, therefore, not so much in any sense of final achievement, as in the sense that the struggle with the material world (including the world of musical material) must continue. Similarly, the deeply ironic reprise of the first movement's graveyard/trans-figuration passage (bars 213–22) seems to function partly to demonstrate within this work that no such reprise is really meaningful, and (paradoxically) partly to hold out some kind of metaphysical hope that trans-temporal monologism may, *pace* Bakhtin, be available to the spirit in some other domain. Poulenc's comment that 'I believe what interested [Prokofiev] most of all was the life and history of religions' (Robinson 1987: 253) may not have been so wide of the mark, even if Prokofiev's own overt pronouncements on the function of art were rhetorically more accommodated to his immediate political, secular circumstances: 'I am convinced that a composer, a poet, sculptor, or painter is called upon to serve man and the people. They must beautify man's life and defend it. Before anything else they must be a "citizen of their art", glorify man's life and lead him to a happy future. Such, in my opinion, is the indisputable code of art' (quoted in Seroff 1968: 355).

The wandering, shell-shocked reminiscence of the last movement's folksy second theme right at the end (bars 227ff.) and the again deliberately evaded full closure of the final cadence (with its emphasis on C♭ as substitute V, the significantly unresolved problem of ♮$\hat{7}$ or ♭$\hat{7}$, and the single occurrence of major $\hat{3}$ rendered ineffectual – see Example 8.18) *appear* to produce a negative conclusion in the context of Stalinist aesthetic ideology. But, as we have observed, the piece is 'about' unachieved potentialities, and whether those potentialities should be construed in terms of the onward march of secular, Stalinist progress or some other, covert, spiritual belief, will probably remain forever disputable – though official approbation of Op. 80 was indeed forthcoming, with the award of the composer's fifth Stalin Prize in June 1947. In any case, the underlying ironic mode of thought, in the extended sense of the term outlined here, has emerged as a powerful creative and critical strategy, one which performers not only can respond to in an interpretative capacity but can actively exploit to change the way in which we hear and think about music and its dynamic processes.[7]

---

[7]   While this chapter was in press, my attention was belatedly drawn to three dissertations whose contents it has been impossible to incorporate into the foregoing discussion: R. Kaufman, 'Expanded tonality in the late chamber works of Sergei Prokofiev' (Dissertation, University of Kansas, 1987); N. Minturn, 'An integral approach to the music of Sergei Prokofiev using tonal and set theoretical analytical techniques' (Dissertation, Yale University, 1988); and M. J. Thibodeau, 'An analysis of selected piano works by Sergey Prokofiev using the theories of B. L. Yavorsky' (Dissertation, Florida State University, 1993).

## REFERENCES

Bass, R., 1988: 'Prokofiev's technique of chromatic displacement', *Music Analysis* 7/2: 197–214.
Bent, M., 1991: 'Deception, exegesis and sounding number in Machaut's Motet 15', *Early Music History* 10: 15–27.
Bishop, L., 1989: *Romantic Irony in French Literature from Diderot to Beckett* (Nashville: Vanderbilt University Press).
Bonds, M. E., 1991: 'Haydn, Laurence Sterne, and the origins of musical irony', *Journal of the American Musicological Society* 44/1: 57–91.
Carpenter, E. D., 1988: 'The theory of music in Russia and the Soviet Union, ca. 1650–1950' (Dissertation, University of Pennsylvania).
Eagle, H., 1981: *Russian Formalist Film Theory* (Ann Arbor: University of Michigan Press).
Holquist, M., 1990: *Dialogism: Bakhtin and His World* (London: Routledge).
Jusefovich, V., 1979: *David Oistrakh: Conversations with Igor Oistrakh*, trans. N. de Pfeiffer (London: Cassell).

Kierkegaard, S., [1841] 1968: *The Concept of Irony, with Constant Reference to Socrates*, trans. L. M. Capel (Bloomington: Indiana University Press).

Lang, C. D., 1988: *Irony/Humor: Critical Paradigms* (Baltimore: Johns Hopkins University Press).

McQuere, G. D., 1983: 'Boris Asafiev and *Musical Form as Process*', in G. D. McQuere, ed., *Russian Theoretical Thought in Music* (Ann Arbor: UMI Research Press), pp. 217–52.

Muecke, D. C., 1982: *Irony and the Ironic* (London: Methuen).

Nestyev, I. V., 1960: *Prokofiev*, trans. F. Jonas (Stanford: Stanford University Press).

Robinson, H., 1987: *Sergei Prokofiev: A Biography* (London: Robert Hale).

Rylance, R., 1987: *Debating Texts: A Reader in Twentieth-Century Literary Theory and Method* (Milton Keynes: Open University Press).

Samuel, C., 1971: *Prokofiev* (London: Calder and Boyers).

Schlifstein, S., ed., [1961]: *Sergey Prokofiev: Autobiography, Articles, Reminiscences* (Moscow: Foreign Languages Publishing House).

Selden, R. and Widdowson, P., 1993: *A Reader's Guide to Contemporary Literary Theory* (Hemel Hempstead: Harvester Wheatsheaf).

Seroff, V., 1968: *Sergei Prokofiev: A Soviet Tragedy* (London: Frewin).

Tull, J. R., 1976: 'B. V. Asaf'ev's *Musical Form as Process*: translation and commentary' (Dissertation, Ohio State University).

Wilde, A., 1981: *Horizons of Assent: Modernism, Post-Modernism and the Ironic Imagination* (Baltimore: Johns Hopkins University Press).

# PART THREE

# Performance as process

■

# CHAPTER NINE

# Performance and analysis: interaction and interpretation

## JOEL LESTER

■

'Players should understand what they play.' This pithy pronouncement, at the start of Donald Francis Tovey's *Companion to Beethoven's Pianoforte Sonatas* (1931: iii), articulates one of the prime rationales for producing and publishing music analyses. Like most analysts, Tovey lists, discusses and graphically depicts both obvious and subtle features of the music, apparently on the assumption that this knowledge will be immediately useful to performers. Occasionally, theorists suggest or even insist on specific performance directions based on their analyses, as Heinrich Schenker does in his 1925 essay on the Largo from J. S. Bach's Sonata in C major for Solo Violin. More recent literature includes two notable books aimed at performers which explain how analysis would help them: Edward T. Cone's *Musical Form and Musical Performance* (1968) and Wallace Berry's *Musical Structure and Performance* (1989), the latter including many more specific performance directions than the former. Within the past decade, additional articles and review-articles specifically address the relation of analysis to performance (especially Schmalfeldt 1985, Dunsby 1989, Rink 1990 and Howell 1992).

I suggest that with rare and quite circumscribed exceptions something is strikingly absent from this literature – namely, performers and their performances. Tovey, Schenker, Berry, Cone and Howell never validate an analysis by referring to singular performances, and Berry even questions the very integrity of any performance which is not based on analytical insight and rigour: 'The purely spontaneous, unknowing and unquestioned impulse is not enough to inspire convincing performance . . . [A]lthough the interpreter's impulsive response to the score can fortuitously hit on convincing approaches through a developed (if often unreasoned) sense of appropriateness, the purely intuitive is unlikely to afford a necessary grasp of – or place in – the comprehended whole' (1989: 217–18).

For these and virtually all analysts, analyses are assertions about a piece, not about a particular rendition. Performers and performances are largely irrelevant to both the analytical process and the analysis itself. If a given performance articulated the points made in an analysis, that would not validate the analysis; rather, the analysis would validate the performance (even when performances differ, like the two described in

Schmalfeldt 1985: 28). If a given performance failed to articulate the points made in the analysis, the performance, not the analysis, would be deemed somehow inadequate (as in Cogan and Escot 1976: 253–4).

Implicit or explicit in all these writings is a view that performance and analysis intersect only when performers follow theoretical edicts or actually become theorists. I have written elsewhere about the pernicious effects that this attitude has had on communication between theorists and performers (Lester 1992). I propose here to challenge the assumption that communication need take place solely when analysts give directions to performers, and to argue that more reciprocal discourse would enhance our understanding of music-theoretical issues as well as performance issues.

Such a challenge could proceed methodologically, questioning Berry's assertion (and its implicit acceptance by many others) of the inherent superiority of cognition in creative performance. Is it right to assume that all those tens of thousands of hours that performers spend honing their skills are entirely mindless, and that it is only when cognitively derived information is explained in words that performers' skills are able to create valid performances?[1]

Additionally, one might question why theorists frequently accede to the 'unreasoned' creative genius of composers but withhold similar approval from 'unreasoning' performers. Theorists regularly acknowledge the acumen of composers who could obviously not have shared our cognitions about musical structure because they lived long before the formulation of the theoretical principles that we now believe to be the very foundation of their works. One could ask why performers are not granted similar status. Theorists criticise harmony texts which lavish care on the author's own musical illustrations rather than on 'real music'. Should we not also fault analyses which apparently are based on the analyst's (imagined?) rendition of a piece rather than on actual performances? After all, most performers have in all likelihood devoted far more time, care and training to realising music in sound than all but a few theorists. (One can raise these points, however, without going so far as Jonathan Dunsby's wry quip, 'More often than not what the analyst is working on is his or her own "performance" in his or her head, and more often than not this performance will be second-, third- or worse-rate' (1993: 8).)

Such methodological approaches to the interaction between analysts and performers would be likely to yield rather abstract categorical statements, no doubt antagonising

---

[1]  Even those recent writers who offer a dialogue between performer and analyst stack the deck in favour of the latter. Tim Howell invites readers of his 'search for a middleground' between analysis and performance to play through Beethoven's Bagatelle Op. 119 No. 1 before reading his analytical prose (1992: 703–14). Unfortunately, this suggests that running through the piece once or twice will help readers understand performance issues; by contrast, a concert pianist living with the Bagatelle for years before performing or recording it will develop a much deeper relationship with it. I realise that it would have been absurd for Howell to tell his readers to spend a few decades learning to play the piano and building a solo career centred around Op. 119 before reading his analysis, but he could have suggested playing the piece as well as studying one or more (recommended?) recordings. Janet Schmalfeldt (1985) is more evenhanded when she formulates her article on analysis and performance issues in the case of two other Beethoven bagatelles as a discussion between her own two personae of analyst and performer (she is an accomplished pianist as well as an analyst). But even she offers an imbalanced dialogue: her pianist-persona is learning to play the pieces, but it is obvious from her prose that her analyst-persona has studied them long and hard.

just as many theorists as there have been performers antagonised by the remarks of theorists. Another way of addressing the issue is to leave aside methodological considerations and propose a more vibrant interaction between analysis and performance – an interaction stressing the ways in which analysis can be enhanced by explicitly taking note of performances, indeed by accounting for them as part of the analytical premise. Such an approach constitutes the body of this chapter.

Whatever difficulties obtain in defining a 'piece of music', it is commonly accepted, I believe, that musical scores are not so much the piece itself as a map of the piece or a recipe for producing it. However different the metaphors *map* and *recipe* might be, they both suggest that a musical work exists beyond its score. Performances are one sort of realisation of a piece (in most cases the sort intended by the composer), and are at once richer and more limited than scores. They are richer in that performances add features never fully notated in any score – myriad nuances of articulation, timbre, dynamics, vibrato, pitch, duration and so forth. Yet each nuance limits the piece by excluding other options for that element. In this sense, a performance is necessarily only a single option for that piece, delineating some aspects while excluding others – just like a single analysis.

Just as analysts use scores as avenues to the pieces they analyse, and refer to other analyses with approbation or disapproval, they can – and should, I would argue – refer to performances in order to get at the essence of the pieces they analyse. To give some idea of how this might work, I shall consider ways in which performances can reflect, reflect upon and inspire analytical statements, and shall then summarise some implications of such an approach.

The first instance concerns an analysis of the Minuet from Mozart's Piano Sonata in A major K. 331 (Example 9.1). Thematically and tonally, this movement resembles a miniature sonata form. The first reprise contains a period in the tonic in bars 1–10, ending with a tonic cadence, and a phrase cadencing strongly in the dominant – a miniature second theme-group – in bars 11–18. The second reprise starts with a tonally mobile development section ending on the dominant in bar 30, while the recapitulation begins with a somewhat recomposed version of the opening period – the antecedent phrase as before, but the consequent reworked to lead to a more emphatic tonic cadence in bars 40–1. In lieu of a complete cadence akin to that in bar 10, however, when the consequent phrase in the recapitulation comes to its end, it seems to elide with the second theme-group on the downbeat of bar 41. This is a common situation in sonata-form movements, even those on a much larger scale than this one, as potentially conclusive tonic cadences are often downplayed in the recapitulation prior to the end of the second theme-group.

Example 9.2 reproduces Schenker's middleground graph of the Minuet. The underlying structure that it asserts agrees with sonata-form structure through the 'exposition', 'development' and beginning of the 'recapitulation': the background motion C♯–B articulates the two key areas of the first reprise, and E is transformed in function from a local tonic at the end of the first reprise to the dominant of A major in the second reprise, all the while prolonging the background B in the first part of an

Example 9.1   Mozart, Sonata K. 331, Minuet, bars 1–18 and 36–48

Example 9.2 Middleground graph of Mozart, Sonata K. 331, Minuet, from Schenker [1935] 1979: Figure 35,1. (Reproduced with permission of the publisher.)

interrupted structural descent. The beginning of the thematic and tonal recapitulation is marked by the restoration of the structural line on C♯. Following this point, however, Schenker's analysis no longer reflects a usual sonata-form scheme. The background structure concludes on bar 41 – the point at which the second theme-group begins. According to this analysis, the remaining bars reinforce the already achieved tonic as in a coda, via the melodic descent through a fifth, and therefore are not essential to bringing the music to its conclusion, at least as far as pitch structure is concerned. They do not play the essential role in the structure of a sonata-form second theme-group or second key area which, in keeping with Cone's 'sonata principle' (1968: 76–7), must be grounded in the tonic key, or which must resolve the 'polarity' of the foreign keys in the exposition, as in Charles Rosen's (1980) description of the essentials of sonata form.

Even without explicitly raising this point, Schenker's analysis implies that bar 41 is a phrasing elision: the cadential dominant of bar 40 resolves on the tonic in bar 41, ending the first theme-group period on the downbeat just as the second theme-group phrase begins. Many performances of the Minuet elide the cadence in precisely this manner, such as Lili Kraus's recording from ca 1966.[2] Others take an altogether different approach. For instance, in his 1966 Carnegie Hall recital Vladimir Horowitz made bar 40 a half cadence rather than continue the phrase into bar 41, with a ritardando, diminuendo and noticeable breath at the end of bar 40 before launching a new phrase in bar 41.[3] In his performance, there is little sense that the right hand's grace note A completes a cadential arrival. Instead, the second theme-group phrase emphatically begins on the E, and the descent of a fifth from this E to the final A is structurally integral and essential, not a mere coda. The dominant in bar 40 concludes an open-ended phrase, moving locally to the phrase beginning in bar 41 but resolving definitively only with the final tonic cadence of the Minuet, which rhymes with the half cadence in bar 40. In effect, the recapitulation's first theme-group period and second theme-group phrase relate as in an interrupted descent, which is not at all what Schenker's analysis shows.

These two ways of arriving at bar 41 reflect different views of the Minuet's form. Specifically, they disagree over whether the motivation for musical structure resides in underlying voice-leading or in themes and key relationships. In effect, Horowitz interprets the Minuet as a sonata form in which the grounding of the second theme-group in the tonic is a significant factor in bringing the movement to a close. Schenker and Kraus, on the other hand, rely on the directed linear motion to the tonic in bar 41 to locate the end of the Minuet's essential structure.[4]

The differences between Kraus's and Horowitz's treatments of bars 40–1, minute as they may be in terms of fractions of seconds and fractions of decibels, are not superficial interpretative details. They raise profound questions about which musical elements are crucial to musical form, where finality is achieved in this Minuet and whether tonal closure occurs at the same time as rhythmic and thematic closure.

These are the very sorts of issues that theorists have been disputing since the notion of musical form and structure evolved from theories of articulated periods in the decades framing 1800. Many different models for these structural aspects have been proposed. Heinrich Christoph Koch, while paying some attention to the roles of themes, suggested that tonally articulated periods were the crucial elements. Adolph Bernhard Marx and others in the generation after Beethoven (and many of their followers up to the present time) placed much more weight on thematic aspects of structure. Tovey and others in the twentieth century scorned the resulting thematic moulds. Schenker argued that underlying large-scale voice-leading was the most crucial factor, with themes playing relatively insignificant roles. Rosen and Cone, as noted above, have proposed their own criteria for the essential underpinning of sonata forms.

When these and other theorists dispute either the nature of form or the structuring of a given piece (such as this Minuet), those of us who follow such disputes (or

---

²  The discography at the end of this chapter provides details of all recordings mentioned in the text.
³  This effect is evident in all three passes through bars 40–1 in the course of the movement, but is most marked in the third rendition, after the trio.
⁴  An analysis of this movement in Westergaard 1975 disagrees with Schenker on many fundamental and interpretative aspects of musical structure, but concurs with him in concluding the essential tonal activity in bar 41.

chronicle them in our implicit or explicit histories of theory) generally regard the resulting interpretative decisions as absolute – Schenker's or Tovey's ideas (or some mixture of both) have displaced and discredited the notions of Marx. If we conceive of these ideas in relation to performance at all, we generally think of how we might coach a performer to be aware of and to project the aspects of musical structure that we are espousing.

But the issues at stake in these theoretical disputes over musical structure and its crucial elements have in fact not been settled, either provisionally or definitively. No matter how much theorists may believe that one position or another is now ubiquitous and that no self-respecting scholar would dare defend a tenet long considered *passé*, the contrasting positions remain very much alive in performances. The renditions by Kraus and Horowitz are no less eloquent than the writings of theorists on the aspects of musical structure just discussed.

Put bluntly, we delude ourselves if we think that disputes over musical structure are either resolved or irrelevant to performance. In fact, in the sense that piano pedagogy (and that of other instruments frequently given leading melody lines) emphasises the shaping and delineation of melodies, it may well be that thematic and sectional theories of musical form carry just as much weight in today's world of performance as they did in the nineteenth-century theories so frequently disparaged in recent scholarly writing.

The criteria that create musical form and the relation between underlying voice-leading and themes are not the only commonly accepted theoretical tenets that are challenged by listening closely to respected performances. Issues concerning metre and phrasing arise in connection with the growing trend in linear analyses to depict metric and hypermetric levels along with pitch levels. One such analysis is Carl Schachter's rhythmic reduction of Chopin's Prelude in G major Op. 28 No. 3 (1980: 202–10). The Prelude (the relevant portions of which appear in abridged form in Example 9.3) is largely a parallel period, bars 3–11 forming the antecedent phrase ending on the dominant, and bars 12–27 forming the consequent phrase ending on the tonic, all framed by a two-bar introduction and brief coda. Schachter's rhythmic reduction (Example 9.4) proceeds from a rhythmic background which reflects the division of the piece into two sections. The antecedent phrase composes out the motion from the opening tonic to the dominant at the half cadence in a regular metre, with an extra bar of dominant at the end. The consequent phrase is more complex, including a long stretch on the subdominant. Schachter discusses at some length the location of primary accents within this subdominant and the following dominant. As he hears the Prelude, the change to the subdominant in bar 18 is metrically relatively unaccented compared with the (relatively accented) reiteration of the subdominant at the beginning of the next phrase-division in bar 20.[5]

---

[5]   Schachter acknowledges (1980: 202n.) that his analysis is based on Figure 76,2 in Schenker 1935, which also graphically illustrates that the arrival on bar 18 is an anticipation of the structural arrival of the subdominant in bar 20.

Example 9.3    Chopin, Prelude Op. 28 No. 3, bars 12–27 (abridged)

Example 9.4   Durational reduction of Chopin, Prelude Op. 28 No. 3, from Schachter 1980: 202. At each level of the analysis, bar numbers refer to the complete Prelude. (Reproduced with permission of the publisher.)

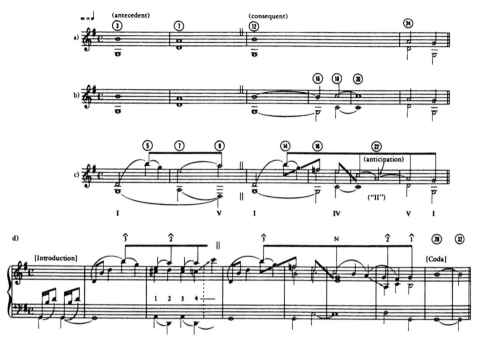

Pianists playing the Prelude typically mark the beginnings and endings of larger rhythmic units and phrases by means of (often slight) ritardandos or pauses immediately before crucial accented bars. Just as Kraus, Horowitz and Schenker express divergent views on the form of Mozart's Minuet, performances of Chopin's Prelude differ in the nature of phrase connections, the metric status of cadences and the location of large-scale accents in general. Among the seemingly innumerable recordings of the Prelude, I call attention to one each by Artur Rubinstein (196?) and Ferruccio Busoni (ca 1920). These recordings treat many aspects of the Prelude differently, but they both disagree with Schachter on the location of hypermetric accents during the subdominant prolongation: both recordings mark the arrival on the subdominant in bar 18 with some emphasis (by slowing noticeably before the downbeat) but proceed with no further ado into the continuation of the subdominant in bar 20.

In answer to questions about which performance(s) his analyses relate to, Carl Schachter has stated that his analyses refer to pieces as he conceptualises them.[6] Most theorists would probably reply in like manner if asked such questions. But when considered with those aspects of Rubinstein's and Busoni's performances that

---

[6]   Schachter made this comment at the City University of New York in Spring 1993 in a discussion following Leo Treitler's reading of the article published as Treitler 1993.

Example 9.5    Durational reduction of Strauss, 'Blue Danube' Waltz No. 1, from Rothstein 1989: 8

contradict his interpretation, Schachter's stance raises troubling issues about what his analysis of this Prelude means. Schachter, Rubinstein and Busoni probably agree that the subdominant interpolation in bars 18–23 is the reason why the consequent phrase of the Prelude is considerably longer than the antecedent (sixteen bars as opposed to eight bars) while remaining a single large phrase. Their disagreement concerns the hypermetric status of the subdominant.

The mutually accepted pitch-structure interpretation of all three musicians is, presumably, a 'given' characteristic of the piece. But the metric status is not, in the sense that these three musicians, who have all had successful careers interpreting this repertoire in contrasting ways, can disagree without losing their position as authorities. As with the bases of form and design raised by the divergence between analyses and performances of Mozart's Minuet, the hypermetric status of this Prelude is by no means a foregone conclusion. The manner in which pitch and metric structuring are inextricably intertwined in Schachter's (and Schenker's) graphing fails to reflect that the former (at least in regard to the subdominant) is an uncontentious issue while the latter is not.

Despite its brevity, Chopin's Prelude is a relatively complex piece in terms of large-scale rhythm. But even in pieces which seem quite straightforward in their larger rhythms, standard performance practice often conflicts with what has become established procedure in the analysis of hypermetre. For instance, William Rothstein regards the four-bar regularity of Johann Strauss's 'Blue Danube' Waltz No. 1 as so universally accepted that he uses it to introduce the notion of hypermetre in the very first rhythmic reduction in his *Phrase Rhythm in Tonal Music* (1989: 8), shown here in Example 9.5. Rothstein explains that 'the four-measure segments . . . are supra-measure units that are perceived *as if* they were measures, because they exhibit a regular alternation of strong and weak "beats" analogous to that of single measures'.

With the consistent four-bar units and their nesting to form eight-, sixteen- and thirty-two-bar units, it would seem that the Waltz is a clear-cut example of the type of hypermetric nesting that Rothstein, Schachter and others believe exists in a wide range of musical styles.

Performances of the 'Blue Danube', however, exhibit a wider range of metric options than Rothstein lays out, especially at the final cadence in bar 32. Among various recordings which articulate the metric status of the cadence relatively weakly (just as Rothstein would predict) is one conducted by Anton Paulik (1956). But that view of the cadence's metric status is far from universal: in a 1966 recording, Eugene Ormandy organises the metrics quite differently, making the cadential arrival in bar 32 the most accentually marked point in the last part of the Waltz.

Other aspects of these two performances suggest that the metric status of the cadence in bar 32 results from more fundamental decisions about the overall form of the cycle. Paulik projects the hypermeasures as analysed by Rothstein by linking the opening two waltzes of the cycle in a single, long-range crescendo of activity beginning in the introduction and crossing the dividing line between the two pieces. To maintain that long line, he downplays the finality of the cadence of the first waltz (bar 32), suspending the gesture into the opening of the second. Ormandy, by contrast, conceives of these first two waltzes more separately. In his rendition, the crescendo of activity during the first concludes at the final cadence; the second waltz begins once again from a relatively low point of activity. The differences between these performance strategies and their relationship to Rothstein's analysis make it clear that even in a dance-movement with regular nested four-bar units, hypermetre is not a factor dictated by the score: it must be interpreted.

The preceding discussions demonstrate that many issues assumed by theorists to be resolved – the bases for musical form and structure, the relationship between underlying voice-leading and musical form, the status of hypermetre – are in fact quite open to debate in today's musical world. For these issues and their manifestations – phrasing, form, hypermetre, structural voice-leading, arrival on crucial structural notes, the balance between connections and articulations, the factors that bring a composition to its conclusion – are the constant concerns of performers. These issues may have been settled, at least provisionally, in theoretical writings, but the very bases of the arguments have barely been broached, let alone resolved, in the sphere of performance.

Performers may not necessarily verbalise or even think consciously about these issues, even to themselves in the privacy of their practice studios. Nor do performers necessarily address them (whether consciously or intuitively) with the purpose of understanding how the piece is put together, how it 'works', how it can be shown to exemplify a particular structure or how it is reducible to more fundamental structures. That is, their goal is not necessarily to analyse the piece. It may well be, for instance, that when Horowitz played a half cadence in bar 40 of Mozart's Minuet from K. 331 he was not consciously aware of anything other than creating an 'effective' performance, however he defined that concept. Indeed many performers may be concerned with little more than achieving an 'effective' performance – one which pleases their sense of

Example 9.6    Mozart, Sonata K. 545, I, bars 1–8

fancy and propriety (stylistic and aesthetic propriety as well as matters of stage decorum) and which is received by their audiences with approval. But in order to realise such a performance, they must deal with the very same features that analysts regularly confront, assuming, of course, that there is some relationship between sounding music and what analysts do when dealing with the range of issues listed in the preceding paragraph. Thus, Horowitz's half cadence in bar 40 comments on the form of Mozart's Minuet and the location of its structural conclusion just as much as Schenker's analysis does. Likewise, Ormandy's strong arrival on the cadence in bar 32 of the 'Blue Danube' speaks to the issue of hypermetre, even though his 1966 recording antedates the first appearance of the term 'hypermeasure' in theoretical discourse in Cone 1968.

Although I have discussed only a few bars in relatively brief movements, the issues raised apply to many levels of structure in larger movements. My discussion also has relied on performance features obvious on first hearing (even when the point under consideration at first seems relatively abstruse, such as whether or not Horowitz articulates a background arrival in a Schenkerian graph). On repeated, closer hearings, many more subtle features can be discerned. Thus, the list of analytical features reflected in performances can extend to include a considerable number, even most, of the elements and entities that analysts treat.

Many such instances are obvious and need no illustration here. But others are more problematic. Consider the first four bars of Mozart's Piano Sonata in C major K. 545 (Example 9.6). Despite its familiarity, this is a puzzling opening. Over a bass which moves only by neighbour motions to articulate each two-bar group, these four bars seem at first like a miniature period, with the antecedent in bars 1–2 and the consequent in bars 3–4. But several crucial features belie this appearance. Both two-bar

Example 9.7   Voice-leading reduction of Mozart, Sonata K. 545, I, bars 1–8

units end on tonic chords, but in contrast to common practice in such periods, it is the melody of the *antecedent* that concludes on the tonic note, while the melody of the *consequent* ends off the tonic note. Additionally, it is not immediately obvious how the consequent relates to the antecedent. True, the melodies of each two-bar unit have similar rhythmic shapes. But that is not a very compelling relationship, especially at the opening of a piece. Common thematic techniques such as sequence, motivic development, ornamentation or diminution are absent.

One compelling relationship linking bars 1–2 to 3–4 is a hidden motif. The melodic outline in the first two bars – C–B–C – is the literal bass line in the next two bars, as shown in Example 9.7. This contrapuntal relationship recurs in expanded form in the next four bars with the C–B–C motion now in the inner voice. In bars 3–4, the soprano adds the A–G–F–E motion over C–B–C. In bars 5–8, the A–G–F–E melodic outline recurs over a new bass (F–E–D–C), while the C–B–C line returns to its original register, as the inner voice. In a sense, the movement opens almost as if it were an accompanied three-part invention.

The remainder of the movement features innumerable variants of the opening motifs and the counterpoint arising from them. Virtually every note in the movement, including all the passagework, derives from the melodic arpeggiation, the C–B–C or $\hat{8}$–$\hat{7}$–$\hat{8}$ motion, or the A–G–F–E or $\hat{6}$–$\hat{5}$–$\hat{4}$–$\hat{3}$ motion. Even the recapitulation in the subdominant is a large-scale reflection of these opening bars: bars 3–4 rework bars 1–2, but with a subdominant inflection at the opening; the recapitulation likewise reworks the exposition, but with a subdominant inflection at the opening. This perspective on the piece incorporates a synoptic view along with the diachronic experiencing of the movement. It can be fleshed out within a Schenkerian graphing or a Schoenbergian development of the opening basic idea.

From either perspective, the subsurface thematic relationship between the melody in bars 1–2 and the bass in bars 3–4 is important. Yet I have never heard a performance or recording which projects this hidden relationship. Indeed, I believe that any attempt to project the bass line in bars 3–4 as a significant feature, let alone a leading feature, would result in a tastelessly unbalanced texture and a most un-Mozartian style. This is one of those analytical insights that may be quite compelling structurally, but must remain a subsurface feature of the piece as realised in sound.

It is therefore unlike the opening motif of Brahms's Intermezzo in A minor Op. 118 No. 1 (Example 9.8), which is sometimes curtailed in performance with deleterious effect if the downbeat of bar 2 in the left hand (marked by Brahms with an accent) is not connected with the preceding right-hand octaves. Projecting the motif as a four-note unit (C–B♭–A–E) clarifies numerous aspects of the Intermezzo. It provides a subtle hint of the final key in the extremely ambiguous tonal climate of the very opening: the complete motif clearly arpeggiates C–A–E, undercutting the sense that bar 1 projects a dominant seventh built on C.[7] It ensures that later variants of the motif are perceived as transformations, not extensions, such as the free inversion of the complete four-note motif that begins the second reprise (G–G♯–A–C), and the final stable statement in bars 36–9. And it enhances appreciation of Brahms's contrapuntal finesse when he introduces the overlapping imitations that connect the opening four bars of the piece to the cadence of the first reprise: the motif might have gone F–E–D♯–A in bars 4–5, but Brahms presents the A along with the D♯, using the A to begin a free imitation of the motif.

The differences between the motivic connections in Mozart's Sonata and Brahms's Intermezzo raise exceedingly difficult issues of analysis and interpretation: deciding when and how to project an analytical finding, and conceptualising the status of an analytical finding which is not projectable. I do not believe that all analytical findings need be projectable or indeed projected. I have argued elsewhere, for instance, that the plot line in Shakespeare's *Romeo and Juliet*, which leads to the death of the two protagonists (and, hence, which makes the drama a tragedy), turns on an undelivered letter (Lester 1982: 267–8). But even though I believe that this event is pivotal to the plot, and I believe that an understanding of that point greatly enhances one's appreciation of Shakespeare's dramatic genius, if I were a director I would never stage the play as a critique of an inefficient postal service in renaissance Italy. Certain structural issues may be highlighted; others are clearly best left for quiet reflection.

What are the consequences of the above discussions? By insisting on their own readings of pieces, many analysts implicitly signal that there is one and only one correct reading of a passage or a piece – hence the sharp pens wielded against predecessors and opponents, even against others within the same theoretical camp (as in the various analysis symposia in the *Journal of Music Theory* some years ago). It is one thing if theorists argue about the 'proper' reading of a passage among themselves, apart from any performances of the piece. But it is something quite different if the disagreement is between the assertions of a theorist and the evidence of a given performance, or, in more extreme cases, the evidence of many or even all performances. For what power can an analytical assertion carry if clearly contradicted by a performance which is widely accepted as 'effective'? Need we be forced to choose between Schenker and Horowitz, between Schachter and Rubinstein/Busoni, between Rothstein and Ormandy? Must we believe that one performance is 'right' and another 'wrong'? Should we accept that analysis has little or nothing to do with sounding music and that these contradictions are therefore inconsequential (see Dunsby 1989 and 1993)?

---

[7]  Cone (1977) cogently discusses the tonal ambiguity of these opening bars. See also Narmour 1988, which echoes many of the points made here.

Example 9.8    Brahms, Intermezzo Op. 118 No. 1, bars 1–6

In addition, the troubling notion that there is only a single 'ideal' or 'correct' interpretation of an artwork, the aroma of hubris that emanates from this perspective and the possible implication that analysis and sounding music are only tangentially related raise purely practical and pedagogical concerns. Briefly put, such a limited and limiting perspective often alienates aspiring performers – the very group who, if we accept Tovey's dictum, should be the primary target for instruction in theory and analysis. Performers and students hoping to become performers will not listen long to scholarly 'authorities' who place themselves in opposition to eminent virtuosos.

Instead of explaining why performances are 'wrong' when they do not agree with analyses, and instead of implying (by ignoring them) that performances are irrelevant to analysis, analysts can usefully incorporate performances as an important ingredient of the analytical process. Common parlance suggests that when performances of a piece disagree with one another, or when analyses of a piece disagree with one another, they are different interpretations of the same piece. That locution can fruitfully be extended to differences of conception between analyses and performances.

Welcoming differing interpretations into analysis need not lead to uncritical acceptance of all points of view and a bland relativism. On the contrary, the reality of performance forces one to realise that choices must be made among alternative approaches to any given issue – at least for a particular rendition. Making choices among various possibilities is an important part of any sort of interpretation, both in analysis and in performance. But in contrast to the way in which analytical decisions are often regarded, performance decisions suggest that many (though certainly not all) possible choices are not so much 'right' or 'wrong' as simply different, leading to varying perspectives (see Schmalfeldt 1985: 28).

In addition, performance decisions are often contingent in the sense that making one decision can tend to obviate others. As noted earlier, Ormandy's interpretative decision to keep the first two waltzes in the 'Blue Danube' relatively distinct seems to be closely related to the way in which he projects the metrics of the first waltz's final cadence. Taking note of performances as part of the analytical process will assist in distinguishing between analytical decisions involving indisputable aspects of structure which should not be contradicted by any analysis and/or performance, and those analytical decisions that are interpretative.

Indisputable statements can go far beyond assertions of mere 'fact' about the music (e.g. that C is the first and last note in the right hand in the first melodic unit of Mozart's K. 545) to comprise elements which are not specifically notated in the score. For instance, no one would deny that there is a tonic cadence at the end of the first waltz in the 'Blue Danube' set – Rothstein, Ormandy and Paulik all agree on that even though there is nothing in the score specifying 'tonic cadence', as the required pitches and rhythms are manifest. Likewise, no one would deny that there is a phrase beginning and ending on the tonic in bars 41–8 of the Minuet from Mozart's K. 331 – Schenker and Horowitz concur on this point even though no score notation specifies that phrase. Any performance not projecting these entities – a performance of the 'Blue Danube' not articulating a dominant-to-tonic motion into bar 32, or a performance of the Minuet from K. 331 failing to render bars 41–8 as a phrase in some sense – could legitimately be regarded as 'incorrect', as failing to follow the score.[8]

Interpretative analytical statements, by contrast, do not describe universals. Rather, they concern a particular conceptual shaping of the piece realised in analysis and (according to the interaction I am advocating) possibly in performance as well. In the 'Blue Danube', Ormandy's performance contradicts Rothstein's assumption that the hypermetre is inherent in the score; likewise, Horowitz's performance challenges Schenker's assertion that the basic structure of Mozart's Minuet necessarily ends in bar 41. As suggested above, these interpretative decisions often reveal different strategies in realising the piece. Rothstein's and Paulik's approaches emphasise the continuity of the waltz cycle; Ormandy's approach makes the first waltz more of an individual statement. Horowitz emphasises the sonata-form structure of Mozart's Minuet, graphically expressing Cone's 'sonata principle' by making the grounding of the

---

[8]   I realise that this formulation adopts a somewhat narrow, positivistic view of a 'piece', sidestepping situations where performers do not play the notes in a score. I refer here not only to ornamentation in music prior to the late eighteenth century, but also to the common practice earlier in the twentieth century (if not in previous periods from which we do not have recorded performances) of altering scores, sometimes substantially. For instance, Béla Bartók's 1922 and 1929 recordings of his *Allegro barbaro* (1911) differ from his own previously published score in the length, pitch content and dynamics of some passages. Such prerogatives were by no means limited to composers playing their own works. Treitler (1993) cites numerous and sometimes extensive changes in the pitch content and form of Chopin works recorded early in this century by Alfred Cortot, Sergei Rachmaninoff and Ignacy Paderewski. This tradition has been perpetuated by at least a few performers until quite recently, as in 1968 when Vladimir Horowitz added several notes to Robert Schumann's *Arabeske* Op. 18, including a right-hand f¹ before the first written note in the score. But even in performance styles where such changes were both common and, presumably, expected, I am not aware of instances where performers tampered with the score so that the types of 'factual' entities referred to above – phrases and cadences – were changed. If these entities had been changed, one could legitimately argue that the performed music was indeed different from the piece in the score.

second theme in the tonic key the motivation for the conclusion; Schenker downplays the thematic aspect and concentrates on underlying voice-leading structures.

No one could argue that any of these approaches is incorrect in the sense that it contradicts the score. Rather, these varying perspectives show that there are different strategies for projecting structural issues in pieces, just as we commonly recognise the existence of various strategies in projecting the affect of pieces – for instance, whether a given passage in Tchaikovsky's Sixth Symphony comes across as resigned or anguished. Deeming such remarks 'interpretative' need not deny their validity to analysts (who often seem to believe that the domain of analysis extends only to definitive statements about 'structure'); rather, they have the potential to refocus analytical activity on the ways in which certain decisions about the music impinge on structural aspects other than those directly under scrutiny. To return to the 'Blue Danube' one last time, it is irrelevant whether Ormandy's primary intention was to accent the cadence in bar 32 or to make the first waltz a discrete unit (or to make some other point, or even not to make any particular point), for both decisions are inextricably interwoven in his performance. What matters far more is understanding how these perspectives are related, determining which one(s) may be more satisfying and establishing the criteria on which such judgements are made.

To be sure, there are analytical assertions which cannot legitimately be disputed even though they seem impossible to project in any performance. One example might be: 'The second key area of Mozart's Sonata in C major K. 545 is G major.' I cannot imagine how any performance would either reflect or deny that statement interpretatively. If the performer declined to play the appropriate notes that establish G major after bar 12, the performer would not be playing the piece. Such statements seem irrelevant to performance concerns.

Likewise, there are interpretative statements which, though not projectable, might affect attitudes towards a given performance. One example is the hidden motivic structure in Mozart's Sonata in C major. Knowledge of these hidden motifs might not predispose performers to emphasise the relevant notes, but could cause them to conceptualise the piece as organically unified. Ignorance of these hidden motifs might result in the ever-new melodies and passagework of the exposition being regarded as a freely associated stream of consciousness. Either approach – developing variation or free association – will affect a host of different performance decisions: whether to seek a relatively wide or limited timbral range, whether to maintain a basic tempo or adopt wide-ranging rubatos, whether to voice the passagework throughout the movement in order to bring out motivic and linear connections with the more homophonic textures elsewhere in the movement or to differentiate the passagework from the more melodic materials, and so forth. One's evaluation of the resulting divergent approaches will depend in part on one's position in the now-fashionable debate between structuralists and post-structuralists.

Acknowledging that performances are relevant to analysis will also dramatically broaden the repertoire that theorists call upon when making analytical assertions. There are a great many more recorded performances of most pieces than there are published analyses (this is probably true even of much-analysed but rarely performed twentieth-century compositions). In addition, performance decisions, because they arise from so many different perspectives, likely reflect a much wider range of structural options than analyses, many of which tend to address a fairly limited agenda. The vast repertoire of recordings remains a resource barely noticed by theoretical discourse.

The ramifications of such an approach extend quite far. If pieces are regarded as composites of seemingly innumerable acceptable interpretative possibilities, the focus of analysis could shift from finding 'the' structure of a piece to defining multiple strategies for interpreting pieces. Performers could enter analytical dialogue *as performers* – as artistic/intellectual equals, not as intellectual inferiors who needed to learn from theorists. Even stylistic and aesthetic questions could be addressed more directly in such analyses than is often the case (see Rink 1990). Consider the first movement of Robert Schumann's String Quartet in A major Op. 41 No. 3. As a sonata-form movement, it exhibits the types of features for which Schumann's sonata forms are often criticised (as in Rosen 1980: 295–315 and Dahlhaus 1989: 158–60). The opening thematic unit of the Allegro molto moderato, a four-bar phrase cadencing on the tonic, appears as the first theme, as the main tune in the transition and as the closing theme. This, along with the fact that much of the new melody launching the second theme-group is built from the very same melodic motions as the opening theme, undercuts the thematic contrast underlying many descriptions of sonata form. In terms of keys, much of the first theme-group is in the dominant, and an extensive portion of the melody that opens the second theme-group reverts to the tonic key of the movement – including the very portion of the second theme that is melodically closest to the opening theme. Thus, the tonal contrast or tonal dissonance at the heart of so many other formulations of classical sonata form is also absent.

Unfortunately, most performances of this movement succeed all too well in bringing the lack of thematic and tonal contrast to the fore. Even while enjoying the enchanting music in these performances, a listener often cannot help agreeing with the common critical assessment that Schumann really did not know how to write successful sonata forms.[9] By contrast, a 1972 recording by the Quartetto Italiano transforms all these supposed problems into assets. By means of carefully nuanced rubatos and shifting timbres, they do not play the movement as a weak example of Mozartian or Beethovenian sonata form. Instead, they produce an evolving thematic and tonal design which challenges us as theorists and analysts to find a new formulation of sonata form more accurately describing Schumann's composition.

In conclusion, let me confirm that I fully agree with Tovey's dictum that 'players should understand what they play'. But to his injunction I append the following: 'Analysts should understand what it is they analyse, especially when the goal of their analysis is to enlighten performers.'

---

[9]  Such performances recall Charles Rosen's description of Schumann's Piano Sonata in F♯ minor Op. 11 as 'beautiful', only to be followed by an extended critique of the work replete with terms and phrases like 'inadaptability', 'anomalies', 'strains', 'fundamentally unclassical' features and 'attack on classical tonality and the integrity of classical form' (1980: 296–315 passim).

REFERENCES

Berry, W., 1989: *Musical Structure and Performance* (New Haven: Yale University Press).

Cogan, R. and Escot, P., 1976: *Sonic Design: The Nature and Sound of Music* (Englewood Cliffs, New Jersey: Prentice Hall).

Cone, E. T., 1968: *Musical Form and Musical Performance* (New York: Norton).

　　1977: 'Three ways of reading a detective story – or a Brahms intermezzo', *The Georgia Review* 31/3: 554–74. Reprinted in E. T. Cone, *Music: A View from Delft*, ed. R. P. Morgan (Chicago: University of Chicago Press, 1989), pp. 77–93.

Dahlhaus, C., 1989: *Nineteenth-Century Music*, trans. J. B. Robinson (Berkeley and Los Angeles: University of California Press).

Dunsby, J., 1989: 'Guest editorial: performance and analysis of music', *Music Analysis* 8/1–2: 5–20.

　　1993: 'Real music', *Newsletter of the Society for Music Analysis* 4: 8–9.

Howell, T., 1992: 'Analysis and performance: the search for a middleground', in J. Paynter et al., eds., *Companion to Contemporary Musical Thought*, 2 vols. (London: Routledge), vol. II, pp. 692–714.

Lester, J., 1982: *Harmony in Tonal Music*, vol. II (New York: Alfred A. Knopf).

　　1992: Review of Berry 1989, in *Music Theory Spectrum* 14: 75–81.

Narmour, E., 1988: 'On the relationship of analytical theory to performance and interpretation', in E. Narmour and R. A. Solie, eds., *Explorations in Music, the Arts, and Ideas* (Stuyvesant, New York: Pendragon), pp. 317–40.

Rink, J., 1990: Review of Berry 1989, in *Music Analysis* 9/3: 319–39.

Rosen, C., 1980: *Sonata Forms* (New York: Norton).

Rothstein, W., 1989: *Phrase Rhythm in Tonal Music* (New York: Schirmer Books).

Schachter, C., 1980: 'Rhythm and linear analysis: durational reduction', in F. Salzer, ed., *The Music Forum*, vol. V (New York: Columbia University Press), pp. 197–232.

Schenker, H., 1925: 'Johann Sebastian Bach: Sechs Sonaten für Violine, Sonate III, Largo', *Das Meisterwerk in der Musik*, vol. I (Munich: Drei Masken Verlag), pp. 63–73.

　　1935: *Der freie Satz* (Vienna: Universal Edition). English translation: *Free Composition*, trans. and ed. E. Oster (New York and London: Longman, 1979).

Schmalfeldt, J., 1985: 'On the relation of analysis to performance: Beethoven's Bagatelles Op. 126, Nos. 2 and 5', *Journal of Music Theory* 29/1: 1–31.

Tovey, D. F., 1931: *A Companion to Beethoven's Pianoforte Sonatas* (London: Associated Board of the Royal Schools of Music).

Treitler, L., 1993: 'History and the ontology of the musical work', *The Journal of Aesthetics and Art Criticism* 51/3: 483–97.

Westergaard, P., 1975: *An Introduction to Tonal Theory* (New York: Norton).


DISCOGRAPHY

Bartók, B., 1922: *Allegro barbaro* (Hungaroton LPX 12334-A).

　　1929: *Allegro barbaro* (Hungaroton LPX 12326-A).

Busoni, F., [ca 1920] ca 1966: F. Chopin, Prelude in G major Op. 28 No. 3 (Everest X-906).

Horowitz, V., 1966: W. A. Mozart, Piano Sonata in A major K. 331 (CBS Records M3K 44885).

　　1968: R. Schumann, *Arabeske* Op. 18 (CBS Records M3K 44886).

Kraus, L., [ca 1966]: W. A. Mozart, Piano Sonata in A major K. 331 (Monitor Records, MCS 2105).

Ormandy, E. and the Philadelphia Orchestra, [1966]: J. Strauss, 'Blue Danube' Waltz No. 1 (Columbia ML 6334).

Paulik, A. and the Vienna State Opera Orchestra, [1956]: J. Strauss, 'Blue Danube' Waltz No. 1 (Vanguard 2VRS-476).

Quartetto Italiano, [1972]: R. Schumann, String Quartet in A major Op. 41 No. 3 (Philips 6703 029).

Rubinstein, A., [196?]: F. Chopin, Prelude in G major Op. 28 No. 3 (RCA Victor LM-1163).

# CHAPTER TEN

# Analysis and the act of performance

## WILLIAM ROTHSTEIN

Every true work of art has but one true performance, its own particular to it . . .

The hand may not lie; it must follow the meaning of the voice-leading.

Heinrich Schenker[1]

This book is testimony to the increased scholarly attention that musical performance is receiving, not least from theorists and analysts. In the early part of the twentieth century, some theorists – including Hugo Riemann and Heinrich Schenker – were deeply engaged with issues of performance;[2] but for several decades the pendulum swung away from such practical concerns, at least in American scholarship. Performance practice became the preserve first of historical musicologists and then of practitioners in the budding historical performance movement. The current renewal of interest in this area among theorists is related, I believe, to a much broader intellectual trend, one which refuses to regard musical structure and its discovery by means of analysis as ends in themselves. One could call this trend 'post-structuralist' in the literal sense. At its most radical, post-structuralism has devalued structure, and has even denied that structure is a relevant issue for certain kinds of music (particularly opera).[3] While most theorists and analysts are unwilling to attack the foundations of their disciplines in this way, many have been drawn to issues which relate structure to other aspects of music: to the history of musical style, for instance;[4] or to human cognitive capacities;[5] or – of most immediate relevance here – to performance practice.[6]

---

[1]  'Jedes wahre Kunstwerk hat nur einen wahren Vortrag, seinen eigenen und besonderen . . .' 'Die Hand darf nicht lügen, sie muß dem Sinn der Stimmführung folgen.' Schenker, 'Entwurf einer "Lehre vom Vortrag"', compiled by Oswald Jonas from Schenker's unpublished notes; Oswald Jonas Memorial Collection, University of California at Riverside. The quoted sentences come respectively from pp. 32 and 21 of Jonas's typescript (my translation). For further information on this source see Rothstein 1984.

[2]  See, for example, both theorists' editions of and writings on Beethoven's piano sonatas, including Riemann 1920 and Schenker [1920] 1972. On Schenker, see also Rothstein 1984.

[3]  See, for example, Abbate 1989.

[4]  Examples include Meyer 1989 and Rothstein 1989.

[5]  See especially Lerdahl and Jackendoff 1983.

[6]  Examples include Burkhart 1983, Schmalfeldt 1985, Cook 1987, Wason 1987 and Berry 1989.

The fundamental question is this: what effect should music's structure have on the way in which music is performed? In particular, how should the results of analysis be conveyed (assuming that they *should* be conveyed) to the listener? One familiar response – at least, the one I have heard most often – asserts that analysis is useful because, knowing what a piece of music contains in terms of structure, the performer can proceed to 'bring it out'. This, in my view, is a dangerous half-truth. Its superficial plausibility is, no doubt, why it tends to be repeated, not least by teachers of analysis. But it is important to think through the issues more carefully. In what follows, I shall present examples in which 'bringing it out' would do a performance more harm than good. I shall also comment on the difference between analytical truth (see the epigraphs above) and dramatic truth; the performer needs to be concerned with both. All of my examples are taken from music for solo keyboard, for no better reason than that the piano is my instrument. Only four composers are represented: Bach, Beethoven, Chopin and Brahms. Nevertheless, I believe that my ideas are applicable to much music of the eighteenth and nineteenth centuries – especially instrumental music – and to some twentieth-century music as well.

Most listeners, I am sure, do not go to concerts or listen to recordings to hear an analytical demonstration. Audiences (and I am referring only to serious music-lovers) quite properly demand something else of the performer, something I can only call 'magic'. The kind of magic that is necessary to a successful musical performance is not essentially different from that required by the other performing arts. The performer must first of all identify with the work and must inhabit it as completely as possible, regardless of the work's genre or tone. Thoughtful observers have expressed unease even with performers as brilliant as, say, Vladimir Horowitz or Laurence Olivier, when they have sensed dissociation between the performer and the work – when the performer's talents have been engaged, so to speak, in *playing with* the work rather than *playing* the work.

But the performer who relies upon detailed analysis is rarely prone to the short-comings of a Horowitz or an Olivier but to another kind of error: the error of pedantry. Here one might compare a musical performance to the public recitation of a poem. A reciter will prove to be at least competent if he or she knows the language being recited, understands the syntax of each sentence and has a firm grasp of the poem's verse structure, metre and rhyme. But correctness in all these areas does not guarantee a convincing recitation. What should be done – to consider just one kind of problem – in the case of enjambment, where syntax and verse structure collide? Analysis alone will not help, because in such a case analysis – which, by definition, involves the resolution of an object into its parts – is not the solution but the very source of the problem.

It is in part for reasons such as this that Schenker eschewed the word 'analysis' (in German, *Analyse*) in favour of 'synthesis' (*Synthese*). In the case of poetic enjamb-ment, what must guide the reciter is an *idea* of synthesis – specifically, a decision regarding what kind of synthesis is needed to integrate the poem's conflicting parts (verse structure and syntax being partial viewpoints in poetry, like harmony, counterpoint and metre in music). Once a piece of instrumental music has been analysed – resolved into its parts – synthesis is even more urgently needed than in poetry, because the lack of words leaves the music's underlying idea more open to uncertainty.[7] The nature of Schenker's 'synthesis' is well known: voice-leading as the carrier of the tonic triad through time and transformation. Thus, in my second epigraph above, it is 'the meaning of the voice-leading' that Schenker takes to be the *real* meaning of the work, the meaning that the performer's hand must not violate. This is indisputably an enormous advance over simplistic ideas of 'analysis' and 'bringing out'. But, as we shall see, even it is not an unerring guide to the performer.

Perhaps the clearest conflict between 'analysis' and 'synthesis' occurs in fugues, above all the fugues of J. S. Bach. When I was a child learning to play the piano, I was taught to 'bring out' the subject of a Bach fugue at each of its entries. In this way (it seems to have been presumed), I would at least not appear to be missing the point of the fugue. But of course that is exactly what I *was* doing. For Bach delights in weaving his subjects into every part of his musical argument – beginnings, middles and ends – and he often goes to great lengths to conceal their entries. To 'bring out' such hidden entries would be to reveal not erudition, but boorish pedantry. No; the performer should play along with Bach, keeping hidden what Bach took pains to conceal. Then the listener will have the pleasure of discovering the subject once it is already under way. Or perhaps the subject will be missed altogether, or only half-noticed, which is by no means the worst possible outcome: it is surely better for the listener to grasp the overall flow of a fugue than to focus solely on its thematic material, and in this respect a fugue is no different from any other piece of music.[8] But the *performer* should be aware of the subject whenever it is present. What I am suggesting, therefore, is not ignorance on the performer's part but active complicity with Bach – a kind of 'acting' in which the performer knows that the subject is there but pretends not to notice, at least at first. The performer, like Bach, is then in the position of misleading the listener in one domain (the thematic) in order to reveal a greater truth which lies elsewhere.

Sometimes Bach alters the head of his subject to help conceal its entry. He does this several times, for example, in the Fugue in A minor from Book II of the *Well-Tempered Clavier*. Example 10.1 is a reconstruction, in three stages, of the middle voice's entry at bar 17. Stage 1 shows an ascent in parallel tenths in bar 16 (note the augmented second F–G♯), followed by a cadence in bar 17.[9] Stage 2 shows the octave displacements caused by Bach's demisemiquaver movement, plus the quaver embellishments of the bass and middle voices. (The bass's quavers relegate the augmented second to a subsurface level of the music.) Stage 3, finally, shows the actual passage,

---

[7]  I am thinking of poetry which is contemporaneous with my musical examples, excluding certain poets of the later nineteenth century (especially the French symbolists, whose purposeful obscurity arose partly from an attempt to imitate the effect of Wagner's music).

[8]  The same thought is expressed by Roger Sessions in Olmstead 1987: 87. Sessions contrasts Bach's fugues with the fugue from Beethoven's Piano Sonata Op. 106; in the latter, he says, the subject *should* be consistently emphasised.

[9]  The E shown in brackets in Stage 1 is actually heard an octave higher. On a larger scale, this E represents a continuation of the bass E heard on the downbeats of bars 13 and 15. E (V) moves to A (i) at the cadence in bar 17, although the bass's figuration obscures the cadence somewhat. My reading of the bass in bar 16 is based partly on the counterpoint with the right hand's registrally displaced ascending third (a²–b¹–c¹) and partly on the voice-leading that the subject's tail exhibits elsewhere in the Fugue.

Example 10.1    Bach, Fugue in A minor (*WTC*, II)

Stage 1: bars 16–17, reduced to crotchets

Stage 2: bars 16–17, reduced to quavers

Stage 3: bars 16–18[1]

with the entry bracketed. Bach has seized the opportunity of the whole-tone resolution in the middle voice (D to C) to begin a version of the fugal answer (compare
bars 3, 9–10, 13 and 25–6). For the keyboard player to 'bring out' this entry – say, by
accenting the fourth quaver of bar 17 – would be ill-advised.[10]

More often Bach conceals his subject while keeping it in plain view, with no
protective alteration – even, sometimes, concealing it where one most expects to find

---

[10]   An extreme example of bringing out concealed entries may be heard in Sviatoslav Richter's recording of
the Fugue in A minor (Le Chant du monde 278 529). In bar 17, Richter plays e[1] on the third quaver rather
than b, and he plays it *fortissimo*; the following d[1] is played *piano*, the rest of the subject again *fortissimo*.
(Harpsichordists are naturally spared the temptation to thump out entries in this way.) Edward Aldwell
(Elektra/Nonesuch 79200-2) accents d[1] on the fourth quaver – he habitually brings out subject entries – but
is more subtle about the entry than Richter; in general, Aldwell's recording demonstrates how entries can be
highlighted with minimal disruption of the musical flow. Among pianists, Andras Schiff (Decca/London 417
236-2) takes perhaps the closest approach to the one I am advocating here.

Example 10.2   Bach, Fugue in C minor (*WTC*, II)

a. bars 1–5¹, reduced

b. bars 1–5²

c. bars 4–5¹, reduction of hypothetical perfect cadence

it. Such a case is the bass entry in the exposition of the Fugue in C minor from Book II (Example 10.2).[11] The bass enters in bar 4, just as the soprano is in the final stage of an octave descent from $c^2$ in bar 2 (embellished with an upper neighbour) to $c^1$ in bar 5. This descent would close with a perfect cadence but for the presence of the subject, which evades the cadence by descending by step from V to $i^6$ rather than by leap from V to i. (As Example 10.2a shows, the descent from $c^1$ (bar 1) ultimately forms a sixth, $c^1$–e♭.) In my opinion, the cadential process should be the focus of attention here, not the subject; in particular, the soprano's line should not be broken by the sudden turning of the spotlight onto another voice. The bass should enter unassumingly, as if to support the soprano's cadence; its opening note, g, is after all a continuation of the g in bar 3. Only the failure of the cadence to complete itself (compare the hypothetical

---

[11]   The analysis in Example 10.2a is similar to one in Renwick 1991, except that Renwick shows the perfect cadence being completed by the bass c on the second half of bar 5's first beat. I disagree; in my view, the cadence is evaded at bar 5 and is successfully completed only at bar 23.

Example 10.2c) should draw the listener's attention to the subject – although it will have been obvious, given the genre, that a bass entry was imminent.

In both these examples, excessive attention to the fugal subject – the result of the way in which fugues are conventionally analysed – can only distort the music in performance. To overcome such baleful results of analysis, the type of synthesis advocated by Schenker is exactly what is needed: attention to the larger spans of the melody (or melodies) and the harmony, as Example 10.2a suggests.[12] The answer to a blinkered analysis – in this case, thematically obsessed analysis – is more and better analysis, with special emphasis on Schenker's concept of 'synthesis' through voice-leading on the medium to large scale. This applies to the performance of fugues in general, although other factors may be relevant to the performance of a particular fugue (characteristic dance rhythms, for example).

Strategic underplaying of important melodic materials is often advisable when those materials are relatively arcane.[13] Beethoven's Piano Sonata in A major Op. 101 provides a good example. This Sonata is permeated through all its movements by a set of three related motifs (see Example 10.3). Motif 1 is a stepwise motion through a fourth, either descending or – less frequently – ascending. Motif 2, a variant of Motif 1, is a 'gapped' fourth, meaning a fourth which is only partly filled; thus a step is followed by a leap of a third in the same direction, or a leap of a third is followed by a step in the same direction. Motif 3 is related to Motif 2 and consists merely of the downward leap of a third, usually from an upbeat to a downbeat; this motif belongs mostly to the finale, although it is foreshadowed earlier. Example 10.3 shows instances of all three motifs, drawn from various parts of the Sonata. I have simplified matters by excluding further variants of the motifs, although such variants are plentiful.[14]

It is of the utmost importance, in my view, that the pianist be aware of these motifs and of the musical drama in which they play leading roles. That this Sonata embodies a kind of programme can be denied, I think, only by the most obtuse adherent of 'absolute music'. The nature of Beethoven's programme is suggested by the extremely important contrast between the descending and ascending forms of Motif 1. The descending form is by far the more common, if one excludes the use of the ascending form in the finale's semiquaver figuration. The ascending motif is reserved for special moments, and it is twice highlighted in a high register: at the end of the first movement, and in bars 30–2 of the second-movement March (note the special colour created by the pedal in the latter statement). These high-register, ascending forms of

---

12  See Schenker 1926: 55–95 and Kalib 1973: II, 246–320. For another relevant (and highly stimulating) discussion, see Harrison 1990.
13  The motifs that figure in Schenkerian analyses are usually of this type, consisting often of a single interval, especially one traversed by step.
14  My analysis of Op. 101 is greatly indebted to Schenker [1920] 1972 and Oster [1949] 1983. Schenker points out many occurrences of Motif 1, and also the foreshadowing of Motif 3 in the first movement's coda. Oster (who does not discuss Op. 101) details a similar motivic drama in Beethoven's *Egmont* Overture and alludes to its presence in the Sonata in C major Op. 102 No. 1 for Piano and Cello.

Example 10.3   Beethoven, Sonata Op. 101

a. I, bars 1–4 (slightly reduced)

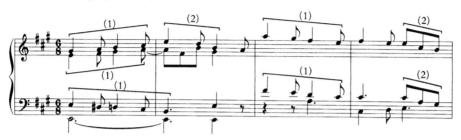

b. I, bars 30–3¹

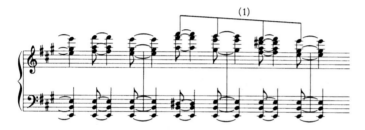

c. I, bars 94–9¹

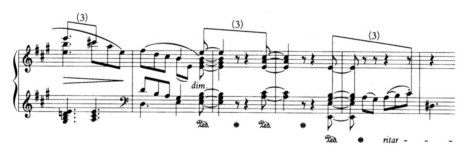

d. I, bars 101–2 (extract)

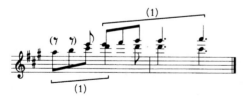

e. II, bars 1–4[1]

f. II, bars 8b–9

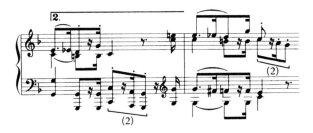

g. II, bars 30–3

h. II, bars 44–5[1]

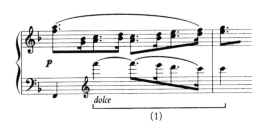

i. III, bars 1–4

j. III, bar 8

k. IV, bars 1–4

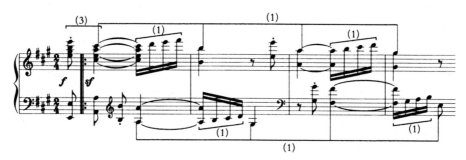

l. IV, bars 57–8

m. IV, bars 78–81[1]

n. IV, bars 273–6

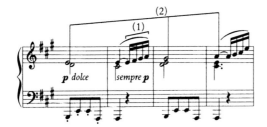

Motif 1 can, I believe, be identified as representing the divine, or possibly human striving for the divine.[15] In the first movement, the final, ascending statements of Motif 1 (see Example 10.3d) reverse the descending statements in bars 31–3 and 83–5, using exactly the same pitches. In the March, the ascending fourth (Example 10.3g) provides a moment of ecstatic contemplation in the midst of grotesque comedy, the latter dominated by the descending form of Motif 1.[16]

Once the pianist is aware of these motifs and their ramifications throughout the Sonata, what is he or she to do about them? To what degree, in particular, should the motifs be 'brought out'? I would suggest a variable approach, depending upon a number of factors. The two chief questions the performer should ask are the following. First, how readily would the motif be heard without the pianist's active intervention? Secondly, what role in the musical discourse does a particular motivic statement play? Is it a foreshadowing, an expository statement, a developmental spinning-out, a culmination or an after-echo? On these bases one can conclude, for example, that the last two bars of the first movement require more active attention to Motif 1 than do bars 31–3, although both statements are important points of culmination. At the end of the movement, both the greater complexity of the texture and Beethoven's notation of the right hand tend to obscure the imitative entries of Motif 1 in its ascending form. While awareness of the motif in the earlier passage will help the pianist to achieve the desired warmth of expression (*espressivo e semplice*), there is nothing here – save the syncopations – to compete with the motif for the listener's attention.

---

[15]  See Kinderman 1985.
[16]  See Schenker [1920] 1972: 35–41. In reading this work, one must remember that the graphic analyses it contains are the first Schenker published. It is not surprising, therefore, that they appear more purely intuitive, and less systematic, than many of his later ones.

A very different situation is presented by the movement's first two bars. Here it is as though the first theme were not yet aware that it *is* the first theme; this tentative statement on the dominant has almost the character of an introduction.[17] It is good for the pianist to know that the descending form of Motif 1 is in the tenor; that Motif 2 is in the soprano in bar 2 (since $e^2$ acts as an appoggiatura, this form of Motif 2 bears the seeds of Motif 3); and that the soprano and alto in bar 1 suggest the ascending form of Motif 1 (although $c\sharp^2$ functions as a passing note leading to $d^2$). Except for the clear statement of Motif 2, however, these are mere foreshadowings. It would be the height of insensitivity – indeed, it would spoil the effect of the opening altogether – if the pianist were, say, to 'bring out' the tenor's statement of Motif 1. The listener should not be *forced* to hear the motif; Beethoven reveals its significance gradually, and the pianist must respect his plan. The next statement of Motif 1 is in bar 3 (soprano and tenor), but it is easier to hear this as an inversion of bar 1 (soprano and alto) than to relate it to the tenor's opening notes. The full significance of those notes becomes apparent only at the beginning of the recapitulation, where the motif's appearance is carefully prepared (the tenor in bars 58–9 grows out of the preceding octave ascent in the bass, and the two registers are linked even earlier). At this point it is the listener's responsibility – and of course the pianist's – to remember and to understand; the pianist might help the listener by playing the tenor here with a certain degree of emphasis. In bars 1–2, by contrast, the pianist should do what I advised in the case of Bach's concealed fugal entries: to be aware but to underplay.[18]

A further problem for the performer of this Sonata is the unusual form of its first movement, particularly its exposition. This is a highly compressed and famously ambiguous example of sonata form; an especial puzzle has been the precise location of the 'second theme'. Schenker had it right, I think, when he wrote that three formal parts are melded together in bars 5–25: the consequent phrase of the first group (*1. Gedanke*), the transition (*Modulation*) and the second group (*2. Gedanke*).[19] For my own sake as a pianist, I have found it necessary to make some decision as to how these bars subdivide; otherwise the lengthy passage, lacking in both perfect and imperfect cadences until the end, can easily sound aimless.

[17] Janet Schmalfeldt, using as her point of departure some remarks in Dahlhaus 1991, has commented perceptively on the analogous situation at the beginning of the Sonata Op. 31 No. 2 ('Form as the process of becoming: the Beethoven–Hegelian tradition', a paper delivered to the 1993 joint meeting of the American Musicological Society and the Society for Music Theory).

[18] Comparison with Henrik Ibsen's *The Wild Duck* is useful in this regard. When the duck is first mentioned, early in Act II, it is not seen by the audience or referred to as a duck, only as something in a basket; nor is its symbolic import made known in any way. In the Sonata, Motif 1 – which proves to be the most important motif in the entire work – is introduced almost as casually. The listener has no way of knowing – and *should* have no way of knowing – what momentous significance these few notes will assume for the Sonata as a whole. For the pianist – likewise the director of Ibsen's play – to try to reveal this significance at its first appearance would be to commit a dramatic error of almost unimaginable crudity.

[19] Schenker [1920] 1972: 15. Those who have placed the 'second subject' at bar 16 are incorrect in my view (see for instance Riemann 1920: 252–6 and Blom 1938: 195–6). Although this is a distinctive melodic idea, bars 16ff. represent what I have called a 'cadential theme', which I define as the final approach to the cadence of a larger group (usually the second group in a sonata form), when that approach is characterised by distinctive melodic material. (See Rothstein 1989: 118.)

Example 10.4   Phrase analysis of Beethoven, Op. 101, I, bars 1–25[1]

My segmentation of the exposition is shown in Example 10.4. The antecedent and consequent phrases of the first group are labelled 1 and 2 respectively. Since the 'proper' or expected completion of the consequent can only be imagined, I have shown two possible ways in which this might happen – one cadencing in the tonic, the other in the dominant. Following the fermata at bar 6 – where the vi triad of A major is reinterpreted as ii of E major – I understand four more segments, all but one of them consisting basically of four bars. The first of these segments, labelled 3, moves from the initial ii harmony, through V and I, to IV; as I imagine it, this segment broadens out in its third and fourth bars (as shown). Segment 4 overlaps the end of Segment 3 and carries the harmony from IV to V; notice that this segment has the proportions of a Schoenbergian sentence, 1 + 1 + 2. Segment 5 overlaps the end of Segment 4 and continues the dominant harmony, leading in five bars to the interrupted cadence in bar 16. The melodic rhythm of Segment 5 imitates that of Segment 4 with an extra bar (the third) added.[20] Segment 6 completes the main part of the

[20]   The first three bars of Segment 5 (bars 12–14) have a parenthetical quality, the result of the continued prolongation of both $\hat{5}$ (b[1]) and the V harmony. As far as the melody is concerned, Beethoven could have proceeded from bar 11 directly to bar 15. The bass of bar 11 connects clearly to the bass B at the end of bar 15, further establishing the parenthetical status of the bars in between. At a deeper level, therefore,

exposition by leading, finally, to the perfect cadence in E major. The latter half of Segment 6 is greatly expanded; when the expansion is removed, this segment also has the proportions of a sentence.[21]

I have said that I find some subdivision of this exposition necessary for purposes of performance. In fact, although the two types of analysis generally influence each other, I find the phrase analysis in Example 10.4 of more immediate utility than a middle-ground voice-leading analysis – which, as yet, I have only partly worked out for this movement.[22] In my mind, the subdivisions of the exposition are connected with changes in the music's imaginary 'orchestration', always an important factor in Beethoven's piano writing.[23] For example, the overlap at bar 12 is connected, for me, with a change from an orchestral to a chamber texture; this requires a new colour from the pianist. But all of these subdivisions and punctuations must be treated with the utmost delicacy in performance. Even if one were to claim that my six segments represent the 'true' form of the exposition – and I am not prepared to claim so much for them – one is discovering the 'truth' only to obscure it again. By subdividing the exposition, I am conducting an 'analysis' in the literal sense. But to perform the analysis is not to perform the piece. Decisions about how to convey the relation between part and whole remain to be made (this is where voice-leading analysis can help). Often, as here, these decisions should be reached in such a way that the listener is carried forward through all lesser punctuations to the larger goal. Here that goal is not even the perfect cadence at bar 25 but the crowning statement of Motif 1 in bars 31–3.

Admittedly, Op. 101 is an exceptionally subtle piece. One of its most remarkable passages contains a motivic reminiscence so discreet that no amount of 'bringing it out' could suffice to make it clear to the casual listener. In the latter part of the finale's coda – thus at the very end of the Sonata – Beethoven works out several ideas at once (see Example 10.5). It is not difficult to hear that the melodic rhythm is derived from the first theme, and that the upper voice traces a filled-in version of Motif 3 (E–D–C♯). The bass reinforces Motif 3 by repeating the contra E that made its first appearance just before the recapitulation (bars 191–9). Since the low E always occurs on an upbeat bar, leading to a tonic downbeat, one's impression is that the movement's first two chords (V–I) are being freely augmented.[24] But, as Example 10.5 shows, a truly amazing event occurs in the inner voice. What is being traced in these bars (315–19) is the ascending form of Motif 1, leading from E to A as it did in the last two bars of the first movement. (The motif was also heard in an inner voice at the end of the recapitulation, bars 267–70.) Motif 1 is then liquidated by being progressively

Segments 4 and 5 could be reduced to a single segment of five bars. On parentheses in general, see Rothstein 1989: 87–92 and passim; on parentheses in Beethoven's late piano sonatas, see Kinderman 1988.

[21] This expansion is discussed in Rothstein 1989: 81–3.

[22] A complete voice-leading analysis of this movement may be found in Korsyn 1983: 13–16. While I find much of Korsyn's analysis compelling, I cannot subscribe to it in all particulars.

[23] See Robert Schumann's comment on this aspect of Beethoven's piano writing (as compared to Schubert's) in Schumann [1840] 1983: 113.

[24] The hypermetric analysis in Example 10.5 is from Schenker [1920] 1972: 98–9, where the presence of E–D–C♯ is also pointed out. William Kinderman (1990) notes the significance of the contra E and makes several other excellent points concerning this Sonata.

Example 10.5    Voice-leading reduction of Beethoven, Op. 101, IV, bars 313–23

compressed, first to F♯–G♯–A and then to G♯–A alone; the latter dyad has already been heard throughout most of the coda, almost as an ostinato.

One can only speculate as to the meaning of Motif 1 at the end of the Sonata. Why is it presented so covertly?[25] I hear the motif – especially its last appearance – as a kind of prayer. While the message of the finale is surely that, given sufficient determination (the movement is marked '*mit Entschlossenheit*'), happiness is possible in this life, Beethoven at the same time seems to be looking surreptitiously – or perhaps subconsciously – upward. So, while $e^3$ leaps down in this coda to the earthly tonic (bars 308–15), and even to the subterranean dominant (the contra E), rather than ascending to heaven as in the first movement's coda, thoughts of God and salvation have not disappeared. The only thing the performer can do is to sing Motif 1 inwardly while playing bars 315–19 and 320–3; at any rate, that is what I do when I play the Sonata. *Möge es wieder – zu Herzen gehen!*[26]

I have mentioned poetic enjambment and the difficulty of reciting enjambed verse. Enjambment exists in music, too, presenting the same sorts of challenges to the performer. The situation arises especially in music of the nineteenth century – particularly its first half, when the relation between European art music and poetry was closer than it had been for centuries (perhaps since the *formes fixes* of the late Middle Ages).

Enjambment is what the principal theme of Chopin's Ballade in G minor Op. 23 is all about (the title 'ballade' of course implies a particularly direct link with poetry). Part of the purpose of the introductory recitative is that the first bar of the theme not only *sounds* like a perfect cadence (as do the first two bars of the trio in Mozart's 'Jupiter' Symphony; see Janet Levy's chapter in this volume) but *is* in fact a perfect cadence – the final cadence of the introduction. From here to the end of the theme (bar 36), the metrical and syntactic structures are consistently enjambed. I have illustrated these enjambments by means of a voice-leading graph (Example 10.6).[27] The three main sections – introduction, antecedent and consequent – are separated

25    I hear another concealed occurrence of E–F♯–G♯–A (Motif 1) at the beginning of the recapitulation's closing theme, bars 248–55. E and F♯ are heard in the upper voice of bars 248–9; G♯ is implied in bar 250 (it is purposely omitted from the left hand); A is reached at the end of bar 251.

26    This quotation is of course from Beethoven's inscription at the beginning of his *Missa solemnis* Op. 123: 'Von Herzen – Möge es wieder – zu Herzen gehen!' ('From the heart – may it return – to the heart!').

27    A middleground graph of the entire Ballade appears in Figure 153,1 of Schenker [1935] 1979 (reproduced in Samson 1992: 48). My analysis of bars 1–36 is consonant with Schenker's, but my reading of the introduction differs in some details from Samson's (: 49).

Example 10.6   Voice-leading reduction of Chopin, Ballade Op. 23, bars 1–36

by double barlines; the halves of the antecedent and consequent are separated by single barlines; the halves of these halves are separated by dotted barlines. Notice how every barline – whether double, single or dotted – falls in the middle of some harmonic or linear motion; only at the end of the theme does one coincide with a cadence.

If we disregard the recitative (which naturally is irregular in its organisation), what the barlines in Example 10.6 represent might be termed the music's verse structure. The smallest unit shown, two bars, corresponds to a single verse; four bars – the amount of music contained between solid barlines – represent a couplet. The antecedent as a whole is a quatrain, and the consequent is a quatrain with its second couplet greatly expanded. What is peculiar about Chopin's enjambments here is that he does precisely what the good reciter of poetry avoids: he pauses at the end of almost every verse by means of the quaver rests in the melody. Thus Chopin seems to invert the Duchess's moral in *Alice in Wonderland*: 'take care of the sense and let the sound take care of itself'. Chopin is apparently telling the pianist to take care of the versification (the sound) and to let musical syntax (harmony and voice-leading) take care of itself.

Should the pianist follow this advice, or would doing so result in the musical equivalent of a nonsense poem? Conflicting elements in this theme require the pianist to maintain a precarious balance; as in the other ballades (for analogous reasons), the main theme is one of the most difficult parts of the piece to play well.[28] The divisions between verses must certainly be respected, as Chopin indicated. And yet the pianist must also *feel* the need for resolution at the end of each verse, a yearning whose quality varies according to the tonal situation: the supertonic sevenths of bars 10, 16 and 18 are poignant in a way the dominants of bars 12 and 20 (which simulate imperfect cadences) are not. One thing the pianist can do about the supertonics is slightly to highlight the upper neighbour $e\flat^1$ (the upper-neighbour motion D–E$\flat$–D is one of the principal motifs of the piece); this will help to maintain tension through the following rest.[29] At bars 12 and 20, the feeling of cadence may be counteracted by a slightly rushed entrance of the seventh, $c^1$.[30] By these means (or others to similar effect), an awareness of the music's syntax can be preserved for the listener despite the counterindications of its verse structure. If syntax is neglected entirely, the result will sound like the singsong recitation of metred poetry, which is nowhere more intolerable than where verses are enjambed.[31] And, of course, the unquiet affect of the theme will have been destroyed.

A similar example is the main theme of Brahms's Intermezzo in A minor Op. 116 No. 2. This is another piece based on popular verse forms; in this case a folk song seems to be evoked.[32] Like Chopin, Brahms pauses at the end of each verse – the verses are as short as one bar – although most verses end with a chord which demands immediate resolution, either a dissonance or a secondary dominant. Brahms treats the issue of enjambment more explicitly than Chopin in that he varies the theme throughout the piece, changing the terms of the conflict with each variation. The first variation (bars 10–18) is especially interesting in this respect. In the antecedent, the voice-leading resolutions are de-emphasised by the lack of nuances in bars 10–11 (compare the swells in bars 1–2). In the consequent, the verse structure is played down and the resolutions promoted by the rhythm, which replaces the minims of the theme with continuous quavers. Throughout the variation, however, Brahms adheres to the verse structure in his slurring. The pianist should strictly observe Brahms's nuances; beyond this, judicious pedalling from dissonance to resolution (or from a secondary dominant to its respective 'tonic') will help to give musical syntax its due. There are passages,

---

[28]  Rothstein (in press) discusses conflicts within the main themes of the second and fourth ballades.

[29]  Schenker believed that *all* upper neighbours should be highlighted dynamically. See Rothstein 1984: 13–14.

[30]  One might take progressively less time with each accented seventh from bar 8, where the tempo has not yet been firmly established, to bar 14, where (uniquely) there is no quaver rest.

[31]  Leichtentritt (1921: I, 5) proves that neglecting the music's verse structure in favour of its syntax is even more disastrous: he 'corrects' the notation of Chopin's theme, shifting it by half a bar so that its verse structure and tonal structure coincide (he begins the theme, wrongly, at the second half of bar 9). The reader is encouraged to play and contemplate this 'corrected' version!

[32]  Schenker noted the folk influence in a review of Brahms's Op. 116 following its publication in 1894; see Federhofer 1990: 65.

though, in which Brahms seems to indicate that syntax – the resolutions – should *not* be respected; this is clearest in the first four bars of the variation in A major (bars 51–4).

An example of a different sort is Chopin's Waltz in A♭ major Op. 42. Whereas Chopin's Ballade and Brahms's Intermezzo present conflicts between versification and voice-leading, this Waltz features a conflict within a single domain, that of hyper-metre.[33] As is typical of waltzes, Op. 42 is composed in units of eight bars, subdivided in halves (4 + 4). There are only two exceptions: a twelve-bar unit (3 × 4) in bars 153–64, and an apparent five-bar unit at the end (bars 285–9). The latter exception is, I believe, more apparent than real: while bar 289 is indeed the fifth bar of a group, I think it rea-sonable to feel three bars of silence following the notated end. The eight-bar divisions and their four-bar subdivisions represent the basic metrical structure of the piece.

Why claim that the four- and eight-bar divisions are *metrical* – that is, that they represent units in some way analogous to single bars? To answer this question fully would take us too far afield, and the issues involved are both intricate and controversial. For present purposes, I suggest that the reader think of the matter in this way: if Chopin's Waltz were choreographed, and the dance were receiving its initial rehear-sals, the choreographer or ballet master would almost certainly count aloud from one to eight, over and over, with one count to a bar. (A waltz as rapid as this would not be counted in three; the crotchets instead represent subdivisions of the main beat, which is the dotted minim.) The regularity of Chopin's scheme ensures that the count would be unbroken except for bars 153–64, where the ballet master would have to count to twelve (or to four three times) rather than to eight. The fact of being counted as 'one' – or, more precisely, the feeling of counting 'one' – is what I mean by a downbeat; if the unit being counted is larger than a single bar (as it is here), the downbeat is termed a hyperdownbeat. The units themselves are called hypermeasures. It is not always necessary to accent a downbeat (or hyperdownbeat) in performance, and a great many should not be so accented.[34] Nevertheless, a series of accents, regularly spaced, will generally cause a listener to infer a metre (or hypermetre). This is how most metres (and hypermetres) are initially established, but they need not continue in this way to remain viable. It takes strong counterindications – accentual patterns which consistently contradict an established metrical pattern – to dislodge one metre (or hypermetre) and establish another.

The eight-bar divisions of the Waltz are thus hypermeasures; these are subdivided into smaller hypermeasures of four bars each. The hypermetre is so consistently main-tained that it constitutes an aesthetic premise of the piece. And yet, in several passages, the hypermetre does not comfortably fit the musical rhythms. While the two-against-three pattern of the Waltz's principal theme has often been commented upon, this conflict between the hypermetre and some of the rhythms it contains is even more remarkable.

---

[33] The literature on hypermetre is large and growing. See especially Zuckerkandl 1959: 98–114 and 131–6; Lerdahl and Jackendoff 1983: 17–35 and passim; Schachter 1987; Kramer 1988: 81–122; Rothstein 1989 and 1995.

[34] According to Roger Sessions, the downbeat is the one beat in a bar that needs no accent (see Olmstead 1987: 188).

Example 10.7    Durational reduction of Chopin, Waltz Op. 42, bars 1–72

The Waltz is episodic in form. After the eight-bar introduction, a series of themes alternates with a sixteen-bar refrain (first heard at bar 41). The first of these themes, beginning at bar 9, functions as the principal one. All sections remain close to the tonic, although other keys are touched upon in passing.

Example 10.7 is a durational reduction of bars 1–72, comprising the introduction, the first theme, the refrain and the second theme. (The refrain begins again at bar 73.)

Example 10.8   Alternative durational reduction of Chopin, Op. 42, bars 55–74

One bar of Example 10.7 represents four bars of the Waltz; double barlines separate eight-bar units. The placement of the barlines, and the distinction between single and double barlines, follows Chopin's hypermetre strictly. For the first theme and the refrain, square brackets are used to show smaller groupings; these form sentence-like patterns of 2 + 2 + 4 bars.[35]

The hypermetre sounds most stable in the refrain. The dominant ninths here act as appoggiatura chords, falling on strong beats and resolving on weak ones. The final dominant ninth, an inverted one (bars 55–6), is extended to two bars; its resolution is thus delayed until the following hyperdownbeat (bar 57). This resolution also marks the beginning of the second theme.

The second theme, like the refrain, features dominant ninths and their resolutions. Partly because of this similarity – but also because of the accented, dotted-minim Gs – there is a strong tendency to hear this theme not in the hypermetre of Example 10.7 but in that of Example 10.8. (I have changed the representation of the music in Example 10.8 to highlight the harmonic rhythm, upon which this alternative hyper-metre is partly based.) In Example 10.8, the ninth chords again fall on stronger beats than their resolutions. If the theme is heard out of context, this hypermetre suits it far better than the other one: in particular, all changes of harmony now fall on strong beats (the first, third, fifth and seventh of eight). A wonderful detail is that, according to Example 10.8, the theme's final cadence (bar 72) falls on the seventh of eight beats, leaving that hypermeasure incomplete; as a result, bar 73 sounds initially like an after-echo to the cadence (the trilled A♭ is analogous to Chopin's earlier quaver triplets). I have reconstructed this echo at the end of the example (see the two beats in brackets).

The first theme exhibits similar metrical ambivalence; I have shown its alternative hypermetre in Example 10.9. The resolution of the introduction's long dominant strengthens the downbeat quality of bar 9, but contradictory signals quickly accumulate. The series of melodic leaps in bars 14–16 fits the alternative hypermetre better than

---

[35]   See Rothstein 1995 for a discussion of the relation between grouping and hypermetre. Symmetrical grouping patterns, such as 4 + 4 or (2 + 2) + 4, tend to support or even determine a passage's hypermetre; I term this principle the 'rule of congruence'. Also discussed is a 'rule of harmonic rhythm', which is relevant to Example 10.8 in the present essay.

Example 10.9   Alternative durational reduction of Chopin, Op. 42, bars 9–40

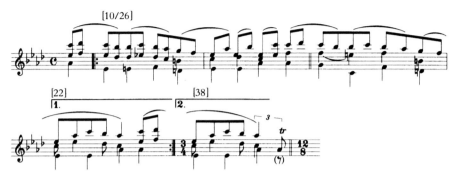

the original one; so does the placement of the cadential $^6_4$ in bars 14 and 22.[36] Perhaps most telling of all is the suspended F in bar 18: in Example 10.9, the suspension pattern (preparation, suspension and resolution) fits the hypermetre perfectly; not so in Example 10.7. The accented passing notes at the beginnings of bars 10 and 12 – which are very like suspensions, having been prepared in the previous bar – also benefit from the alternative hypermetre: they sound more expressive if one hears those bars as strong ones within their respective hypermeasures.

Despite the evidence of Examples 10.8 and 10.9, it remains my contention that Example 10.7 represents the 'true' or governing hypermetre of the Waltz. The alternative hypermetres I have proposed are prominent – especially in the second theme – but essentially secondary; the term 'shadow metre' has recently been coined to describe such secondary metrical patterns.[37] It is the consistency of the eight-bar scheme as a whole that is decisive.

The existence of contradictory metrical schemes within the same passage raises acute problems for the pianist. Which hypermetre (if any) should be 'brought out' when each has a certain validity – one operating locally, the other defining the pattern of the whole? If Example 10.7 represents the principal hypermetre, should one accent the music in such a way as to 'bring it out', suppressing alternatives as potentially misleading? Or should one be so bold as to follow Chopin – who accented the dotted minims in the second theme – and allow the listener to be misled?

It is impossible to prescribe a single solution, but some version of the second option is surely necessary. It is vital that, to some degree, the pianist keep *both* hypermetres alive in the first and second themes, for to surrender completely to either one would be to slight the complexity of the music. To 'bring out' exclusively the hypermetre of Example 10.7 would sound pedantic and wooden; to ignore it entirely would be to sever a thread which holds the work together. One must make it possible, somehow, for the listener to entertain both possibilities. What will probably work best is for the

---

[36]   See Aldwell and Schachter 1989: 298–9. The authors note that weak-beat cadential $^6_4$s are relatively common in the early nineteenth century.

[37]   The term originates with Frank Samarotto, who introduced it in a paper delivered to the Second International Schenker Symposium (New York, March 1992).

pianist to keep the main hypermetre firmly in mind but to play against it in certain passages. In the first theme, for example, the sentential subdivision might privilege the main hypermetre in bars 9–16, while the suspension in bar 18 might tip the balance in favour of the secondary or 'shadow' hypermetre for bars 17–24. (To my ear, the ascending tonic arpeggio in bars 24–5 keeps the balance tipped that way for the remainder of the theme.) But even as the pianist seems to favour one hypermetre, suggestions of the other can be provided: in bars 10 and 12, by playing the dissonances expressively; in bars 25–40, by stressing the sentential organisation of the melody. In the second theme the focus must surely be on the shadow hypermetre, but the left hand is free to remind the listener of the principal hypermetre by, for example, giving a slight weight to the bass's A♭ in bars 57 and 65 (in bar 65 this is also advisable for the sake of the suspension).

Instrumentalists too often forget something which most singers know instinctively: that musical performance is, by its very nature, a species of acting. It is the performer who controls the way in which virtually every aspect of the work is conveyed to the listener. Which features of the music are 'brought out', which are concealed, which are allowed to speak for themselves – these are only some of the decisions the performer must make. Determining what those features are is the task of analysis – analysis which is best carried out through a combination of intuition, experience and reason.

Enacting a play is not the same thing as diagramming its plot or analysing its characters in a lecture, but the actors who are to perform the play need to understand both plot and character if they are to do the play justice. In the same way, performing a musical work and analysing it are activities of very different kinds, but the performer needs to understand both the work's 'characters' and its 'plot' if the performance is to be a compelling one. The performer's aim in undertaking an analysis is not only to understand the work for its own sake – performance is not so disinterested an activity as that – but to discover, or create, a musical narrative. Given the lack of verbal content in instrumental music, it is probably most accurate to say that the performer synthesises this narrative from all he or she knows and feels about the work; listeners, in turn, will construct their own narratives, guided by the performer. One performer's narrative may differ radically from another's for the same work, and not all will accord equally with the composer's intentions; most musicians would agree (all nonsense about 'the intentional fallacy' and 'the indeterminacy of the text' aside) that the composer should have considerable say in these matters.[38] But a narrative there must be, even if it is one which cannot be translated into words, and it is the performer's job to come up with it.[39] Analysis provides a set of tools – actually, many sets – to help do the job.

[38]  A well-known example of a compelling musical narrative which is openly at variance with the composer's expressed intentions is Sergei Rachmaninoff's recording of Chopin's Sonata in B♭ minor Op. 35. In the slow movement (the famous *Marche funèbre*), Rachmaninoff expresses the image of a funeral cortège first approaching and then receding from an observer. The dynamic means that he uses to present this narrative openly flout Chopin's dynamic indications. The performance is magnificent in its own terms, but Chopin evidently had a different narrative in mind.

[39]  Recent writings on narrativity in music include Cone 1974, Newcomb 1987, Maus 1988 and Abbate 1991. In earlier times – especially the seventeenth and eighteenth centuries – musicians spoke instead of 'musical rhetoric'.

What kind of analysis – which set of tools – is best? I have suggested four in this chapter: analysis based on themes and motifs; metrical analysis (including musical versification); phrase analysis; and voice-leading analysis of the Schenkerian sort. Traditional harmonic analysis is not included here, although it informs all of the approaches I have listed, and the list is by no means exhaustive (texture, for example, has not been addressed). Exclusive reliance on any one approach can be dangerous, as I have argued; analysis must lead to synthesis. (Voice-leading analysis has the virtue of being synthetic in its essence, but even it alone is not enough.) Each approach has much of value to contribute, if carried out sensibly, and each can serve as a corrective to the others. Each can help, too, in the construction of the story the performer will tell.

Many performers deliberately construct narratives, tableaux and programmes for the works they play, but – probably wisely – they rarely speak of them in public. I have already suggested, in my discussion of Beethoven's Op. 101, how motifs, for example, can act like characters in a drama, and what kind of story that Sonata may be trying to tell. The shifting hypermetres in Chopin's Waltz may be used as a starting point to construct a narrative for that work; so also the interaction between subject entries and voice-leading in a Bach fugue. Analysis, in short, helps to provide the raw material; the performer's imagination, and empathic identification with the work, must do the rest.

In telling a story, the performer is not merely laying out facts. An important tool of the story-teller is deception. It is one thing to be convinced that something is true analytically, quite another to decide how – even whether – to disclose such information to one's listeners in a performance. Sometimes, I have argued, it is better for the performer to suggest something which is 'false' – or more precisely, something which is 'true' only from a certain, partial vantage point – than to spell out everything one knows. In that way, the performer adopts temporarily the viewpoint of one or two characters in the drama, so to speak, rather than assuming omniscience at every moment. Dramatic truth and analytical truth are not the same thing; a performance is not an *explication du texte*. The performer's task is to provide the listener with a vivid experience of the work, not an analytical understanding of it. But experience – the more vivid the better – will give the listener an avenue towards understanding.[40] Neither the performer's part in this process nor the listener's need be fully conscious for the process itself to succeed; professional analysts, too, do not work through conscious reasoning alone.

Schenker's dictum in the first epigraph is almost certainly wrong: every musical work, like every play, has many 'true' performances. But an analysis which is sympathetic to the work in all its facets gives the performer a firm basis upon which to build a convincing re-creation. Analysis, transmuted by imagination and a certain amount of cunning, can help to inspire that magic without which even the greatest music cannot fully live.

[40]  See Sessions [1950] 1971.

REFERENCES

Abbate, C., 1989: 'Opera as symphony, a Wagnerian myth', in C. Abbate and R. Parker, eds., *Analyzing Opera: Verdi and Wagner* (Berkeley and Los Angeles: University of California Press), pp. 92–124.

    1991: *Unsung Voices: Opera and Musical Narrative in the Nineteenth Century* (Princeton: Princeton University Press).

Aldwell, E. and Schachter, C., 1989: *Harmony and Voice Leading*, 2nd edn (New York: Harcourt Brace Jovanovich).

Berry, W., 1989: *Musical Structure and Performance* (New Haven: Yale University Press).

Blom, E., 1938: *Beethoven's Pianoforte Sonatas Discussed* (London: Dent).

Burkhart, C., 1983: 'Schenker's theory of levels and musical performance', in D. Beach, ed., *Aspects of Schenkerian Theory* (New Haven: Yale University Press), pp. 95–112.

Cone, E. T., 1974: *The Composer's Voice* (Berkeley and Los Angeles: University of California Press).

Cook, N., 1987: 'Structure and performance timing in Bach's C major Prelude (WTC I): an empirical study', *Music Analysis* 6/3: 257–72.

Dahlhaus, C., [1987] 1991: *Ludwig van Beethoven: Approaches to His Music*, trans. M. Whittall (Oxford: Clarendon).

Federhofer, H., 1990: *Heinrich Schenker als Essayist und Kritiker* (Hildesheim: Georg Olms).

Harrison, D., 1990: 'Rhetoric and fugue: an analytical application', *Music Theory Spectrum* 12: 1–42.

Kalib, S. S., 1973: 'Thirteen essays from the three yearbooks "Das Meisterwerk in der Musik" by Heinrich Schenker: an annotated translation', 3 vols. (Dissertation, Northwestern University).

Kinderman, W., 1985: 'Beethoven's symbol for the deity in the *Missa solemnis* and the Ninth Symphony', *19th-Century Music* 9/2: 102–18.

    1988: 'Thematic contrast and parenthetical enclosure in Beethoven's Piano Sonatas, Opp. 109 and 111', in H. Goldschmidt and G. Knepler, eds., *Zu Beethoven*, 3 vols. (Berlin: Verlag Neue Musik), vol. III, pp. 43–59.

    1990: 'Beethoven', in R. L. Todd, ed., *Nineteenth-Century Piano Music* (New York: Schirmer Books), pp. 55–96.

Korsyn, K., 1983: 'Integration in works of Beethoven's final period' (Dissertation, Yale University).

Kramer, J. D., 1988: *The Time of Music: New Meanings, New Temporalities, New Listening Strategies* (New York: Schirmer Books).

Leichtentritt, H., 1921, 1922: *Analyse der Chopin'schen Klavierwerke*, 2 vols. (Berlin: Max Hesses Verlag).

Lerdahl, F. and Jackendoff, R., 1983: *A Generative Theory of Tonal Music* (Cambridge, Massachusetts: MIT Press).

Maus, F., 1988: 'Music as drama', *Music Theory Spectrum* 10: 56–73.

Meyer, L., 1989: *Style and Music: Theory, History, and Ideology* (Philadelphia: University of Pennsylvania Press).

Newcomb, A., 1987: 'Schumann and late eighteenth-century narrative strategies', *19th-Century Music* 11/2: 164–74.

Olmstead, A., 1987: *Conversations with Roger Sessions* (Boston: Northeastern University Press).

Oster, E., [1949] 1983: 'The dramatic content of the *Egmont Overture*', in D. Beach, ed., *Aspects of Schenkerian Theory* (New Haven: Yale University Press), pp. 209–22.

Renwick, W., 1991: 'Structural patterns in fugue subjects and fugal expositions', *Music Theory Spectrum* 13: 197–218.

Riemann, H., 1920: *L. van Beethovens sämtliche Klavier-Solosonaten*, 2nd edn (Berlin: Max Hesses Verlag).

Rothstein, W., 1984: 'Heinrich Schenker as an interpreter of Beethoven's piano sonatas', *19th-Century Music* 8/1: 3–28.

1989: *Phrase Rhythm in Tonal Music* (New York: Schirmer Books).

1995: 'Beethoven "mit und ohne Kunstgepräng"': metrical ambiguity reconsidered', in J. Webster and G. Stanley, eds., *Beethoven Forum*, vol. IV (Lincoln: University of Nebraska Press, forthcoming).

in press: 'Ambiguity in the themes of Chopin's first, second and fourth ballades', *Intégral* 8.

Samson, J., 1992: *Chopin: The Four Ballades* (Cambridge: Cambridge University Press).

Schachter, C., 1987: 'Rhythm and linear analysis: aspects of meter', in F. Salzer and H. Siegel, eds., *The Music Forum*, vol. VI, part 1 (New York: Columbia University Press), pp. 1–59.

Schenker, H., [1920] 1972: *Beethoven: Die letzten Sonaten. Sonate A-dur Op. 101*, 2nd rev. edn, ed. O. Jonas (Vienna: Universal Edition).

1926: *Das Meisterwerk in der Musik*, vol. II (Munich: Drei Masken Verlag).

[1935] 1979: *Free Composition (Der freie Satz)*, trans. and ed. E. Oster (New York and London: Longman).

Schmalfeldt, J., 1985: 'On the relation of analysis to performance: Beethoven's Bagatelles Op. 126, Nos. 2 and 5', *Journal of Music Theory* 29/1: 1–31.

Schumann, R., [1840] 1983: 'Schubert: Symphony in C major', in *On Music and Musicians*, trans. P. Rosenfeld, ed. K. Wolff (Berkeley and Los Angeles: University of California Press), pp. 107–12.

Sessions, R., [1950] 1971: *The Musical Experience of Composer, Performer, and Listener* (Princeton: Princeton University Press).

Wason, R., 1987: 'Webern's Variations for Piano, Op. 27: musical structure and the performance score', *Intégral* 1: 57–103.

Zuckerkandl, V., 1959: *The Sense of Music* (Princeton: Princeton University Press).

# CHAPTER ELEVEN

# The pianist as critic

## EDWARD T. CONE

■

I

'So far as it is alive, [it] is made again at every instant. It is made afresh as part of the process of being known afresh; what is permanent is what is always fresh, and it can be fresh only in performance – that is, in reading and seeing and hearing what is actually in it at this place and this time . . . Or put another way, the critic brings to consciousness the means of performance' (Blackmur 1955: 199). When R. P. Blackmur wrote that, he was of course referring to literature. Using the quotation for my own purposes (Cone 1989: 108), I have tried to establish the critic of music as a kind of performer, whose 're-creation of a composition is, as it were, an ideal imaginary performance' (: 102). But, as I pointed out, one can equally well view the performer as a kind of critic: 'To put it aphoristically: the performance criticizes the composition' (: 101).

The significance of my title should now be clear. By calling attention to the pianist as critic, I am not implying that he spends his spare time dashing off reviews for the daily press or producing more serious essays for the scholarly journals – although he may very well do so. What I mean is that, if he is a serious musician, his piano-playing itself is a critical endeavour – that each performance is an implied act of criticism. By singling out the pianist, I advance no special claims for his instrument or its music. I chose him for practical and personal reasons, for he is the only performer of whom I can speak from first-hand acquaintance. (For that reason, too, I hope my unfashionable use of masculine pronouns will be tolerated.)

The critic's task, again according to Blackmur, is 'the job of putting the audience into a responsive relation with the work of art: to do the job of intermediary' (Blackmur 1955: 183–4). It is thus much more than simply positive or negative evaluation. Judgement has its place, but as only one – perhaps emotionally the first but logically the last – of the critic's duties. 'The critic', says Leonard Meyer, 'does not come to praise masterpieces' (nor, I should add, to condemn failures), 'but to explicate and illuminate them' (Meyer 1973: ix–x). In a word, to interpret them.

Interpretation: that is the obvious link between critic and performer. The same resources that lead to valid critical interpretation inform intelligent practical interpretation – i.e. performance. Both critic and performer, when approaching a musical work, depend first of all upon intuition guided by experience; but in each case, the interpreter, in order to produce more than just an idiosyncratic response, must rely on a combination of sound technical analysis and relevant musicological scholarship. To be sure, it is neither necessary nor even desirable that such background support leave immediately perceptible marks on the finished product: indeed, when the sources of a performance in historical or analytical studies are obtrusively obvious, we call the interpretation 'academic'. Yet the performer, like the critic, ignores those sources at his peril.

If every performance is an implied act of criticism, it follows that the pianist who plays in public assumes certain responsibilities towards his auditors. He makes, as it were, certain commitments to them. The first concerns the worth of the work he is playing. Its appearance on the programme is an indication of the pianist's faith in its value – not necessarily eternal value, but value for this audience, here and now. One aim of the performance should be to convince each member of the audience of that value: by confirmation, in the case of a work commonly known and loved; by conversion, in the case of a new work or one hitherto generally scorned.

In the case of the familiar masterpiece, the pianist's guarantee of its value is almost bound to involve a further commitment on his part. He implies that the piece has not been exhausted by all its previous performances, and he promises an interpretation which is somehow novel – which will impart news to this audience, at this place, at this time. Today the pianist sometimes makes, by implication, a further claim. When he plays a work from the past – say from the early nineteenth century – he may be trying to demonstrate its viability on a modern pianoforte, probably a concert grand. Or if he is a purist, playing the less aggressive instrument of an earlier day, he is making the even more daring assumption that sounds originally designed to be heard by musical professionals and amateurs in the salons of Restoration Paris or Biedermeier Vienna can produce a comparable effect upon a large and varied audience in a modern concert hall.

Musical performance thus differs from verbal criticism in one important respect. The verbal critic can either praise or condemn the object of his criticism, or even maintain a neutral stance; but the pianist who chooses a composition for performance is normally praising it by that very act. There can of course be exceptional circumstances: one may have a didactic purpose in playing music of which one disapproves. And the condition of choice is important because some selections may be externally dictated. In the absence of such constraint, however, a corollary to the pianist's original guarantee applies to the make-up of an entire programme. Since he is requiring the chosen works to appear in one another's company, not only is he vouching for each one individually but he is also assuring his audience that all the compositions are of roughly comparable, although not necessarily equal, artistic value – that they all inhabit, as it were, the same musical world. Serious programme-making is itself a critical act, for it enables each work to influence one's perception of its companions. Thus, even though the pianist who plays an old favourite may make no startling revelations about the piece in and of itself, he may accompany it by others which illuminate it or are in turn illuminated by it.

Schubert's Impromptu in A♭ major Op. 142 No. 2 (to cite a work which will later concern us at some length) presents a useful example. Although obviously playable as a self-contained composition, it was originally one of four members of a single opus; and there has been consequent speculation as to whether Schubert conceived of them as a whole, like the movements of a sonata or of a more loosely connected suite. But a letter of 21 February 1828, from Schubert to the publishing house B. Schott's Söhne, offers 'Four Impromptus for pianoforte solo, which might be published separately or all four together' (Deutsch 1947: 739). There is thus no compelling historical reason for playing the entire opus as a unit; nevertheless, such a performance might well enable No. 2 to converse with its companions. (As a result, one might perceive a close connection between the textures of the tonic A♭ in No. 2 and those of the mediant A♭ in No. 1 – as opposed to the very different sound of the mediant A♭ in No. 4.) On the other hand, a pianist might group No. 2 with other short pieces by Schubert, selected perhaps from the Impromptus Op. 90 or from the *Moments musicaux*. Going further afield, he might present Schubert among his contemporaries, or indicate his points of contact with later composers.

It is unfortunately true that many performers fail to exploit such possibilities. All too often their own critical standards are shown up by selections which indiscriminately mix masterpieces with trifles. Artur Schnabel once described such programmes as 'arranged like a foreign visitor's day in Paris – from cathedral to night club; in other words, from the highest downward' (Schnabel 1942: 65). What he advocated, of course, was 'a program containing exclusively music of one quality, namely the best' (: 73).

Another difficulty arises with respect to the performance of contemporary music. Ideally, new music should be carefully surrounded by music in more familiar styles with which it can, so to speak, enter into a fruitful critical dialogue. All too often new compositions are quarantined, consigned to programmes consisting entirely of unfamiliar works equally hard to comprehend on first hearing. Under such circumstances, intelligent programme construction is impossible. The audience, numbed by excessive novelty, cannot hear the interrelationships between the compositions. Even the performers may have had no opportunity of thoroughly learning works which they did not choose but accepted on assignment.

The ideal programme, however, will have communicated a great deal of critical evaluation to the audience even before a single chord has been heard – evaluation which has resulted, one hopes, from long and close study on the part of the performer. Now, in Wonderland fashion, evidence must be produced for the verdict already pronounced. That evidence is, of course, the performance of each work, or more precisely, the personal perception of that work embodied in the performance.

## II

In a musical culture based on oral tradition, on learning by rote and on improvisatory elaboration, perception of a musical work depends on aural memory. That is no doubt the most natural way of comprehending music; but the culture that has produced our own serious music is more sophisticated – or more artificial. We accept the authority of the written score. Unlike some contemporary theorists, I do not consider the composition to be identical with the score; nevertheless, I have insisted that 'the composition is at least the score . . . and from a purely objective point of view that may indeed be all that the composition is . . . The score is the ultimate source of all our perceptions' (Cone 1989: 99).

The performer's first obligation, then, is to the score – but to what score? The autograph or the first printed edition? The composer's hasty manuscript or the presumably more careful copy by a trusted amanuensis? The composer's initial version or his later emendation? The first German edition or the first French edition? An original edition or one supposedly incorporating the composer's instructions to his pupils? Those involved in the attempt to establish a canonic text of Chopin's works face all those decisions.

Admittedly, Chopin's music presents an exacerbated case; nevertheless, the problem it exemplifies in exaggerated form is a general one. Nor do the difficulties necessarily end with the establishment of a widely accepted text. An accurate score is useless unless it is read accurately; and accurate reading depends not only on familiarity with the notational conventions of the period but also on insight into the composer's personal attitude towards those conventions. For example, what principles govern slurring and phrasing? How are the embellishments to be realised? Are dotted rhythms to be played exactly, or assimilated – e.g. to triplets? In the absence of specific indications, to what extent are the pedals to be used? To answer such questions the performer need not be a scholar, but he must be able to recognise and make judicious use of sound scholarship.

The performer's responsibilities thus begin with what I call his obligation to the score – but they do not end there. Even if the score is, as I have claimed, 'the ultimate source of all our perceptions', it is not their object: rather,

> it is the perceived composition that is the object of critical and interpretive thought . . .
> Perception in this context means, of course, not the physical act of hearing the work, but the *way* one hears it, in actuality or imagination. Perception includes not only one's view of the musical structure but one's reaction to its expressive power as well . . . In other words: one's *perception* of the composition is the source of one's *conception* of its performance. And while the score remains one authoritative measure of the validity of all such conceptions, it can never have been so completely and perfectly notated as to permit only one re-creation as uniquely correct.                 (Cone 1989: 99–100)

Although the performer's fidelity to the score is necessary, it is never sufficient. It must always be put to the service of what I call the convincing, as opposed to the merely correct, performance: the projection of a conception or interpretation reflecting a deeply felt personal involvement with the musical thought of the composition. Moreover, our notation – any notation – can be only approximate. In fact, it is exactly the space cleared by that approximation, an area of indeterminacy, that is the locus of the performer's prime interpretative activity.

Although we pride ourselves on the precision achieved by modern Western notation, our system accommodates wide deviation. We demand accuracy of pitch and have standardised the semitones of our tempered chromatic scale; yet most of our instruments permit minute variations which are deliberately cultivated by performers, and we prize a judicious vibrato. We indicate relative durations as accurately as possible; yet we decry metronomic performance. As for accents, dynamic levels and gradations of tone colour, our scores indicate them in only the most general terms.

The realisation of any score thus requires decisions at every point – decisions which are critical in both senses of the word. Pianists, however, are denied – or spared – one set of such decisions; for once the piano has been tuned, no deviations of pitch are possible (unless one is using the instrument in an abnormal manner). In the areas of dynamics and rhythm, however, the pianist has wide control. He can and must determine each tone's point of attack, relative strength and duration. One particular set of decisions in this realm is crucial for the pianist as for every performer: those that establish tempo. It is on those that I shall now concentrate.

## III

Tempo is obviously a determinant of musical expression. Equally important, however, and logically prior, are its formal aspects. For that reason I find the order that Schumann adopted for his own critical categories suggestively relevant. His essay on the *Symphonie fantastique*, it will be recalled, treated his subject according to 'the four points of view from which a musical work can be examined: *form* [*Form*] (of the whole, of each movement, of period, of phrase), the *compositional fabric* [*musikalische Composition*] (harmony, melody, continuity, workmanship, style), the *specific idea* [*besondere Idee*] that the artist wanted to present, and the *spirit* [*Geist*] that rules over form, material, and idea' (Schumann [1835] 1971: 226). Of these categories, the first two most obviously refer to the formal aspects of music; the last two, to the expressive. My discussion of tempo will follow that outline.

'Musical form', I once wrote, 'is basically rhythmic' (Cone 1968: 25). I had in mind the way the elements of rhythm in detail – relative accent and duration – collaborate at intermediate levels to produce phrase-articulations, and are transmuted at still higher levels into proportions among thematic, harmonic and dynamic areas. But all of those relationships remain imprecise until they are realised in a specific tempo or set of tempos. Formal structure is fully determined only when tempo is fixed.

The truth of that statement is obvious if it is taken to refer to relative tempos, whether among movements or among sections of a single movement. How many speeds does a given composition embody? If more than one, how do they relate to one another? One's answers significantly affect one's perception of the unity, proportions, interconnections and rhythmic patterns of the work, regardless of its absolute time-scale. As I have argued elsewhere, temporal ratios, to be effectively perceptible, need not be exactly commensurable (Cone 1987: 144–7). On the other hand, a precise relationship among disparate tempos can sometimes reveal the underlying unity of a superficially loose structure, as Arthur Mendel convincingly demonstrated in his analysis of Bach's 'St Anne' Fugue (Mendel 1959).

The simplest ratio between tempos is that of equality; and many compositions, though sectional in form, depend without question on a single tempo. Others are more ambivalent. In the absence of specific indications performers often feel free to emphasise sectional contrast by tempo changes. Sometimes, to be sure, such a decision is justified. Often, however, it depends on the kind of tradition that Mahler characterised as *Schlamperei*.

The elegance of Chopin's Polonaise in A♭ major Op. 53 is frequently marred by pianists who insist on playing the octaves of the central section at an increased speed to display their virtuosity. They have overlooked Chopin's recommendation of a unitary tempo through his reminiscence of the octaves in the final bars of the coda. Although the motivic connection is recognisable in any case, it is certainly more cogent when supported by uniform velocity.

What of absolute tempo? Some have tried to insist that it can have no influence on form, for a composition exhibits the same structure at every speed. Its patterns of musical relationships are invariable regardless of the elapsed time its performance may require. To a pure formalist, or (what probably comes to the same thing) a pure relativist with respect to musical content, absolute tempo would thus appear to be a matter of personal choice, unconstrained by structural considerations.[1]

This argument is faulty. Fifty years ago, the opening chorus of Bach's *St Matthew Passion* was usually taken at a pace so ponderous that one was forced to hear it as a dialogue between two choruses, into which the phrases of a chorale were occasionally interjected from afar. At best it sounded formally loose and episodic; at worst, interminable. Today's more realistic tempos reveal it as an imaginatively wrought chorale-fantasy; the chorale phrases, far from being interpolations, are the controlling elements of the form. Paradoxical though it sounds, absolute tempo governs our perception of the relative importance of each musical event, and thus our comprehension of form.

At this point the discussion is moving from Schumann's first category, *Form*, to his second, *Composition*, or as I call it, compositional fabric, for by this term Schumann meant form in its more detailed aspects, as he indicated by his references to 'continuity' and 'workmanship'. It is the tempo which determines what elements of the fabric the performer can project, and how much the listener can take in: which metrical units

---

[1] Nelson Goodman once argued in a lecture that a musician actually 'performed' a composition if and only if he or she produced all its pitches correctly and in exact rhythmic relationship, regardless of tempo. It was pointed out to him that in consequence a pianist who played one wrong note in an otherwise perfect rendition of a piece did not perform it, whereas another pianist playing the same piece without error but at a snail's pace (say, one bar per hour) did perform it!

Example 11.1 Handel, 'Dead March' from *Saul*, bars 5–8 and reductions

Example 11.2 Chopin, Impromptu Op. 66, bars 5 and 43–4

represent the basic pulse; which elements are to be regarded as structural, which ornamental; which attacks count individually, which in groups; which passages are to be followed in exact detail, which passed over impressionistically; which linear and harmonic connections are binding, which tenuous.

For example, a harmonic progression which works at one tempo may fail at another. In the 'Dead March' from Handel's *Saul*, a suitably slow pace permits the hearer to make sense of the V[7] of IV in bar 6: it is an appoggiatura-chord to IV$^6_4$, which is a neighbour to the tonic (Example 11.1a). But if one plays the March a little too fast, the chord of resolution loses its identity and the entire bar sounds like an extended dominant seventh – a musical solecism because its syntax is never explained (Example 11.1b).

Important melodic relationships may also be concealed by injudicious choices of tempo. One often hears pianists – especially young ones – play Chopin's so-called 'Fantasy-Impromptu' Op. 66 at a speed which obscures the thematic connection between the opening and central sections (Example 11.2), whereas a less frenetic Allegro agitato clearly asserts the melodic contour.

In brief: if relative tempo governs unity, contrast and proportion, absolute tempo establishes the limits of intelligibility. Both are formal tasks. But absolute tempo has an important expressive task as well. It is crucial to the definition of what may be called musical character – whether that is understood in terms of abstract motion or human emotion, whether it is considered to be movement or mood, whether it is implied or made programmatically explicit. As manifested in individual works, character is thus closely allied with Schumann's third category, *Idee* – 'the specific idea that the artist wanted to express'.

More problematic is the relevance of tempo to Schumann's last category – mainly because his explanation of *Geist*, 'spirit', is so vague. I have glossed it as 'that mysterious quality that somehow reflects the outlook of the individual, the social milieu, and the age that produced [the work]' (Cone 1989: 101). If I am right, *Geist* refers to style in its broadest sense – the style of a composer, of a period, of a country – just as Schumann's second category, *Composition*, refers to style narrowly defined – the style of the individual work. 'Spirit' in this sense is bound to be affected by tempo, for the range of available speeds is one of the most salient characteristics of an historical style. The opening chorus of the *St Matthew Passion* is again a case in point. The conception of the work that eventuated in the change of tempo noted above was not due to formal considerations only. It was also the effect of new – and, one hopes, more penetrating – insights into the style of Bach and his period. One might well wonder in which direction that development proceeded. Did a new understanding of 'form' result in, or from, a new interpretation of 'spirit'?

Here as elsewhere, contemplation of tempo reveals the indivisibility of musical form and expression. That is why the performer's most important critical task may well be to derive, from his perception of form and content, as accurate a conception of tempo as possible. But that conception will in turn permit a sharper perception of structure, a perception which will point to a more exact conception of tempo. The process thus continues indefinitely.

I have chosen two examples to illustrate in greater detail the problems involved in determinations of tempo: Schubert's Impromptu in A♭ major Op. 142 No. 2, and Chopin's Etude in E major Op. 10 No. 3. The treatment of the first will emphasise the influence of relative tempo on form; that of the second will focus on the establishment of absolute tempo and its effect on expressive character. Yet in both discussions the interpenetration of the formal and expressive aspects should exemplify the indivisibility stressed above.

## IV

The Schubert Impromptu exhibits few problems with regard to the establishment of a text: there is one autograph, easily accessible (in the Pierpont Morgan Library, New York); it was the source of the original and subsequent editions. Even so, there are a few questionable details: the exact rhythm of the ornament in bar 27, the auxiliary of the trill in bar 76 and the ambiguous status of the possibly duplicated coda (bars 144$^3$–8).[2] More important to our concerns is the silence of the score on a crucial

---

2      Bar 27: most editions print the right-hand turn as four equal notes. According to the autograph, it consists of two demisemiquavers plus two semiquavers.

Bar 76: no auxiliary is indicated for the trill, but most editions suggest G♯$^1$. G♮$^1$, however, is possible, and it sets the following A♭$^1$ in greater relief.

Coda: in the autograph, it is placed after the first song-form, before the trio (i.e. beginning as a continuation of bar 46). The direction *zum Schluss* was evidently added to this passage only later; it is possible that this emendation was not Schubert's. (See Schubert 1984: 165–6.)

question of relative tempo: should the principal thematic contrast be supported by a change of speed?

The pattern is the familiar song-form with trio. There is a short transition between trio and reprise, and there is a short coda at the end. The sole tempo indication is Allegretto; the metre is a uniform 3/4. Although a trio may be assigned a contrasting tempo, that is not the case here. Did the composer intend one anyway? Most pianists have seemed to think so. Recordings indicate a preference for an opening at $\downarrow$ = 100– 108 and a trio at $\downarrow$ = 132–144.[3] Against that tradition, the fact that Schubert does on occasion specifically designate a new tempo for a trio suggests that the absence of such a marking here implies uniformity. Moreover, there is no tell-tale ritardando stipulated for the short, rhythmically uniform passage returning to the initial song-form (bars 97–8). But such negative indications are insufficient without the support of positive evidence derived from the music itself.

A first attempt in this direction, namely an examination of the Impromptu's overall proportions, leads to inconclusive results. To be sure, uniformity of tempo produces a rough equivalence between song-form and trio: 2 × 46 and 2 × 44 bars respectively. That is neat but not precise. It is certainly not interesting enough to substantiate a claim to musical superiority, and the critical pianist will therefore have to move from Schumann's first category to his second and search the details of the compositional fabric for further clues. What does he find?

The first song-form presents a theme of great charm and apparent simplicity which nevertheless conceals a subtle rhythmic conflict. The underlying pulse is the crotchet of the 3/4; but in the first two bars of each phrase both melody and inner voices lengthen the second beat, producing a pattern which, at a slower pace, would be sarabande-like. (The second-beat stress was originally even stronger, involving the bass as well, as altered passages in the autograph attest.) The resulting agogic stresses are supported by melodic slurs in both the opening and the returning statements of the song-form. (Indeed, in view of the *sempre ligato* explicitly enjoined at the outset, those slurs would be redundant were it not for their rhythmic function.) At the same time, however, the frequent appoggiaturas (e.g. on the first beats of bars 2, 3, 6 and 7) imply harmonic accents supporting the normal metrical stress. That articulation is further underlined by the crescendos into bars 14 and 44, as well as by the indicated accentuations of the more forceful central section (bars 17–30). The ambiguity between the two varieties of accent is temporarily resolved at each cadence in favour of the metrical stress – an outcome eventually confirmed by the coda (certainly after the da capo but possibly before the trio as well[4]).

---

[3]  *Recording*                                    *Opening*      *Trio*

Alfred Brendel (Vox PL-12390; n.d.)        $\downarrow$ = 108    $\downarrow$ = 144
Edwin Fischer (Pathé COLH-68; 1938)        $\downarrow$ = 100    $\downarrow$ = 132
Walter Gieseking (Angel 35533; n.d.)        $\downarrow$ = 100    $\downarrow$ = 132
Artur Schnabel (Victor LVT-1019; n.d.)      $\downarrow$ = 100    $\downarrow$ = 144

[4]  See note 2 above. Today the coda is almost invariably played only at the end. That version accords well with my interpretation, for the coda can confirm the supremacy of the original song-form over the trio.

The trio, for its part, tries to impose a contrary resolution even though the effort is foredoomed; but that is the 'story' of the piece. The trio retains the crotchet pulse but subdivides it into triplets, replacing the right hand's block chords by arpeggios. This contrast of rhythm, texture and consequent mood is what the usually adopted tempo emphasises – or exaggerates, for the contrast is clear even if the original tempo is retained. That tempo, moreover, makes an important contribution to the trio's attempt to resolve the rhythmic ambiguity in its own way: the metrical connection between song-form and trio may be broken in the absence of a common beat.

The retention of a common beat, on the other hand, reveals that in the trio the song-form's tentative stress on the second beat has become an obsession. Now, despite a normal rhythm of harmonic change on the downbeats, almost every bar gives the second beat special emphasis – by the crests of the arpeggiated melody and by the cross-rhythm of the interior dominant pedal. Both kinds of detail are signalled by marks of accentuation. The trio's *fortissimo* climax differs significantly from the high point of the song-form. There the first beats of bars 25 and 27 were marked *ffz*; here four successive bars (69–72) insist on the supremacy of the second beat – in the left hand by an exaggeration of the sarabande rhythm, ♪ ♩ , in the right hand by the successive application of *fz* to its melodic crests. That overemphasis defeats itself, however, for the cross-metre dissolves into an ametric equalisation in bars 73–4, enabling order to be restored by the resumption of the normal harmonic rhythm in bar 75. Now a less aggressive second beat (without added accent) foreshadows the neutrality of the two-bar transition to the da capo reprise.

Throughout that rhythmic development, a uniform tempo offers an opportunity for what may be called contrast within correspondence. It is unfortunate that this interesting relationship is so often vitiated in performance. The search for a convincing speed to encompass both song-form and trio uncovers an interesting connection between absolute and relative tempo. The trio, with its arpeggiated passagework, cannot sustain the slow versions of Allegretto usually chosen. Probably ♩ = 126–132 is the lower limit of permissible speed. Is the same tempo possible for the song-form as well? Actually, it confers on that section a more characteristically Allegretto flavour. Moreover, when the arpeggios can be heard as chords moving at the same rate as those of the opening, the composition discloses – or confirms – a unity of texture, and even of motif, concealed beneath the surface contrast. Compare, for example, the cadences at bars 37–8 and 57–8: they are related by melodic inversion (Example 11.3).

The performance thus suggested, which takes issue with what might be called the standard renditions, represents a twofold act of criticism. First, it projects a thoroughgoing critical reinterpretation of the composition. At the same time, it embodies an indirect critical judgement on most other performances of the same piece.

## V

It would be comforting but misguided to believe that the advent of the metronome enables us to put an end to differences of opinion as to tempo. Many composers prefer

Example 11.3   Schubert, Impromptu Op. 142 No. 2, bars 37–8 and 57–8

not to impose such strict limitations on their interpreters, fearing that their instructions will be taken too literally. Others may designate exact tempos, only to modify them later on, as Stravinsky notoriously did in the last movement of the *Symphony of Psalms*. (A passage marked ♩ = 48 in the original 1930 version was altered to ♩ = 72 in the 1948 revision. Later performances conducted by the composer effected further changes.) Some composers have indicated tempos considered so outlandish that they are generally disregarded. Thus musicians used to insist that Schumann's metronome was defective, and that Beethoven's deafness prevented him from realistically imagining speed. (Consequently, a conductor can create a sensation by announcing his intention of following Beethoven's instructions in the Ninth Symphony.)

Chopin's Etude Op. 10 No. 3 is a case in point. The sources are typically confusing. There are two autographs, of which one (in the R. O. Lehman Collection, Pierpont Morgan Library) is a draft, differing in detail from the second, a definitive version (at the Chopin Society, Warsaw). The first French edition (Paris: Schlesinger, 1833) and the first German edition (Leipzig: Kistner, 1833) offer still further readings.[5] Their confusion embraces the domain of tempo. The two autographs specify Vivace and Vivace ma non troppo respectively; by the time of publication those had become Lento ma non troppo. Did this represent a change in the composer's conception, or merely a more precise wording? 'Not too lively' and 'not too slow' are, after all, reasonably proximate. Nevertheless, further evidence suggests that Chopin came to prefer a somewhat slower pace. Both autographs retain a uniform tempo throughout; in the printed editions, the middle section of the ternary form is to be played *poco più animato* (bar 20), as if to restore to this passage the bravura that would otherwise now be lost.

Just how fast is this Lento ma non troppo? The first German edition indicates an unlikely ♩ = 100 – surely a misprint. The first French edition gives ♪ = 100, which has been generally accepted ever since – at least in print, although not in practice. Does anyone play the opening at that speed? Typical recorded performances hover between ♪ = 56 and ♪ = 72. (I say 'hover' advisedly, for lavish rubato makes precise clocking impossible.)[6] But if Chopin knew what he was doing and meant what he wrote, he intended a mood of passionate intensity rather than of nostalgic regret. In

---

[5]  The conflicting versions of bars 30–1 and 34–5 are notorious. Most pianists ignore all four sources, preferring the emendation of Chopin's pupil Carl Mikuli.

[6]  *Recording*                                                    *Opening*

Claudio Arrau (Angel 35413; n.d.)                       ♪ = 56
Alexander Brailowsky (Victor LM-6000; n.d.)      ♪ = 60
Alfred Cortot (Pathé COLH-39; 1933)                   ♪ = 60
Maurizio Pollini (DG 2740 230; 1981)                   ♪ = 72

view of the tradition built up over the years, it may be impossible to play the Etude at full speed today; but one might at least begin a trend in that direction with a performance which would again criticise not only the piece, by revising our estimate of its content, but also other performances, by showing up their 'inauthentic' sentimentality.

A closer approach to metronomic fidelity would present not only a mood but also a form more in accord with Chopin's conception. Whereas traditional performances are forced to adopt a much faster pace for the central section,[7] a brisk initial tempo permits the *poco più animato* to emphasise the *poco* rather than the *più*. The central section can thus be construed as modifying the basic tempo instead of establishing a new one of its own, and the entire Etude can be heard as the development of a single impulse.

The improvement is especially noticeable in the passage (bars 54–61) that follows the *con bravura* cadenza. Those bars are bound to embarrass the pianist who, following tradition, must use them to effect a retransition, not only to the opening theme, but also to its slow tempo. Whether one interprets the passage as a premature return to that tempo or as a long ritardando, it seems sluggish and repetitious. But if the contrast between the two tempos is minimalised, the *poco più animato* can prevail until the *smorzando* and *poco rallentando* of bars 60–1. In that case the melody, with its subtle reminiscences of the theme introduced in bar 21, can offer a gradual détente from the cadenza, supported as it is by harmonies which continue to develop the climactic dominant. But the lower voices also refer to the original accompaniment of the principal theme, foreshadowing its return. Thus the tonic downbeat of bar 62 represents an elision, for it both resolves the tension of the central section and initiates the reprise. And the double meaning of that chord points in turn to the double meaning of the entire passage in question: those eight bars not only prolong the dominant of the preceding section in suspensive preparation for its resolution, but also turn it into an upbeat of the section to come. In performance, a recognition of the elision makes it possible to sustain a momentum there which will animate the rest of the piece – again in contrast to the usually prevailing mood of sad resignation. (In support of the foregoing interpretation, I should point out that Chopin signals the return of the theme at bar 62 not by a 'Tempo primo', but by a simple *a tempo*.)

One detail which our hypothetical pianist would have to consider closely is the final cadence. Neither the opening statement nor the reprise of the theme achieves the full tonal closure that Heinrich Schenker, if not our own musical intuition, has taught us to expect. There is no perfect authentic cadence; both times, a climactic $I_4^6$ –V resolves deceptively, initiating a descent to the tonic through the sequence vi–iii, IV–I (bars 17–20 and 70–3). In the reprise the plagal effect is extended by the minor subdominant (bars 73–4), but there is still no final V–I. Most pianists create one by so stretching the indicated rallentando (bar 75²) that the last semiquaver of the penultimate bar (an

---

[7]   They also noticeably accelerate up to the cadenza (bars 46–54¹). The following speeds introduce the section:

| | |
|---|---|
| Arrau | ♪ = 84 |
| Brailowsky | ♪ = 112 |
| Cortot | ♪ = 100 |
| Pollini | ♪ = 92 |

Example 11.4    Chopin, Etude Op.10 No. 3, bars 76–7 and reduction

octave B–b) can be heard as implying an entire dominant chord (Example 11.4). The required slackening of pace might be justified at the tempo usually taken, but at or near Chopin's metronomic speed it would sound tastelessly exaggerated. The whole problem vanishes, however, in the second, definitive autograph, which instructs one to play the succeeding Etude (in C♯ minor, Op. 10 No. 4) immediately: *attac[c]a il presto con fuoco*. If Chopin considered Nos. 3 and 4 as constituting a single composition in two movements, a full close at the end of No. 3 would be unnecessary. Since we do not know why the printed editions dropped the instruction, we cannot know Chopin's final intention; but the pianist who dares play No. 3 up to tempo might well consider linking it with No. 4.

By dwelling on questions of tempo, I have meant to belittle neither the importance nor the difficulty of other aspects of rhythm. Attack, phrasing, accentuation, dynamic gradation, rubato: all present problems whose solutions are essential to convincing performance. But no interpretative decision links the performer's appreciation of expressive content with his perception of formal structure more firmly, and enables him to project that connection more effectively, than choice of tempo. That is why it is a model act of criticism.

REFERENCES

Blackmur, R. P., 1955: *The Lion and the Honeycomb* (New York: Harcourt Brace).
Cone, E. T., 1968: *Musical Form and Musical Performance* (New York: Norton).
    1987: 'Twelfth night', *Journal of Musicological Research* 7/2–3: 131–56.
    1989: *Music: A View from Delft*, ed. R. P. Morgan (Chicago: University of Chicago Press).
Deutsch, O. E., 1947: *The Schubert Reader* (New York: Norton).
Mendel, A., 1959: 'A note on proportional relationships in Bach tempi', *The Musical Times* 100: 683–5.
Meyer, L. B., 1973: *Explaining Music* (Berkeley and Los Angeles: University of California Press).
Schnabel, A., 1942: *Music and the Line of Most Resistance* (Princeton: Princeton University Press).
Schubert, F., 1984: *Franz Peter Schubert, Neue Ausgabe sämtlicher Werke*, series VII/2: *Werke für Klavier zu zwei Händen*, vol. IV, ed. W. Dürr and C. Landon (Kassel: Bärenreiter).
Schumann, R., [1835] 1971: 'A Symphony by Berlioz', in E. T. Cone, ed. and trans., *Hector Berlioz: Fantastic Symphony* (New York: Norton).

# CHAPTER TWELVE

# Playing in time: rhythm, metre and tempo in Brahms's *Fantasien* Op. 116

## JOHN RINK

The growing literature on analysis and performance should be approached with caution by the enquiring performer: prolonged exposure might induce a state of confusion or despondency. Two contradictory tendencies characterise this literature: first, an authoritarian school of thought advocating 'serious' analysis of the score as the basis of interpretation;[1] and secondly, a pessimistic view expressing doubt that analysis and performance have much or anything of substance to offer each other.[2] Needless to say, some authors have sought a middle ground between these extremes,[3] and the present chapter is conceived in just such a conciliatory spirit. Specifically, it attempts to show that analysis and performance can indeed be intimately linked – and in ways directly impinging on the act of interpretation, not just in some wishfully conceived, theoretically motivated fashion. It also defines a novel kind of 'historical performance practice' as a strategy for interpreting the music of Brahms.

Briefly put, the central goal of this study is to evaluate the intuitions that guided my own performance of Brahms's seven *Fantasien* Op. 116 about two years before this essay was written:[4] I shall reconstruct the analytical framework that unconsciously

---

[1]  See for instance Narmour 1988 and Berry 1989.

[2]  Dunsby 1989 best exemplifies this tendency. See Rink 1990 for discussion of the terminological inconsistencies that dog the analysis-and-performance literature, especially surrounding the word 'analysis'.

[3]  See Howell 1992 and Rink 1994b, in addition to other chapters in this volume. Compare also the analyst/performer dialogue in Schmalfeldt 1985.

[4]  In broaching the topic of intuition I acknowledge the controversy surrounding it in recent literature, as well as the lack of understanding evinced by some authors who dismiss out of hand its relevance to 'intelligent' performance. For instance, Howell (1992: 698ff.) treats intuition and analysis as mutually exclusive, failing to appreciate that any 'intuition', whether the analyst's or the performer's, reflects a process of learning and of experiencing. In short, intuition is an 'immediate apprehension or cognition', or 'the power or faculty of attaining to direct knowledge or cognition without *evident* rational thought and inference' (in the words of *Webster's New Collegiate Dictionary* (Springfield, Massachusetts: Merriam, 1974), p. 607; my emphasis), but deriving from *past* 'rational thought and inference'. My own term, 'informed intuition', reflects a broad range of experience and the exploitation of theoretical and analytical knowledge, as well as historical understanding, at the 'submerged level of consciousness' described by Wallace Berry (see Rink 1990: 324 for discussion). I accept, however, that intuitions are not always 'right': although the experienced, sensitive performer can usefully rely on them 'automatically' when they have arisen through prolonged consideration of stylistic, historical, analytical and technical factors, some intuitions are misleading and would benefit from retrospective reassessment and refocusing. This is where analysis can be valuable, helping to fill those gaps where intuitions

shaped the performance, thereby testing the 'performer's analysis' that I have defined elsewhere.[5] The project on which the chapter is based had three stages: first, preparation of the *Fantasien* for a public recital in March 1991; secondly, detailed analysis of the set; and finally, reassessment of the performance in the light of the analysis. The investigation differed from much research on analysis and performance in that I learned the music on the basis of intuition alone, rather than adopt the procedure advocated by some authors – that is, conceiving the performance in terms of the analysis, a process which typically inspires dubious imperatives to the performer to 'bring out' a given motivic parallelism or structural harmony, often in violation of the spirit of the music, however that may be understood. In contrast, the approach taken here afforded an intimate knowledge of the score comparatively free from theoretical bias. The second stage of the investigation was also unusual as my analysis was predicated on issues of direct relevance to the performer, not on broader analytical concerns nor a particular methodology, the intention being to discover specific ways in which analysis can help – rather than constrain – the performer. Two aspects interested me especially: the 'problem-solving' role of analysis in performance,[6] and its potential to shape an entire interpretation. The first enabled me to resolve certain difficulties which had arisen while learning the music, in particular the treatment of hemiolas and other implied rebarrings, as well as the manipulation of phrase rhythm. As for the second, analysis provided insight into tempo relations between the seven works in the set and into large-scale rhythmic procedures.

It is no accident that the analysis consistently focused on elements involving musical time – specifically, rhythm, metre and tempo – for these more than any other compositional parameter directly affect the performer, whose most essential concerns are forward impulse, timing and 'shape'. Another reason for such a focus stemmed from the lack of attention to rhythm, metre and tempo in the abundant literature on Op. 116, even in the most exhaustive study of the opus, Jonathan Dunsby's essay on 'the multi-piece in Brahms',[7] which serves as a point of departure for this chapter. Notwithstanding the set's complicated compositional history,[8] Dunsby adduces

---

fail or prove inadequate. For further discussion of intuition in performance see Berry 1989, Rink 1994b and David Epstein's chapter in this book.

[5]  See Rink 1990; compare Jonathan Dunsby's comment (1982: 8) that 'the moment we perform something other than a copy of someone else's performance we are, if we choose to be articulate about how an interpretation is devised, analysing the music'.

[6]  This is one of the few points of contact between analysis and performance enthusiastically endorsed by Dunsby (1989: 9ff.).

[7]  Dunsby 1983. Op. 116 is also studied in Evans [1936], Mastroianni 1970, Matthews 1978, Musgrave 1985, Cai 1986, Kraus 1990 and Lewin 1990.

[8]  Initially it comprised only five works; two pieces were added after 20 October 1892 (when Brahms sent Simrock *Stichvorlagen* of the original five works from Op. 116, as well as the eventual Op. 117), with publication of all seven pieces to follow later that year. On the basis of correspondence between Clara Schumann and Brahms, Camilla Cai (1986: 177) deduces that the original five were Nos. 2–6 and that Nos. 1 and 7 were the later additions (in contrast to Max Kalbeck's hypothesis (1915: 282) that Nos. 6 and 7 were added to Nos. 1–5). The title *Fantasien* was also adopted at a late stage, apparently at Kalbeck's behest (see Cai 1986: 177). Although Brahms never insisted on their being performed together, he did want the seven pieces to appear in one volume (rather than the two *Hefte* in which they were actually published): in Kalbeck's words (1915: 282), 'Die Phantasien sollten wohl, schreibt er [Brahms], am besten in einem Heft erscheinen.'

compelling formal, tonal and motivic evidence to suggest that the seven numbers constitute a 'multi-piece', that is, a 'large homogeneous work' made up of 'small, heterogeneous pieces' (1983: 168). Within a tonally closed framework defined by motion from the 'tonic' D minor in No. 1 through No. 2's 'minor dominant' (A minor), No. 3's 'subdominant' (G minor) and the 'supertonic' (E major or E minor) in Nos. 4, 5 and 6 back to the 'tonic' in No. 7, Brahms establishes an extraordinarily coherent network of motivic relationships, among them a progression in thirds plus linear variants thereof (see Musgrave 1985: 256–60) and a 'turn-figure embedded in an arpeggiated six-four' (Dunsby 1983: 183). Dunsby observes that 'the music is saturated with these shapes . . . the fundamental materials are related in something like the way to be found in conventional large forms' (: 184).

There seems little reason to doubt the set's coherence as a multi-piece, whether or not Brahms's original intention was to produce a unified cycle, but for the performer many questions follow on from this conclusion. First of all, the relevance to the pianist of the motivic correspondences adduced by Dunsby and Musgrave is anything but obvious, and this of course reflects a broader dilemma faced by any analytically minded performer: how to use the results of one's analysis – for instance, how (if at all) to convey a sense of motivic unity in live performance. Just because a given motif is found throughout a work or set of pieces does not mean that the performer should necessarily *do* anything about it: trying to project motivic unity in sound by 'bringing out' all the motivic connections that inhere in a 'unified' work would result in an absurd distortion of the music.[9] What is of undeniable importance to the performer, however, is an aspect of Op. 116's motivic unity virtually ignored by most analysts: *the actualisation in time of the principal motifs* – in other words, *their contexts in the music's unfolding narrative.* And it is not just the temporal settings of these motifs that matters to the pianist: other aspects of the music's shaping in time are equally relevant to meaningful performance. Just as Brahms bases the seven pieces on a small number of cells, he 'motivically' exploits recurrent rhythmic and metrical devices (such as large-scale hemiola-related processes and extension and contraction of the hypermeasure) to control forward impulse; furthermore, disparate tempos may be defined in terms of a few related pulses extending through the opus. Insofar as one can make such a statement without lapsing into the insidious 'language of exigency' employed in much analysis-and-performance literature, I would claim that the performer's chief responsibility in interpreting this multi-piece is to grasp and somehow articulate in performance the intraopus rhythmic 'system' devised by Brahms, for an understanding of rhythm (in the broadest sense) lies at the heart of convincing interpretation.[10]

---

[9] For an example of this kind of approach see Berry 1989: 31–2 and passim. Various problems associated with such a procedure are discussed in William Rothstein's chapter in this book; see also Joel Lester's essay.

[10] In Edward Cone's words (1968: 31), the key to achieving 'valid and effective performance' lies in 'discovering and making clear the rhythmic life of a composition'. As I have written elsewhere (Rink 1994b: 228), Cone 'is referring here to *all* rhythmic aspects of a work: phrase rhythm, harmonic rhythm, formal rhythm, etc. – in short, the unfolding temporal profile of every active parameter, the composite of which could be thought to constitute the music's "rhythmic shape"'. See Cone 1968 and Rink 1994b: 226–35 for exemplification of this point; see also Cone's chapter in this volume.

Such an understanding is by no means easy to achieve, however, despite David Epstein's claim to the contrary that the 'mechanisms of motion' in Brahms's music speak for themselves, that 'the music in a fundamental sense is performance proof': 'Let the performer play the notes and the rhythms as they are written and the music must move . . . motion is built into the notes themselves, the inevitable product of their structure', which 'exerts its own control' (1990: 198–9). That this view needs further refinement can be shown not only by comparing the fundamentally different interpretations of Op. 116 available on commercial recordings, but also by attempting to devise a performance strategy for what Walter Frisch (1990) terms 'the shifting bar-line in Brahms's music' – specifically, whether one subordinates a notated metrical organisation to an implied rebarring, allows the original time signature to prevail or combines more than one metrical scheme for the sake of tension and ambiguity. Another thorny problem typical of Brahms's music arises from unspecified internal tempo relationships, as in Op. 116 No. 7, which has no fewer than four time signature changes without any indication as to pulse equivalence.

Clearly there are difficult decisions to be made in interpreting this music: however much the 'correct' interpretation may be implicit within the notes, other strategies could work – or appear to work – equally well, thus requiring the performer to exercise discrimination in responding to the 'mechanisms of motion' in Op. 116. Even if the music seems to 'exert its own control', interpretation always involves choice, and the basis for choosing, for discrimination, must be musically – that is, historically, stylistically, analytically, technically, expressively – viable. Spelling out the basis for choice in interpreting this set is the goal of the next two parts of the chapter.

## TEMPO AS STRUCTURAL FRAMEWORK

If Op. 116 is the integrated 'multi-piece' Dunsby would have us believe, it is almost inconceivable that the tempo relationships between individual numbers were arbitrarily defined by Brahms or left simply to the performer's will. This seems particularly unlikely given the findings of previous studies of tempo relationships in Brahms's music, which have discerned logical schemes underlying tempo changes in single compositions like the Haydn Variations (see Forte 1957) and in works with several movements such as the symphonies. In his most recent study of the temporal properties of Brahms's multi-movement compositions, David Epstein concludes on the basis of analytical evidence that

> a steady basic pulse runs continuously throughout a work of Brahms, underlying all segments, sections, and movements of the work and serving as the referential basis – indeed, the temporal module – for explicit changes of tempo. New tempos relate to this basic pulse in . . . simple ratios . . . for the most part 1 : 1, 1 : 2, 2 : 3, 3 : 4, and their inverse. This is in fact the principle of the *tactus* found in Renaissance music . . . [whereby] changes of movement within all parts of a piece were *tactus*-bound through a system of mathematical proportions.[11]     (1990: 204–5; compare Epstein 1979, 1985 and 1995)

[11] Historical evidence to support Epstein's hypothesis about the *tactus* is somewhat elusive, with regard to both actual renaissance practice and Brahms's understanding thereof. Focusing here on the latter (the former is

Table 12.1   *Tempo markings in Op. 116*

FAST

| | | |
|---|---|---|
| 1. *Capriccio* | 3. *Capriccio* | 7. *Capriccio* |
| Presto energico | Allegro passionato | Allegro agitato |
| | Un poco meno allegro | |
| | Allegro passionato | |

MODERATE

| | | |
|---|---|---|
| 2. *Intermezzo* | 5. *Intermezzo* | 6. *Intermezzo* |
| Andante | Andante con grazia ed | Andantino teneramente |
| Non troppo presto | intimissimo sentimento | (originally Andante |
| Andante | (originally Allegretto | grazioso, then Andante |
| | in Hamburg MS) | teneramente in Hamburg |
| | | MS) |

SLOW

4. *Intermezzo*
Adagio

From this hypothesis follows an intriguing proposition relevant to our investigation: if indeed the *tactus* principle applies to single compositions by Brahms (either sets of variations or works in several movements), and if Op. 116 constitutes a single 'multi-piece', then by extension the *tactus* principle should influence tempo relationships in this set – in other words, simple tempo ratios like those found by Epstein and Forte elsewhere in Brahms should link the seven heterogeneous works under scrutiny here. If true, this would naturally have important implications for performance.

To ascertain what tempo relationships do exist between the individual numbers, one must first consider Brahms's tempo markings in both the one surviving manuscript and the first edition of Op. 116.[12] Table 12.1 groups these as fast, moderate or slow; as it affects an entire 3/8 bar, No. 1's Presto is classed with the Allegros in Nos. 3 and 7, and thus all three Capriccios fall into the same category. Note the original markings of No. 5 (Allegretto) and No. 6 (Andante grazioso, then Andante teneramente), respectively slightly faster and slower than the final tempos. Although it suggests a rough temporal symmetry centred on the formally anomalous No. 4 (see Dunsby 1983: 175–6), such a diagram says little about the progression of pulse from

beyond the scope of this study), there is no substantiated proof that in his own music Brahms attempted to follow what he would have regarded as standard sixteenth-century practice, although circumstantial evidence (e.g. compositional features such as the motivic relationships found here in Op. 116 and by Epstein and Forte in other works of Brahms) and the rhythmic techniques of some composers who influenced him, such as Schütz (see Mendel 1960), J. S. Bach (Mendel 1959), Mozart (Zaslaw 1974) and Beethoven (Kolisch 1943), suggest that *at least* carefully defined tempo relationships, and possibly even proportional ones, guided his own compositional method.

12  McCorkle (1984: 465–8) catalogues the sources, first editions and first performances of Op. 116 and cites relevant correspondence.

one piece to the next. To determine that, there are two possible sources of information: empirical evidence (for instance, as embodied in commercial recordings) and analytical evidence.

Before examining either of these, it will be instructive to consider 'internal' tempo relationships in those three works with changes of time signature or tempo designation – Nos. 2, 3 and 7. Although No. 2 is straightforward, in that Brahms indicates a constant pulse at the changes to 3/8 and back to 3/4 (Example 12.1), the tempo changes within No. 3 are quite problematic (Example 12.2). Epstein proposes maintaining the minim pulse more or less throughout the work: 'The two tempos [Allegro passionato and Un poco meno allegro] . . . are virtually the same – at most, slight flexible variants of the basic pulse' (1990: 211). Were this the case, however, the second section would sound very rushed indeed, whereas motivic relationships – and general musical factors – argue for a noticeably broader tempo: in my view, the bracketed crotchet figures in the example (which constitute a significant link between the sections – see Kalbeck 1915: 284) should be played at approximately the *same* speed, resulting in a new tempo for the middle section *two-thirds* that of section A.[13] As for No. 7's time signature changes, for which no equivalences are given (as mentioned above), the pulse of the 3/8 passage towards the end (where the opening melody returns, greatly compressed) can be deduced from the surrounding 2/4 sections. (See Example 12.3.) Although three relationships are possible – ♪ = ♪, new ♩. = former ♩ (whereby the *beat* length is preserved, if the 3/8 is counted in one) or new ♩. = former ♩ (which maintains the *bar* length) – the first is preferable, as it allows the hemiola emerging later in the 3/8 section to reestablish the crotchet pulse of the 2/4 conclusion to follow, a rhythmic link employed elsewhere in the set and indeed often by Brahms (see Epstein 1990: 206, 210). That Brahms had this link in mind can be inferred from the hastily notated Hamburg manuscript (transcribed in Example 12.4), in which, presumably by mistake, he failed to reinstate bar 90's 2/4 and omitted the double barline present in the first edition, thus implying a continuous beat between the hemiola passage and the three-bar conclusion. The change in time signature at bar 21 is more awkward, which explains the plethora of recorded interpretations. (See Example 12.5.) Two possibilities exist: maintaining the quaver (which means a slower pulse in the new section), or keeping a steady beat – i.e. new ♩. = former ♩ (which produces a faster quaver in the new section). Both are satisfactory, although, again, the first seems preferable as it allows the tenor melody (see Cai 1989: 66–7) and the all-important cadential figuration in bars 42–3 (discussed below) to be stated at the original 2/4 pulse. It also preserves the quaver as a subpulse and thus would support Epstein's hypothesis that 'changes of movement' within a work by Brahms are '*tactus*-bound' in simple proportions – once again, a 3 : 2 ratio between the first and second sections (i.e. based on metronomic values; the inverse ratio applies to the beat duration). Table 12.2 shows how the various pulses in No. 7 are related when the quaver is kept constant throughout.

---

[13]   This 3 : 2 ratio between old and new tempos (based on the metronomic values of the beats) is corroborated by the empirical evidence adduced later.

Example 12.1   Op. 116 No. 2

a. bars 17–20

b. bars 49–51

Example 12.2   Op. 116 No. 3

a. bars 1–2

b. bars 35–6

Example 12.3   Op. 116 No. 7, bars 72–7

Example 12.4    Op. 116 No. 7: transcription of Hamburg MS, bars 86–92

Example 12.5    Op. 116 No. 7, bars 19–23[1]

Table 12.2    *Relationship between pulses in Op. 116 No. 7*

| Bar: | 1–20 | | 21–46 | | 47–73 | | 74–89 | | 90–2 |
|---|---|---|---|---|---|---|---|---|---|
| Time signature: | $\frac{2}{4}$ | | $\frac{6}{8}$ | | $\frac{2}{4}$ | | $\frac{3}{8}$ | | $\frac{2}{4}$ |
| Pulse: | ♩ | | ♩. | | ♩ | | ♩. | | ♩ |
| Ratio (between metronomic values): | 3 | : | 2 | : | 3 | : | 2 | : | 3 |
| 'Tactus' | ♪ | = | ♪ | = | ♪ | = | ♪ | = | ♪ |

When this line of enquiry is extended beyond Nos. 2, 3 and 7, a fascinating scheme of tempos between the individual pieces emerges if the 'logical' temporal relationship exemplified by No. 3 is assumed to link other principal motifs. I do not of course mean by this *all* the unifying motifs identified by Dunsby, as some are less relevant than others to the music's narrative process (however cogent their connections appear on paper, what matters most to the performer and the listener is their audible relationship in a 'live' context). I am referring specifically to the two most important cells from the performer's perspective: the chains of (usually descending) thirds plus linear variants thereof, which are particularly prominent in Nos. 1, 3, 4 and 7, and the short–long, or iambic, rhythm found especially in Nos. 2, 5, 6 and 7, as well as No. 4.

Example 12.6    Motivic relationships at hypothetical proportional tempos

a. descending/ascending thirds and linear variants

(i) at ★ = x

b. iambic rhythms
(i) at ★ = 3y

(diminution of figure in
1ff. – see below)

(ii) at ★ = y

If my hunch is correct and if Epstein's hypothesis of proportional tempos has any bearing on this multi-piece, these motifs, which operate more or less throughout the opus, will in some *intrinsic* way relate to one another when the music is brought to life: in other words, these omnipresent motivic cells will become temporally 'aligned' if and when the constituent pieces are played at 'correct' tempos.[14]

Let us assume on the basis of what we have discovered in No. 3 that the most significant motivic correspondences in the set are equivalent in duration, and let us observe the fascinating relationships that ensue. Example 12.6a shows the first of the all-important motivic 'germs' – descending or ascending thirds occasionally joined linearly – unfolding at the same speed (attack rate = metronomic value x, marked by a star in the example) in Nos. 1, 3, 4 and 7, those works in which the motif most conspicuously appears. This temporal pattern, established in both hands at the start of No. 1 and repeated in various guises throughout the piece (as in the left hand, bars 9–12), resurfaces in No. 3 at the climax of sections A and A', where minims (also at x) conclude a process of rhythmic augmentation from quavers at the opening through crotchets near the middle of the two sections. In No. 4, falling thirds at $\flat$ = x function cadentially in bar 8 and thereafter embellish the melody (as in 15–17), while in No. 7, in crotchets, they assume a thematic function in the two A sections and the turbulent second section (respectively, bars 1ff. and 42ff.). Furthermore, this important motif is heard in diminution in Nos. 3 and 7 at a speed four times as fast (i.e. 4x – part ii of Example 12.6a), thereby enhancing the connection between these Capriccios.

The other unifying motif of significance is the short–long rhythm especially prominent in Nos. 2, 5 and 6 – that is, the three works *not* reliant on the thirds motif – as well as the last piece, which, like Brahms's codas in general, has a multifaceted summarising function in Op. 116.[15] Example 12.6b relates the iambic patterns heard in No. 2's middle section, the distinctive over-the-barline impulse on which No. 5 is based in entirety (see Lewin 1990: 18–24) and the rocking rhythm at the climax of No. 7 (which, though slurred long–short, assumes an over-the-barline iambic character (see Cooper and Meyer 1960: 12ff.)). All of these are durationally equivalent ($\flat$ = 3y in each case), as are the crotchet–minim patterns of Nos. 2 and 6 shown at the bottom of the example ($\flat$ = y), a pattern also implied by the harmonic rhythm at the start of No. 6.

It is within No. 7 that the relationship between these hypothetical tempos x and y is defined once and for all (giving further credence to my claim that the final Capriccio 'summarises' the entire multi-piece). As we have seen, the tensions created

---

[14]   By 'correct' I mean a *range* of suitable tempos, rather than specific fixed values. Epstein observes that
        'right' tempo is a universal concern, for without it a performance is handicapped, at the least. Tempo
        exerts a master control over the unfolding of all elements of a work – themes, phrases, harmonic
        progressions, sections, overarching relations, proportions. Unfolded at the 'right' pace these fit together
        naturally. Likewise our physiology, on whose coordination this performance depends, functions naturally.
        In brief, we 'breathe', and so does the music.          (1985: 35; see also Epstein 1979, 1990 and 1995)
[15]   See Dunsby 1983: 187 and Forte 1957: 193 and 198. The short–long rhythm also occurs in Nos. 1, 3 and 4,
        but these manifestations are far less striking, possibly because of the 'competition' from other intentionally
        more prominent motivic material.

by the change to 3/8 at bar 74 (Example 12.3) are resolved by the return to 2/4 at bar 90 (Example 12.4), where the hemiola in the preceding eight bars anticipates the 'new' crotchet pulse. Given that the tempo of the 3/8 passage is $\textarial{.}= y$, and that of the 2/4 $\textarial{} = x$, this hemiola/crotchet equivalence means that *y is precisely two-thirds of x*, i.e. x : y = 3 : 2. Accordingly, extrapolating from this, we find that *the same ratio applies to all of the contexts in which these motivically derived hypothetical tempos are found*.

The large-scale tempo implications of this conclusion can be seen in Table 12.3, which displays pulses and subdivisions for the entire opus in terms of the two basic tempos and multiples thereof that can be extracted from the principal motifs when related as above. Correspondences are indicated by the horizontal boxes, the broadest of which occurs at metronomic value 2x = 3y, extending as the basic *tactus* unit virtually throughout the set. This will be discussed shortly; for now, note that the broken lines represent either the temporary suspension of a particular duration – as at y, where No. 2's pulse is bracketed with that of No. 3's middle section – or, in the case of Nos. 5 and 7, alternative readings. The different possibilities in No. 7 have already been discussed; as for No. 5, suffice it to say that most pianists adopt a slower tempo than Brahms's specified Andante (let alone the original Allegretto), and this chart depicts proportional relationships effecting both the slower 'norm' (right-hand column) and the more lilting tempo apparently desired by the composer.

Having derived hypothetical proportional tempos on the basis of the principal motivic material as articulated in time, we can now define a tempo strategy for performing this multi-piece. The pianist need conceive of only one tempo at the start of No. 1 – but that tempo, or something close to it, will eventually have to serve for Nos. 3 and 7 to ensure the temporal alignment of the descending-third motif. Thus some long-term planning must occur when choosing the tempo of the first Capriccio. Although the *tactus* plays no part in the opening work (a later compositional date than for Nos. 2–6 might explain this anomaly), the stringendo from bar 189 establishes a much quicker pulse, possibly as fast as $\textarial{.}= 2y$, which is the value of No. 2's quaver as shown in Table 12.3. This would establish a simple 2 : 1 ratio between the end of the first piece and the start of the second. Once the main pulse ($\textarial{} = y$) is established in No. 2, the tempo relationships between sections take care of themselves (although the rhythmic foreground is highly complex, as we shall see), the hemiola towards the end preparing the pulse of No. 3. The third piece leads into its successor via the rhythmic augmentation that presents the thirds motif in minims at x (bars 99–103), which are played at the same pulse as the quaver setting of the motif in No. 4 (bars 8 and 15–16 *et seq.*). To get from No. 4 to No. 5, the pianist can link the former's semiquaver to the latter's (triplet) quaver, producing a flowing Andante at $\textarial{.} = y$, a pulse also maintained in No. 6. The triplet quaver of the latter serves as the join to No. 7, where the semiquaver figuration at the opening is played at the same tempo as the analogous shape starting No. 3, thus effecting another large-scale connection.

Although this strategy for producing a temporally coherent rendition of the seven *Fantasien* might seem highly contrived in print, the succession of tempos described here is a perfectly natural one when 'intuitively' activated in performance (i.e. at a 'submerged

Table 12.3  *Intraopus pulses and subdivisions*

| | 1. Presto energico | 2. Andante | | | 3. Allegro passionato | Un poco meno allegro | Allegro passionato | 4. Adagio | 5. Andante con grazia ed intimissimo sentimento | 6. Andantino teneramente | 7. Allegro agitato | | | | | |
|---|---|---|---|---|---|---|---|---|---|---|---|---|---|---|---|---|
| Time signature: | 3/8 | 3/4 | 3/8 | 3/4 | 2/2 | | | 3/4 | 6/8 | 3/4 | 2/4 | 6/8 | | 2/4 | 3/8 | 2/4 |
| Metronomic values: | | | | | | | | | OR | | ♪ = ♪* OR ♩. = ♩ | | | ♪ = ♪* OR ♩. = ♩ OR ♩. = ♩ | | |
| ½ x | | | | | | | | ♩ Pulse | ♩. Pulse | | ♩ Super-Pulse | | ♩ Super-Pulse | | ♩. Pulse | ♩ Super-Pulse |
| y | | ♩ Pulse | ♩. Pulse | ♩ Pulse | | ♩ Pulse | | | ♩. Pulse | ♩ Pulse | | ♩. Pulse | | ♩. Pulse | | |
| x | ♩. Pulse | | hemi-ola ♩ | hemi-ola ♩ | ♩ Pulse | | ♩ Pulse | ♪ | | | ♩ Pulse | hemi-ola ♩ (in 3/4) | ♩. Pulse | ♩ Pulse | hemi-ola ♩ | ♩. Pulse | ♩ Pulse |
| 2y | ♩. Pulse after *stringendo*, 189ff.? | ♪ | | ♪ | | ♩ | | | | ♪ | | | | | | |
| 2x = 3y (*tactus*) | ♪₃ | ♪ | ♪₃ | ♩ | ♩₃ | ♩ | ♫ | ♪ | | ♪₃ | ♪ | ♪ | ♪ | ♪ | | (♪) |
| 4x | | ♫ | | ♪ | | ♪ | | | | | | ♫ | | ♫ | | |

Equivalence implied by Brahms

*Preferred equivalence          *Preferred equivalence

level of consciousness'). And no musician would argue that these hypothetical tempos had to be adhered to with metronomical exactitude in order for the performance to work (in any case, research suggests that the tempos could vary by as much as $\pm 5$ per cent and still be audibly 'the same' – see Epstein 1985: 40–3). What counts is the *perceived* relation between pulses, which as a matter of course will be greatly deviated from throughout a performance even though listeners would sense that the music was being played at one tempo.[16]

To put these conclusions to the test, I conducted a survey of recordings at the National Sound Archive in London. The (admittedly subjective) procedure involved the use of a metronome to determine the 'main tempo' – i.e. the implied principal pulse (*not* the average) – of a performance after several listenings to each rendition. Data from nine commercial recordings plus my own recital are listed in Table 12.4,[17] the figures representing a metronomic value for the prevailing pulse in each work or section thereof, with average tempos at the far right. (The numbers in brackets were calculated by excluding anomalous tempos,[18] which are italicised, as in the case of Wilhelm Kempff's exceptionally slow No. 1.) Interesting observations emerged from this comparison. For instance, the middle section of No. 3 was generally played much more slowly than the outer sections (despite the Un poco meno allegro marking); No. 4 (Adagio) was often faster than No. 5 (Andante); and successive tempos in the notorious No. 7 were inconsistent. Table 12.5 groups the averages according to the fast–moderate–slow classification of Table 12.1, except that No. 5's average 56 (54) belongs to the slow category. Taking another average *within* the three classes, the respective means are 115/72/58, or, again discounting anomalies, 114/74/57, which, as indicated at the bottom of the table, are related in almost exact whole-number ratios: $114 : 74 \approx 3 : 2$ (*proportio sesquialtera*), $114 : 57 = 2 : 1$ (*proportio dupla*) and $74 : 57 \approx 4 : 3$ (*proportio sesquitertia*). These results echo those obtained in the motivic study above: i.e. $x : y = 3 : 2 \approx 114 : 74$, and so forth.

It is noteworthy that the empirical evidence conflicts with the motivically derived tempo scheme in the case of No. 5. Table 12.3 proposes a pulse of $\downarrow. = y$ and a moderate tempo rather faster than that taken by most pianists – in fact, all but one of those listed in Table 12.4. The odd man out, Stephen Kovacevich, plays No. 5 at $\downarrow. = 80$ in a pert but cogent interpretation closer to Brahms's Andante marking – not to mention

---

[16]    Gabrielsson and Bengtsson distinguish four different types of tempo:
> (a) the abstract *mean tempo*, calculated as the total duration of a music section divided by the number of beats in the same section, (b) the *main tempo*, being the prevailing (and intended) tempo when initial and final retardations as well as more amorphous caesurae are deleted, (c) *local tempi*, maintained only for short periods but perceptibly differing, and (d) *beat rate* . . . describing minor fluctuations, which may not be perceptible as such.                (quoted in Gabrielsson 1988: 33)

I am obviously considering 'main tempo' here.

[17]    As Table 12.4 indicates, the performances in question were recorded between 1954 and 1991. It is likely that less consistent results would have been obtained had it been possible to compare performances from up to 100 years ago, due to the narrowing of interpretative practice in the latter part of this century.

[18]    In cancelling out individual interpretative idiosyncrasies (which is not of course to deny the aesthetic legitimacy of differing interpretations), we arrive at an ostensible expressive norm for some forty years of Brahms playing.

Table 12.4   *Tempos of recorded and live performances*

| Piece and tempo marking | Time signature | Pulse | JK | WG | WK | MR | GO | SK | PR | JD | EG | JR | AVERAGE |
|---|---|---|---|---|---|---|---|---|---|---|---|---|---|
| 1. Presto energico | 3/8 | ♩. = 108 | | 104 | *80* | 112 | 112 | 120 | 112 | 120 | | 100 | ♩. = 108 (111) |
| 2. Andante | 3/4 | ♩ = 63 | | 76 | 69 | 69 | 69 | 72 | *50* | 63 | | 69 | ♩ = 67 (69) |
| 3. Allegro passionato | 2/2 | 𝅗𝅥 = 108 | | 108 | 104 | 108 | 126 | 120 | 100 | 120 | | 100 | 𝅗𝅥 = 110 |
| Un poco meno allegro | | 𝅗𝅥 = 84 | | 76 | 72 | 80 | 76 | 76 | 76 | 76 | | *58* | 𝅗𝅥 = 75 (77) |
| Allegro passionato | | 𝅗𝅥 = 108 | | 116 | 104 | 108 | 126 | 120 | 100 | 120 | | 100 | 𝅗𝅥 = 111 |
| 4. Adagio | 3/4 | ♩ = 60 | | 54 | 63 | 63 | 50 | 65 | 48 | 66 | | 63 | ♩ = 59 |
| 5. Andante con grazia ed intimissimo sentimento | 6/8 | ♩. = 52 | | 59 | 56 | 42 | 60 | *80* | 56 | 52 | 52 | 56 | ♩. = 56 (54) |
| 6. Andantino teneramente | 3/4 | ♩ = 54 | | 76 | 100 | 69 | 84 | 84 | 50 | 69 | 84 | 76 | ♩ = 75 |
| 7. Allegro agitato | 2/4 | ♩ = 120 | | 126 | 120 | *150* | 138 | 126 | 120 | 126 | | 120 | ♩ = 127 (124) |
| | 6/8 | ♩. = 80* | | 86* | 80* | 120 | 126† | 112† | 108† | 116† | | 108† | ♩. = 104 |
| | | | * i.e. ♪ = ♪ | | | | † i.e. ♩. = ♩ | | | | | | |
| bars 47–61 | 2/4 | ♩ = 152 | | 144 | 126 | 176 | 176 | 126 | 126 | 132 | | 112 | ♩ = 141 |
| bars 62–73 | | ♩ = 120 | | 138 | 120 | 150 | 144 | 120 | 126 | 126 | | 120 | ♩ = 129 |
| | 3/8 | ♩. = 100 | | 72 | 76 | 100 | 126 | 92 | 84 | 104 | | 70 | ♩. = 92 |
| | 2/4 | ♩ = 100 | | 92 | 88 | 120 | 108 | 100 | 84 | 108 | | 92 | ♩ = 99 |

JK  = Julius Katchen – Decca SDD 533 (1964)     WG = Walter Gieseking – Columbia CX 1255 (n.d.)

WK = Wilhelm Kempff – Decca LXT 2935 (1954)    MR = Mikhail Rudy – EMI 7475562 (1986)

GO = Gerhard Oppitz – EMI 057-30806 (1978)     SK = Stephen Kovacevich – Philips 411 137-1 (1983)

PR  = Pascal Rogé – Decca SXL 6786 (1977)      JD  = Jörg Demus – Westminster XWN 18802 (1958/9)

EG  = Emil Gilels – Supraphon 1111 2550 (1973)    JR  = John Rink – Recording of 1991 recital

Table 12.5   *Average tempos (fast, moderate and slow) and proportional relationships*

FAST

| No. 1: | 108 | No. 3 | 110 | No. 7: | 127 | AVERAGE | = | 115 |
|---|---|---|---|---|---|---|---|---|
| | (111) | (A & A'): | | | (124) | | | (114) |

MODERATE

| No. 2: | 67 | No. 3 (B): | 75 | No. 6: | 75 | AVERAGE | = | 72 |
|---|---|---|---|---|---|---|---|---|
| | (69) | | (77) | | | | | (74) |

SLOW

| No. 4: | 59 | No. 5: | 56 | | | AVERAGE | = | 58 |
|---|---|---|---|---|---|---|---|---|
| | | | (54) | | | | | (57) |

APPROXIMATE RATIOS BETWEEN PULSES (USING BRACKETED AVERAGES):[a]

| *Pulse:* | 114 | | 74 | | 57 |
|---|---|---|---|---|---|
| *Ratios:* | 6 | : | 4 | : | 3 |
| | 3 | : | 2 | | |
| | 2 | | : | | 1 |
| | | | 4 | : | 3 |

a   In Tables 12.4 and 12.5, averages in brackets have been calculated by excluding anomalous tempos (i.e. those in italics in Table 12.4).

the original Allegretto – than the walking-on-eggshells renditions of most performers (including myself). To preserve the *tactus* unit shown in Table 12.3 and to align the piece with No. 2's Andante and No. 6's Andantino, I would advise a brisker tempo for No. 5 than is the norm; of course, the challenge at this speed is to capture the graceful, intimate mood required by the composer.[19] A slower-than-usual tempo for No. 7 might be in order for similar reasons.

These recommendations certainly apply to my own interpretation of the set. In addition to speeding up No. 5 (as well as Nos. 1 and 3) and slowing down No. 7, I would now play the middle part of No. 3 at a tempo capturing the motivic connection shown in Example 12.2, and I would aim to preserve the quaver *tactus* within No. 7. There would be other small adjustments as well. I hasten to add, however, that these changes would not be adopted simply to make the rendition conform to some 'theoretical' scheme of proportional tempos in Brahms's music; rather, their intention would be to align the motivic connections detailed above so that the essential unity of this multi-piece could come to the fore. Any choice of tempo will have implications for the listener's perception of unity,[20] and by devising a

19   According to Cai (1986 and 1989), the 'con grazia ed intimissimo sentimento' marking, like all character indications in the set (*energico, passionato, teneramente* and *agitato*), pertains only indirectly to tempo.

20   Related issues are discussed in Rink 1990, 1994a and 1994b; see also Cone's essay above. Nicholas Cook's chapter in this volume makes similar points regarding Furtwängler's interpretations of Beethoven's Ninth Symphony.

comprehensive network of proportional tempo relations on the basis of the principal motifs in Op. 116, the performer imbues his or her interpretation with an all-encompassing sense of structure or architecture. I am not of course arguing exclusively for *these* fast, moderate and slow tempos (other proportional values could work just as well) or claiming that deviation from the proposed tempos in one or more numbers is necessarily 'unmusical' – as I have implied, a range of interpretations might convince, although some less than others. Nor would I ever insist that the performer slavishly attend to the tick of the metronome at any given tempo. But if proportional tempos in this set *are* effected, they will enable the performer to demonstrate the unity of this 'multi-piece' in a unique way beyond the analyst's power: in a sense, the performance thus takes on an important 'analytical' function – the performance becomes an *act of analysis*. As I see it, the pianist's best strategy is to aim for roughly proportional tempos and let the durationally equal motivic correspondences 'speak for themselves' (to that extent allowing the in-built structure to 'exert its own control'), rather than attempt to 'bring out' motivic connections per se: the unity of pulse can be communicated and perceived far more readily than motivic unity as normally understood, which is best demonstrated in notated analysis, not aurally. The alignment of tempo relationships in performance results not only in the durational correspondence of the principal motifs (as seen in Example 12.6), but also in the logical succession of pulses shown in Figure 12.1, where fast and moderate tempos alternate more or less throughout, with a slow tempo at the heart of the set for either Nos. 4 and 5 (Figure 12.1a) or No. 4 alone (Figure 12.1b). By adopting this varied scheme, the performer in essence lays the foundation for a series of complementary affective responses, moving 'from one affect to another' as in the eighteenth-century free fantasies of C. P. E. Bach.[21] In this way tempo acts as a structural framework and a foundation for the manifold tensions that, in typically Brahmsian fashion, rack the rhythmic foreground.[22]

## RHYTHM, METRE AND THE EXPRESSIVE MICROSTRUCTURE

Having established a rhythmic background for the set, I shall address middle- and foreground temporal issues, specifically phrase structure and implied rebarrings such as hemiolas. In analysing phrase structure, I employed a method accessible to any performer with a modicum of academic training, the intention throughout this project being to work towards a practical analytical approach to performance with realistic pedagogical potential. The first step was simply to parse the music into phrases, the

---

[21]  See Bach [1753] 1949: 153. The same result characterises the succession of 'thematically defined' tempos that Jon Finson (1984: 471–5) shows to be a central part of late-nineteenth-century performance practice.

[22]  It is instructive to compare Chopin's approach to tempo: according to Berlioz, he could play his mazurkas with a 'thousand nuances of movement' but without losing the pulse, and to Liszt his unique rubato was like the 'trembling' leaves of a tree whose trunk remained solid and stable. See J.-J. Eigeldinger, *Chopin: Pianist and Teacher as Seen by His Pupils*, trans. N. Shohet with K. Osostowicz and R. Howat, ed. R. Howat (Cambridge: Cambridge University Press, 1986), pp. 49–51 and 71–3.

Figure 12.1    Relationship between average pulses in Op. 116

a. No. 5 played at a slow tempo, as in most recorded performances (see Table 12.4)

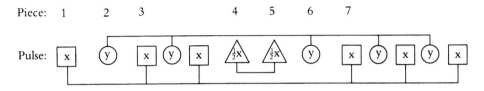

b. No. 5 played at a moderate tempo, as per Brahms's 'Andante' marking (see Table 12.1)

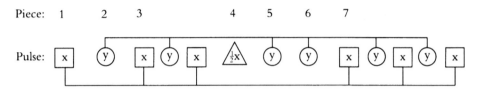

second to look for systematic processes or patterns like extension, contraction or elision of defined units. In doing so I discovered a scheme of alternating regular and irregular phrase structures extending through the opus: No. 1 for instance is propelled by a virtually incessant hypermetric accent every four bars, whereas No. 2 is constantly in a state of flux, particularly in its middle section. This alternation continues from piece to piece, organising the set in the manner of the alternating tempos described before, and also functioning in tandem with an opposition between duple and triple metric units or subdivisions thereof to be considered shortly.[23]

Two case studies will illustrate possible performance strategies in works with regular or irregular phrase structures. In No. 1, as in all four 'regular' works, the accent pattern impels the music forward, the four-bar hypermeasure being abandoned in only a few places, which, by contrast, take on special significance. These include a nine-bar written-out 'ritardando' (bars 123–31) just before the reprise in this 'symmetrical sonata form' (Dunsby 1983: 175); a five-bar momentum-generating passage (184–8) launching the drive to the final cadence; and three six-bar phrases based on a *ritmo di tre battute* principle (see Cai 1986: 379), which I shall single out for examination, as the performance issues they pose call for a solution of relevance to the interpretation of the entire opus.

First, however, consider the opening bars of No. 1 (Example 12.7), where Brahms exploits the instability caused by the left-hand syncopations and right-hand over-the-barline impulses in bars 1–4 by shifting the metric accent to the third quaver in bars 4–7 (note the *sfs*), returning to the notated metre via the emphatic 'regularising'

---

[23]    See Forte 1957 for discussion of two-against-three oppositions in the Haydn Variations.

Example 12.7   Op. 116 No. 1, bars 1–9[1]

Example 12.8   Op. 116 No. 1

a. bars 53–9[1]

b. bars 164–76[1]

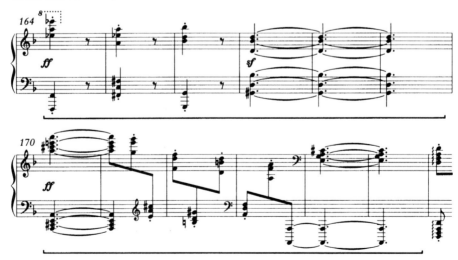

gesture joining the end of bar 7 to the strong downbeat in bar 9. This brief passage violently pulls at the musical fabric and catapults the listener into the opus, provided that the pianist makes full use of the metrical implications latent in bars 1–4 which are then made manifest in 4–7. Exploitation of latent implications gradually made manifest is in fact a key strategy in performing the whole set: a progression from latent through emergent to manifest states characterises not only brief passages like this, but also larger spans like the *ritmo di tre battute* phrase extensions just described, as well as intraopus processes related, for instance, to hemiolas. The six-bar phrase in 53–8 divides logically enough into two three-bar groups (Example 12.8a), but simply to stress the implied 'metric downbeats' in 53 and 56 would miss the point. My own approach to 53–8 (which follows a sixteen-bar tension-building passage driven by an octave pedal on C tolling every four bars) is to maximise ambiguity by regarding the *ritmo di tre battute* as only latent for the time being, giving the F major chord in 55 cadential emphasis and treating the $ii^6_5$ in 56 as if it were a *one*-bar approach chord to the dominant extended by two additional bars in order to generate momentum. This 4 + 2 interpretation can simultaneously hint at the 3 + 3 organisation implicit in the passage, which, surfacing again in bars 164–9, at last prevails in 170–5 just before the reprise (Example 12.8b).

Note that these six-bar phrases relate to No. 1's standard four-bar hypermeasure in a 3 : 2 ratio, which is not only that of the hypothetical fast and moderate tempos proposed earlier − x : y − but also the ratio between the triple and duple metrical schemes in opposition throughout the set, as in the middle section of No. 2, which serves as the next case study. Here again the latent–emergent–manifest principle helps the performer control the extraordinarily complex phrase structure depicted in Example 12.9, which redrafts bars 19–50 in terms of the crotchet pulse from the opening section, rather than Brahms's new 3/8 time signature. Disparate groupings inherent in the music vie for prominence, defined respectively by the composer's slurs, the right-hand melodic units and the left-hand accompaniment patterns, which set up the at times conflicting metrical implications shown on the diagram. Observe in particular the 2/4–3/4 juxtapositions (both horizontal and vertical, as in the highly unstable bars 24–30) which generate considerable inner tension (see Cai 1986: 379–80), along with the hemiolas in bars 40–3, 45–6 and 47–50; note also the extension or truncation of established patterns (particularly in the left hand) and the ambiguity surrounding metric accents, which are often held in abeyance to propel the music towards resolution at bar 51 (following the arrival on A of the motivically important octave progression). The performer is advised to refer simultaneously to as many different organisational schemes in operation at a given point as possible, perhaps practising each separately and then combining them in a rhythmic counterpoint transcending allegiance to any one grouping, with elements of each surfacing here and there to tantalise the listener with hints of stability in that particular direction, only to have the music turn immediately towards another. Such twisting and turning – which defies precise notation and can be captured only in sound – creates a marvellous floating effect, a metrical void, a kaleidoscopic temporal 'neutrality' clearly intended by Brahms (note the huge left-hand slur), maximised by the high, suspended tessitura

Example 12.9 Op. 116 No. 2: phrase structure of bars 19–50

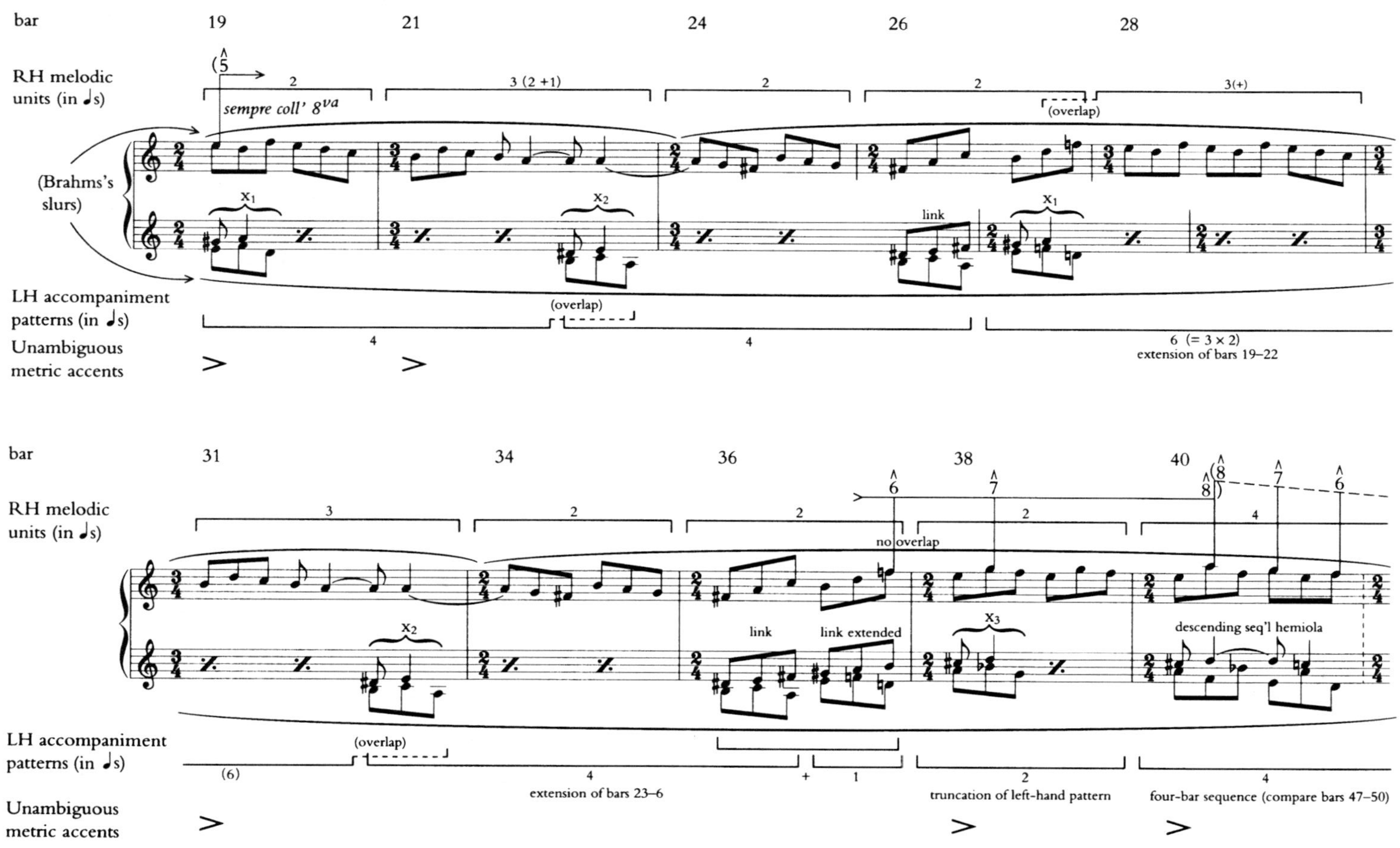

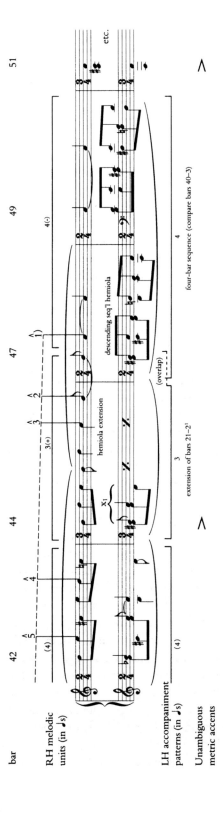

Table 12.6   *Hemiolas in Op. 116*

| Piece: | 1 | 2 | 4 | 6 | 7 |
|---|---|---|---|---|---|
| Bars: | 21–36 | 40–3 | 27–8 | 25–42 | 21–46 |
|  | 132–47 | 45–6 | 31–2 | 57–60 | 74–5 (implied) |
|  | 185–9 | 47–50 | 50–1 |  | 82–9 |
|  |  | 79 |  |  |  |
|  |  | 81 |  |  |  |

and the broken-octave semiquaver figuration whose convoluted contour enhances the sense of breathless urgency.

Exploiting tensions between latent, emergent and manifest states is a useful strategy in performing the notorious hemiolas and metric shifts that infiltrate the music. Brahms disposes the former in a symmetrical pattern spanning the opus: as Table 12.6 indicates, hemiolas appear in Nos. 1, 2, 4, 6 and 7, gradually increasing in significance – that is, in disruption to the notated metre – as the set unfolds, thus lending a goal-directed dimension to these normally discrete rhythmic devices. In No. 1, the strong four-bar hypermeasure cushions the hemiola's impact in bars 21–36 and 132–47 (more detailed discussion of these passages follows below), while the much briefer hemiola some forty bars later generates momentum towards climax, at the same time preparing the two-quaver beat division in No. 2, just as No. 2's left-hand hemiolas in bars 79 and 81 emerge from triplets to foreshadow the following Capriccio's duple pulse (attack rate = x in Table 12.3, p. 266). Whereas in Nos. 2 and 4 hemiolas are confined to short bursts of activity (their destabilising potential temporarily kept on hold), in No. 6 they pervade the entire middle section, and for the first time in the opus the hemiola-defined metre virtually supplants the notated one, again assuming priority for a few bars just before the end. Stability in No. 7's middle section is even more threatened by the out-of-phase juxtaposition of a 6/8 accompaniment and a 3/4 melody, which capitalises on the two-against-three duality present throughout the opus in numerous parametric contexts and at various levels. As noted already, tensions reach a peak with the change to 3/8 at bar 74, the implied hemiola in 74–5 manifested in the climactic eight bars redefining the 2/4 metre in which the piece ends, resolution limited to just three bars. In summary, then, a comprehensive hemiola process based on the latent–emergent–manifest principle builds upon tensions implicit at an early stage to reach their full disruptive potential in the final Capriccio.

Earlier I alluded to possible performance strategies to cope with hemiolas and other rebarrings: one can submit the notated metre to an implied one, allow the original time signature to prevail or, as in No. 2's middle section, combine more than one metrical organisation such that none predominates. Although contexts vary, in general I advocate keeping a toehold on the notated metre (compare Cai 1986: 371), even when an alternative scheme obscures or threatens it, for the pull between the two energises the music (as in No. 5, which thrives on the conflict between a texturally dense chordal anacrusis and a thinner, dissonant downbeat; here the performer would completely miss the point by accenting the upbeat and thus disregarding the time signature). Implicit reference to the time signature was surely Brahms's general intention, for he did not hesitate to change it when he wanted a different metre to prevail, as in Nos. 2 and 7. When the original time signature is maintained, it should not be completely effaced, meaning that simply rebarring Brahms's music to show implicit alternative metrical schemes, as some analysts do, inadequately defines a performance strategy.[24] In bars 21–36 of No. 1, for instance, rather than adopt the hemiola-inspired 3/4 wholesale, I initially suspend the metric accent, relying on the four-bar hypermeasure for stability until, at bar 25, the hemiola is allowed to surface in the left hand against a right hand syncopated in the original 3/8. The metrically neutral ascent in the treble then climbs against the hemiola accompaniment in 29–32, which exerts greater force as the passage closes. The same procedure applies to the counterpart to this passage, bars 132–47, which is renotated in Example 12.10 to reflect this performance approach.

As stated above, the middle section of No. 6 is more seriously racked by conflicting metrical implications. Three systems operate in the passage (Example 12.11): the notated 3/4; an implied 2/4 with downbeat on the last crotchet of bar 24; and a different implied 2/4, whose downbeat falls on the first crotchet of 25. One performance approach, proposed by Cai (1986: 378), is 'to deemphasize all metrical accent', producing 'an unaccented, smooth stream of notes – for which no clear notation existed in Brahms's time'. In essence this means playing the passage without barlines, as in the previous example, a strategy with which I generally agree. Nevertheless, even if barlines are suppressed, it is important to allow innate metrical tensions between the 3/4 and the 2/4s to surface when appropriate. The very life of these passages derives from a seemingly random oscillation between conflicting systems competing within the neutral background aptly described by Cai. In practical terms, this means isolating each organisational scheme in rehearsal and then 'contrapuntally' juxtaposing them without any one assuming priority, relying on Brahms's slurs to shape the metrical void.

Such a suspension of metre, which I also observe in the middle section of No. 2 (as mentioned earlier), is a viable interpretative possibility again in the middle section of No. 7. Here a two-bar hypermeasure operates (defined in part by the up-and-down quaver motion), providing stability at a further remove from the notated 6/8 (shown in Example 12.5, p. 261), which clashes throughout with the implied 3/4 in the right hand (the innate ambiguity resolving only briefly in the first ending, bar 44a – see Example 12.12). Rather than explicitly tie the passage to either the 6/8 or the 3/4 (as some performers do, often ignoring the 6/8 pulse altogether), I transcend allegiance to both, responding to the hypermetrical lilt and imbuing the staccato crotchet melody with an unsettled, syncopated feel to capture its out-of-phase character, starting as it

---

[24]   See Frisch 1990: 144 for a critique of Schoenberg's analyses of rhythm in Brahms.

    Compare these comments with the discussion of Chopin's Waltz Op. 42 in William Rothstein's chapter, which (like Janet Levy's essay) similarly advocates the projection of ambiguity in performance rather than its eradication.

Example 12.10   Op. 116 No. 1, bars 132–49[1]

Example 12.11   Op. 116 No. 6, bars 22–8

Example 12.12   Op. 116 No. 7, bars 41–4a

were a quaver too late. The effect, as in other passages, is one of hovering (see Evans [1936]: 226), that is, the 'kaleidoscopic temporal "neutrality"' described before, which again can be achieved by practising the two systems in isolation and then combining them within a metrical void.

It is telling that so many passages like this occur in the set: I would even venture to describe them as a unifying device like the other more conventional motifs that 'saturate the music'. Unlike their counterparts, however, these rhythmic 'motifs' can be realised in performance alone: not only do they defy precise notation, but their unifying powers are activated only as the music itself comes to life in sound. In this regard performance again assumes the mantle of analysis, able to illuminate aspects of musical structure which cannot be fully grasped or represented on paper.

As with any 'analysis', various interpretations are of course possible (see Cone 1968: 34 and Schmalfeldt 1985: 28): mine are by no means the only ones available. Nevertheless, like the hypothetical proportional tempos discussed earlier, there are compelling reasons for favouring the interpretative approach proposed here – that is, the maximising of ambiguity and inner tension within a metrical void where no bar-lines operate. These reasons have to do with the historical context and possible origins of Brahms's rhythmic technique, which will be explored in the final part of the chapter.

## FANTASIES OP. 116, THE ART OF IMPROVISATION AND 'HISTORICAL PERFORMANCE PRACTICE'

The title of this set – *Fantasien* – has inspired considerable speculation: its implications are explored, for instance, in Dunsby 1983 and Kraus 1990, particularly with regard to form and harmony. Although chosen at a late stage, apparently on Kalbeck's advice (1910: 195), the title aptly summarises the approach to rhythm outlined here, which in many respects is indeed fantasy-like. While formal and tonal liberties were the most widely recognised features of eighteenth- and nineteenth-century improvisation, rhythmic freedom was an equally essential stylistic component, particularly in the free fantasy, the improvisatory genre *par excellence* noteworthy for its lack of barlines and unspecified metre, which enabled it to plumb depths of expression unattainable in 'ordinary' compositions. C. P. E. Bach writes in the *Versuch*:

> Unbarred free fantasias seem especially adept at the expression of affects, for each meter carries a kind of compulsion within itself. Consider in comparison the accompanied recitative, where tempo and meter are frequently changed in order to rouse and still the rapidly alternating affects. The metric signature is in many such cases more a convention of notation than a binding factor in performance. It is a distinct merit of the fantasia that, unhampered by such trappings, it can accomplish the aims of the recitative at the keyboard with complete, unmeasured freedom.[25] ([1762] 1949: 153)

This does not mean that the free fantasy was rhythmically illogical: Bach also stresses that 'although no bar lines are employed, the ear demands a definite relationship in the succession and duration of the chords themselves . . . and the eye, a relationship in the lengths of notes so that the piece may be notated' (: 430). As with harmony and form, therefore, rhythmic liberties in the free fantasy apparently were exercised in an ordered manner. This was consistent with the principle of *vernünftige Betrügerey* (rational deception) at the heart of Bach's improvisatory practice.

---

[25]   Certain details of Mitchell's translation have been altered to conform more closely to Bach's original.

These passages from the *Versuch* apply with almost uncanny accuracy to Brahms's *Fantasien* Op. 116, alluding to the essential rhythmic quality of the metrically free passages discussed in this essay, which unfold against the 'background' provided by the scheme of proportional tempos and, on a smaller scale, by the notated time signature. The relevance of Bach's remarks is not entirely surprising: Brahms's rhythmic technique could be linked to Bach's via Beethoven, whose improvisatory music reveals important points of contact with Bach's not only in terms of form and tonality, but also in terms of rhythm (particularly in the highly 'improvisatory' late piano sonatas: for instance, the Largo of Op. 106; the Adagio espressivo interruptions in the first movement of Op. 109, as well as their counterparts in Variation 6 in the last movement; and, above all, the Adagio ma non troppo and *Recitativo* of Op. 110, with its well-known *Bebung*). Although the free fantasy had declined as an independent genre by the early nineteenth century, its spirit was thus perpetuated by Beethoven, his assimilation of the 'improvisatory' into composed music having incalculable influence on both improvisation and composition throughout the nineteenth century – surely one of his most important legacies. Brahms's rhythmic technique is but one example of that influence.[26] The link proposed here between rhythm in the free fantasy and in the *Fantasien* Op. 116 is possibly only part of the picture: the connection could also lie behind the innovative rhythmic style embodied in other works by Brahms, meaning that the 'historical performance' approach developed in this chapter might potentially be relevant to Brahms's music in general. In any case, it would be worth exploring in greater detail whether or not this seminal aspect of Brahms's 'progressive' compositional technique,[27] like so many features of his style (including proportional tempos), was in fact essentially retrospective.

---

[26] Other influences on Brahms's rhythmic technique include Schumann and J. S. Bach; see Epstein 1979 and Frisch 1990 for discussion.
    Studies of the C. P. E. Bach/Beethoven connection are cited in Clark 1988. As for the link between Brahms and Bach, Brahms anonymously edited three keyboard concertos and two violin/keyboard sonatas by Bach and openly admired his music in general (as well as the *Versuch*), of which he possessed several scores.
[27] Note Schoenberg's remark ([1946] 1975: 131): 'When Brahms demanded that one hand of the pianist played twos or fours while the other played threes, people disliked this and said it made them seasick. But this was probably the start of the polyrhythmic structure of many contemporary scores.'

## REFERENCES

Bach, C. P. E., [1753, 1762] 1949: *Essay on the True Art of Playing Keyboard Instruments* [*Versuch über die wahre Art das Clavier zu spielen*], trans. W. J. Mitchell (New York: Norton).

Berry, W., 1989: *Musical Structure and Performance* (New Haven: Yale University Press).

Cai, C., 1986: 'Brahms' short, late piano pieces – opus numbers 116–119: a source study, an analysis and performance practice' (Dissertation, Boston University).

    1989: 'Brahms's pianos and the performance of his late piano works', *Performance Practice Review* 2/1: 58–72.

Clark, S. L., 1988: 'C. P. E. Bach in literature: a bibliography', in S. L. Clark, ed., *C. P. E. Bach Studies* (Oxford: Clarendon), pp. 315–35.

Cone, E. T., 1968: *Musical Form and Musical Performance* (New York: Norton).

Cooper, G. and Meyer, L., 1960: *The Rhythmic Structure of Music* (Chicago: University of Chicago Press).

Dunsby, J., 1982: 'Editorial', *Music Analysis* 1/1: 3–8.

    1983: 'The multi-piece in Brahms: *Fantasien* Op. 116', in R. Pascall, ed., *Brahms: Biographical, Documentary and Analytical Studies* (Cambridge: Cambridge University Press), pp. 167–89.

    1989: 'Guest editorial: performance and analysis of music', *Music Analysis* 8/1–2: 5–20.

Epstein, D., 1979: *Beyond Orpheus: Studies in Musical Structure* (Cambridge, Massachusetts: MIT Press).

    1985: 'Tempo relations: a cross-cultural study', *Music Theory Spectrum* 7: 34–71.

    1990: 'Brahms and the mechanisms of motion: the composition of performance', in G. Bozarth, ed., *Brahms Studies: Analytical and Historical Perspectives* (Oxford: Clarendon), pp. 191–226.

    1995: *Shaping Time: Music, the Brain, and Performance* (New York: Schirmer Books/ Macmillan).

Evans, E., [1936]: *Handbook to the Pianoforte Works of Johannes Brahms* (London: Reeves).

Finson, J., 1984: 'Performing practice in the late nineteenth century, with special reference to the music of Brahms', *Musical Quarterly* 70/4: 457–75.

Forte, A., 1957: 'The structural origin of exact *tempi* in the Brahms-Haydn Variations', *The Music Review* 18/2: 138–49.

Frisch, W., 1990: 'The shifting bar line: metrical displacement in Brahms', in G. Bozarth, ed., *Brahms Studies: Analytical and Historical Perspectives* (Oxford: Clarendon), pp. 139–63.

Gabrielsson, A., 1988: 'Timing in music performance and its relations to music experience', in J. A. Sloboda, ed., *Generative Processes in Music* (Oxford: Clarendon), pp. 27–51.

Howell, T., 1992: 'Analysis and performance: the search for a middleground', in J. Paynter et al., eds., *Companion to Contemporary Musical Thought*, 2 vols. (London: Routledge), vol. II, pp. 692–714.

Kalbeck, M., 1910 (vol. III) and 1915 (vol. IV): *Johannes Brahms*, 2nd edn, 4 vols. (Berlin: Deutsche Brahms-Gesellschaft).

Kolisch, R., 1943: 'Tempo and character in Beethoven's music', *Musical Quarterly* 29/2–3: 169–87 and 291–312.

Kraus, D., 1990: 'Brahms' op. 116: das Unikum der sieben Fantasien', in K. and R. Hofmann, eds., *Brahms-Studien*, vol. VIII (Hamburg: Patriotische Gesellschaft), pp. 49–60.

Lewin, D., 1990: 'Brahms, his past, and modes of music theory', in G. Bozarth, ed., *Brahms Studies: Analytical and Historical Perspectives* (Oxford: Clarendon), pp. 13–27.

Mastroianni, D., 1970: 'Elements of unity in *Fantasies*, opus 116 by Brahms' (Dissertation, Indiana University).

Matthews, D., 1978: *Brahms Piano Music* (London: BBC).

McCorkle, M., 1984: *Johannes Brahms: Thematisch-Bibliographisches Werkverzeichnis* (Munich: Henle).

Mendel, A., 1959: 'A note on proportional relationships in Bach tempi', *The Musical Times* 100: 683–5.

    1960: 'A brief note on triple proportion in Schuetz', *Musical Quarterly* 46/1: 67–70.

Musgrave, M., 1985: *The Music of Brahms* (London: Routledge and Kegan Paul).

Narmour, E., 1988: 'On the relationship of analytical theory to performance and interpretation', in E. Narmour and R. A. Solie, eds., *Explorations in Music, the Arts, and Ideas* (Stuyvesant, New York: Pendragon), pp. 317–40.

Rink, J., 1990: Review of Berry 1989, in *Music Analysis* 9/3: 319–39.

    1994a: 'Chopin's Ballades and the dialectic: analysis in historical perspective', *Music Analysis* 13/1: 99–115.

    1994b: 'Authentic Chopin: history, analysis and intuition in performance', in J. Rink and J. Samson, eds., *Chopin Studies 2* (Cambridge: Cambridge University Press), pp. 214–44.

Schmalfeldt, J., 1985: 'On the relation of analysis to performance: Beethoven's Bagatelles Op. 126, Nos. 2 and 5', *Journal of Music Theory* 29/1: 1–31.

Schoenberg, A., [1946] 1975: 'Criteria for the evaluation of music', in *Style and Idea*, ed. L. Stein, trans. L. Black (New York: St. Martins Press), pp. 124–36.

Zaslaw, N., 1974: 'Mozart's tempo conventions', in *Report of the Eleventh [IMS] Congress Copenhagen 1972* (Copenhagen: W. Hansen), pp. 720–36.

# Index

Lightning Source UK Ltd.
Milton Keynes UK
UKOW031807111011

180121UK00005B/46/A

9 780521 619394